NEWNES'
PICTORIAL KNOWLEDGE

VOLUME THREE

NEWNES'
PICTORIAL KNOWLEDGE

General Editors
R. H. POOLE
PETER FINCH, M.A.
WALTER SHEPHERD

Art Editor
A. H. J. HUMPHREYS

VOLUME 3

GEORGE NEWNES LIMITED
CARLTON HOUSE, GREAT QUEEN STREET,
LONDON, W.C.2

PRINTED IN GREAT BRITAIN
BY THE WHITEFRIARS PRESS LTD., LONDON AND TONBRIDGE, AND
BOUND BY HAZELL, WATSON & VINEY LTD., AYLESBURY AND LONDON
N.P.K. 7055. W.P. 5316

CONTENTS OF VOLUME THREE

THE STORY OF THE WORLD AND ITS PEOPLES—
LANDS, NEAR AND FAR, OF OUR COLONIAL EMPIRE

Colour Plates

Photo=tone Supplements

The Story
of the
World and
its Peoples

Our Homeland—
England, Wales,
Scotland
and Ireland

AN ENGLISH VILLAGE

Topical Press.

Wherever you go in the world, you will find nothing to surpass the peaceful charm of England's villages. Their beauties are typified in this picture of old-world Welford-on-Avon, in the county of Warwickshire, where thatched roofs, beam and plaster walls, grass verged lanes and the old church tower combine in a rural loveliness that is uniquely English

THE HOME OF THE BRITISH

ONE of the most wonderful stories in history is that which tells how a little group of islands, which were inconsiderable and far away in the outer world of the Greeks and the Romans, became the Motherland of the greatest Empire that the world had ever seen.

That little group of islands is the British Isles—our Homeland, and the Motherland of the Overseas Dominions, themselves the homes of peoples of the Commonwealth who look towards the Motherland with affection as the real home of the Commonwealth to which they are proud to belong.

There must be something remarkable about these islands inasmuch as they have become the centre of a great Commonwealth of Nations whose lands occupy over one-quarter of the globe and whose peoples total at least a quarter of the world's population.

People and Geography

What is it? Is it the people themselves? It is true that the British race has most of the qualities of empire builders, but it is also true that Britons possess these qualities largely because of the geography of their Homeland.

That is one of the reasons why geography is interesting. Geography, of course, tells us of strange lands and peoples, and of the wonderful things that are being done in other parts of the world. But, in addition to this, it does help to explain what the peoples of a land have done in the past, and what they are doing at the present time; and it may help us to foresee what they can do in the future—if they choose. *If they choose*—that is important, for some peoples have not taken advantage of the geography of their land, perhaps because they did not choose, perhaps because they have not been able and energetic enough. Geography often shows us what splendid chances nations have missed, as well as those which they have taken and used to make their country a better place in which to live.

The British race must have used most of the advantages which Nature gave them when she made the British Isles as she did, and placed the islands where they are.

It is a fact that we have in our Homeland one of the best climates in the world. Yet we often grumble at our weather—more often in fun than in real anger—and look upon it as a series of practical jokes played upon us by Mother Nature, all through the four seasons.

The Fortunate Islands

Have you friends abroad? Listen to what they say on coming " Home " for a holiday—for most of the citizens of the British Commonwealth look upon the Motherland as home, even if they were not actually born there, and long to visit it.

One will say, " Thank God for a sight of fields of living green once more "; another will love to feel the beat of the rain upon his face and the bluster of the wild west wind ; for

Will F. Taylor.

LAND'S END

Land's End, the westernmost tip of England, is some 293 miles from London. It is a familiar landmark to travellers. Those who are homeward bound welcome it as marking the entrance to the English Channel, and outward bound voyagers feel that it is here that they really bid farewell to England. The lighthouse just off Land's End is known as the Longships. The longest continuous journey that can be made in the British Isles is from Land's End to John o'Groats, a distance of more than 800 miles.

Photochrom.

THE NEEDLES

These famous rocks are landfall to many a traveller to England, for past them steam the great ocean liners using the deep-water port of Southampton. They can be seen at the westernmost tip of the Isle of Wight, not far from Alum Bay. They are the remains of a tall pillar of chalk which crumbled into the sea nearly 200 years ago. Notice the top of the lighthouse protruding above the tip of the farthest rock.

these men have come from thirsty lands of blazing sunshine where water is the most precious thing on earth.

Yet another from a country where winters are bitter and cruel will say how fortunate he is to come home for Christmas, knowing he will have no need to fear frostbite if he goes out, and that if he journeys by road or by rail his car or his train will not be buried deep in snow drifts.

It is true that occasionally the weather is unpleasant ; but it does not last long, and better weather soon wipes away disagreeable memories of the bad days that precede it.

You have only to journey—even a little—in other lands to know what a wonderful little Homeland is yours, and what a good climate it has for work and for play.

Mineral Wealth

Besides the advantage of a genial climate, the British Isles possess rich stores of coal and iron as well as other useful minerals.

Luckily most of the coal is near enough to the sea to make it easy for cargoes to be sent away to other lands for sale ; and what is more important still, the iron is near enough to the coal for the best use to be got out of both.

Iron makes the steel for machinery of all kinds, and coal provides the power to drive it. Our factories, our railways and our steamships to-day are still largely coal-driven, although electricity and oil are playing an increasingly important part in manufacture and in transport. It is our wealth of coal and iron that has made Britain a great manufacturing country, and dotted the seaways of the world thickly with British steamers made of British steel, driven by British coal, carrying British goods to all parts of the world that can be reached by sea-going vessels, and bringing home again the foodstuffs for Britain's millions of workers and raw materials for her busy factories.

When we think over all the advantages possessed by the land in which we live we see that very few countries are as fortunate as ours in their natural

A PANORAMA OF THE HARBOUR AT DOVER—

Known to the Romans as Dubris, Dover is one of the most historic of the Cinque Ports which, from the time of Edward the Confessor until the fifteenth century, had the task of providing warships for the defence of the kingdom. In this picture (left) we see part of the Castle within whose walls are the remains of a Saxon fort and a Norman lighthouse.

wealth, their fertility, their climate and their position in the world of to-day.

In the visits we shall make to different parts of our Homeland in the following pages, we shall understand many things if we remember that all things we have and use are the gifts of the Earth, and that the rocks of which our land is built up decide not only its particular types of scenic beauty, but very often the kind of work people do and the ways in which they live and move and have their being.

The Changing Face of Britain

This well-worn phrase was never more apt than at the present time. As a result of the Second World War and the national and international problems that have arisen from it, life in these islands of ours has changed enormously and is still changing at a tremendous rate. War swallowed up the wealth we had accumulated abroad; war com-

pelled us to increase the number and productivity of our factories and, in some cases, to disperse them from their old accustomed centres; war, too, led to the development of new industries and new methods, and took our women-folk from their homes into the work-shops and factories in unprecedented numbers. When peace came, we could see that something very like a quiet revolution had taken place, and changes in the management of our resources and in our ways of life have since increased the speed of that revolution considerably.

In recent years we have seen the coal-mines, railways, the gas industry, and the production and distribution of electric power pass into public owner-ship. The development of these indus-tries under State control has brought many changes. We have also seen the redistribution of some of our old indus-tries, and the establishment of new ones

Topical Press.

—MOST FAMOUS OF THE CINQUE PORTS

During the Second World War, Dover was in the front line. It was bombarded repeatedly by long-range German guns along the French coast near Calais, and heard the roar of its own heavy guns replying to these attacks. To-day, it has returned to its happier life as the starting-point for many a holiday in Europe for those who like the short sea-crossing from Dover to Calais.

in the neighbourhood of large towns and cities where there is good transport and adequate electric power is available from the National Grid. Town and Country Planning is creating new towns as dormitories for people from such old over-crowded areas as London and as centres of new industrial ventures. Many towns in Britain are following the examples of London and Paris and are developing on their outskirts industrial belts where a great variety of manufactures is produced. For modern transport—by road, rail and air—no longer compels industries to be sited near the sources of their raw materials or near the ports by which these raw materials enter the country. Readily available power and transport are important keys to the location of our industries to-day, although—as you will learn in the following pages—the old, traditional centres retain their prime importance.

To-day, Britain strives to be the workshop of the world. Modern Britain lives by her trade, and so we have often been forced to deny ourselves the fine things that British craftsmanship produces in order that these things may be sold and shipped abroad to pay for the food and raw materials without which we cannot live.

Old Gives Way to New

For such reasons we are expanding our industries as much as possible and thoroughly modernising them where this has not already been done. Old is giving way to new as up-to-date machinery is installed in mine and mill; and our urgent need for such minerals as iron and coal has led us to supplement the products of the mines with those of the open-cast system, sometimes paying as the price of our industry the temporary disfigurement of our countryside.

But the slag heaps, grime and

TWO OF ENGLAND'S GREAT SEAPORTS

Liverpool, Lancashire, on the right bank of the River Mersey and some three miles from the sea, is one of the greatest trading centres of the world and the principal port in the United Kingdom for the Atlantic trade. Cereals, sugar, timber, cotton, oil and fruits come to Liverpool by sea.

The great docks at Southampton cover some hundreds of acres and are steadily being enlarged. They stand at the mouths of the Rivers Itchen and Test and the open sea is reached either by the Solent, north-west of the Isle of Wight, or by Spithead, round the Ryde and Bembridge corner.

LIVERPOOL AND SOUTHAMPTON DOCKS

Topical.

Liverpool's beginning as a port goes back to Norman days and its history has been largely concerned with merchant shipping. From Liverpool the famous clippers sailed to China, India and Australia and some of the earliest steamships made the Atlantic crossing.

Fox Photos.

In this photograph we have another view of the docks at Southampton, showing a number of ocean liners at the quayside while in the right foreground can be seen a liner in the graving dock for repair. Southampton is the home port of the *Queen Elizabeth* and *Queen Mary*.

scarification that are inevitable to much of our industry do not mean that we have forgotten or cast aside the beauties of our Homeland.

To-day they are safeguarded by such means as green belts with which our town planners encircle modern cities, and by such schemes as those for National Parks and Forests. Such bodies as the National Trust play an important part in preserving our beauty-spots and historic places—for these things of beauty which are our heritage are essential to the British scene. They provide the relaxation that all of us need and help us to earn our living by bringing to our Homeland thousands of foreign tourists every year. Indeed, catering for tourists is a growing British industry.

As you read on, you will discover more about the people and places which go to make our Homeland, and you will find much of which you can be proud. For Britain is as beautiful as she is industrious, and it is within our power to build for her a future even more glorious than her past.

British Council.

SHAKESPEARE'S CLIFF, DOVER

Everyone making the Channel crossing from Calais to Dover knows Shakespeare's Cliff, whose sheer, white sides form part of the " White Walls of Old England." The cliff is of chalk and rears its great bulk to a height of more than 350 feet above the beach and above the railway which pierces its massive base. The cliff is one of our famous coastal landmarks which welcome the visitor and speed the parting guest.

LONDON AND THE THAMES BASIN

BUCKINGHAM PALACE, THE EAST FRONT

Associated Press.

Buckingham Palace, the London residence of British Sovereigns for nearly two centuries, stands on the site of the old Mulberry Garden where James I tried to encourage a national silk industry. Originally built as a red brick mansion by John Sheffield, Duke of Buckingham, the Palace was later bought by George III. It was rebuilt in 1825 by John Nash ; the East Front was added about 1847 and later remodelled.

" I go hence
To London, to the gathering place of
Souls."—*E. B. Browning.*

LONDON is the heart of the British Commonwealth and first port of the Commonwealth. The great city stands astride the river Thames, the river that has been called " the highway of the world."

Although for sheer size and population London is closely rivalled by New York, London has what New York can never possess—a wonderful history that can be traced in her buildings and monuments in almost unbroken sequence from Roman times to the present day. We could fill this book with the tale of London, and still leave the story unfinished.

The beginnings of London were in the little village that grew up by the first London Bridge, which was built by the Romans and was crossed by the Roman road that we know as Watling Street. Even then London was a port for ships carrying goods brought by traders from different parts of the country and sent to the Continent by the Romans. But many long years had to pass before it had grown enough in size and importance to become the capital of England.

The Tower, built by Bishop Gundulf under William the Conqueror, reminds us that it was in the Norman period that London became the centre of government ; and from the Conqueror's time until now the Tower has been a storehouse of history. Westminster Abbey, re-built in the eleventh century—" our national Valhalla," as it has been called —is a monument that enshrines within its walls historical memories that reach back in a continuous chain to the very day on which its foundation stones were laid.

William Gordon Davis.

THE MONUMENT

Towering over Billingsgate's fish markets, the Monument commemorates the Great Fire of London of 1666.   Its height is 202 feet, this being the distance of the Monument from the Place in Pudding Lane where the fire began.

The name London really belongs to the City, which extends from where old Temple Bar once stood, to Bishopsgate and Aldgate, and from Thames-side north to the lines formed by Finsbury Square, Barbican and Holborn.   To-day there is also the County of London, which in 1951 had a population of 3,348,336 people while Greater London had 8,346,137.

What is London ?

But London to most people now means the mighty growth of human settlement that includes the distant suburbs and still day by day is pushing its way outwards in every direction where there is land for it to grow. This Greater London is still the greatest town the world has ever seen.

London is the focus of British roads and railways ; all the world's seaways lead to it, and its docks provide accommodation for ships of all the seafaring nations of the globe.   It is an airways centre, too, whose old airport of Croydon is now used only by light 'planes.   London Airport at Heathrow, now one of the finest in the world, is used chiefly for inter-continental traffic, while Northolt, not far away, deals mainly with home and European traffic.   A third airport at Bovingdon is chiefly for freight, while a fourth at Blackbushe, near Camberley, is a relief airport for use in bad weather.

It is claimed that when London Airport is complete, it will be the largest and best-equipped in the world. The cost of the building works has been estimated at £21 millions, and in September, 1953, when the plans for the central terminal buildings were made public, it was announced that by the end of 1960 the airport would be handling double the traffic that used both London Airport and Northolt during 1952.   The main arrival and departure building will be able to take 1,200 passengers an hour.   The six main runways, which are linked to the buildings by subways and an access tunnel, will take the

THE TOWER OF LONDON

Fox Photos.

The Tower takes its name from its oldest part, the White Tower built by William the Conqueror. The White Tower walls, 11 to 15 feet thick, are 90 feet high. Beyond the Tower is the famous Tower Bridge the " leaves " of which can be raised to allow ships to enter the Pool of London.

Planet.

Wearing Tudor uniform, the Yeomen Warders escort the Governor of the Tower on a ceremonial occasion. Heading the procession is the Chief Yeoman Warder, who carries the Tower Mace, which is surmounted by a silver model of the White Tower.

largest airliners, and the two rows of aircraft stands on the central site will accommodate between 64 and 71 airliners at a time. Between three thousand and four thousand electrical circuits are being installed for the airport lighting, and on the runways and tracks alone there will be some 25,000 lights.

London is a great business and banking centre whose interests are not only British, but world-wide. It is a great manufacturing centre, too, with a wider variety of products than any other manufacturing city in the world. It is the centre of a government that is still a model for the liberty-loving nations of to-day, and the home of a Parliament that is known all the globe over as "the Mother of Parliaments." It is the capital of all the self-governing nations and colonies which are united in the British Commonwealth of Nations.

You will often hear sailors speak of the Thames as "London River," for to them the river is the sea gateway to the capital and its important docks. The largest ships use the docks at Tilbury, which are nearest the sea and are linked by good roads and railways with London itself. The docks farther up the river are much larger; the Royal Victoria and Albert and the King George V docks are probably the most important. But some ocean-going ships unload their cargoes in the very heart of the capital, making their way up river and passing through Tower Bridge into the "Pool of London" with its busy wharves.

Few visitors to London realise that it possesses factories of many kinds. South London has its glass and metal works, potteries and breweries; the East End, its clothing factories; the north-east, its furniture factories. Many of the main roads leading into the capital are bordered by works of all kinds and sizes turning out a wide variety of products from biscuits to wireless sets. In or near London, too, are our chief film studios.

A. Louis Jarché.

"THE ROOM" AT LONDON'S INTERNATIONAL GRAIN MARKET

London's international grain market is The Baltic Exchange and the main place of business in the building is "The Room," where ships for carrying grain are chartered. Like Lloyd's, the Exchange began in a coffee house, "The Virginia and Baltic."

A GREAT BANKING CITY

Seven important streets converge at the Bank of England whose buildings are seen on the left in this picture. The Bank is sometimes referred to as "the Old Lady of Threadneedle Street." Facing us is the Royal Exchange, the third to be built here since its foundation in 1571.

A stock exchange is where the stocks and shares of public companies and Government securities are bought and sold. The picture shows us the "Floor of the House" at the London Stock Exchange while business is in progress. The London Stock Exchange was founded in 1773.

WHITEHALL, CENTRE OF GOVERNMENT

Charles E. Brown.

This fine aerial picture shows (left) part of St. James's Park, and beyond, the Horse Guards Parade. To the right of the Horse Guards is the War Office, and nearer to us are various other Government departments and ministries, all of which flank Whitehall.

Walter Scott.

One of London's best-loved statues is that of Eros which surmounts the fountain at Piccadilly Circus. Eros seems to symbolise London itself, and whenever there is thanksgiving or rejoicing Londoners gather round the fountain which he dominates.

"WE WILL REMEMBER THEM"

Bippa.

On Remembrance Day each year the leaders of the nation, together with many ordinary citizens, gather at the Cenotaph in Whitehall, London, to pay homage to those who died in two World Wars. In this picture the Queen is seen as she steps forward to place a wreath on the Cenotaph.

Central Press.

On November the Ninth each year, the Lord Mayor rides to the Law Courts to receive the Royal Assent to his election. He is seen here accompanied by his mace-bearer and the mace, in his famous coach, escorted by members of the Honourable Artillery Company in pikemen's uniform.

TWO LONDON EXCHANGES

Lloyd's is an insurance market and the world centre of shipping information. Its name originated from the use by underwriters and merchants of a coffee house kept by Edward Lloyd in the seventeenth century. Insurance business is still transacted in the manner of 250 years ago.

A. Louis Jarché.

The New London Corn Exchange in Mark Lane was opened in June, 1953, and takes the place of the original building which was destroyed during the Second World War. Our picture shows the interior of the Exchange on a typical market day.

WESTMINSTER BRIDGE AND BIG BEN

"Big Ben" is actually the bell upon which the hours are struck, but many people give the name to the Clock Tower in which the bell hangs. The Clock Tower is one of London's best-known landmarks and is part of the New Palace of Westminster, the official name of the group of buildings forming the Houses of Parliament. The old Palace in which Parliament met was destroyed by fire in 1834, and the present buildings were designed by Sir Charles Barry in 1840. Westminster Bridge, opened in 1750 as the second bridge built across the Thames in London, was rebuilt about the middle of the nineteenth century.

Specially painted for this work.

THE POOL OF LONDON

If you stand upon London Bridge and turn your face towards the Tower Bridge, you are looking down upon the Pool of London, one of the most historic stretches of waterway in the world. Here you may see ocean-going ships being loaded and unloaded by huge cranes, which pick up the merchandise as with a giant's hands. In the view you will be able to include the Tower of London, Custom House and a great many churches and other interesting buildings.

Planet.

Air raids destroyed many buildings near St. Paul's Cathedral, thus providing this new view of Sir Christopher Wren's masterpiece. The Cathedral occupies the site of an earlier one irreparably damaged in the Great Fire of 1666. The Cross on its dome stands 365 feet above London.

Topical Press.

The new Waterloo Bridge seen in this picture was begun in 1937 and completed in 1944 ; it replaced an older bridge built by John Rennie which had served London for over a century. Parts of Rennie's bridge went to his Scottish birthplace to form a memorial to the great engineer.

The London Basin

London in its local relation is the centre of the " London Basin," which is really the lower basin of the Thames, extending from the gap in the chalk hills west of Reading to the sea, and lying between the chalk ridges of the Chilterns and the North Downs, through both of which roads and railways find their way by gaps in the hills, from the London Basin to the rest of Britain. As well as farmlands, the Lower Basin has such manufacturing towns as *Dunstable*, an engineering centre, and *Luton*, where there are large engineering and industrial plants and where hats are made: *High Wycombe*, which makes beech from the Chilterns' woods into chairs and other furniture: and, along the Essex shore, the great new oil refinery at *Coryton*, and at *Dagenham*, a great car and tractor works: and on the Kentish shore, at such places as *Dartford* and *Greenhithe*, paper mills fed with raw material from the forests of Canada and the Baltic.

Reading is the " biscuit town " of the south. It has engineering works and iron foundries, too, and brews ale. Within its ruined abbey, " Sumer is i cumen in "—the first English song, it is said—was composed. From Reading British Railways main lines diverge to Oxford and the Midlands, and to the west *via* Swindon, the railway engineering and aircraft industry town, or *via* Hungerford to the west country.

Above Reading, and beyond the gap which the Thames has cut between the Marlborough Downs and the Chilterns, is the Upper Thames Basin, which includes the fertile plain of Oxford, and

Topical Press.

AUSTRALIA HOUSE, LONDON

All the member nations of the British Commonwealth have headquarters in London, the Commonwealth capital. Along the Strand you will find the offices of the Governments of most of the various States of the Commonwealth of Australia. At the eastern end of Aldwych, where it joins the Strand, is Australia House itself.

TWO FAMOUS MUSEUMS

A. F. Kersting.

The Natural History Museum at South Kensington is one of several which came into being after the Great Exhibition of 1851 when it was decided to set up permanent collections in London. Thus we have the Victoria and Albert Museum, the Science Museum, and the Natural History Museum.

Mirrorpic.

The British Museum was first opened in 1759, but the present building was erected during the nineteenth century. The Museum Library is the largest and most valuable in the world ; its ticket-holders use the famous Reading Room which has seats for over 450 readers.

2—2

stretches westward to the beautiful Cotswold Hills, whence flow the " seven springs " that unite to form the young Thames. This Upper Basin is very different from the Lower Basin at whose heart lies the great metropolis— with its busy docks and markets, its factories and business centres, and its Thames, murky with the tide of commerce and clamorous with the voices of ships and men of all trading nations of the world.

City of Spires

The centre of the Upper Basin is the lovely city of Oxford, the ancient home of culture and learning, rich in history and in art—a city of beautiful towers and spires, set in a green and pastoral countryside, and one of the most famous cities in the world. Every one who can, goes to see Oxford ; and those who go, long to return. Oxford has played an important part in England's history : not so much because of its famous University, as its key position on the routes north and west of London. Indeed, its fame as a stronghold and a trade centre was widespread some time before it became known as a University city. From the times of Canute onwards, Oxford was the scene of many a great assembly in English history; its name is given to the Provisions of Henry III's reign which are so important in our constitutional history; it was at Oxford that Charles I held court during the Civil War; it was to Oxford that the second Charles went when the Great Plague swept through London.

Topical Press.

LONDON'S BEST-KNOWN SQUARE

The world knows Trafalgar Square, where Nelson surveys the capital of the British Commonwealth from the top of his famous column. The overall height of the column is 170 feet, 2 inches, and the figure of the famous admiral is three times life size. Beyond the column we see South Africa House, then (left) the church of St. Martin-in-the-Fields and the National Gallery. The most recent additions to the monuments in the square are memorials to Lord Jellicoe and Lord Beatty.

Walter Scott.

Planned and, for the most part, built by Henry III, the Abbey Church of Westminster is the most historic of our churches. Here English sovereigns are crowned and here the famous men of our country, who have served the nation well, are laid to rest. The noble proportions of the Abbey are clearly seen in this picture of the Choir, Sanctuary, and High Altar. The Altar is modern, but the mosaic pavement before it consists of the restored remains of that brought from Rome about 1263.

WHERE KINGS AND QUEENS ARE CROWNED

Albert Hester.

Since Norman times, England's kings have been crowned before the High Altar of Westminster Abbey. The mosaic of the Last Supper is wrought in Venetian glass ; above it are the words " The Kingdoms of the World are become the Kingdoms of our Lord and of His Christ."

H. N. King.

Banners hang over the stalls of the Knights of the Bath in the Henry the Seventh Chapel at Westminster Abbey. The order of the Bath, conferred for military or civil service to King and Country, is one of the greatest honours that can be bestowed. It was re-instituted by George I in the year 1725.

INSIDE THE HOUSES OF PARLIAMENT

Walter Scott.

In this photograph you obtain a very clear idea of what the House of Lords is like inside. In the centre, the two raised chairs are the thrones, with the distinguished strangers' gallery just above. The galleries at the sides are for peeresses. Just beyond the table you see the woolsack occupied by the Lord Chancellor. For centuries a sack of wool has been the official seat.

W. G. Davies.

On the night of May 10th, 1941, the House of Commons, which had been in use for nearly a century, was destroyed by enemy bombs. For nine years the " faithful Commons " sat mostly in the House of Lords. The new House of Commons, seen above, was opened by King George VI on October 26th, 1950. Many gifts from the Parliaments of the British Commonwealth countries enhance its importance as the Mother of Parliaments.

To-day, however, we know the city best from its great University whose many historic colleges and other buildings are places of pilgrimage for visitors from near and far. We know Oxford, too, for its pleasant waterways, and for the beauties of the surrounding countryside. Not many miles north-west of the city is the small town of Woodstock where stands the great Palace of Blenheim built for that inspired soldier, the Duke of Marlborough, and named after the most famous of his victories.

But Oxford is considerably more than a rural centre or a University town. You have only to see the busy traffic in the "High," as the High Street is called, to realise that the city does not dwell in the past. Oxford has industry; its suburb of Cowley contains one of the largest car manufacturing plants in the country.

Oxford, like nearby Aylesbury, is an old market-town, and in this pleasant vale which geographers call the Upper Basin of the Thames, farming is still the main business. Aylesbury is noted for its dairy produce and poultry, and the Cotswold Hills for their sheep. Remnants of the ancient wool trade survive at *Witney*, famous for its blankets, and you can go to wonderful old towns and villages in the Cotswolds whose fine churches and monuments tell the story of a once great and flourishing woollen industry, and of the days when Cotswold woollen manufacturers were merchant princes, and Cotswold towns among the most important in the land.

It is the grey Cotswold stone that makes the towns and villages here so attractive: the grey stone and the fresh bright green of the Cotswold pastures.

Topical Press.

CLEOPATRA'S NEEDLE

Brought to England from Alexandria, Egypt, in 1878, this 3,500-year-old relic of Ancient Egypt now stands upon the Victoria Embankment, London. Cut from red granite and weighing about 186 tons, the Needle has a companion obelisk in Central Park, New York. Both once stood at Heliopolis. Despite its name, the Needle on the Victoria Embankment has no connection with the famous Queen Cleopatra.

IN WESTMINSTER CATHEDRAL

This picture, taken at a solemn moment during the celebration of Mass at the High Altar of Westminster Cathedral, shows the ornate splendour which characterises the interior of the largest Roman Catholic church in Britain. Built in the Byzantine style and completed externally in 1903, the Cathedral is the church of the Cardinal-Archbishop, who is seen in the picture in his robes kneeling before the Altar at the sacred moment of consecration.

TOWARDS THE WEST END

Topical Press.

Facing each other across Trafalgar Square are the offices of two Commonwealth nations. The Union of South Africa shares the east side with St. Martin-in-the-Fields. On the west side is Canada House, shown in the picture.

Walter Scott.

Like Regent's Park, Regent Street came into existence as part of the Prince Regent's plan for a fine villa linked to Carlton House by a stately road. Nash, the famous architect, had a hand in this scheme, but the present modern thoroughfare is best known for its fashionable shops.

PARK AND PALACE

Hyde Park is the most famous of London's open spaces and occupies an area almost as great as that of the City of London itself. In this picture we see the Serpentine, the lovely stretch of water within the Park, which was formed from the ponds of the old West Bourne by Queen Caroline.

The London residence of the Archbishop of Canterbury is the last of the capital's old riverside palaces. Originally the manor house of Lambeth, the palace has buildings which date in part from the thirteenth century. The gatehouse seen in this picture was built about 1490.

LONDON'S GOVERNMENT AND LAW

The County, as opposed to the City, of London, is governed from the County Hall on the banks of the Thames. This Hall, shown above, was begun in 1912 and was formally opened by King George V in July, 1922. It stands almost opposite the Houses of Parliament.

Photos : Topical Press.

The four Honourable Societies of the Inns of Court were formed in the early fourteenth century and constitute what is virtually a university of English Law. Here we see Lincoln's Inn which was once the London estate of the third Earl of Lincoln. The buildings include the sixteenth century Old Hall and gatehouse.

BESIDE THE THAMES

On the Thames, immediately opposite Windsor, is Eton College, one of our great public schools for boys which dates from the reign of King Henry VI. Part of its buildings has stood since 1448, but here we see the sixteenth century Lupton's Tower and the main schoolyard.

Another magnificent Thames-side building is Hampton Court Palace which was built by Cardinal Wolsey and presented by him to King Henry VIII. This picture shows part of the palace kitchen, which is kept exactly as it was in Wolsey's time. Notice the curious cooking implements of those bygone days and the spits upon which large joints were roasted before the open fire.

Exploring beyond Stow-on-the-Wold and lovely Burford on the little river Windrush, we find such quaintly-named places as the Slaughters and the Swells, delightful villages and hamlets that make this one of the most beautiful districts in our islands.

The Seven Streams

The Windrush is one of the small streams which give their waters to make the larger river, our Thames. The others include the Churn, on whose course lies Cirencester, which, as Corinium, was the fourth largest town in Roman Britain : the Evenlode and the Coln : and the Cherwell, which joins the Thames at Oxford. Some say that the Seven Springs are the source of this, the chief river of England, but many consider that the true source of the Thames lies at Thames Head, three miles from Cirencester.

The Thames is rich in both history and beauty. From ancient Oxford, it flows through the regatta towns of Henley and Marlow, where oarsmen from many parts compete, to reaches—or stretches of the river—that have won fame through the sheer loveliness of their scenery. On goes the river to Royal Windsor, where the magnificent castle of our kings and queens rises nobly upon a chalk cliff overlooking the stream. On the opposite bank is Eton, whose college, one of our great public schools for boys, dates from the reign of King Henry VI. Thence the Thames flows past Runnymede, where King John granted the Great Charter, to Cardinal Wolsey's splendid palace of Hampton Court, and so to London.

Overlooking the historic fields of Runnymede from the crest of Cooper's Hill is the memorial to 20,455 airmen of the British Commonwealth forces who lost their lives in the Second World War and have no known grave. The memorial was unveiled by H.M. Queen Elizabeth II on October 17th, 1953—" On Cooper's Hill eternal wreaths shall grow, While last

William Gordon Davis.

THE STATUE OF PETER PAN

Peter Pan, the " boy who would not grow up," is known to us all as the hero of Sir James Barrie's immortal fairy story. Sir George Frampton's statue of Peter, near the Long Water in Kensington Gardens, shows him surrounded by the fairies who were his companions and is one of the most famous and delightful of London statues.

TOWERS AND SPIRES OF OXFORD

Many famous colleges and other buildings are seen in this aerial view of the ancient University city.
It is easy to understand why Oxford is often called " the city of spires." Notice the Great Quadrangle
of Christ Church, the college founded by Cardinal Wolsey.

The Great Quadrangle of Christ Church is the
most spacious in Oxford. " Tom Tower," rising
above the Great Gate, takes its name from its
massive bell.

The Radcliffe Camera was built in 1737-49 and
now serves as a reading room of the Bodleian
Library. More than a million books are housed
in its underground store.

the mountain or while Thames shall flow."

The Thames Estuary

East of the capital, where Tilbury and its important docks now stand, Queen Elizabeth I spoke stirring words of encouragement to her troops before the defeat of the Spanish Armada. The Nore is remembered for the naval mutiny of 1797; here, too, in 1667, came the Dutch fleet to enter the river Medway, which flows into the Estuary at Sheerness, and burn ships and dockyard at Chatham, the important naval base; and during the Second World War, the Estuary was the assembly place for brave convoys of merchantmen and mighty invasion fleets.

Fortunately, its business to-day is much more peaceful. The Thames Estuary has its holiday resorts, bright seaside places such as Southend and Margate, and its waters are a highway for merchant shipping taking their car-goes to and from London.

Its great importance as the sea-gateway of London and the stirring events which have happened along its course make the Thames the chief river of England and one that is known throughout the world. Its length, from Thames Head bridge to the Nore is 209 miles, but from Seven Springs, the distance to the mouth is greater by some miles. In the estuary, between Sheerness and Shoeburyness, the width is about $5\frac{1}{2}$ miles.

The Name, "Thames"

Around Oxford you may hear people refer to the Thames as "the Isis." No satisfactory reason for this local name has ever been given. And although we do not know exactly how the name "Thames" came into being, we have been told by Cæsar that when he came to Britain the river was called "Tamesis." We know, too, that in Saxon times, it went by the name "Thamis."

Topical Press.

TRYING TO "BUMP" THE BOAT IN FRONT

Twice a year "bump" races take place on the Thames at Oxford; similar races are held on the river Cam at Cambridge. Crews from the different Colleges race on a course a little over a mile long, starting a set distance apart from one another and each trying to "bump" the boat in front.

Specially painted for this work.

THE HOME OF ENGLAND'S SOVEREIGNS

For nearly nine centuries, Windsor Castle has been the home of England's Kings and Queens. Founded by William I on the site of an earlier fortress, it was largely rebuilt by Edward III, and later sovereigns extended it. In St. George's Chapel, seen on the right, are the stalls and insignia of the Knights of the Garter, while the Round Tower is to the left. The residential parts of the Castle contain a rich store of artistic treasures.

Specially painted for this work.

ONE OF BRITAIN'S SEA GATEWAYS

The Royal Liver Building, its cupolas surmounted by figures of the mythical liver bird, has seen many a heavily-laden merchant ship proceeding up or down stream on its business of carrying part of Britain's trade. Liverpool, upon whose Merseyside this famous building stands, is the third largest city in England and is second only to London in the amount of trade it handles as a seaport. Shipping of all nationalities uses its spacious docks and wharves along the Mersey, or passes through the Eastham lock into the Manchester Ship Canal for the cotton capital.

THE GARDEN OF ENGLAND

THE " SEVEN SISTERS " OF SUSSEX DOWNLAND

The Sussex Downs, from Cuckmere Haven to Birling Gap, come sloping to meet the sea in the form of tall chalk cliffs which are known as the " Seven Sisters." They are true " White Walls of Old England," familiar to everyone who passes up or down the English Channel, and extend practically from Seaford to Eastbourne. To prevent these landmarks from being disfigured by buildings they, and the Downs immediately behind, have been purchased for the Nation.

AT least two favoured regions of south-eastern England call themselves " The Garden of England "—one, the fair county of Kent, and the other the Isle of Wight —and both of them have excellent rights to the title ; for both are beautiful and fertile lands in the sunniest quarter of our Homeland, where fruits and flowers come to perfection and where the climate is delightful throughout the greater part of the year.

Both belong to the beautiful Downland region between the Thames and the English Channel. From Salisbury Plain (which is really rolling chalk country, with valleys and hollows in it big enough to conceal large bodies of the troops who use it as a manœuvring ground), two great ridges of chalk hills run eastward, (1) the North Downs with Dover and Shakespeare's Cliff at their seaward end, and (2) the South Downs coming to the sea by way of Hampshire and Sussex at the high cliff of Beachy Head, from whose top Shakespeare says:—

" The fishermen upon the beach appear like mice."

Castle Towns

Both of these chalk ridges are cut by streams, many, like the Blackwater, Wey and Medway, finding their way to the Thames ; and many, like the Arun and the Sussex Ouse, to the English Channel. In the gaps which these rivers have cut in the chalk ridges, stand old castle towns—Guildford on the Wey, Rochester on the Medway, Canterbury on the Kentish Stour, Arundel on the Arun, and Lewes on Sussex Ouse, all of which still have their ancient strongholds. To-day such towns still command the gaps as important route centres on roads and railways. The whole of the south-eastern corner of England is dotted with ruins of many castles built there, because this was the nearest part of Britain to the Continent. To this day it plays an important part in our land and sea defences—Chatham (with its suburb, Gillingham) and Sheerness, Dover and Portsmouth are great naval stations ; Canterbury, Winchester and Aldershot are military centres.

Between the Downs

Canterbury, however, is more famous as the seat of the Primate of All England, and many still go on pilgrimage to visit its wonderful Cathedral, and the ruins of the first Christian Church in England.

Between the North and South Downs is the Weald of Sussex and Kent— the *Anderida Silva* of the Romans and the *Andredsweald* of the Saxons—

with the Forest Ridges in the middle rising to over 800 feet in Crowborough Beacon. The Weald still retains remnants of the ancient forests, and here and there you may yet see traces of the old charcoal burners' fires where the charcoal for smelting the Wealden iron was made. The British iron industry, however, has long since gone north to the coalfields ; but there are working collieries in East Kent behind Deal and Dover.

All along the Kentish and Sussex shores are sunny seaside towns, well known to weary Londoners—Herne Bay, Margate and Ramsgate, Deal, Folkestone, Hastings, and Eastbourne; Brighton—known as " London by the Sea "—Worthing, Littlehampton and Bognor Regis. Important channel

Mirror Features.

REFLECTED IN THE STILL MOAT WATERS

Leeds Castle, Kent, has no connection with the city of Leeds in Yorkshire. Its name comes from Led, or Ledian, an Anglo-Saxon who built the first fortress on this site about the year 850. Parts of the present castle, which is still inhabited, have been standing for more than 600 years. Henry V imprisoned Joan, his stepmother, here for practising witchcraft, and it was here that the same king received the Emperor Sigismund.

SHEPHERD AND HARVESTER

Topical Press.

This flock of lambs is on its way to the annual sheep fair at Tenterden, an ancient market town in Kent. Many sheep fairs take place in July, when farmers buy and sell ewes and lambs for fattening or for breeding. Notice that although the shepherd has three helpers, he still brings his faithful dog.

Central Press.

This rich crop of ripe corn stretches for more than two hundred acres over the rolling Sussex Downs. It is being harvested by self-binders, which reap the corn and bunch it into tied sheaves. The sheaves will be built up into stooks and later brought in from the field by trailer and tractor.

3—2

A FARM IN " THE GARDEN OF ENGLAND "

This oast-house farmstead nestling in the heart of its orchards is typical of Kent, the lovely county which is often called " The Garden of England." Oast-houses are really kilns in which hops or malt are dried ; and Kent is Britain's principal hop-growing region, although hops are also grown in Sussex, Hampshire, Hereford and Worcestershire. Hops were not originally a crop native to our islands ; they were imported from Holland many centuries ago.

ferry towns there are, too ; *Dover*, for Calais, Ostend and Dunkirk ; *Folkestone*, for Boulogne, and *Newhaven*, for Dieppe. The ancient port of Richborough, which lies between Sandwich and Ramsgate, was neglected for many years, although it was of importance during both World Wars. But recently efforts have been made to bring the port back to life as a terminal for a Continental car ferry service. Richborough is where the Romans landed for the Claudian invasion of England.

Kentish Fruit and Hops

Hops grow best on well-drained, sunny slopes; Kent is hilly and sunny, and so grows more hops than any other part of Britain. Tall poles and many lengths of wire and string are necessary to support the plants; and in fields that have exposed sides, trees are planted to form a wind-break, or an artificial wind-screen of canvas or sacking is put up.

In orchard lands and hop-fields a limited number of men are at work all the year round, for the trees must be tended, the hops must be planted, and the ground must be kept in order. But when the fruit-picking and the hop-picking seasons begin, large numbers of additional workers are required. Many of these are local folk, especially women and children ; but thousands come from the large towns to spend the

IN A KENTISH HOP GARDEN

By courtesy of Rotary Hoes Ltd.

Hops grow best on well-drained, sunny slopes. They are grown from " cut setts," or root cuttings, which are planted out in rows when they are about a year old. The hops seen here are still young and have not climbed the 12 ft. high network of poles, wires and cords which has been prepared for them. Between five and ten bines will be allowed to climb upwards from each stool and by September the maze of cords and wires will be lost in the dense foliage of the mature plants. Kent and Sussex form one of the main areas of hop-growing in Britain, the other being Hereford and Worcester. In the former the hop fields are called " gardens," in the latter, " yards."

Fox Photos.

Although mechanical pickers have been invented, many hops are still picked by hand. Every September sees gangs of pickers from London, Birmingham and South Wales busy in the hopyards and gardens, pulling down the bines and taking them to the " cribs " (canvas containers) where they strip off the hop cones. The picking season lasts about three weeks and during that time the pickers live in camps or temporary huts. Their pay varies according to the amount that they pick.

fruit-picking and the hop-picking seasons in the country. Train-loads of hop-pickers go to Kent from London during the late summer.

Not all Kent is devoted to orchards and hop-fields ; there are parts which are quite unsuitable for fruit-growing or general agriculture. The high chalk hills (Downs) are mainly covered with grasses, although here and there suitable slopes are cultivated. This rich grassland is used for grazing sheep, which flourish on the crisp downland herbage.

South-eastern England—particularly the county of Kent—is noted for its orchards. Other famous orchard lands of the south-east are those of Essex, Sussex and Hampshire—all in the south-eastern portion of England.

This part of Britain is so good for fruit-growing and hop growing because (1) the soil is rich and well-drained ; (2) there is usually the right amount of rain at the right time of the year; (3) it is one of the sunniest parts of Britain, and receives its full share of the summer sunshine ; (4) it is quite near London and its suburbs, where the fruits find a ready market. Soft fruit must be got quickly to markets and shops, for it has to be sold fresh, or it cannot be sold at all, and this is an important reason why soft fruit growers always have their farms near regions where large numbers of people live.

Around Romney Marsh

We cannot leave this part of our homeland without looking briefly at Romney Marsh, once the home of smug-

Will F. Taylor.

IN CANTERBURY CATHEDRAL

For 1,000 years Canterbury has been the centre of our religious teaching. In the photograph above we see the door leading from the cloisters into the north transept of the Cathedral. The four knights who murdered Thomas à Becket hurried through this very doorway, meeting the Archbishop just beyond and brutally killing him to gain favour with their royal master, Henry the Second.

A LIBRARY IN CHAINS

Will F. Taylor.

At one period printed books were so precious and so liable to be stolen that they were secured to their places on the shelves by means of chains. Here is the famous Chained Library of the Minster Church at Wimborne, in Dorset. To read a book one may place it upon the lectern, but the strong chain prevents its removal. The library was formed nearly 250 years ago. Even the Bibles were secured by chains in many of our churches in olden times. There is another collection of chained books in Hereford Cathedral.

glers, and the old towns round about, such as Rye. Rye is now two miles from the coast, but the rock on which it stands was once washed by the sea. Winchelsea, too, is another ancient place which, like Rye, was later added to the original five towns (Hastings, New Romney, Hythe, Sandwich, and Dover) comprising the Cinque Ports, but which is now only a village.

For centuries Romney Marsh has been noted for its rich pasture lands which to this day support large flocks of sheep. But much of the Marsh was ploughed up during the War and the amount of cultivated land is now seven times greater than it was in 1939, while the sheep are not so many. So it is that tulips, tomatoes, potatoes and wheat now grow where once sheep grazed.

In this corner of England you can find many reminders of the times when our country was threatened with invasion. At Sandgate and Camber are the remains of Tudor castles and, scattered along the low coast, the Martello towers built in 1804 to guard the shore against Napoleon. Cutting across the Marsh on the landward side is another relic of the Napoleonic wars, the Royal Military Canal, constructed as part of the defences in those times.

Lympne, which long ago ceased to be a seaport and now lies comfortably inland, is another point from which we might set out for the Continent. Here we could drive our car into a waiting transport aircraft and be flown swiftly across the Channel.

The Hampshire Basin

The Hampshire Basin is almost cut in two by the deep Southampton Water—the estuary of the Itchen and Test, with the great port of Southampton at its head. Southampton has a history which goes back to the centuries before the Conquest, and its charter of incorporation was granted by Henry I. Southampton also has the advantage of

Crown Copyright.

A VILLAGE BAKERY IN DORSET

Although it does not resemble the huge bakeries in the towns and cities, the bakery in the Dorset village of Sydling can produce all the loaves, cakes and buns needed locally. From four to five hundred loaves are baked in the ovens every week.

CASTLE AND COTTAGE

It has been said that Corfe village, in Dorset, lies at the foot of its ancient fortress " like a faithful hound." The castle itself was never taken by storm, but during the Civil War it was betrayed to Cromwell's men, who afterwards destroyed its towers and walls.

Photos : Leonard and Marjorie Gayton.

In the extreme north-east of Wiltshire is the old village of Castle Combe, which has been owned by the Scrope family for some six hundred years. Here lived Sir John Fastolf, the original of Shakespeare's character, Falstaff.

double tides—four a day—which give it practically average high-water conditions most of the time. That is why it is the home port of some of our finest liners, especially those sailing to the Americas and to South Africa.

Old Cathedral Cities

Two lovely old cathedral cities in the Hampshire Basin are Winchester and Salisbury, the former the ancient capital of England and the city of King Alfred the Great ; the latter near the ancient fortress of Old Sarum. Salisbury stands on the edge of the great plain to which it gives its name. More plateau than plain, this rolling Wiltshire downland is a region of sheep pastures where farms are few because the soil is so poor. Not far

from one of the larger military camps on the Plain is one of the most remarkable ancient monuments in Britain, the massive circular group of stones which we know as Stonehenge. Surrounded by an earthwork some 300 feet in diameter, this strange temple of some long-dead people was once thought to have been built by the Druids. But modern archæologists fix the date of its construction as about 1700 B.C., when these great stones were brought, by some means unknown to us, from a Welsh bluestone quarry, and erected in their present form—as a temple to the sun-god, perhaps. No one can say exactly why or when Stonehenge was built, but even in these days of motoring and air travel, when modern artillery thunders on the ranges not far

Central Press.

SOUTHAMPTON'S GREAT OCEAN TERMINAL

" An ocean terminal without rival in the world " was the description given to the impressive reception station which was opened at Southampton Docks at the end of July, 1950, for Transatlantic passengers. It was used for the first time by the biggest ship in the world, the *Queen Elizabeth*, seen in this photograph as she was being manœuvred alongside the new Terminal.

Topical Press.

ENGLAND'S STONES OF MYSTERY

Stonehenge (the actual meaning of the word is " the hanging stones ") stands on the edge of Salisbury Plain and has probably been in existence since about 1700 B.C. No one can say exactly why Stonehenge was built, or how the great stones of which it is made were transported from a Welsh quarry many miles distant : but this strange monument is believed to have been a temple to the Sun.

from the megaliths and trilithons of Stonehenge, there is a chill, mysterious atmosphere about this site of ancient practice and religion that conveys itself to even the most cynical visitor.

In North Wiltshire, at the village of Avebury between Marlborough and Devizes, are the remains of another great work of early man, a vast earthwork and ditch which once had a great circle of stones over 1,000 feet in diameter. A mile away is the 130-foot high Silbury Hill, the largest artificial mound in Europe built for a purpose which remains secret to this day.

The Isle of Wight, now separated from the mainland by the Solent (yachting at Cowes) and the Spithead (naval anchorage and reviews), was

ages ago part of the mainland ; its chalk backbone is a continuation of the Dorset chalk heights, and the famous Needles at its western end are broken-off fragments. The real business centre of the Island is Newport. Much better known, however, are the delightful resorts along its coasts— Ventnor, Shanklin, and Ryde. On the mainland west of the Isle of Wight is the seaside health resort of Bournemouth with its splendid pine woods and sands. On the north-west mainland, too, are the leafy glades and heaths of the New Forest, where majestic oaks, beeches, firs and other trees provide cover for ponies, fallow deer, and other forest animals. This was once the hunting ground of kings, and you can see " the Rufus stone "

INSIDE AN ANCIENT TITHE BARN

Until the Tithe Commutation Act of 1835 it was common for English farmers to pay a tithe to the Church ; that is to say, a tenth part of their produce. The corn, wool, or whatever it was that the local farmers paid, was often stored in a special barn until such time as it was needed for use or for sale. One of these barns can still be seen at Tisbury in Wiltshire. As the picture shows, it is strongly built of stone with a roof of thatch and timber.

where William the Red fell victim to a crossbow arrow.

A feature of the Dorset coast is Portland Isle, connected to the mainland by the Chesil Beach or Bank, a long natural groyne of shingle that shelters Weymouth and its naval and channel-ferry harbour.

Dorset is a county of old towns such as Dorchester, Shaftesbury, Corfe and Blandford. Its Portland stone and Purbeck marble have enriched many a fine mansion and palace. Thomas Hardy, the great writer who made " Wessex " the background of much of his work, was born at Upper Bockhampton. It is the county of " The Oldest Thing in Britain "—the great figure of the Cerne Giant cut in the Dorset chalk.

ENGLAND'S RIVIERA & THE WEST COUNTRY

Fox Photos.

LOOKING ACROSS DARTMOOR FROM HYNE DOWN

Dartmoor is the largest piece of open land in the south of England. Its hills and tors, combes and streams, have such a wild and rugged beauty that it has become a very popular holiday haunt. From the high ground, or tors, of Dartmoor's great expanse of rock and heather, you get such lovely views as this, with a moorland village and its fields and a green countryside that stretches to the horizon.

WHO has not heard of Devonshire cider, of Cornish pasties and pilchards, and of the spring flowers of the Scillies? Some of us, perhaps, have been fortunate enough to spend holidays there, and know what lovely English counties Cornwall and Devon are.

They form a long peninsula that juts out well into the Atlantic, so that no part of it is far from the sea. The west winds from the ocean bring plenty of moisture that keeps the fertile valleys and grassy slopes green for the dairy cattle from whose rich milk Devonshire butter and Cornish cream are made. These winds bring cool air from the sea in summer; and in winter, when the sea is much warmer than the land, the westerly breezes make this peninsula milder and warmer than any other part of the British Isles. In the lovely gardens of Penzance and other towns grow palms and bamboos, and beautiful hydrangeas flourish in the open air. No wonder many people who dread cold weather go to Devon and Cornwall to spend the winter, instead of visiting more expensive winter resorts of foreign Rivieras. The winter climate of our English " Riviera " is just as good, and actually less liable to cold spells, for it has no *mistral* to chill one's marrow, and no dust.

The warm moist air of Cornwall and the Scilly Islands makes spring come earlier there than anywhere else in Britain ; that is why we look to these parts of our islands for our first supplies of spring flowers and vegetables.

The Moors

Cornwall and Devon are very hilly, as we see when we go through them in the train. The railway follows the valleys, and avoids the high lands where the hard old rocks have been raised into the moors for which this

45

Will F. Taylor.

TINTAGEL CASTLE

These are the ruins of Tintagel Castle, in North Cornwall. The Castle, in legend, is associated with King Arthur, but the stone-work you see here dates from the thirteenth century.

western peninsula is famous. *Exmoor*, in Somerset and North Devon, is made of hard sandstone, and stands up sharply in Dunkery Beacon; *Dartmoor* and *Bodmin Moor* are great bosses of hard old granite, which has been much worn by wind and weather, leaving very hard parts upstanding as " tors." Yes Tor (2,028 feet) is the best known, but High Willhays overtops it by nearly a dozen feet. They say that a man who has not tramped over Dartmoor and seen its magic sunsets has yet one of the best things in life to enjoy.

In veins in some of the hard old rocks of Cornwall and Devon there are tin and copper, lead and zinc; but they have been worked so long ago that there is not much metal left to be easily got. The chief mines are in the neighbourhood of Tavistock, St. Ives, and Camborne. Old workings used by the Romans, and even by people who were in Britain before the Romans came,

are still to be seen in contrast to the modern equipment of such mines as South Crofty. The quarrymen of Cornwall and Devon get out fine slate and beautiful granite from the rocks for use in building. From the granite, too, china clay is got; much of it goes to the Potteries for making china, and some is used in preparing calico in Lancashire, or in glazing paper in Kent, or even in making false teeth in America! *Fowey* is one of the ports which sends away this china clay in many directions. Pitchblende, which is radio-active, is also found in Cornwall.

A Lovely Coastline

The coastline of this south-western peninsula is very beautiful, with its rocky cliffs, deep coves and sandy bays, and its water of Mediterranean blue, that sometimes becomes a sea of emerald shot with deep indigo. In former times it extended into the Atlantic, for the Scillies are the up-

Will F. Taylor.

STEEPLE ROCK

If you were to visit the Lizard in Cornwall, you would find a rocky coast of great beauty. The pillar shown above is known as " Steeple Rock," and may be seen at Kynance Cove.

A SHELTERED BAY IN DEVON

Planet News.

The sheltered bay in this picture, with its holiday-makers, its bathing huts, its boats, and its pebble beach, is a scene of great activity as sailing craft of various sorts and sizes make ready for the Annual Regatta. The scene is typical of Beer, the pleasant holiday resort near Seaton in south-east Devon. Beer is one of the few places along the coast of that lovely county where the cliffs are made of chalk.

CORNWALL'S CURIOUS CHEESEWRING

Both Devon and Cornwall are very rocky counties whose quarries yield fine slate and beautiful granite for use in building. In some places, some whim of Mother Nature has produced curious rock formations such as the " Cheesewring," near Liskeard, in Cornwall. We know that this incredible formation was in existence at least 300 years ago, but none can say how it came to be assembled in this peculiar manner.

THE VILLAGE STOCKS

Will F. Taylor.

If we go right back to Saxon times we find that stocks were in use as a form of punishment. Men (and women, too) were held fast by the ankles, the stocks being made to open like a book to receive the unfortunate person's limbs. Here are the well-preserved stocks to be seen in the churchyard at Ottery St. Mary, Devon. Often we can find ancient stocks on village greens as relics of days that have passed ; and, more frequently still, in churchyards. This is because people who failed to attend church regularly were often punished in such a manner.

49

4

standing remnants of a sunken land that tradition says was part of King Arthur's lovely land of Lyonnesse. The ruins of Tintagel Castle remind us of the great King of the legends and of his famous Knights of the Round Table.

Fishing is an important business along this coast. Immense shoals of pilchards and mackerel visit the shores at certain times of the year, and fishing fleets from Mevagissey and Penzance, St. Ives and Newlyn, Plymouth and Falmouth, reap rich harvests. From Brixham, on the opposite side of Tor Bay to Torquay, the renowned Brixham trawlers go out into the Channel for flounders and plaice, turbot and brill, skate and hake.

The biggest town in south-western England is *Plymouth*, which, with Devonport and Stonehouse, forms the famous "Three Towns" of the West Country. Plymouth is a naval port commanding the Channel approaches, and also a port of call for large liners from which passengers and mails are landed for speedy transit to London by the expresses of British Railways. Its harbour is protected by a strong breakwater, and the Eddystone Lighthouse, a few miles off, flashes its welcome and warning to the ships. West of Plymouth the railway crosses the famous Saltash Bridge on its way to Bodmin, Cornwall's county town, Truro, with its fine cathedral, and Penzance.

The English Naples

Torquay, "the English Naples," on beautiful Tor Bay, is visited yearly by many thousands in successful quest of health, recreation and sunshine. Its counterpart in North Devon is Ilfracombe, twenty miles due west of which is rocky Lundy, an island about $2\frac{1}{2}$ miles long and a mile broad, with a population of some 50 people. Smaller

Fox Photos.

BADGWORTHY WATER IN THE DOONE COUNTRY

Many parts of the British countryside have associations with our great novelists and poets ; and as we look along Badgworthy Water towards Doone Valley, we think at once of Blackmore and the Doones of Exmoor who live so vividly in the pages of his immortal romance *Lorna Doone*. Doone Valley is within easy reach of such northern Devon holiday centres as Ilfracombe and Lynton.

British Council.

A DEVONSHIRE BEAUTY SPOT

Most visitors to Torquay know the forge, or blacksmith's shop, at the nearby village of Cockington which you see in this picture. Its leafy lanes, thatched roofs and wash walls make it one of the most attractive of Devon villages. Notice the garden walls cleverly built of shaped stones without mortar or cement.

but very beautiful holiday places lie on both coasts of the south-western peninsula.

Exeter, an old Roman city, built where the Britons had a great fortress, stands where many roads and the railways converge to cross the Exe by its bridges. Its cathedral and its castle are well worth seeing, and so is its Elizabethan Guildhall which reminds us of Exeter's powerful guilds in Tudor times.

But, go where we will, there is a perpetual feast of interest in this well-named English Riviera. In Cornwall we soon find that the beauty spots are dotted along the expansive line of rugged coasts, with the busier industrial and workaday parts nearer to the backbone of the county. Redruth and Camborne are both concerned closely with engineering and mining, and each has an inland setting. At the latter place Richard Trevithick invented and ran upon the king's high-

way a locomotive propelled by steam. Near the former is the great circular arena with its grassy steps upon which the people sit and where John Wesley himself preached to congregations of miners. Some of the tin-mines in this area are actually 3,000 feet in depth.

Down the Tranquil Fal

If we visit *Truro*, with its quaint and narrow streets, it will not be long before we find ourselves gliding down the River Fal by steamer on the way to Falmouth, than which there are few more fascinating places in the country. Here we find the old and the new grouped side by side, the busy commercial and seafaring section sharply divided from the part that forms a great modern holiday resort and yachting centre with everything to attract the visitor and nothing to offend.

In days that have now receded well into the historic past Falmouth was in truth our foremost port for mails from overseas. Into its sunswept harbour sailing vessels from the south and far west put in and the letters they brought were dispatched in post-haste style by road to London and other parts. St. Mawes Castle and Pendennis Castle are both within easy reach of Falmouth, a town which went by the name of Penny-come-Quick until the year 1660.

On the north coast is Newquay, another fine town that forms a magnet to thousands of tourists and holiday-makers. The " new quay " after which the town is named was actually constructed more than 300 years ago, but the place as we know it to-day is indeed a jewel in Cornwall's crown, for it looks full out into the Atlantic and ocean breakers come pounding in for countless surfriders on the sandy beaches. From here we can reach easily enough the famous Bedruthan Steps (a staircase made by nature leading down the cliffs)

or go to inspect the sands and caverns of Watergate Bay.

A little further to the south and still on the bracing north coast Cornwall has another gem in Perranporth, and if we go there we shall see Perran Round, a curious and quite impressive amphitheatre. Perhaps we may hear then of the old Cornish miracle plays, some of them taking three days to perform, which were given in this very Round and at other places. Or we may even inspect the site of St. Piran's Church, buried some 1,200 years in shifting sands of the dunes and rediscovered but little more than a century ago.

Our Most Southerly Point

The Lizard is the most southerly point on English shores, just as Land's End is the most westerly, and if you stand on high ground at a favoured spot along the centre of the county you can have the glittering sea within

Will F. Taylor.

THE CAVE AT MULLION COVE

Cornwall's rocky coast suggests smugglers, wreckers, and other like characters of historical romance, but to-day its caves and sands are the favourite haunts of British holiday-makers. Here is the cave at Mullion Cove its arched entrance forming a frame for Mullion Island beyond the rocks and sands.

Leonard and Marjorie Gayton.

ONCE THE HAUNT OF SMUGGLERS

More than one link with the smugglers of old can be found in the small fishing town of Mevagissey. The town stands on the beautiful coast of south Cornwall, about six miles from St. Austell. Its harbour, which is seen in this picture, is the home port for pilchard and mackerel fisherman, who can reap a rich harvest off the rocky coast at certain times of the year.

sight in front of you and behind as well. Over thirty miles to the west are the Scilly Isles which we can reach by boat or air. The people are few in number because the islands are so small, but they are famous for their fine flowers and bulbs and early vegetables, which they send to London and other great market towns. Their climate is a mild one ; in January, when we in England are huddling round our fires, the average temperature in the Scillies is 45°.

That Cornwall is of immense antiquity is proved by the existence of stone circles, monoliths and ancient crosses and one cannot go far without seeing some traces at least of these monuments of days almost before history began. Long in advance of the Romans there came to this western peninsula Phœnicians, who must have been inspired sailors and adventurers. They acquired from the Britons who

dwelt in these parts lead, tin and other metals precious to them and gave in exchange wares brought from their own eastern Mediterranean land of Phœnicia.

Devon, too, has everything of interest, its rocky, northern coast brisk and bracing, whilst its southern shores are warmer and far less boisterous. Here is a county of rich and well-kept farms, especially in the valleys or combes, and of cattle that compare for quality with any in the kingdom. Many people rank Devon second to Yorkshire in size but this is incorrect, the right order being Yorkshire, Lincolnshire and then Devon, the last-named being only thirty-six square miles behind as it takes third place.

Raleigh, Drake and Gilbert were all three men of Devon, whilst Dartmouth and Bideford have both joined handsomely with Plymouth in contributing to the maritime story of this county.

Mention of Bideford is a reminder, too, that *Westward Ho !* was written in this fine old town which has put up a statue to the author.

Trout Streams of Devon

The chief rivers of the county, many of them renowned for their trout, are the Tamar (which marks the boundary with the sister county), Exe (rising on Exmoor), Dart, Teign, Taw, Tavy and Torridge. Some of these rivers have their sources on Dartmoor and they are mostly swift-running. Taw and Torridge flow into Bideford Bay, whilst Plymouth Sound comes at the mouth of the broad Tamar. As for Cornish rivers, the most important are the Tamar, Fal, Fowey and Camel, the last-named running into Padstow Bay.

Like Cornwall, Devon's coastline is closely studded with popular holiday resorts. Ilfracombe and Lynton (within easy reach of the romantic Doone Valley) are on the rocky, northern shore looking across the broad Bristol Channel to the coast of South Wales. On the south, Sidmouth, Exmouth, Dawlish and Teignmouth form a notable quartet, each offering its particular attractions.

The Thatched Cottages

The whole of this English Riviera is a district of picturesque villages with many cottages wearing their snug bonnets of thatch. Wide spacious moorlands offer both solitude and the prospect of adventure, whilst there is always the romance of the sea-rovers of other days, as well as that of smugglers, ship-wreckers and their kin.

To accept these south-western counties merely as one immense pleasure or health-giving resort, however, would be to render them a great injustice. The wealth of agricultural and market garden produce of Devon and Cornwall, the hundreds of thousands of tons of kaolin (china clay) ; the fisheries, mines, stone quarries and so forth, all contribute an adequate share to

Copyright.

TRURO CATHEDRAL

Truro Cathedral stands upon the site of the church of St. Mary and was built between the years 1880 and 1910. The old church actually forms the south aisle of the Cathedral which itself is built in the early English style.

Gerald Wilson.

MONT ORGUEIL CASTLE

Go to Jersey in the Channel Islands and you will see this stern Norman stronghold overlooking Gorey Harbour. The Dukes of Normandy began building the Castellum de Gurrit, as it was first called, in the tenth century. Its present name was bestowed on it by the Duke of Clarence, son of King Henry IV. The little town of Gorey, nestling at the foot of the castle hill, is noted for its oysters.

the trade and industry of this fair land of ours.

The Channel Islands

Across the English Channel, clustering together west of France's Cap de la Hague, are the Channel Islands, the only parts of the old Duchy of Normandy which remain under the English Crown. Many British holiday-makers will know Jersey, Guernsey, Alderney, the feudal island of Sark, and perhaps the smaller islands of the group as well. For the Channel Islands are a famous holiday centre, especially in the spring when *St. Helier* in Jersey and *St. Peter Port* in Guernsey are focal points for visitors from both France and Britain.

Those of us who cannot go to see the lovely spring flowers of the Channel Islands may yet taste the early fruit and vegetables for which the islands are famous, for these are flown and shipped for sale in English markets.

A Great Novelist

Linked with the Islands is the name of Victor Hugo, the famous French author, whose *Toilers of the Sea* tells of the fisherfolk of these isles, and who himself lived for fourteen years in Hauteville House, Guernsey, where he wrote *Les Misérables* and other famous works. You can still visit this house where Hugo lived with his parents and where there are carved chairs whose Latin inscriptions may have been cut by the novelist himself.

These islands, which the French call appropriately enough *Îles Normandes*, have their own laws and customs. No enactments of the British Parliament have effect in the Channel

Islands unless special reference is made. So we find the offices and institutions of old alive to-day—the Bailiffs who preside over the Royal Courts : the Jurats who are the life-elected members of the Courts : and the States Assemblies. Sark, an island in the bailiwick of Guernsey, has been described as " the only purely feudal State remaining in the world." Its laws come from the Seigneur and its Parliament (called the Chief Pleas) which meets three times a year, but more frequently if circumstances demand it. The population of the islands is over 103,000. Though English is the language in daily use, French is the official language and a *patois* is used which has survived from Norman times. Not so very many years ago it was Sark's proud boast that there was no public debt, no income tax, no unemployment, " and best of all no politicians " on the island, and we who live in a larger,

higher-geared industrial community may wonder whether progress has really brought us all the advantages we think it has.

Most holiday-makers reach the Channel Islands by steamer from Southampton or Weymouth, but nowadays fast air services operate from London Airport (Heathrow) and Southampton to Channel Island airports on Guernsey, Jersey, and Alderney. Look at an air route map of the British Isles and you will see that all our distant parts—the Channel Islands, the Scilly Isles, the Shetlands, Orkneys, and Outer Hebrides—are linked with the mainland by regular and rapid air services.

The West Country

We travel now from the rugged beauty of Devon and Cornwall and the Channel Islands to the fresh, green pastures of the West Country : to the

Topical Press.

THE LITTLE HARBOUR OF A FEUDAL ISLAND

Sark, the small but lovely island in the Channel Islands group, is still governed by feudal laws and customs almost as old as the island itself. Creux Harbour, shown in this picture, lies on the eastern side of its rocky coast at the base of perpendicular cliffs through which tunnels have been cut to the interior of the island.

Leonard and Marjorie Gayton.

AN OLD MARKET TOWN IN THE WEST COUNTRY

The Yarn Market at Dunster, in Somerset, was where the famous " Dunsters " (broadcloth) were once sold. Rising proudly above this quaint little market town is Dunster Castle, which was bought by the Luttrell family in 1376 and which still remains in their hands.

counties of Dorset and Somerset where dairy and mixed farming are important and where cheese and other processed and tinned dairy products are made.

Going north-eastwards from the Blackdown Hills, we cross the pasture lands of the Plain of Somerset. Upon the plain is the old castle and market town of Taunton where Monmouth was proclaimed king in 1685. Farther away to the north, near Bridgwater, is Sedgemoor where in that same year Monmouth's pitiful forces were destroyed by the troops of James II.

The Plain itself continues as far as the Mendips, the range of hills running north-west from the broadcloth town of Frome towards Weston-super-Mare, the popular holiday resort on the Bristol Channel. The Mendips were once an important lead mining region, with more than 100 mines at the time of greatest mining activity here. But to-day, we know these hills better for their scenic wonders such as the Cheddar Gorge

which is really no more than a huge gap torn by water in the limestone Mendips.

The dissolving action of running water upon limestone rock is also seen in the numerous channels and caverns which streams have made in this part of the country. The best-known is the stream which disappears down a swallow, or swallet, hole near the village of Priddy to travel underground and re-emerge in the famous Wookey Hole about three miles from Wells and about half-way between Wells and Westbury. Wells itself, famous for its beautiful cathedral and moated Archbishop's palace, has a history going back more than 1,200 years to King Ina of Wessex. North-east of the city, on the other side of the Mendips, is Radstock which is one of the centres of the Somerset coalfield.

Wells is not the only site of ancient Christianity in Somerset. To the south is Glastonbury which has rightly been called " a cradle of the English Church."

VILLAGE CRAFTSMEN AT WORK

Central Press.

The ancient craft of roof thatching is dying out. Only in the country districts are skilled thatchers found, but there is still a steady demand for their services.

Fox Photos.

Skilled thatchers can work their reeds into cunning shapes and patterns, neatly trimming the thatch once it has been securely fastened in position.

J. Dixon-Scott.

Basket-making is but one of the old crafts and rural industries that still flourish in Britain's country-side. Here, in his small "factory" on King's Sedge Moor, the basket-maker deftly weaves dried withies into stout baskets of all shapes and sizes in much the same way as his ancestors did.

CIDER MAKING

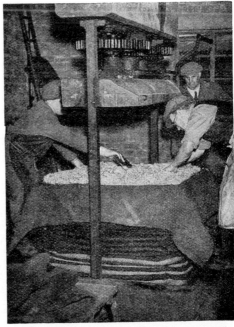

The apples in this picture have come from Devon orchards to a Norfolk factory where they ripen before being crushed into the pulp. The best cider apples are grown in the West Country.

Worcestershire is another county where cider is made. At this cider mill the fruit is pulped electrically and the juice squeezed from the pulp in the presses.

Photos : Fox Photos.

For the most part, cider is made by thoroughly up-to-date machinery ; but in some parts of Gloucestershire, old stone mills such as the one seen above are still used. The horse knows exactly what is required, and plods round, working the grindstone which crushes the apples into pulp.

The Abbey at Glastonbury is the oldest religious foundation in the country and dates traditionally from A.D. 63 when it was founded by St. Joseph of Arimathea whose staff, plunged by the saint into the ground, took root and became famous as the Holy Thorn.

This again is King Arthur's country. The Holy Grail for which he and his knights searched is said to be buried at the foot of Glastonbury Tor, and Glastonbury itself—so the legend runs— is Avalon, seat of the Knights of the Round Table and burial place of King Arthur and Guinevere, his queen.

Their burial place is said to have been discovered in 1191, while Henry de Soliaco was Abbot of Glastonbury. In the trunk of a hollow tree, the bones of King Arthur were found, as was the flaxen hair of Guinevere. Nearby was a cross made of lead which bore the words " Here lies buried the renowned King Arthur in the Isle of Avalon with Guinevere." Relics were certainly found about this time, but were they really those of King Arthur? It depends on whether or not you believe the legend.

North-east of Glastonbury, on the banks of the River Avon, stands the old Roman city of Bath, often called " Queen of the West Country."

Bath owes its fame to its mild winters and, above all, to its famous hot springs which made it a favourite resort of the ancient Roman conquerors, who saw perhaps in its gentle climate something that reminded them of their distant homes in Italy. A large Roman bath, built about the first century, can still be seen.

But the period of Bath's greatest glory was the eighteenth century when the city became the resort of fashionable society, when such as Beau Nash were supreme in the Grand Pump Room. The stately qualities of those times are preserved

Planet News.

THE ABBOT'S KITCHEN AT GLASTONBURY

Glastonbury is the oldest religious foundation in England. The Abbey that was once a house of the Benedictine monks is now in ruins, and of its domestic buildings only the Abbot's Kitchen remains. Here food was prepared for pilgrims and guests and cooked over four fires, one at each corner of the building; the chimneys from these fires carried the smoke out at the eight-sided lantern on top of the stone roof.

UNUSUAL ARCHES IN WELLS CATHEDRAL

Planet News.

Wells Cathedral has been called the "most beautiful thing on earth." The crowning glory of the Cathedral is the West Front, upon which there are some 300 carved figures each about 8 feet high. On entering, one is immediately impressed by the double arches seen in this picture, which meet to form a St. Andrew's Cross and were so built in 1338 to strengthen the central tower.

for us in many of the buildings of this lovely city which, standing in its amphitheatre of hills, is still visited by thousands who come to drink of the healing waters and bathe in the warm pools.

Georgian Bath

Bath is one of our oldest cities and was known to the Romans as *Aquæ Sulis*, meaning the Waters dedicated to Sul, a goddess of those times. Besides its relics of Roman times, Bath has a fine Abbey Church, upon whose West Front some mason of bygone time has carved the story of Jacob's Ladder.

But as one might expect, Bath's greatest architectural beauties belong to Georgian times, when it was fashionable to drink the waters of the spa whether one was ill or not. The worthy citizens of Bath of that time were aware of the leisured life led by men and women " of Quality," and, by providing a round of tasteful entertainment at the spa, lured the rich from their more familiar haunts in London. When Richard Nash—Beau Nash, as he came to be called—became Master of Ceremonies at the spa, its popularity grew so great that more houses were needed. Accordingly the Woods—father and son—were employed, the one designing the North and South Parades, and the Assembly Rooms, and the other, the Royal Crescent. The latter is a particularly fine example of the architecture of the time, and we who look upon it to-day find it hard to realize how little public opinion favoured Royal Crescent when it was new.

Another of the sights of Bath is the Pulteney Bridge which, since it is walled in, reminds us

J. Dixon-Scott.

BUILT BY THE ROMANS AT BATH

The Ancient Britons knew of the properties of the waters of Bath for curing ill-health, and their conquerors the Romans actually built the bath seen in this picture. Many centuries later, when coaches were the chief means of getting from one place to another, Bath was a great meeting-place for the leaders of society and for famous literary persons. Behind the Roman Bath in this picture is Bath Abbey Church, whose west front bears the story of Jacob's Ladder carved in stone.

A. F. Kersting.

TO COMMEMORATE A GREAT DISCOVERY

This is Bristol seen from the Cabot Tower on Brandon Hill, erected to commemorate the " fourth centenary of the discovery of America by John Cabot, and sons Lewis, Sebastian, and Sanctus." In the foreground is the Memorial Tower of the University. This is 200 feet high and contains a bell weighing 10 tons.

of those days when bridges in England, like the Ponte Vecchio in Florence, had shops and houses upon them. Beneath the bridge flow the waters of the Avon, and if we followed them down to the river mouth, we should come to the largest city in the west of England— Bristol, with its important deep-water docks at Avonmouth.

Bristol is the port whence the Cabots sailed in Henry VII's reign to discover Newfoundland, an exploit that is commemorated by the Cabot Tower on Brandon Hill. To-day, it is an important industrial city, making many kinds of products, from aircraft to chocolates, cocoa and cigarettes, textiles and leather. The docks at Avonmouth, where the river enters the estuary of the Severn, are a fruit trade centre (especially for bananas) for cargoes from Central and South America and the West Indies.

Across the Severn from Avonmouth are Newport and the South Wales coast.

At one time the only way to travel by rail from Bristol to Newport was through Gloucester. But construction of the Severn railway tunnel put an end to this roundabout route, cutting the journey from Bristol to Newport from eighty to twenty-six miles.

The Severn Estuary

The Severn Estuary is rather like a funnel in shape and this causes great differences between high tides and low tides. Flood tides pile up in the estuary until at last they rush up the Severn in the famous " bore." A similar bore, called " the Egre," can be seen upon the River Trent. Some day our engineers may build a big dam across the Severn so that its waters can be used to provide electricity for South Wales and the Midlands.

It is also proposed to build a giant suspension bridge across the upper reaches of the Severn Estuary.

EAST ANGLIA

Fox Photos.

HARVESTING IN THE MODERN STYLE

East Anglia contains field after field of splendid tall, strong wheat, especially in its northern region. When the heavy ears are golden-red, the farmer harvests his crop making increasing use of the modern machinery that simplifies his work. Here, for example, is a combine harvester which performs simultaneously all the operations from cutting to threshing.

EAST ANGLIA got its name from those Angles who, in the sixth century A.D., pushed up the tidal river estuaries in their longships, overcame the Britons, and established their own simple civilisation on the ruins of the Roman-British culture they found there. Originally Norfolk and Suffolk, East Anglia to-day usually includes the county of Essex as well. It is part of the rich agricultural lowland of south-eastern England, and, geologically at any rate, belongs to the London Basin.

In the west is the chalk country of the East Anglian Heights which come to the sea in the steep cliffs of Hunstanton Point. Most of it is the broad gentle slope from those low chalk hills to the North Sea, to which flow sluggish rivers with marshland along their lower courses, and deep estuaries up which the sea-tides make their ways. Connected with the lower Yare are the Norfolk Broads, wide sheets of shallow water formed by the barring of the old estuary by sandpits and mudbanks, and to-day a favourite summer resort for those who love sailing and camping and fishing.

The Sunshine Coast

Orwell and Stour combine their estuaries to form the deep-water harbour of *Harwich*, a naval station guarded by the forts and seaplane base near Felixstowe, and an important ferry-town for the Continent. Mail steamers ply regularly between Harwich and the Hook of Holland and Antwerp. One of the earliest train ferries to be started in Britain runs between Harwich and Zeebrugge. It is employed in goods traffic only. Truck-loads of goods from the Continent can be shunted on board the ferry, taken to Harwich and run off to the main line railway to Liverpool Street or the North.

The coast of East Anglia is low and

marshy towards the south, but from Thorpe Ness northwards it has cliffs of firm gravel and sand. The whole coastline has undergone subsidence, and the ruins of several of the old towns and villages now lie beneath the sea. Ancient Dunwich was an important city and port in the Middle Ages, with many churches, monasteries and a king's palace ; to-day all that is left of it is a small fishing village nestling behind a steep cliff on whose brink totter the few ruins of its former greatness. Aldeburgh, now a pleasant but small seaside resort, and once an important port, is another town that has suffered in the past from the inroads of the sea.

This is the drier and sunnier side of Britain, and the whole coastline is studded with popular seaside resorts— Southend, Walton, Clacton-on-Sea, Dovercourt, Felixstowe, Aldeburgh, Southwold, Lowestoft, Yarmouth, Sheringham, Cromer and Hunstanton.

Yarmouth and *Lowestoft* are the headquarters of great British herring and sprat fisheries in autumn, when Scots lassies come south to deal with the catch, cleaning the fish, grading them and packing them into barrels with salt, with the amazing speed born of long practice. Many other fish, too, are caught and landed at these and many smaller ports along the coast. Colchester oysters from the oyster-beds of the Colne estuary are almost as famous as Yarmouth bloaters and kippers.

A Farming Region

East Anglia is mainly a farming region, where a good deal of our home supplies of meat, wool, grain, fruit and vegetables, butter and milk are produced. The Lea Valley market gardens are an important source of market produce for London and have one of the largest glasshouse areas in the

Leonard and Marjorie Gayton.

A VILLAGE GREEN IN ESSEX

One of the most charming villages in Essex is Finchingfield. Indeed, it has been called " one of the four loveliest villages in England." Here we see the village green. The road which crosses it is carried over the brook by a narrow-backed bridge and then climbs gently up the hill to the old church of St. John Baptist.

British Commonwealth. They supply such London markets as Covent Garden, Spitalfields, and the Borough with choice fruit, flowers and vegetables. The famous orchard centre of Essex is Tiptree with its important jam factories and vegetable canneries.

In the Middle Ages East Anglia was the home of flourishing woollen industries; worsted got its name from Worstead, near Norwich, where the Flemish weavers settled in Anglo-Norman times. Great churches, all too large for their villages and small towns, bear witness to ancient days when their population was much larger than it is now.

To-day, the woollen manufactures have gone chiefly to the coalfields of the Midlands and the North, and the old East Anglian woollen towns engage in other business—milling, brewing and distilling, and manufacturing the goods and machinery needed by an agricultural population. Most of them are market towns to which country folk bring their produce, and from which they take home things they need but cannot grow or make for themselves. The very names of some of them—Newmarket (famous for its " Heath " and its horse races), Stowmarket, Needham Market —prove how long they have been market towns.

Ipswich has iron foundries and engineering works ; it makes agricultural implements and garden tools, and so does *Norwich*, the lovely old Cathedral and castle city on the Wensum, where woollen goods and boots and shoes are made, and also chocolates and confectionery, beer and mineral waters, as

Mirror Features.

BILLINGFORD MILL, NEAR DISS

In January, the hedgers and ditchers get to work, trimming back the hedges with their sickles and billhooks and clearing the ditches so that the water can run freely. Here we see them at work by Billingford Mill, a post mill that recalls the days when wind and water were the power for grinding the corn of every farmer in the country.

FROM TUDOR TIMES

Planet News.

These beam and plaster houses recall the days of the Tudors when the country town of Lavenham in Suffolk was an important centre of the cloth trade. An even more impressive relic of its greatest days is the Hall of the Guild of Corpus Christi in the market-place.

A. F. Kersting.

When James I visited Audley End, he declared that " it was too much for a King, but it might do very well for a Lord Treasurer." Thomas Howard, first Earl of Suffolk, then held that office and it was he who built this wonderful mansion near the old Essex town of Saffron Walden.

well as mustard from locally-grown supplies of seed.

In Essex and nearer London, several modern factories have been set up, notably those for making rayon (artificial silk). But it is as grainland that East Anglia is most important—field after field of splendid tall strong wheat, heavy with gold-red ears, especially in the northern half of the region, where beautiful old thatched houses are perhaps commoner than anywhere else in Britain.

Golden Grain

Why is south-eastern Britain the place where most British wheat is grown ?

First of all, the land there is rich enough and the soil stiff enough to grow fine, tall, heavy wheat. Much of this soil is fine earth made by prehistoric glaciers grinding over the rocks and powdering their surfaces into fine " rock flour," which was left behind when the ancient ice melted and streams washed it down and spread it out over the plains of the east.

But good soil by itself is not enough; to grow fine wheat the fields must have just the right amount of rain and sunshine at the right time.

Wheat needs rain when it is springing up and sprouting, and when the ears of grain are forming. After that, it requires long bright sunny days to ripen the ears, and then to give the farmer a chance to reap and harvest the grain during fine dry weather.

This is exactly what happens in most years in East Anglia and in other parts of south-eastern Britain. The rains of spring and early summer sprout the wheat, make it grow tall and strong, and swell the ears. The

Fox Photos.

SAILING ON THE NORFOLK BROADS

The Norfolk Broads and their connecting rivers form one of Britain's favourite holiday haunts. The calm waters make the Broads a paradise for the more cautious yachtsmen who like to be certain of a comfortable berth at night. Scenes such as this, of well-rigged craft proceeding under full sail, are common enough on the Broadland waterways where yachts, wherries, and motor cruisers are available to the holiday-maker.

MAKING SUGAR FROM BEET

Sugar beet is now cultivated widely in Britain, particularly in East Anglia, where there are also the factories to deal with the crop. Harvesting takes place about October, when the beets are lifted, their green tops cut, and carted to roadside dumps whence lorries take them to the factory.

Photos : Fox Photos.

A lot of earth is lifted with the beet when they are harvested. This is one of the reasons why high pressure water is used to unload the lorries when they reach the factory.

In the factory the beet is washed by such special machines as this before it passes through the various processes which extract the sugar and separate it from the water and waste.

long sunny days of late summer and early autumn ripen the grain and give the farmer a sunshine harvest-time.

Sugar Beet

Sugar beet is now cultivated widely in East Anglia, and sugar factories have been set up, for sugar beet grows just as well there as on the opposite side of the North Sea.

Harvest time in the sugar beet fields is the late autumn when the fat, white beet are " lifted " and their green tops lopped off with a sickle. They are actually a muddy white in colour, for quite a lot of earth is lifted with them. Go along East Anglian roads during October and you will see dumps of lifted beet waiting for the lorries which will take them to the sugar beet factory. There intricate machinery will wash them and process them, extracting the sugar from the beet and separating it

from the water and waste. The raw sugar which results has to be refined, of course, and the process used includes the dissolution of the sugar in water, its treatment with charcoal, and its boiling.

How do you reach Norfolk and Suffolk where the beet is most widely grown ? There is a fine road from London to Norwich as well as the main line train routes.

One main route of British Railways goes *via Chelmsford*, the market centre and county town of Essex, through *Colchester*, once a fine Roman city and now an important military and market centre, to *Ispwich*, whence two main lines branch—one to serve the east coast watering-places, the other to Norwich and the north coast. Another main line cuts north by way of the Lea Valley, Bishop's Stortford, Cambridge, and Ely to Norwich and to King's Lynn.

Topical Press.

OUTWARD BOUND FROM HARWICH

Harwich, one of England's gateway ports to the Continent, is also a centre for international yacht racing. In this picture we see the start of a race from Harwich to Kristiansand in Norway, in which yachts from England, Norway and Holland took part. A fine breeze on the starboard quarter enabled the craft to show their paces watched by enthusiasts on the pierhead.

THE FENLANDS

Will F. Taylor.

OLIVER CROMWELL'S HOUSE

The so-called " Isle of Ely " was for long the camp of refuge for English freedom, for hereabouts Hereward the Wake had his stronghold. Oliver Cromwell, who was born at Huntingdon, also spent much time in these parts, and you see above the photograph of an old house at Ely which was for a while in the occupation of the Lord Protector.

THIS is the country of Hereward the Wake, who, secure in his Camp of Refuge amid the marshes, long defied Norman William, who in the end went to great lengths to make peace with him. The story of this grand old Anglo-Saxon is told in Charles Kingsley's " Hereward the Wake," where you may read of the fenland, of the men who fought there in Hereward's days, and of those who lived there in Kingsley's time:—

" Such was the Fenland—hard, yet cheerful ; rearing a race of hard and cheerful men, showing their power in old times in valiant fighting, and for many a century since in the valiant industry which has drained and embanked the land, till it has become a very garden of the Lord. And the highlander who may look from the promontory of Peterborough, the ' golden borough ' of old time; or from that Witham on the Hill which once was a farm of Hereward the Wake's ; or from the heights of that Isle of Ely which was so long the camp of refuge for English freedom—over the maze of dykes and lodes, the squares of rich corn and verdure, will confess that the lowlands, as well as the highlands, can at times breed gallant men."

The English Holland

The Fen country is the low land round the large inlet of the Wash, into which flow several long slow rivers. At their seaward ends these rivers are filled with tide-water from the sea when the tide is high ; but when the tide is low their water is shallower and their smaller streams flow between wide steep banks of soft mud. For miles they have banks built by men to keep them in their channels when the water is high, or they would overflow the surrounding country, which is at a lower level there.

When there were no banks, these streams overflowed and created great swamps, which were the homes of myriads of water fowl. Reeds and coarse vegetation choked the rivers and overran the swamps. But here and there were patches of higher and firmer

71

land that stood up a little above the marshes, like islands (as indeed they came to be called). In later times towns arose on these fenland "islands"; some of these are important to-day—the cathedral cities of Ely and Peterborough, for example. It was on just such a high and dry spot that Hereward's "Camp of Refuge" was made.

In years to come, the Wash may cease to be a feature of the Fenland coastline. As the Fens themselves were turned from swamp into fertile farming land, so may the Wash be reclaimed from the sea to provide thousands more fertile acres. Much has already been done, and by April, 1949, such projects as the Wainfleet Scheme and the Holbeach Scheme had, within a space of three years, reclaimed nearly 10,000 acres of rich farming land. One of the pioneers of land reclamation in the Wash was no less a person than King George VI whose Sandringham estate was the scene of pre-war experiments in reclamation. Reclamation is also being done by the Norfolk Estuary Company and will result from the River Nene Catchment Board's plan to extend the restraining walls of the Nene river farther into the Wash.

Cambridge

The first towns grew up on the borders of the Fenland, where higher ground provided good sites. The University town of *Cambridge*, for example, commanded the ridge of downland which in early times formed the only means of communication between East Anglia and the Midlands. To the north lay impassable fenland; to the south impenetrable forest. In the Middle Ages Cambridge was one of the chief distributing centres of England; but when the silting up of the Wash closed its ports, trade declined, and its great annual fair—" Stourbridge

Reece Winstone.

LINCOLN CATHEDRAL AND THE EXCHEQUER GATE

Although a church is said to have stood on this site as long ago as A.D. 627 and the cathedral of Bishop Remigius was built here in 1074, Lincoln Cathedral as we see it to-day was not begun until 1192. This picture shows us the towers of the West Front rising above the ancient Exchequer Gate which is a relic of the walls that surrounded the Minster Yard.

SCENES AND SIGHTS OF CAMBRIDGE

Photochrom.

The beautiful old Colleges and their chapels are the chief attractions for visitors to Cambridge. King's College Chapel, illustrated above, is an architectural wonder of the world.

Will F. Taylor.

The River Cam flows placidly through the grounds of many Cambridge colleges. Here we see St. John's, which possesses two bridges, one known as the " Bridge of Sighs."

Will F. Taylor.

Many Cambridge colleges have verdant lawns and beautiful gardens leading right down to the edge of the River Cam, and the ancient buildings thus appear in a setting at once dignified and restful. In this picture we see the grounds of King's College, with Clare College beyond.

Fair "—became but a shadow of itself. It is the University that makes it important to-day ; and the beautiful old colleges and their chapels are the chief attraction for visitors. King's College Chapel is one of the architectural wonders of the world. As one would expect in a University town, printing and bookbinding is an important industry, but Cambridge is also important as a market centre for the farmers of the surrounding country-side and for its radio industry.

The Fertile Fens

The Fens form " a vast level of black peaty soil 2 feet to 6 feet deep, resting on clay," and stretching into several English counties. This region is kept drained by windmills and pumping stations where water is lifted into drainage channels to find a natural way to the rivers and the sea.

A great deal of fenland is now used by farmers, and intersected by " droves " or straight roads that lead from village to field. The Fen country is famous for its heavy crops of potatoes, its fine celery, and its splendid vegetables.

More interesting still are the orchard lands. Acres and acres of strawberries and raspberries, plums and apples, and other fruit provide work for fruit-pickers from June to October. At some of the towns and villages (*e.g.*, Histon and Shippea Hill) large jam factories, fruit canneries and vegetable canneries have been built.

The oolite Northampton Heights (whose rich iron deposits feed the blast furnaces of Wellingborough, our second largest iron producer) bound the Fens on the west, and the chalk hills of the Chilterns to the East Anglian Heights bound them on the south and east. Other important iron-smelting towns on the fringe of Fenland are *Scunthorpe* in Lincolnshire, and *Corby* in Northamptonshire.

F. Dixon-Scott.

AT TRINITY COLLEGE, CAMBRIDGE

The charm of old buildings, in a perfect setting, could never be better seen than in this picture of Trinity College, Cambridge. Our view shows the Great Court with its lawn and fountain. As one would expect in a University town, printing and bookbinding is one of the chief industries of Cambridge.

THE HEART OF ENGLAND

Walter Scott.

ANNE HATHAWAY'S COTTAGE, SHOTTERY

Anne Hathaway, wife of William Shakespeare, was the daughter of a farmer. The charming cottage shown in this picture was once her home, and was inhabited by generation after generation of Hathaways, the descendants of Anne's family living here until 1911. The cottage is at Shottery, within comfortable walking distance of Stratford-on-Avon.

THE very centre of England, they say, is in Warwickshire, the county of beautiful woods and gardens, through which the Avon flows on its way to the Severn. This is Shakespeare's country, for on the Avon is Stratford, where the greatest poet and dramatist of all time was born in 1564, and where you can visit the house and go into the very room in which the " Bard of Avon " first saw the light. The town is visited by large numbers of people every year ; they come from all parts of the civilised world to see the birth-place of Shakespeare and the wonderful collection of Shakespeare relics in its rooms, the old Grammar School which he is said to have attended and the cottage at Shottery near-by, where he courted and won Anne Hathaway.

In the neighbourhood are still the remnants of the Forest of Arden, which Shakespeare loved ; and in the towns and villages are lovely old Tudor houses that remind us of the days of Good Queen Bess when Shakespeare was doing some of his finest work. Beneath the shadow of Warwick Castle, which is finely preserved, are the beautiful old Tudor houses of Mill Street ; and not far away is Kenilworth Castle, where Leicester entertained Queen Elizabeth I with splendid hospitality.

The Red Plain

Warwickshire is part of the English Midlands, which geologists call " The Red Plain." It *is* red—red in the fertile fields when it has been newly turned up by the plough, red in its wayside walls and in the mellow stone of its old cottages, country seats and ancient castles. For the whole of this heart of England is floored with the New Red Sandstone, which is the

75

colour of old-rose ; from it the fertile red soil has been formed, and from it the stone for building has been taken. But in places humps of much older and harder rocks have thrust through this New Red Sandstone floor—in Charnwood Forest and in Cannock Chase, for example—and it is in and around such old rocks as these that the great coalfields of the English Midlands lie.

The boundaries of this Midland region are clearly shown in any good map. The oolite (limestone) ridges which can be traced from the Cotswolds through Edge Hill and the North-ampton Heights to Lincoln Edge and the Humber form its southern bound-ary. Its western limits are the Welsh Highlands, along whose edges are the old " Marches " or border lands held in the Middle Ages by the " Lords Marcher "—stout fighters with strong bands of retainers to keep back the Welsh raiders.

In the north the Pennines project far into the plain, above whose floor they stand like a giant promontory of limestone thrust into a sea of sand-stone. From the Pennines, beautiful streams like the Dove and Derwent flow down through the lovely dales to swell the lordly Trent that sweeps on past Burton, the home of the best English ales, past Nottingham, the busy town of the hosiers and boot-makers, past the old castle town of Newark and through farm lands and factory centres to the deep estuary of the Humber.

The Midland Sea Gates

The English Midland Plain has three great gateways through which the pro-ducts of its mines and busy factories pour to the wide world. The china and crockery of the Potteries ; the boots and shoes of Stafford, Northamp-ton, Nottingham and Leicester ; the iron and other metal goods of the

W. G. Davis.

THE MEMORIAL THEATRE, STRATFORD-ON-AVON

This modern building, reflected in the calm waters of the River Avon, is the Memorial Theatre whose festival performances of Shakespeare's plays bring visitors from all parts of Britain and the world. Built of red brick, it forms a striking addition to the scenery of the river banks.

Leonard & Marjorie Gayton.

THE " LEYCESTER HOSPITAL " AT WARWICK

The gabled, half-timbered building on the right of this picture is the " Leycester Hospital," which was endowed as a home for old soldiers by Robert Dudley, Earl of Leicester, in the year 1571. Originally the hall of three local religious guilds, the Hospital stands close by the West Gate and still serves as a home for veterans of the wars.

Black Country ; the motor cars, agricultural machinery and cycles of Coventry and other centres ; and the goods from the engineering shops and electrical works of Rugby and its neighbours all use these gateways. They are sea-gates— one, the Mersey gate at which stands the great city-port of *Liverpool*, with its ship-building sister-town of Birkenhead across the water. Another is the Humber gate, with the important port of *Hull* (or Kingston-upon-Hull as we should rightly call it if we keep to its old name), and its sister-port of *Goole* farther up the estuary. The third is the Severn gate where are *Newport* and *Cardiff*, which serve not only the Midlands, but also the busy coal and metal businesses of the South Wales coalfield; and on the other side of the estuary, the city-port of *Bristol* on the Bristol Avon (with its outport for deep-water ships at Avonmouth), which is itself an important manufacturing centre with sugar refineries, tobacco factories, paper, timber, and

leather industries, and cocoa and confectionery plants.

Ways Across the Red Plain

South-eastwards, across the oolite ridge and the clay vale on the other side, and then over the chalk Chilterns several great main railways provide highways to *London*, the great estuary port where gather the ships of the seven seas. These main routes cut across the eastern side of the Red Plain, serving Northampton, Nottingham, Leicester and Derby on their way to the north by the eastern flanks of the Pennines. Other main routes pass through the heart of the plain and serve its western borders, too. The western route to Scotland cuts through the Midland Gate (in which is the great railway junction and engineering town of *Crewe*) between the Pennines and Welsh mountains to reach the busy plain of South Lancashire. A main railway line crosses the Red Plain by way of the

L. E. A.

A LINK WITH GEORGE WASHINGTON

Sulgrave Manor is in Northamptonshire. It was rebuilt about the year 1540 by Lawrence Washington, a direct ancestor of George Washington, the first President of the United States. The north courtyard is formed by the Tudor and Queen Anne wings of the house and by a building that was once used as a brewhouse.

and some can only admit "monkey-boats" of about 30 tons. On these the canal folk live with their families, every member of which takes a part in the work almost as soon as he or she can run about without fear of falling overboard. Horses are still used to tow the barges along, but in recent years steam barges and motor barges have become common on most of our leading canals.

On some of the continental canals, barges of a thousand tons and more are in common use. British canals might be made much more valuable if they were deepened and widened, and already on some of the more important—the Grand Union, for example — the work of reconstruction and improvement is well in hand.

The Red Plain has rich soil, and abundant grasses suitable for cattle and sheep — cattle (especially dairy cattle) on the plains of Staffordshire and Cheshire, but sheep on the higher and drier ground of the hills, especially the slopes of the oolite ridge. The hides from its cattle and the wool from its sheep, the clear water and power from its running streams gave rise in early times to the great boot and shoe industries and the woollen industries which have long had their home there, and which grew by leaps and bounds when the rich coalfields of the Midlands were opened up.

Black Country to Shrewsbury, from whence another main line goes up the Severn Valley into the very heart of Wales.

Our Canals

It is in the Midland Plain, too, that our canals spread their closest network. The main canal routes form a kind of X with Mersey, Humber, Severn and Thames at the extremities of its four arms. Near the crossing of the arms lie the Black Country and the Potteries, where the system of canals is closer than anywhere else in Britain.

Our canals are not nearly so flourishing as those of the Dutch, the Belgians, the French and the Germans, for many have been allowed to fall into disuse,

In the Coalfields

The coalfields, as we have already seen, are chiefly on and around the humps of ancient rocks that in past ages forced themselves through the level floor of New Red Sandstone.

Each of them has its own particular business, which began in the first place because of special local advantages.

There are, first of all, the coalfields of the Pennine flanks—the North Staffordshire, and the Derby and Nottingham fields. The former is universally known as the "Potteries" because its characteristic manufactures are of china, earthenware and pottery of all kinds. The chief centres are "The Five Towns" (though there are really six, all now included in the city of *Stoke-on-Trent:* Burslem, Hanley, Longton, Tunstall, Fenton and Stoke itself). The Derby and Nottingham fields together form part of the extension into the Midlands of the great Yorkshire coalfields, and here are the iron and steel and engineering works of *Derby* and *Chesterfield,* the woollen and cotton hosiery and boot business of *Nottingham* and *Mansfield,* and the silk manufactures of *Derby* and its neighbourhood.

In the very heart of the Red Plain are three coalfields: (1) the "Black Country" or South Staffordshire coalfield ; (2) the Warwickshire coalfield ; (3) the Leicestershire coalfield.

The first gets its name from the "black" industries carried on beneath a pall of smoke from factory chimneys, and from its grimy canals and giant heaps of black and grey waste from the coal mines or of slag from many blast furnaces. The great city of *Birmingham* is near the south-eastern edge of the coalfield and not on it. It makes all

Fox Photos.

STOKE-ON-TRENT FROM THE AIR

In this picture the kilns, shaped like dunces' caps, give the clue to the important industry for which this great manufacturing town is famous. Stoke-on-Trent is really six towns (Stoke, Burslem, Hanley, Tunstall, Longton, and Fenton) in one, and it is the famous centre of the North Staffordshire pottery industry, with more than 300 pottery works within the city boundaries.

kinds of metal goods, cocoa, chocolate, soap, machinery, motor-cars, explosives and many other manufactured things, and is the business heart of the Black Country.

It has many splendid buildings, and like most of the big industrial towns of the Midlands and the North, much beautiful country around it, and within easy reach of the city. Other towns in the Black Country, Wolverhampton, Walsall, Wednesbury, Dudley and West Bromwich, for example, engage in various branches of the iron and steel trades and in working in metals as well as in engineering and chemical industries. Each, however, has its own special business, which is more important than the several others carried on there.

We must bear in mind that when we speak of a certain town as carrying on a special manufacture, it is the *chief*, and by no means the only, business conducted by its workers. Large factory towns, especially in the Midlands and the North, engage in very many different industries, because most of them have been built on or near the coalfields.

Yet Other Coalfields

The Warwick coalfield is near enough to Coventry and Rugby to be an advantage to both; *Coventry* specialises in motor engineering, but also has important rayon factories, and *Rugby* in the making of electrical apparatus and general engineering. The Leicestershire coalfield is some few miles from Leicester; it is purely a coalfield, and has no great manufacture which has made its home upon it; it has no large industrial cities like most of the other coalfields, but many mining villages and small towns. Ashby-de-la-Zouch is the most important of them. *Leicester* itself is a highly important woollen hosiery manufacturing centre, whose industry dates back to the time when the wool of the Leicester breed of sheep first became famous.

On the western borders of the Midland Plain are three other coalfields —the Flint and Denbigh fields, with ironworks at Wrexham, the Shropshire or Mid-Severn coalfields, and the Forest of Dean, which, like the Leicestershire coalfield, is a field pure and simple, and not the home of any great manufacturing industry.

The Forest itself is very beautiful, especially where the Wye comes down from its deep wooded and winding valley past the ruins of Tintern Abbey to Chepstow Castle and the Severn estuary. Tintern Abbey was founded in 1131 by the lord of the castle at Chepstow for Cistercian monks, and was built according to the Cistercian rule: " None of our houses is to be built in cities, in castles, or villages; but in places remote from the conversation of men."

Before leaving the coalfields of the Midlands, a word must be said about the working of deposits occurring near the surface. During and since the Second World War, the need for coal has been so great that quarries, or opencast mines have been worked. This has usually meant tearing open great tracts of land, but luckily this is done in such a way that once the coal has been extracted, the removed soil can be replaced and, after a time, cultivation resumed.

The Salt Towns

The western side of the Midland Plain, also has rich salt deposits and brine springs. In Cheshire, along the line of the Weaver valley, are the salt towns, Northwich, Middlewich, Winsford and Nantwich. These are the towns of the Cheshire salt field which, some hundred and fifty years ago, was the only large salt field that had been discovered in Britain. Since salt was needed as a raw material for making soda and other chemicals, it was natural for these salt towns to become centres of a great chemical industry, and to-day many of the important chemical factories in our country are gathered in and around the salt towns where they are near raw materials and good trade and

Planet News.

THE RUINS OF COVENTRY CATHEDRAL

Coventry, the Warwickshire manufacturing city noted for its cars, farm machinery and bicycles, had a rich architectural heritage much of which was destroyed during the terrible air raid of November, 1940. Among the priceless buildings destroyed was the beautiful Cathedral of which only ruins remain. Lawns and flowering rock gardens have been laid out where once the citizens of Coventry worshipped.

shipping centres. Their products are sent by the Weaver and the Manchester Ship Canal to Liverpool for export and to the manufacturing towns of South Lancashire.

Bores are sunk into the rock-salt, water is admitted, and the brine is pumped up to be used in chemical manufacture, or, by evaporation, converted into the household salt we know so well. The subterranean hollows created by brine pumping cannot be propped up and the result is that in places large subsidences occur. Houses lean or sink to a low level, but, being built on wooden framework, are raised every so often. There is a special local authority which deals with this.

In Cheshire, too, at Stanlow, is the big new plant for producing solvents, *i.e.,* chemical preparations used to dissolve or extract substances. The new plant is said to be the largest of its kind in the world.

Farming in the Midlands

There is so much to be seen in the towns and cities of the Midlands and in their busy factories and engineering works that it is easy to forget the farms and villages of these " middlelands of England." But there is beautiful countryside away from the big towns, and here the farmers maintain dairy herds, raise pigs, and grow orchard fruits, potatoes and grain. Malt made from their barley is used by the brewers of Burton-on-Trent, who get their hops from the " yards " of Herefordshire and Worcestershire.

You can probably name quite easily some of the delightful things which come from these rich farmlands—the delicious Cheshire and Stilton cheeses, the Pershore plums, cider from Hereford, and the famous pies to which Melton Mowbray has given its name.

It is not surprising to find in these farmlands old market towns, some of which are now thriving cities. Such places are Gloucester, Hereford and Worcester, cathedral cities all. Nor should we forget the ancient walled city of Chester, which, like Shrewsbury and Hereford, was one of the great fortresses of the border lands.

At Chester can be seen relics of Roman times, when the city was Deva, or Devana Castra; beautiful half-timbered buildings that recall the days of the first Elizabeth; and those unusual stone corridors called " the Rows " : and massive walls and towers.

The Marches

These western parts of England were generously provided with castles at one time; in the early Middle Ages, a triple line of fortresses stood along the Marches. Several still stand proudly, and probably the most interesting and imposing of these is Ludlow, whose massive square keep is thought to have been built during the reign of Henry I.

J. Dixon-Scott.

THE RUINS OF TINTERN ABBEY

Founded by Walter de Clare in 1131, Tintern Abbey has been called " the most perfect ruin in England." For even the decay that has overtaken it since the monks were driven out in the reign of Henry VIII cannot destroy the faultlessness of its Early English style and the beauty of its proportions. To-day, its noble grace adds to the charm of the Wye Valley in which it stands.

THE BUSY NORTH

SHEFFIELD, ENGLAND'S CITY OF STEEL

Nothing could better typify our busy North than this picture of industrial Sheffield, where fine steel cutlery and tools are made. Smoke from the chimneys and fire from the blast furnaces stain the sky in sombre greys and vivid reds. Yet within the boundaries of this same city is some of the loveliest moorland scenery. For there is natural beauty as well as industry in the busy North.

NORTHERN ENGLAND is the home of many of Britain's most important industries, for it is well supplied with coal and iron, which are the basis of manufactures, and it has many splendid harbours with large and thriving ports from which the manufactured goods can be exported to all parts of the world, and through which foodstuffs to feed the teeming millions of workers and raw materials to supply the mills and factories can be imported.

Beautiful Scenery

But we shall make a sad mistake if we suppose that the North of England is a region blighted by endless mines and factory chimneys, covered with an everlasting pall of smoke. The North of England is a beautiful district. Those who have wandered over the Yorkshire moors, or explored the pretty dales of Yorkshire, Durham and Northumberland, or tramped over the Pennines, will bear eager witness to that. And linked to the Pennines by the "saddle" of Shap Fell is the English Lake District, which has more real beauty of mountain and dale, lake and fell packed into its small compass

than any other region of the same size anywhere on the globe.

There is wonderful scenery within half an hour's ride from many of the big industrial centres; some, indeed, like Sheffield, have beautiful moorland scenery actually within their boundaries. We have only to go north by train to see green fields, deep woodlands or fine hill scenery separate mines and factory towns.

On the eastern flanks of the Pennines are the three counties of Northumberland, Durham and Yorkshire, well watered by rivers like the Tyne, Wear, Tees and Yorkshire Ouse, which are very beautiful in their upper courses, although they become busy industrial rivers near their mouths.

The Coaly Tyne

Two great coalfields are there: the Northumberland and Durham, and the Yorkshire coalfield, which sends more coal to London and the south than any other in Britain.

Through the very heart of the first runs the "coaly" Tyne, on which stands the great coal-exporting and ship-building port of *Newcastle*, with

6—2

its sister town of Gateshead across the river on the southern bank—the two linked by a high railway bridge, carrying the trains north for Scotland. The banks of the Tyne from Newcastle to the sea are lined with chemical, glass and other factories, iron and steel works, ship-building yards and engineering shops. At the mouth stand Tynemouth, North Shields and South Shields, which share the coal export trade with Blyth farther north, and with Sunderland at the mouth of the Wear, in Durham.

Through the Tyne Gap runs the railway from Newcastle to Carlisle, and following it fairly closely is the old Roman wall of Hadrian, which in places is still sufficiently well-preserved to show what it must have been like during the Roman occupation—walls, turrets and forts and camps can be traced to this day.

Durham, with its ancient castle and fine cathedral built on high ground in a loop of the Wear, is one of the most interesting cities of the North.

Cleveland Iron

At the mouth of the Tees is *Middlesbrough*, in the North Riding of Yorkshire—the home of Britain's greatest iron and steel industries. Steel from Middlesbrough has gone to make some of the finest ships, the largest steel-frame buildings, and the most wonderful bridges in the world. The great bridge across Sydney Harbour in New South Wales was built by a Middlesbrough firm.

Good iron from the Cleveland Hills behind the town, good coal from the Durham field to provide the coke for the blast furnaces, and plenty of limestone with which to smelt the ironstone are within easy reach of the industry. Often, indeed, the steel-making firm

Topical Press.

THE LOVELY COUNTRYSIDE OF THE BUSY NORTH

This beautiful stretch of the Pennine Way is part of the descent from Great Shunnor Fell (2,340 feet) to the little village of Thwaite, almost entirely hidden by trees in the centre of this picture. On either side are the fields that generations of farmers have wrested from the heather and bracken. This is the valley of the Swale, which many declare is the most beautiful of the Yorkshire dales.

MANCHESTER: THE COTTON CAPITAL

British Council.

The Manchester Ship Canal provides a seaway to the very centre of the British cotton industry. The canal is thirty-five miles long and has twelve miles of wharves. Special apparatus is available to remove and replace ships' masts and funnels, if these are too tall to clear the bridges over the canal.

Fox Photos.

Raw cotton comes to Manchester to be distributed to the Lancashire cotton towns, for very little cotton is actually manufactured in Manchester, although some of it is processed there. In this picture we see Piccadilly, one of the busy centres of the cotton capital.

has its own supplies of ironstone, and its own limestone quarries, as well as its own ships on the Tees.

Stockton and Darlington, farther up the Tees Valley, share in the iron and steel business; *Darlington* specialises in railway plant and is one of the centres where engines and trains are made.

Farms and Mills

Yorkshire is the largest of the English counties and is divided into three " Ridings " (an old word, meaning " thirds ")—the West Riding, which is by far the busiest and most thickly populated ; the North Riding, which is partly manufacturing and partly agricultural ; and the East Riding, which is mainly agricultural. Yorkshire men are proud of their county—and they have every reason to be.

The West Riding is the home of our biggest woollen industry, which grew up there in the old days because plenty of wool could be got from the sheep grazing on the hillsides ; and there was sufficient clear running water to wash it, and many streams to turn the mills. Nowadays, however, much of the wool comes from Australia, New Zealand, South Africa and the Argentine, and it is manufactured into all kinds of woollen goods in great mills and factories, most of which are driven by steam power from coal. The Yorkshire coal has done more than anything else to make the industry so important, but we must bear in mind that the woollen business was already there when the coalfield began to be widely opened up.

Will F. Taylor.

'A ROMAN STATION AS IT IS TO-DAY

The Roman Emperor Hadrian built his marvellous wall in the year 122. It was constructed of freestone blocks with a rubble core. Severus, a Roman Emperor, repaired it in 208, and walls, turrets, forts and camps can be traced to this day. Here is the Roman station of Cilurnum at Chesters, in Northumberland. The ruins are those of barrack-rooms, each accommodating about ten men.

J. F. Corrigan.

BUILT BY THE ROMANS

Between Newcastle-upon-Tyne and Carlisle road and railway follow fairly closely the old Wall of Hadrian, which in places is still sufficiently well-preserved to show what it must have been like during the Roman occupation. The original wall, built to defend England's northern frontier, ran from Solway Firth to the Tyne, and was upwards of 70 miles in length. Can you think of the place where the wall ended on the east ? Why, at Wallsend-on-the-Tyne, of course.

As we saw in the Black Country, the towns of the West Riding each produce a special kind of goods, or do some particular branch of the work. *Leeds*, the metropolis of the woollen country, makes more ready-made clothing than any other centre in the world ; *Bradford*, the second largest of the woollen towns, specialises in mohair fabrics; *Halifax* has the world's biggest carpet factories ; *Dewsbury* is the place for heavy woollens, and *Huddersfield* for worsted cloth and for dyeing. Leeds stands at the meeting-place of many routes that converge upon it to pass through the gap in the Pennines made by the Aire tributary of the Yorkshire Ouse.

Through the Aire gap run the trains on their way to Carlisle and Scotland; and the Leeds and Liverpool Canal, which is the water-link between the woollen towns of the West Riding and the cotton towns of South Lancashire. There are many railways and roads, however, across the Southern Pennines connecting these two leading factory districts of Britain.

" Sheffield Make "

In southern Yorkshire another great industry has long been established—the steel cutlery and plate industry of *Sheffield* and Rotherham on the Don. All the world recognises the imprint " Made in Sheffield " as the hall-mark of excellence on cutlery. Here, again, we find a great business growing up because of the local advantages of coal and iron, grindstones from the mill-stone grit of the Pennines, and power from the river ; and growing so huge

Topical Press.

WHERE GRIMSBY'S FISHERMEN DOCK

The seaborne trade of the River Humber is shared by four ports—Hull, Immingham, Goole, and Grimsby. Grimsby is the noted fishing port whose trawlers bring in the harvest of the sea for supply to many parts of the country. It is from Grimsby that the " Grimsby Fish," a special night train, runs non-stop to London with supplies for the markets of the capital. But Grimsby is not only a port for trawlers ; timber, iron ore and wood pulp are also handled here.

that local iron is not sufficient, and it becomes necessary to import the finest Swedish and Spanish iron ores to make the steel. At the present time, British steel production is about $17\frac{1}{2}$ million tons a year, but when the present expansion and modernisation of the industry is complete, British steel plants will be able to produce about 20 million tons a year.

The city of *York* (the old Roman *Eboracum*), in the midst of the broad and fertile Vale of York, has a history that reaches back to early British times, and buildings that take its story from Roman times to the present day.

The Humber Ports

The great port of *Hull* is the sea gate of the busy West Riding, the whole of the basin of the Trent and the English Midlands. It specialises in trade with Australia and New Zealand, but ships from all the great ports of the world enter its spacious docks. *Goole* is a growing port farther up the estuary, and carries on a big business in oil-seed and palm-kernel crushing. The vegetable oils thus obtained go to make margarine, or soap and candles.

Grimsby, like Hull, is a huge fishing port and market on the opposite side of the Humber mouth. It is in Lincolnshire. Not far from it are the large docks of *Immingham*, a port for Baltic lands. Some few miles inland are the blast furnaces of the iron-smelting centre of Scunthorpe. All derive advantage from being near the Humber ; so we mention them here in that connection.

For pleasure and recreation, the toilers in the mills and factories, ship-yards and chemical works, steel and iron works and engineering shops of the factory towns look to the Pennine

AIR FOR THE MERSEY TUNNEL

Herbert J. Rowse.

Opened by King George V in 1934, the Mersey Tunnel links Liverpool and Birkenhead, running for nearly three miles beneath the river. This picture shows us one of the six ventilating stations, each of which contains blower and exhaust fans to force fresh air into the tunnel at the rate of two and a half million cubic feet per minute and withdraw a similar amount of stale air at the same time.
The Mersey Railway Tunnel was opened in 1886 by King Edward VII, when Prince of Wales.

dales and moors on the west, or perhaps more often to the many beautiful seaside holiday towns strung like beads upon the coastline. The chief of these are Scarborough and Whitby.

A Leading Industry

Now let us look at the other side of the Pennines, which is much wetter than the eastern flanks because it faces the prevailing moist winds from the North Atlantic, and therefore grows potatoes and other root crops rather than grain. The moist air is important even in the manufactures, for it enables cotton to be spun without much risk of the fibres cracking and breaking.

The cotton manufacture has long been Britain's leading industry. *Liverpool,* at the sea gate of the Mersey, has always been convenient for the importation of raw cotton from the United States, our chief source of supply ; and since the making of the Manchester Ship Canal, cotton steamers can go right up to the great business heart of the cotton towns. In January, 1954, a new oil dock was opened at Eastham, near the entrance to the Canal. Named after our Queen, the dock is the largest in Britain and reflects the growing importance of Manchester as an oil-refining centre from which petroleum products are exported.

The Cotton Towns

Manchester, indeed, is a first-class *sea* port, with splendid dock equipment, within reach of all the great factory towns of the North and the Midlands. You have not to draw a very large circle round Manchester before you have one big enough to include several millions of people. All these have to be fed, and both Liverpool and Manchester import huge quantities of meat and grain and fruits, besides other foodstuffs.

Each of the cotton towns, like the woollen towns of the West Riding and of the Black Country, has its special business. Wigan is a great coal-mining

centre. Manchester is the business rather than the cotton-manufacturing city. As the natural centre of the roads and railways and canals of the cotton towns, it is the place where cotton goods are collected and marketed ; it is a port, too, as we have already discovered.

Some cotton towns, like Oldham, spin chiefly coarse cotton " counts," while places like Bolton spin finer " counts." Blackburn workers are chiefly weavers; the Bolton people specialise in bleaching ; the St. Helens and Widnes men do a great deal of the dyeing ; and the machinery is made at centres like Oldham and Manchester. Textile machinery made in Lancashire finds its way to all parts of the world where the manufacture of textiles is carried on on a factory scale. We have to think of Manchester and the largest towns not merely as centres of the cotton trade, but as huge manufacturing areas, making many other kinds of goods as well.

Liverpool, too, is not only a cotton and foodstuff port, but a fine city that is the headquarters of many of the leading steamship lines in our Homeland, especially those running regular services to Canada and the United States, to South America and the West Indies, and to West Africa. Liverpool's water-front is one of the wonders of the world. Large liners can come right alongside its great floating landing-stage. Like Heysham, it is one of the ferry ports for Ireland.

Holidays for Lancashire

Where can Lancashire workers take their holidays ? There is the string of pleasant seaside resorts on the Lancashire coast, *e.g.*, Blackpool and Morecambe ; another in North Wales, *e.g.*, Llandudno and Rhyl ; and there are others like Douglas, in the beautiful Isle of Man. For those who love mountain, moorland, or lake, there are the Pennine Moors, the mountain land of North Wales and the Lake District.

THE LAKE DISTRICT

Will F. Taylor.

THE LANGDALE PIKES

The English Lake District is one of the most beautiful parts of our Homeland, and is visited by thousands of tourists every year. In the background of the above landscape we see the famous Langdale Pikes, with Elterwater nearer to us. Elterwater is a beautiful lake because of its setting, and its surface is nearly 200 feet above sea level. It is only one of nearly a score of lakes in the neighbourhood, of which Windermere is the largest.

THE Lake District is one of the most beautiful parts of our Homeland, and is visited by thousands of tourists who go there to catch glimpses of scenes immortalised in verse by Wordsworth, Southey, Coleridge and others of the " Lake Poets."

William Wordsworth was born there, and lived his boyhood days among the lakes and mountains, wandering over the fells of Windermere and Coniston. You remember his poem about the daffodils ? The lake by which he saw " a host of golden daffodils . . . fluttering and dancing in the breeze " was either Grasmere or Rydal Water, near which he lived for many years.

The Lake District has its sterner aspects, too. Its height gives it severe winters and its position on the rainy side of Britain often makes it wet in summer, and swept by snowstorms in winter. Seathwaite, below the Sty Head Pass, is said to have the heaviest rainfall in England. Read Wordsworth's poem " Helvellyn," which paints wonderful word pictures of storm and sunshine, and of the awe-inspiring loneliness of the steep mountain.

Lovely Lakes and Falls

If you look at the Lake District on a map of England you will notice that in some ways it is a district set apart from the rest of the country. Although Shap Fell links it in the south-east with the Pennines, the long Eden Valley cuts off Lakeland from most of the Pennine Chain. Morecambe Bay in the south and the Solway Firth in the north complete the seclusion of this lovely part of England.

The lakes themselves are ribbon-lakes in the narrow valleys that radiate like the spokes of a wheel from the central knot of mountains. The largest is Windermere, but there are others which Nature-lovers think more beautiful. Thirlmere, on the western side of Helvellyn, supplies Manchester with pure water.

Southey and Lodore

There are many beautiful waterfalls, most of which are at their best after the rain. The poet Southey thus describes the Cataract of Lodore:

" Gleaming and steaming and streaming and beaming,
And rushing and flushing and brushing and gushing,
And flapping and rapping and clapping and slapping,
And curling and whirling and purling and twirling,
Retreating and beating and meeting and sheeting,
Delaying and straying and playing and spraying:
Advancing and prancing and glancing and dancing,
Recoiling, turmoiling, and toiling and boiling,
And thumping and flumping and bumping and jumping,
And dashing and flashing and splashing and clashing—
And so never ending, but always descending,
Sound and motions for ever and ever are blending,
All at once and all o'er, with a mighty uproar—
And this way the water comes down at Lodore."

Scafell Pike (3,210 feet) is the highest peak in England, and in the same central knot lie Scafell, Great End and Bowfell. Helvellyn, and the great slate peak of Skiddaw lie farther north. To the east of Helvellyn, Ullswater drains to Penrith and the Eden Valley, along which is the main line from St. Pancras to Carlisle, the most important railway junction of the north of England.

Keswick is the chief centre for the northern valleys, but for people coming from the south, Ambleside is the main centre.

Around Ambleside and Grasmere is Wordsworth-land. At Grasmere is Dove Cottage, where the poet lived with his sister, Dorothy, and to which he later brought his bride, Mary Hutchinson. Here, too, the Wordsworths entertained Sir Walter Scott.

But how can you best reach this lovely region?

Take the express from London to the north, change at Kendal for Windermere if your train has not a " through " carriage, and you are in the Lake District. Go on by 'bus or car through Ambleside to Longdale, and stay in one of the hotels in the valley below some of the finest of the mountains. Get up early some morning and make your way up " the Band " to the top of Bowfell.

The View from Bowfell

Look around you and notice the wonderful golden-green of the fells and deep valleys. All the mountains seem to you to be about the same height. That is because they have been formed by ancient glaciers and streams carving out deep valleys in an old plateau, leaving parts still standing out as mountains.

To the west you can see the Irish Sea, and perhaps catch a glimpse of the high Isle of Man ; to the south-west—almost at your feet, it seems—you see the tall chimneys of the iron and steel works at Barrow and Millom, where the ore got from the mountains is made into all kinds of iron and steel goods.

Barrow-in-Furness, to give it its full name, has large shipbuilding yards and engineering works. Farther north beyond your vision is another and larger strip of " black country "—the Cumberland coalfield along the coast from Maryport to Whitehaven. Some of the workings run far under the sea.

A little to the north-east of Barrow-in-Furness stand the ruins of Furness Abbey, which was founded by King

BOWFELL AND BORROWDALE

Esk Hause affords this view of Bowfell (2,960 feet) and the famous Langdale Pikes. " Hause," " fell " and " pike " are Lakeland terms. " Hause " means the summit of a pass ; " fell," a mountain, or sometimes merely common land; and " pike," a prominent peak on the fells.

Photos : Leonard & Marjorie Gayton.

Borrowdale is sometimes called the " loveliest valley in England." The valley stretches from Derwentwater to the Borrowdale Fells and the remote passes at its farthest end. Below Seathwaite Fell is Stockley Bridge, which is seen in this picture.

Fox Photos.

SPRING TIME IN THE LAKE DISTRICT

This charming picture was taken not far from Rydal in Westmorland. Sheep farming on the Fells
is the main occupation of the people in the Lake District, and the Herdwick breed of sheep which
can stand the cold winters has been developed.

Stephen and which was, in its heyday, the largest Cistercian monastery in England and one of the wealthiest monastic houses in the country. But in 1537, the great Abbey fell a victim to King Henry VIII, who ordered its suppression. The lead roof was stripped from the massive sandstone walls and melted down into lumps bearing the royal mark.

Lake District Folk

Most of the people of the Lake District are farmers who rear sheep on the fells and cattle in the dales. The sheep are usually of the famous Herdwick breed that can stand the bleak weather of the fells. In such country sheep-dogs are of the utmost importance, for the sheep roam far and often reach spots more or less inaccessible to shepherds, but not to their dogs. The sheep-dogs of the lake country have almost uncanny intelligence; sheep-dog " trials " are held every year, and draw many farmers to witness them.

Hedges are rare; pastures and fields are divided by rough stone fences like those which form the boundaries of most of the highways.

The land as a rule is too wet for successful agriculture, and the small amount of plough-land makes this branch of farming the exception and not the rule.

Some of the people are quarrymen, getting out the fine slates and building stones ; or miners working in the iron mines, or winning the few lead and other metal ores from veins in the hard old rocks.

The Isle of Man

When we were standing on top of Bowfell and looking westwards we caught a glimpse of the Isle of Man. Like the Channel Islands, the Isle of Man has its own laws administered by

GRASMERE AND SADDLEBACK

Near Grasmere, in the Rothay Valley, is Score Crag Farm, which is seen in this picture. The Rothay is one of the chief tributaries of Windermere. Rising above Dunmail Raise, and linking Grasmere and Rydal, the Rothay joins the Brathay near Croft Lodge to flow into the head of the Lake.

Photos : Leonard & Marjorie Gayton.

Beyond the ancient " Druid Circle," Saddleback (Blencathra) rises to a height of 2,847 feet. There are many relics of early history in the Lake District. From the top of Saddleback, there are wonderful views of the Crossfell and Helvellyn ranges, the Scafell Group and Skiddaw.

its own institutions—the Court of Tynwald and the House of Keys. The Manx people are of Scandinavian and Celtic origin, with a language of their own which survives to this day. Their island is still divided administratively into sheadings (a word of Scandinavian origin which means a " ship-district ").

Some Manx Legends

The rock structure of the Isle of Man is similar to that of the Lake District. Most of the island's land is pasture, and farming is the traditional industry. But the Isle of Man is a famous holiday resort, and many Manx get their living from the tourists who fly to the island or come by ship from Fleetwood and Liverpool to *Douglas*, the chief holiday centre where a third of the island's people live.

Like all places with long and ancient history, the island has a wealth of folk-lore and legend, and if you visit the grim ruins of Peel Castle, you will probably hear the story of the Manthe Doog, which—so the story runs—haunts the castle guard-room.

Castle Rushen, at Castletown, also has its legends and, if these are to be believed, a mysterious underground room which has never been found. Once the seat of the Kings of Man, the castle is said to be haunted by a giant who periodically returns to the island from which he and his kind were driven by Merlin, the magician of King Arthur's court. But the present castle dates from the year 1344, although in earlier times Vikings had a stronghold on this same site. Relics of their days, and of days still more remote, include remarkable Scandinavian and Celtic crosses which are found in many parts of the island.

Leonard & Marjorie Gayton.

SCAFELL AND SCAFELL PIKE

This picture shows the rugged skyline of Scafell and Scafell Pike as you would see it from the summit of Bowfell. Scafell Pike rises to 3,210 feet and is the highest peak in England. Its summit commands magnificent views of this beautiful part of our country. At times, both the Isle of Man and the Mourne Mountains in Ireland can be seen.

The Story
of the
World and
its Peoples

Among the
Welsh Hills,
Valleys
and Coalfields

F. Dixon-Scott.

CONWAY CASTLE

The ways into Wales by the river valleys, like those by the northern and southern coast plains, were commanded in medieval times by strong castles. Some, such as Conway Castle, still remain externally in a good state of preservation. This romantic building was commenced in the reign of Edward I, and could tell stories of bitter siege. Its mighty walls stand firm upon foundations of solid rock.

THE PRINCIPALITY OF WALES

AT first sight a population map is a very dull thing. But when we read it with knowledge and use our imagination a little, it springs to sudden life, and becomes an interesting human record of the country it represents.

Look at the population map of Wales, for instance. Two facts catch your eye at once: (1) the very densely peopled region of South Wales; (2) the large patches of very thinly populated country in the middle and north.

Why are there so many people in South Wales? The county of Glamorgan alone contains nearly half the people in Wales; and if we examine the population figures for Welsh counties and towns we make the surprising discovery that the city of Cardiff has a bigger population than any Welsh county, except the one in which Cardiff is situated. Evidently, then, there must be special opportunities for people in South Wales to get a living.

The South Wales Coalfield

The secret of it all is that in this part of the Principality lies the rich South Wales coalfield, which covers at least a thousand square miles and extends into the counties of Glamorgan,

Brecon, Monmouth, Carmarthen and Pembroke. It has steam coal for ships, any amount of bituminous coal for homes and factories, and the best anthracite ("smokeless" coal) in the world. In places the sea has cut deep inlets into the coalfield (*e.g.*, at Swansea, the second town of Wales), making it easy for coal export; and the richest part of the coalfield is deeply seamed by streams whose valleys provide easy ways for the coal-trains to the great ports of Cardiff, Newport, Swansea and Barry.

Workers in Metal

When the coal exporting business is good, there is prosperity in South Wales, for it gives employment to miners and other workers, numbering hundreds of thousands. For Cardiff, with Newport and Swansea next, is the most important export centre for the South Wales coalfield. At all of these ports expensive and wonderful coal-handling machinery has been set up to deal with huge quantities of coal in a short time.

Such a rich coalfield is bound to become the home of great manufactures, especially if it has iron as well. There is iron in the South Wales field, but nowadays Welsh ironmasters prefer to import high-grade but cheap iron ores from Spain and Sweden rather than spend more money in getting the local iron. The iron and steel industry of South Wales is enormous; the chief centres are Merthyr Tydfil, Cardiff, Port Talbot, Dowlais, Ebbw Vale, Tredegar, Aberdare and Blaenavon.

This has attracted other great metal industries. The tin-plate business—manufacturing thin steel sheets and coating them with tin to prevent rust—is the biggest in the world. The tin is imported chiefly from Burma, Malaya, Bolivia and Nigeria. Even the United States itself, a great metal-working country, buys Welsh tin-plate. The

Fox Photos.

A WELSH MINING VILLAGE

Cilfynydd, with its rows of terrace houses disappearing into the dusty mist and its pithead gear silhouetted against the sky, is typical of the villages of the Welsh mining valleys. The coal that is mined feeds, among other things, the enormous iron and steel industry of South Wales.

HISTORIC CARDIFF CASTLE

Robert Fitz-Hamon seized Cardiff about the year 1090. The Motte, or artificial hill, on which Robert built his stockade, still stands, but—as this picture shows—it is now crowned by a thirteenth-century shell keep of stone.

Photos: Topical Press.

Cardiff Castle owes much to alteration or restoration in comparatively recent times. The clock tower (left), for example, is quite modern and is one of the additions made by the Bute family, owners of the castle, who presented it to the city of Cardiff in 1947.

huge increase in the use of "tinned" and "canned" meats, fish, fruits and vegetables, has resulted in demands for tin-plate from every important part of the globe. Swansea, Llanelly, Port Talbot and Pontypool lead in the tin-plate industry. Pontypool has new importance as the centre of British nylon production.

Much is being done now to expand and thoroughly modernise the steel industry of South Wales. At Margam, near Port Talbot, great new rolling mills began work in July, 1951, making the plant there the largest and most modern in Europe. Future extensions include work at Velindre, Llangyfelach, near Swansea, and at Port Talbot. At Trostre a new tinplate works is now in operation.

There are besides oil refineries, large copper, zinc and nickel works, factories in which fire bricks are made for furnaces, or where patent fuel is made, or where the coal by-products are extracted and used. All these industries help one another in some way, and each depends upon *coal*. Cardiff is one of the most important ship-repairers in the world, largely because of the advantages offered by the industries of South Wales in providing the necessary materials.

How South Wales is Fed

Food must be brought to this dense

Will F. Taylor.

THE CASTLE OF CARNARVON

Carnarvon Castle, like that at Conway, was begun in the reign of Edward I, and was not only a fortress, but also a royal residence. In olden days there was long-continued guerrilla warfare; and when the English conquered a portion of Wales, they set a castle in some strong place to control the ways. Edward II, the first Prince of Wales, was born in the stronghold illustrated above, which stands on the Menai Strait.

AFTER FIVE HUNDRED YEARS!

Will F. Taylor.

Known as "The Aberconwy," the extremely interesting residence pictured above is not only the oldest house in Conway, but also in the whole Principality, as the sign now swinging at the entrance up the rugged steps proclaims. The house stands at the corner of High Street and Castle Street, its sturdy framework and beams of oak blackened with age.

population in enormous quantities—and it should be remembered that Cardiff and Newport are gates to the industrial Midlands as well for food products. This helps to explain the gigantic flour mills at the four leading ports of South Wales. Oil and timber also come in large quantities from overseas.

All these industries, and the transport by railways and roads, by inland waterways and the sea, which keeps them alive, employ large numbers of people. That is why South Wales supports more than five-eighths of the Welsh people.

The Real Wales

But this is not the Wales of the bards and poets, who have never ceased to sing the glories of her mountains and valleys, and to tell of the wonders of her changing skies above the high and broken horizon. If we wish to see the real Wales of poetry, song, and story, we must visit those regions which show up on the population map as being of little account to busy modern industries and the question of employment. These quiet places are, in fact the spots more visited by those who go to enjoy the beauties of Welsh scenery, or to recover their lost health in some site of mineral springs and the towering hills.

The mountains of Wales have played a very important part in Welsh history. To the mountain fortresses of the west fled the Britons when wave after wave of invaders conquered the eastern plain lands. From them are descended the Welsh, who lived among their hills and crags apart from the English who for centuries did no more than penetrate the wide southern plain. But those same

Reece Winstone.

LLANDAFF CATHEDRAL, NEAR CARDIFF

Framed by a ruined arch of the Bishop's palace which Owen Glendower burned in 1402 is Llandaff Cathedral whose long history dates from the earliest times of the Christian Church in Britain. The first bishop of Llandaff was St. Dubricius, whose successor (about the year 540) was St. Teilo. The tombs of both may be seen in the Cathedral which was rebuilt in 1120, later fell into ruin, and was not restored until 1836.

SCENES AT A NATIONAL EISTEDDFOD

The National Eisteddfod (pronounced i-steth-vod) is the famous Welsh gathering held each year alternately in North and South Wales. This picture shows the scene at a typical Eisteddfod with the Archdruid (right) receiving the Horn of Plenty.

Photos: Keystone.

Clothing of supposed Druidical origin is worn by this bearer of the Horn of Plenty, and by the Gorsedd, or assembly, of Bards.

The highest honours competitors win are the "Crown" and the "Chair." Here we see the winner of the "Crown" and (left) the trumpeter.

mountains which bred love of liberty and independence proved in the end the undoing of the Welsh, for they so barred off tribe from tribe and valley from valley, that strong united action against the invading forces of Edward I. was impossible.

In spite of long-continued guerrilla warfare, the English conquered Wales piecemeal and set their castles in strong places to control the ways.

The Welsh spirit, however, still lives and so does the Welsh language, which is taught in Welsh schools, and spoken by many of the people of the Principality. All that is finest in Welsh poetry, music and song is heard at the National Eisteddfod, the greatest and most famous of Welsh festivals, which is attended by people from all parts of the Principality and of the world.

Eisteddfodau are occasions when Welsh people from all walks of life meet to observe ancient ritual, to compete in verse and song, and to honour those of their nation who have made some outstanding contribution to science or the arts.

Amidst Welsh Mountains

The Welsh Highlands, like those of Scotland and the Lake District, have been formed by streams and prehistoric glaciers carving out deep valleys in an ancient plateau, leaving other parts standing as mountains. The finest scenery perhaps is in Snowdonia, where Snowdon, the highest peak south of the Tweed, rears his head 3,560 feet above the sea. Eighty per cent. of the slate quarried in Wales comes from this region, especially from the famous quarries of Bethesda, Llanberis and Blaenau Festiniog. The slate is exported in coasting craft from Bangor and Carnarvon.

The deep valley of the Upper Dee (the Vale of Bala) separates the Berwyn Mountains from the northern masses, giving a route from Chester and Wrexham by way of Llangollen and

Topical.

IN ONE OF BRITAIN'S NATIONAL PARKS

This view was taken from Freshwater Bay, looking along the Welsh coast towards East Moor Cliff, and it shows part of the area, comprising about 225 miles, which has been designated as the Pembrokeshire Coast National Park.

Tattersall.

THE PRECIPICE WALK AT DOLGELLEY

Dolgelley, in Merioneth, was once noted for its cloth. Near the town, on either side of the river Wnion, there are many beautiful walks, the most noted being the beautiful Precipice and Torrent Walks, which climb the mountain ridge and give fine views of the Wnion valley. This picture shows a typical view across the river valley to the far distant mountains of Snowdon.

Lake Bala to Barmouth and other pleasant seaside resorts on Cardigan Bay.

The Vale of Powys (Upper Severn) affords a route for road and railway from Shrewsbury through the very heart of Wales to Aberystwyth, and separates the Berwyn mass from Mynydd Bach and Clun Forest. In this valley are Newtown and Welshpool, both old centres of the Welsh woollen industry.

Ways into Wales

Another valley giving entrance to Wales from England is the Wye Valley from Hereford, an ancient cathedral town in the midst of beautiful scenery, and its Plain.

These ways into Wales, by the river valleys, like those by the northern and southern coast plains, were commanded in medieval times by strong castles, the ruins of many of which still remain.

Some, like Conway Castle, are yet in a good state of preservation.

Wales supplies two great English cities with pure water that is conveyed many miles in iron pipes. Liverpool gets its water from Lake Vyrnwy; Birmingham from the lake-reservoirs of the Elan Valley.

Farming in Wales has neither the scope nor the possibilities offered in the genial counties that fall to the south of the Bristol Channel. For one thing, much of the agricultural area is on very high ground, and these breezy upland regions have only thin, poor pasture, some of it stone-strewn moorland. In many parts, however, one can find well-drained slopes where, despite heavy rainfall, the ground keeps moderately firm and is thus the ideal range for flocks of sheep. Not less than three millions of these animals are kept in Wales, and there is an outlet for wool in flannel mills at Welshpool and in a cloth-making industry along the Teifi Valley. The acreage under wheat has in recent years tended to increase, but the thickly-populated workaday south demands milk and dairy produce from the farmer rather than grain and cattle.

Rather less than a hundred years ago George Borrow, author of " The Bible in Spain," " Lavengro " and works that have now become classics, made tours in our little sister country over a period of three or four years. He then wrote a famous book which he called " Wild Wales," and so slightly have many of the districts changed that you might take it to-day as a guide of your very own as you set forth to explore the more remote parts. The scenery appealed especially to Borrow, and he brings out its grandeur in his noble pen pictures, telling of leafy glens, lovely waterfalls and gem-like lakes as well as of the mountains, gathering human interest from almost everyone he meets and even setting forth what they said to him.

If you decide to tour in this glorious land you will find history not only in the castles and stories but in the strange cromlechs, Celtic crosses and ancient monoliths.

Before long you will discover that Anglesey was the final stronghold of the Druids, priests of the Celts of centuries ago, who fought almost to the last man against the Roman invaders and with their backs to the Irish Sea.

South Stack Lighthouse

Anglesey is both an island and a Welsh county, and here originated that proud family the Tudors, from which came Elizabeth I. and other British sovereigns, five of them altogether, and just before the Stuart line. Amlwch, Moelfre and Rhosneigr are just a trio of the small resorts strung along the island coasts. Beaumaris is the county town, the old castle here having been erected by Edward I. in 1295. As for

Telford's graceful suspension bridge, over 1,700 feet in length, it was built as long ago as 1826 to carry the famous Holyhead Road, a highway that runs for some of its length over ancient Watling Street. As a neighbour it has the tubular bridge set up by the railway engineer Stephenson, and this came into being a quarter of a century afterwards.

Holyhead is Anglesey's great port for steamer traffic to and from Dublin and it is the biggest town on the island. The flashing beacon guide to incoming and outward-bound vessels is the South Stack Lighthouse built on a humped tongue of land jutting out from the rock-bound coast. Mon was the old name of Anglesey, to be written in rather later times as Mona. The Isle of Man is also Mona, but Anglesey appears to be the first to claim the title.

That part of the Principality known as Snowdonia is perhaps the wildest of all the regions of real Wild Wales. We know that Snowdon rears its head to a height of 3,560 feet, but it is a mistake to regard this noble mountain as having only one peak. The loftiest of them all is known as Y Wyddfa. Next there comes Carnedd Ugan, 3,476 feet, followed by Crib Goch, 3,023 feet, Lliwedd, 2,947 feet, and Aran, 2,451 feet. Of the neighbouring heights Carnedd Llewelyn and Carnedd Dafydd both exceed 3,400 feet, and there are five others that overtop the 3,000 feet mark.

Just at the base of Snowdon we can find Llanberis, which is a placid but enjoyable township for those who wish to ascend the peaks. Many of the hardy ones do make the ascent in three or four hours on foot, marvelling at the scenery unfolded from every angle of the pathway. Others take the rack railway, which makes the climb in about an hour. One can travel in the evening to enthuse over entrancing sunsets, or make the journey in the small hours and watch the sunrise,

IN THE WELSH SLATE QUARRIES

Most things in North Wales seem to be made of slate, even the gateposts and garden fences: and it is claimed that the famous Penrhyn quarry, part of which is seen here, is the largest of its kind in the world. The quarry has been worked for hundreds of years.

Photos: *Topical Press.*

With the aid of a strong rope a rockman lowers himself to the working point where he will prise away at the loosened slate.

Blaenau is another famous slate quarry where the quarrymen drill and cut slate a thousand feet below the ground surface.

either experience being something never to be forgotten.

Capel Curig is yet another of Snowdonia's little gems, a centre for viewing lakes and rapid-running streams or for climbing the lofty mountain summits. Only a few miles away is Bettws-y-Coed, a health resort sheltered by pine-clad hills. The name means simply a " sanctuary in the wood," and here we meet the rivers Llugwy and Conway with stepping stones across the former stream. It is upon the Llugwy, too, that we shall see the famous Swallow Falls. On the western side of the lovely Vale of Conway are the power station and aluminium works of Dolgarrog. To the east and parallel with the Vale of Conway is another beautiful valley, the Vale of Clwyd, at whose sea end is Rhyl.

The Passes of Snowdonia are scarcely less interesting than the peaks. The Aberglaslyn Pass, for instance, is a wooded ravine deeply set in walls of rock 700 feet in height and with a crystal stream running at the bottom. This is not far from Beddgelert, named after the grave of Gelert, Llewellyn's faithful hound. Then there is the Llanberis Pass winding among the slopes of Snowdon itself and the Nant Ffrancon Pass cut like a narrow ribbon among the towering hills.

Only Welsh Spoken

In this part of Carnarvonshire we are likely to meet mostly sheep farmers and such folk; and, rather, as Borrow did in his time, we shall find they have little English to offer, for the tongue they know best is their own native Welsh. When we get nearer the coast, however, we come upon large, spacious towns that gather holiday-makers from all parts and offer not only magnificent scenery but plenty of man-made amusement as well. Llandudno is such a place.

Fox Photos.

THE HIGHEST PEAK SOUTH OF THE TWEED

Snowdon is the highest peak south of the Tweed and gives its name to the wonderland scenery of Snowdonia, of whose beauties the Welsh bards and poets never cease to sing. This view of the 3,560 ft. high mountain shows how it dominates the Welsh highlands.

SNOWDONIA'S WILD BEAUTY

J. Dixon-Scott.

Nearly 3,000 feet high, Cader Idris overlooks the Mawddach river in west Merionethshire. Cader means seat or chair, and Idris is the name of a giant who—according to the old bardic writings—made the mountains his observatory.

British Council.

In the distance loom the rolling mountains of Snowdonia; to the right are the crumbling towers of Harlech's famous castle which overlooks the broad sands and foam-crested waves of Tremadoc Bay. This beautiful coastland is now preserved for the nation by the National Trust.

VALLEYS OF WALES

A. F. Kersting.

In a valley between the grey-green Radnorshire hills lies the little village of Doldowlod. Here we are in the borderlands and are not far from Rhayader, on the Wye, whose name means " the Falls of the Wye " (Rhaiadr Gwy) although there are now no falls to be seen there.

British Railways.

Near Bettws-y-coed the Vale of Conway divides into three further valleys where wood and mountain combine in unforgettable beauty. These are the lovely Swallow Falls near Bettws-y-coed, formed by the river Llugwy as it cascades over giant boulders on its headlong course to the sea.

BAYS ALONG THE COAST

Here, we look down from Constitution Hill to the Three Bays and the town of Aberystwyth on the Cardigan coast. The National Library of Wales is at Aberystwyth, and so is the University College of Wales whose buildings can be seen (right) just beyond the pier.

Llandudno stands on the shores of a crescent-shaped bay whose tips are guarded by the headlands of the Great Orme and the Little Orme. In this view we are standing, beneath the shadow of the Great Orme, in the Happy Valley looking across the town towards the Little Orme.

Here we find St. Tudno's Well, Happy Valley, and countless other interests and attractions, together with Great Orme's Head rising close on 700 feet, forming a headland some seven miles round. It was here, in this romantic setting and at a place called Gogarth Abbey, that Lewis Carroll wrote "Alice in Wonderland." Colwyn Bay, Bangor, Penmaenmawr (the mountain rears its head 1,550 feet above the sea), Criccieth and Pwllheli are other resorts, the two last-named on Tremadoc Bay.

"White Coal"

North Wales is one of the areas of the British Isles where " white coal " can be produced. " White coal " is another name for electricity produced by harnessing the waters of mountain streams and rivers. In North Wales, this power —hydro-electric power, to give it the correct name—is produced at such places as Dolgarrog, Maentwrog, and Cwm Dyli, whose output saves the country some 55,000 tons of coal each year.

Schemes are now planned to extend the plant at Dolgarrog and Maentwrog, and it has been suggested that " white coal " might also be produced at Rheidol, Snowdon, Mawddach and other places, but many say that such developments would disfigure the countryside and spoil the scenic attractions of the area.

Perhaps you are wondering how Wales came to be called by this name. The early invaders, who drove the Britons from the eastern lands into the mountain fastnesses of the west, spoke of them as *wealas*. This was the early English word for ' foreigners,' and to it we owe the modern name, Wales. The Welshman who proudly speaks his native tongue, however, will call his beautiful country, *Cymru*. You can see this name on the roadside when you enter the Principality.

Reece Winstone.

THE HIGHEST RAILWAY IN BRITAIN

This title belongs to the single track railway which ascends Snowdon, the mountain which gives its name to the wildest of real Wild Wales. There are loop halts on the railway where right of way is given by a staff passed from driver to driver; and this is happening in this picture. The ratchet brakes between the lines automatically lock the train in the event of engine failure.

Specially painted for this work.

HISTORIC HARLECH CASTLE, FAMED IN WELSH SONG

Built by King Edward the First to overawe his freshly-won principality of North Wales, Harlech Castle was one of the most powerful of his strongholds. Its walls and towers resisted the attacks of the Welsh under Madoc and yielded to Owen Glendower in 1404 only after lack of food and sickness had reduced the garrison to twenty-one men. During the Wars of the Roses, the castle held out for eight years against Yorkist attacks, and an episode of this long defence is said to have given rise to the famous song *March of the Men of Harlech*. During the Civil Wars, Harlech was the last of the northern Welsh castles to be attacked by the Parliamentary forces; although it was surrendered, the Parliamentarians never dismantled it.

Topical Press.

EDINBURGH CASTLE

Edwin of Northumbria gave his name to the famous Rock thirteen hundred years ago, and it is probable that even then the Rock had long been used as a stronghold. To-day the stern walls of the castle are among the best-known landmarks of "Auld Reekie," as the Scottish capital is sometimes called. Within the castle is the oldest building in Edinburgh, the Chapel of Saint Margaret, Queen of Scotland, who died there in 1093. There, also, you can see the old Parliament Hall and the Scottish Crown, Sceptre, and Sword.

The Story
of the
World and
its Peoples

A Tour of
Caledonia's
Mountains, Glens
and Cities

Oscar Marcus.

THE FLYING SCOT THUNDERS OVER ROYAL BORDER BRIDGE

This magnificent bridge spans the river Tweed about a quarter of a mile from the ancient Border town of Berwick-upon-Tweed. Designed by Robert Stephenson and opened by Queen Victoria in 1850, the bridge has twenty-eight arches and is 126 feet high, and forms one of the chief gateways into Scotland.

THE LAND OF THE SCOTS

TWO great main natural ways lead from London and the English Midlands into Scotland: the East Coast route by way of Doncaster, York, Newcastle and Berwick-on-Tweed, and the West Coast route by way of the Plain of Lancashire, Shap Fell and Carlisle. Between these natural routes rise the long Pennines.

One railway (formerly the L.N.E.R.) follows the eastern route, which is by far the easier from the point of view of the railway engineer. The old L.M.S. line follows the western route by way of Crewe, Wigan, Preston, Lancaster and Penrith. A second main line (also a former L.M.S. route) first reaches Leeds on the eastern side of the Pennines, and then cuts through the Aire Gap to Settle and the Shap, thus meeting more natural obstacles than either of the other two.

The border between England and Scotland is difficult country for roads and railways. The actual boundary runs from Solway Firth and along the crest line of the Cheviots to the Lower Tweed, which enters the North Sea near Berwick-on-Tweed. It is easy for roads and railways to avoid the Cheviots by following the coast plains at their seaward ends ; but beyond the Cheviots and the boundary lie the Southern Uplands of Scotland, which must be passed before travellers can reach the Scottish Midland Valley— the busiest and richest part of Scotland.

Border Forays

These Southern Uplands rise in places to over 2,000 feet, and the hills that go to form them are made of hard old rocks, some harsh and gritty, some slaty. Their slopes are covered chiefly with the short, crisp grass that sheep love ; their valleys are floored with rich soil formed of rock-meal made by the grinding of the ancient glaciers over the rocks, or of fine silt washed down by the mountain streams. In some places among the hills there are wide areas of peatland, and bogs that will probably in time become peat beds.

The country on both sides of the border is thickly sown with ancient battlefields, and the approaches to it on both sides are marked by the ruins of many an old-time castle, tower and fortress. But even these could not prevent the border forays frequent in the old days when raiding and fighting were common and profitable amusements for the sturdy warrior-lords of the borderlands—and by no means dishonourable occupations. Many an old ballad still lingers to tell the tale of border warfare and sing the praises of the proud chieftains and border earls to whom battle and pillage were the spice of life.

The Southern Uplands were once an old high plateau, which for ages has been cut up by many streams into deep valleys, leaving parts upstanding as the hills and mountains of to-day. The highest point is Mount Merrick (2,764 feet) in the west. But it is the valleys that are most important to the road-makers and railway-builders, for they provide the only easy ways across this difficult country, except for those along the coastal plains. Fortunately, the Southern Uplands lie so that a number of streams run south and a number run north. These roads and railways can use valleys up the

J. Dixon-Scott.

ON THE FIELD OF BANNOCKBURN

The battle of Bannockburn was fought near Stirling in 1314 and ended with the defeat of the English forces. Visitors to the battlefield can still see the Bore Stone, shown above, where Robert Bruce planted his standard. The story of the fight is told vividly in Sir Walter Scott's *Tales of a Grandfather*.

SCOTTISH LITERARY SHRINES

Photochrom.

All lovers of the writings of Sir Walter Scott will recognise this fine mansion as Abbotsford, the home that he built himself beside the Tweed in a district rich in history and romance. The study at Abbotsford, with Scott's writing-desk and armchair, is almost exactly as the great novelist left it.

Will F. Taylor.

On January 25th, 1759, Robert Burns was born at this homely cottage at Alloway which is much the same to-day as it was in the times of Scotland's great National Poet. The counties of Ayrshire and Dumfriesshire are those most associated with Burns.

southern slopes and then descend the northern slopes by the valleys leading down to the Scottish Midland Valley.

Ways North from Carlisle

From Carlisle three main railways pass northwards: (1) by the " Waverley " route up Liddesdale down to the valley of the Tweed, up the Gala Valley and down to Waverley Station at Edinburgh; (2) by the Caledonian route up the valley of the Annan and down the valley of the Clyde to Glasgow and Edinburgh; (3) by the south-western route up the valley of the Nith and by a long journey over the plain of Ayrshire to Glasgow. The last two are the former L.M.S. routes ; the first (the old L.N.E.R.) is called the " Waverley " route because it passes through the historic district where Sir Walter Scott lived and wrote his novels.

As we cross the Southern Uplands in the train we notice that towns and villages are few, and that, on the whole, there are not many people living in this part of Britain. Those who do make their homes there are chiefly farmers, who keep flocks of sheep on the grassy hillslopes, or grow grain, roots and vegetables in the rich soil of the valleys in which most of the farmsteads lie.

Wool from the sheep of the Southern Uplands goes to make the tweeds (" twills ") manufactured at Hawick, Selkirk, Galashiels and Peebles.

Lead is mined in the Southern Uplands at the villages of Leadhills and Wanlockhead, a little to the west of the Caledonian route. They are said to be the highest villages in Scotland, and stand on open grassy moors amid the hills.

The Heart of Scotland

Eight-tenths of the people of Scot-

J. Dixon-Scott.

MELROSE ABBEY

Melrose, on the banks of the Tweed, takes its name from the Celtic *maol ros*, meaning " bare moor." The famous Abbey shown here was founded in 1136, destroyed by Edward I in 1322, rebuilt, and again destroyed by Protector Somerset in 1545. Beneath its high altar, the heart of that courageous King, Robert the Bruce, was buried, and the east window was immortalised by Sir Walter Scott in his *Lay of the Last Minstrel*.

British Council.

BLACKFACE SHEEP

With long curved horns, black faces, and shaggy fleeces, these sheep pose placidly for the cameraman. The great sheep-farming area of Scotland is the southern uplands, and the Blackface variety can live on the higher and more exposed pastures and form some sixty per cent. of the sheep of Scotland.

land live in the Midland Valley, which has only one-tenth of Scotland's total area. For there is the most fertile land, and there also are the great Scottish coalfields which support many busy industries. The rest of Scotland is largely filled with mountains (except for the eastern coastal plain, whose old red sandstone floor has given rise to rich soil), and therefore cannot support a very large population.

How is it that Scotland's coal and most of her richest plough-land lie in the Midland Valley instead of being scattered in various places over the country?

Geological Accidents

It is due to what we may call a series of geological accidents which caused two great lines of faults or cracks in the earth-crust to develop— one along a line joining Stonehaven on the east to the Firth of Clyde, and the other from St. Abb's Head on the east to a point south of Ayr on the west. Along both of these lines are multitudes of more or less parallel faults penetrating to great depths.

In past ages, and long before Britain was ready for the coming of the first men, the stretch of earth-crust between these two great lines of faulting sank, and in the rift valley thus created other rock material gathered, covering up the coal measures. When the moving glaciers of the Ice Age ground heavily over most parts of Scotland, planing off the upper rocks and among them most of the coal, the coal measures of the Midland Valley lay snug and untouched beneath their covering of younger rocks, to prove real hidden treasure for the enterprising people who, ages afterwards, were destined to dwell there.

We must not imagine the Midland Valley, however, as a more or less continuous " Black Country " with belching factory chimneys, grimy canals and a landscape everywhere blighted by monster heaps of waste from mines and blast furnaces and with every green thing seared by the hot breath of chemical works. There *are* spots like this, of course, for they are part of the price men must pay for the profits and advantages of mining and manufacture. But most of the Midland Valley is pleasant country with a quiet beauty all its own, and half an hour's ride by car or train from the biggest city will take you to spots as delightful as any lover of the real countryside could wish to see.

Beauty of the Lowlands

The Midland Valley is often called " The Lowlands," and that gives some of us the impression that it is more or less flat. Nothing could be farther from the truth, as we can see if we look at a good map showing the height of the land.

Across the middle of the Midland Valley runs a line of volcanic hills, with here and there wide, deep breaks, through which the rivers have cut their way. The Sidlaws overlook the long Firth of Tay, along whose northern shores, sheltered by the Sidlaws from cold north winds, stretches the fertile Carse of Gowrie, famous for its grain and its fruits.

To the south-west of the Sidlaws rise the crests of the Ochils ; and between the two the lordly Tay has made its way, giving a gap through which approach to the Highlands is easy. In that gap sits the fair city of Perth, near which is Scone, the ancient coronation-place of the Kings of Scotland.

Reece Winstone.

STIRLING'S CASTLE ROCK IS RICH IN HISTORY

Commanding the main route between the Highlands and the Lowlands, Stirling Castle figured prominently in the wars between Scots and English. It was captured by the English, recaptured by William Wallace, and besieged by Edward I. Kings of Scotland were born in the castle palace, but Stirling Castle ceased to be a royal residence when James VI of Scotland went south to rule both Scotland and England from London.

"THE ATHENS OF THE NORTH"

Edinburgh has such beauty and grandeur that the city is known as " the Athens of the North."
This picture shows Princes Street, the most famous thoroughfare and the pride of Scotland's
capital. This, " the finest street in Europe," is many a visitor's introduction to Edinburgh, for
at its east end is the Waverley Station and at its west end the Caledonian. Fashionable shops and
pleasant gardens border the street which has as its foremost monument that raised in memory of
Sir Walter Scott.

Look south-west again from the tops of the Ochils, and you see another hill-mass—the Campsie Fells, with the winding Forth making its way between the Ochils and the distant hills. In that wide and fertile gap is *Stirling*, with its grand old castle high-perched on an isolated rock which was once the lava-plug that sealed the throat of a prehistoric volcano, after its last dying eruption. Stirling is another important gateway to the Highlands; and many a stern fight contested the passage of its famous bridge over the Forth, whose multitudinous windings are known as " the Links of Forth."

From Earl's Seat

Now climb to Earl's Seat on the top of the Campsie Fells, and look south to where the great city of *Glasgow*, with its busy shipyards, factories and engineering works—the home of more than a million people—stands on its wide valley at the head of the estuary of the Clyde. Far away to the south-west across the Clyde estuary rise the outlines of another hill-mass; and westward is lovely Loch Lomond and its majestic encircling peaks, of which Ben Lomond is perhaps the best known. Glasgow and its neighbours, Greenock and Dumbarton (another shipbuilding town with an ancient castle perched upon just such a rock as that upon which Stirling Castle is built), are also well-known gateways by which approach to the Highlands is fairly easy.

North of this central line of hills is the broad and fertile Plain of Strathmore—the "great valley"—between the Highland edge to the north and the volcanic hills to the south. On the

J. Dixon-Scott.

HOLYROOD PALACE, EDINBURGH

The way from Edinburgh Castle, perched on top of the famous Castle Rock, to the old Royal Palace of Holyrood at its foot is known as the " Royal Mile." Many a regal personage passed along it in the days of Scotland's glory as an independent kingdom. Holyrood has been used by our Sovereigns since George IV on their visits to the Scottish capital.

FOR SCOTLAND'S FALLEN

F. C. Inglis.

In Edinburgh Castle, as befits the capital, is the Scottish National War Memorial, erected to the memory of Scots men and women who lost their lives in the conflict of 1914–18. Above is a picture of the shrine with seven stained-glass windows and a Casket containing the names of the Fallen in the two World Wars. In the Hall of Honour all the Scottish Regiments are mentioned.

southern side of these hills there is not so much plain land, for the ground rises more or less gradually to the Southern Uplands—the Border Lands of the old ballads famous in Scottish song and story. *Edinburgh*, the capital of Scotland, with the port of Leith, is on the coastal plain of the Forth. The Pentlands, the Moorfoot Hills, and the Lammermoors rise in a semicircle to the south, broken here and there by gaps used by the roads and the railways. All are within easy reach of the capital.

The British Athens

Edinburgh grew up on and around its famous Castle Rock, which is yet another old volcanic stump. The way from the Castle at its summit down the long slope to the old royal palace of Holyrood at its foot is known as the "Royal Mile," for many a royal personage passed along it in the days of Scotland's glory as an independent kingdom. There are other noble hills, too, within the precincts of the city. So splendid is Edinburgh that it is known all over the world as the "British Athens." You must go far indeed before you find a nobler thoroughfare than Princes Street, or a finer view than you can get from the Castle Rock. Leith nowadays is virtually part of Edinburgh; busy streets connect the two, making them one continuous city. The fine docks at Leith and Granton are the sea gates of Scotland's capital, and give harbour and wharfage accommodation to vessels from all the leading sea-trading countries of the world. Through these ports and others on the deep long inlet of the Firth of Forth come much

Photochrom.

WHERE A QUEEN WAITED VAINLY FOR HER KING TO RETURN
The ruined walls of Linlithgow Palace, about 17 miles from Edinburgh, are charged with tragedy. Here that unhappy person, Mary Queen of Scots, was born: and here Queen Margaret waited vainly for James IV to return from the battlefield of Flodden. Linlithgow, the palace of Scottish sovereigns, was mercilessly sacked by English troops in 1745.

F. C. Inglis.

In the First World War deep tunnelling under the ground for the laying of mines and other military operations necessitated the use of canaries and white mice, mainly to test the purity of the air. These humble creatures are not forgotten in the Scottish War Memorial at Edinburgh.

of the foodstuffs and the raw materials to feed the workers and the mills and factories of the Scottish Midland Valley.

Glasgow and the Clyde

On the western side of the Midland Valley is another deep estuary—that of the Clyde, which is even more important as a sea gate, because it faces the Atlantic and the New World, from which Britain gets vast amounts of foodstuffs of all kinds, as well as raw materials for her manufactures.

Not far west of Edinburgh is the famous Forth Bridge, which carries the eastern route expresses over the estuary on their way to the north.

The Clyde estuary from Glasgow to Greenock is lined with large ship-building yards and engineering works. The estuary is carefully buoyed, so that large vessels can reach the docks; for, like Liverpool, Glasgow is the headquarters of famous steamship lines and vessels from all parts of the world unload and load cargoes there. Like other large ports in Britain, Glasgow has a wide variety of industries, many based on raw materials from the Americas, for trade with which this port is exceptionally well placed. This fine city is very largely the growth of the past century, although it has always been an important centre at the meeting-place of several routes. It was trade with the Americas which caused a sudden and great increase in its population; for when the Glasgow people realised its possibilities, they enlisted the services of the most prominent engineers of the day and deepened the Clyde to admit large ships. There are still living people whose grandfathers waded across the Clyde, where now some of the biggest vessels can lie in safety.

West of Glasgow and not many miles from its boundaries are Renfrew and Paisley, in which cotton manufacture is the leading business. Like the textile industries of South Lancashire and the West Riding of Yorkshire, those in this neighbourhood are of many kinds, utilising different raw materials. Where one textile industry is firmly established, others are likely to follow it.

Photochrom.

GLASGOW UNIVERSITY

While St. Andrews is the oldest University in Scotland, both Edinburgh and Glasgow have great universities. The present buildings of the University of Glasgow, (founded 1450), date from 1868 and were designed by Sir George Gilbert Scott. They stand on Gilmorehill which is part of the 85-acre Kelvingrove Park bought by the Corporation of Glasgow in 1852.

BUILDING A LINER ON THE CLYDE

This photograph gives you a splendid idea of what a modern shipbuilding yard is like. The picture was taken from the air and shows a 40,000-ton ocean liner nearing that stage in her construction when she can be launched into her proper element. Starting with the keel-plate, the monster ship is built girder by girder and plate by plate with the aid of giant cranes.

Thirty miles south-west of Glasgow and about four miles from Ayr is Prestwick, one of the most important airfields in the British Isles, the starting-point for trans-Atlantic services to Gander, Newfoundland, and Montreal, with air links with London, the Continent, the Baltic capitals and Iceland.

Scotland's Busy Heart

The Midland Valley has three great coalfields: (1) the Lanark coalfield, chiefly in the valley of the Clyde, with Glasgow as its outlet, but with other outlets on the Firth of Forth, for it extends really to Clackmannan on the other side of the river; (2) the Ayr coalfield, with the coal shipping ports of Troon and Ardrossan on the west coast ; and (3) the coalfields of the Firth of Forth—the Fife coalfield in the north, and the Lothian coalfield on

the south of the estuary, beneath which they are doubtless connected.

The Lanark field is by far the largest and the most important. Its coal gave rise to the iron and steel industries, the engineering works, and other great businesses which grew amazingly when imported iron and raw materials from the Americas were brought in large quantities to supplement the local supplies. Many large towns have grown up on this coalfield—Lanark, Coatbridge, Airdrie, Motherwell and Falkirk, for example, to say nothing of Glasgow, the second largest town in the Homeland. But supplies of coal from the Lanark field are now growing less and recently development has been concerned with the east coast deposits in Fife and the Lothians, which will lead to the setting up of new industries north and south of the Forth estuary.

An important centre of development is Grangemouth, near Falkirk, which now handles a larger tonnage of goods than any other Scottish port except Glasgow and has important chemical works making dyestuffs, drugs and other products. At Grangemouth, too, oil is refined, ships are built and repaired, and timber imported and worked.

The Ayr coalfield supports the smelters of Irvine and the manufacturers of Kilmarnock in and around which town industrial activity has grown considerably during recent years. The Fife coalfield, with its coal port of Methil, supports the linen mills of Dunfermline and the linoleum and oilcloth industries of Kirkcaldy, as well as the linen, marmalade, and jam business of Dundee and neighbouring towns. The Lothian coalfield is convenient for ships using the ports of Leith and Granton, and for the city of Edinburgh's big paper, printing and biscuit industries.

The Forth and Clyde Canal provides a narrow waterway between the two great estuaries but a proposal for deepening and widening it to form a ship canal from the North Sea to the Atlantic has been abandoned.

Famous Scottish Universities

Edinburgh and Glasgow have great universities. The ancient town of St. Andrews on the coast of Fife has a famous university, too, and picturesque ruins of its former greatness on a rocky platform almost entirely sea-girt on which the old city grew up as a stronghold.

Farmers of the Lowlands

The main routes to the north from Edinburgh and the Forth Bridge cut across Fifeshire, one crossing the Tay by the Tay Bridge, also a triumph of British engineering, and going *via* Dundee and Montrose to Aberdeen, the " Granite City," the home of another famous Scottish university and of Scotland's leading fishing and fish-exporting business. Dundee, like Dunfermline, is a centre of the linen industry, whose mills are fed with flax from the Continent. Raw jute comes here, too, to be made into sacks and bags, and Dundee is famous for its jams and marmalade. The other route crosses the Tay at Perth, the lowest bridge-point on the river, and the centre of important dyeworks.

Many people of the Midland Valley get their living by farming. In the wetter west root-crops are more frequent than grain ; the best grain country is in the drier and sunnier east.

Cattle are more numerous than sheep on the western pastures, but sheep are more numerous than cattle on the eastern pastures, which have less rain than those of the west.

Farming in this part of Scotland is very thorough, and the fertile soil is made by diligent and careful attention to yield richer crops than most other parts of the British Isles.

Fox Photos.

A SCOTTISH HERO

Sir William Wallace, one of the great fighters for Scottish independence, is commemorated in Aberdeen by this statue made of bronze which stands in Union Terrace Gardens.

GRANITE FROM ABERDEEN

Aberdeen is known as " The Granite City " because its granite industry is one of the most important in the world. The pictures on this page are of the Rubislaw quarry and we see (above) a seven ton block of granite after cutting.

Photos: D. McLeod Smith.

How was that block cut? Holes were drilled in the manner shown in this picture. After drilling a long crowbar was inserted in one of the holes. A little pressure applied to the crowbar by one man was sufficient to split the granite.

FISHING AND FORESTRY

" The Times."

Fraserburgh, the important herring fishing port of north-east Scotland, is a gathering place for large numbers of fishing craft from all parts during the season. In this picture, the craft putting out to sea bear Inverness and Lowestoft registration marks respectively.

Wm. S. Thomson.

A poet once wrote of Glen Nevis as a " long, wild, waste glen," and at times it does seem a sombre place. Here, we are looking across the Glen towards the height known as Sgurr a'Mhaim. The slopes are thickly planted under the reafforestation schemes of the Forestry Commission.

By courtesy of British Railways.

BY LOCH LOMOND'S BONNIE BANKS

Lomond is the largest loch, and one of the most beautiful, in Scotland. It has a length of about twenty-four miles and is some five miles across at the widest point. Among the thirty or so islands within the loch is Inchlonaig, the " Island of Yew Trees," where yews were planted to provide bows for the archers of Robert the Bruce. If you visit Lomond, which lies between Stirlingshire and Dumbartonshire, you will notice how the landscape is dominated by majestic Ben Lomond. The mountain has a height of 3,192 feet.

Barnabys Ltd.

A BEAUTIFUL VALE IN THE EMERALD ISLE

There are many lovely vales in County Wicklow, in south-east Ireland, but the most celebrated is probably the Vale of Avoca, part of which is seen in this picture. The Irish poet Thomas Moore sang the praises of this narrow and thickly wooded vale in one of his *Irish Melodies*. His " meeting of the waters " can be seen at Lion's Bridge, where the Avonmore and Avonbeg rivers unite to form the Avoca, or Ovoca, river which flows down to the Irish Sea at Arklow. Summer is the time to see Avoca, when the clear waters ripple between the banks of vivid green.

CLIMBERS OF THE COBBLER

Fox Photos.

The majestic peaks of the Scottish Highlands provide both beauty for the eye and a challenge to such climbers as those seen in this picture looking down upon Loch Long from the craggy height known as the Cobbler. Loch Long opens out into the Clyde Estuary and attracts artists from all parts of the world. The Cobbler, with the peaks of Beinn Ime, Ben Vane, and Ben Vorlich, forms the mountain rampart of the Loch which, from Arrochar to its mouth, is nearly twenty miles long.

The Scottish Highlands

The most beautiful part of Scotland lies north of the Midland Valley in the Scottish Highlands, which fill the greater part of the country north of a line drawn from the Firth of Clyde to Stonehaven on the east coast.

When you enter the Highlands at Dunkeld or at Callander you feel that you are entering a new country, so different is it from the great valley you have just left. From Dunkeld (on the Highland Railway from Perth) you can follow the route through the famous Pass of Killiecrankie up Glen Garry past Dalnaspidal, the highest railway station in the British Isles, and over the Drumochter Pass (1,484 feet)— the highest railway summit—to the valley of the Spey at Kingussie, and on

via Aviemore to Culloden Moor and Inverness.

All the time you have travelled through magnificent highland scenery unrivalled anywhere else in the Homeland.

The Beautiful Trossachs

From Callander, on the railway from Stirling, a visit can be paid to the Trossachs and lovely Loch Katrine, which Sir Walter Scott describes in " The Lady of the Lake." King James V. has climbed to a high viewpoint:—

" Where, gleaming with the setting sun,
One burnished sheet of living gold,
Loch Katrine lay beneath him rolled
In all her length far winding lay,
With promontory, creek, and bay,
And islands that, empurpled bright,

Reece Winstone.

HYDRO-ELECTRIC POWER FOR AN ALUMINIUM WORKS

The Laggan Dam, seen above, is part of the Lochaber water power scheme. Its power house near Fort William supplies the nearby North British Aluminium Co. factory. The Glen Affric scheme, opened by the Duke of Edinburgh in October, 1952, is one of the most recent hydro-electric developments in Scotland.

Robert M. Adam.

THE PEAKS AROUND DALNESS

These guardian peaks will greet you if you visit Glen Etive in the Western Highlands. Nearby is Glencoe, the historic glen where, in 1692, the Macdonalds of Glencoe were massacred by Captain Campbell of Glenlyon and his men. The main scene of the massacre is now occupied by Glencoe Village.

Floated amid the livelier light;
And mountains, that like giants stand,
To sentinel enchanted land.
High on the south, huge Ben Venue
Down on the lake in masses threw
Crags, knolls, and mounds, confusedly hurled
The fragments of an earlier world;
A wildering forest feathered o'er
His ruined sides and summit hoar,
While on the north, through middle air,
Ben An heaved high his forehead bare."

From Loch Katrine the tourist can go by motor coach to the shores of island-studded Loch Lomond, the largest lake in Scotland, where a lake steamer will take him southwards past lofty Ben Lomond to Balloch at the end of the lake, within a short train journey of Glasgow.

" Caledonia, Stern and Wild "

Bolder scenery is to be found in the Grampians, where Ben Macdhui and at least three other peaks rise above 4,000 feet, and where splendid pine forests are to be seen in the valley of the Spey. These are in the Central Highlands. The Northern Highlands, lonely and desolate, with wilder and sterner scenery than anywhere south, lie to the north of Glen More, a deep trench created by faulting in the rocks.

In the bottom of Glen More lie Loch Lochy and Loch Ness with their rivers; and sea, lakes and rivers have been joined by the cutting of the Caledonian Canal from Inverness to Fort William beneath the great hump of Ben Nevis, the highest peak in the United Kingdom. The Canal is used chiefly in summer for tourist traffic. At the Falls of Foyers on the southern side of Loch Ness, and farther to the south-

A HIGHLAND GATHERING—

Aboyne and Braemar are among the places in Scotland famous as the scenes of Highland Gatherings. Ancient in origin, these gatherings draw clansmen and their womenfolk and visitors from all parts of the world.   The picture shows a Highland Gathering at Braemar.

Photos: Topical Press.

A feature of Highland Gatherings is the music of the pipe bands. This picture shows the massed March Past, in which six pipe bands took part, which opened a gathering at Braemar attended by a Royal party from Balmoral.

—PIPING AND DANCING

Central Press.

Highland dancing is an art that has to be learned at an early age. This little four-year-old girl on the left is dancing the Highland Fling with her twelve-year-old sister in the Highland Games at Kilgraston, Bridge of Earn, Perthshire.

Sport & General.

These dancers are competing in the Ballater Highland Games held in the beautiful setting of Monaltrie Park, Ballater, Aberdeenshire. The dance they are performing is the Highland Fling, perhaps the best-known of Scottish dances and certainly one of the most lively to watch.

THROWING THE HAMMER—

To the music of Scotland's national instrument, the bagpipes, Highland dancers compete at the Braemar Gathering. Notice the different tartans worn by the dancers which show the clans to which they belong.

Photos: Central Press.

Throwing the Hammer is always one of the events of Highland Games. This picture, taken at a Braemar Highland Gathering, shows a competitor about to throw in the 22 lb.-hammer class. He won the event with a throw of 94 feet.

—AND OTHER FEATS OF STRENGTH

Central Press.

This competitor threw the 28 lb. stone over 29 feet at a Braemar Gathering, winning the event by this throw.

Sport & General.

This picture was taken at Aboyne, scarcely less famous than Braemar as the scene of Highland Gatherings.

Central Press.

This is another event that you will see at a Highland Games gathering. One man will toss the caber, but two men bring it back for the next competitor.

Sport & General.

Young enthusiasts watch admiringly a competitor in the piping competitions at a Braemar Gathering. Music, dancing, and sports are all part of a Gathering.

west at Kinlochleven, water-power has been utilised for large aluminium works.

The Scottish Crofters

Not many people live in the Highlands, especially in the lonely west and north where plough-land is scarce, and mountain and heathery moors are everywhere. Time was when the few crofters or farmers lived in their small " crofts " in sheltered glens, more or less cut off from the rest of all the world, growing oats and potatoes, rearing a few cows for milk, butter and cheese, and poultry for eggs, and perhaps sheep on the hillside to provide the wool which was spun, woven and dyed for cloth by their wives and daughters. Such humble folk can still be seen in the west and by the sea, and on the lonely isles of the Inner and Outer Hebrides, where crofters are fishermen and farmers too, living on the joint harvests of the sea and the land. They depend upon the small steamers that call periodically for their flour and groceries, and their newspapers and the mails. Their small homes are built of stone from the hills, thatched with heather, or with straw from their small crofts, and timbered perhaps with driftwood picked up on the beaches.

In the north are wide, open heathery moorlands, which are let out to wealthy folk as deer forests or grouse moors, to be visited for deer-stalking and grouse-shooting by gay parties at certain seasons of the year.

But to-day some parts of the Highlands have many large sheep farms, large areas covered by the reafforestation schemes of the Forestry Commission, and such industries as the aluminium works at Kinlochleven and the famous herring fisheries of Lochfyne. The thatched crofters' cottages are disappearing from these areas and the strongest link with the past is in the Gaelic language which Highlanders are proud to use and keep alive. Many of the crofts that remain are lit and powered by electricity, for the Highlands now have hydroelectric schemes, which harness loch and river waters. Of these, one

Scottish Field.

THE PALACE OF FALKLAND, FIFE

Sixteen miles from Perth, upon ground that was associated with the Kings of Scotland as early as the 12th century, stands the Palace of Falkland. The Palace was completed in 1540 by James V to take the place of the original castle. It was here that James died two years later.

IN THE SCOTTISH HIGHLANDS

Planet.

Built probably between the years 1566 and 1572, Barrogill Castle, also known as Castle of Mey, in Caithness, is one of Scotland's oldest inhabited houses. On a clear day Scapa Flow and all the southern part of the Orkneys can be seen, with ships of many nations passing through the Pentland Firth. The Castle is now the Scottish home of the Queen Mother.

British Council.

The turbulent flood waters of the Conon rush headlong in their swift journey through the Highland valley to Cromarty Firth and the sea. Many a Highland stream and river will be as boisterous as this when spring comes and on the mountain peaks the snow melts.

THE TROSSACHS AND BALMORAL

Every seeker of fine scenery and every fisherman in Scotland knows the beauties of the Trossachs, the famous region of lake and mountain around Lochs Lomond and Katrine where wooded slopes hem in the placid waters and where tower such majestic peaks as Ben Lomond.

Photos: Fox Photos.

Standing on the banks of the Dee in about 20,000 acres of deer forest, Balmoral Castle is the Highland home of our Royal Family. The castle was enlarged and almost entirely rebuilt by Queen Victoria. The name comes from the Gaelic and means " majestic dwelling."

SCOTLAND'S RUGGED COASTS

Wm. S. Thomson.

Scotland has many pleasant holiday resorts, both inland and coastal: and one of the most popular is Oban, in Argyllshire. Nestling between the waters of the Firth of Lorne and a range of hills, Oban is a holiday centre and a port. This view of the town was taken from Pulpit Hill.

" The Scotsman."

Here we are standing on a clifftop on the Aberdeenshire coast looking down on Cove, whose tiny harbour lies a few miles south of Aberdeen. The harbour is hemmed in by craggy cliffs from which thin, jagged fingers of rock protrude into the sea almost barring the very entrance.

Robert M. Adam.

WHERE BONNIE PRINCE CHARLIE RAISED HIS STANDARD

The Glenfinnan Monument stands at the head of Loch Shiel, near Fort William, Inverness-shire, on the spot where Prince Charles Edward raised his standard to proclaim the start of the Jacobite Rising of 1745. The Monument was built in 1815 and is surmounted by the figure of a kilted Highlander.

of the most recent is the Glen Affric scheme, whose Fasnakyle power station was formally opened by the Duke of Edinburgh in October, 1952. It has been estimated that when all the schemes in hand have been completed, 4½ million tons of coal will be saved each year.

Despite these developments, most crofters live a precarious life. A few years ago, a special commission was appointed to examine the problems of the crofters. Its report, published in 1954, stated that most crofters live by farming and that many of the crofts are no larger than five acres. The housing of the crofters is improving, but there are still many crofts without electricity or proper water supply. Although some crofters are skilled farmers and stock-breeders, many have still to learn the modern ways which will enable them to produce better crops and stock.

The Highlands are not without modern holiday resorts such as Oban and Dunoon.

Oban, on the coast of Argyll, is a favourite tourist and yachting centre in summer; and many visitors from all parts of Britain go to see the wonderful Fingal's Cave in the island of Staffa, and the holy isle of Iona where St. Columba built his church and monastery in the sixth century A.D. and began his work of spreading Christianity in Scotland.

To The Hebrides

Far out in the Atlantic is the lonely isle of Saint Kilda now denuded of its population.

Scottish islands are indeed romantic, yet only comparatively few southerners ever have the privilege of visiting the Hebrides, for example. You will find the latter on your map flanking the north-east coast and you will see that there are both the Inner and the Outer Hebrides divided by Little Minch, a strip of water only a dozen miles across at one point. Skye, Mull, Islay and Jura are four of

OVER THE SEA TO SKYE

Violet Banks.

South Uist, in the Outer Hebrides, is an island that is " fair enough in summer; but in winter it is open to the Atlantic, bleak, windswept, cold." Its people gain a hard living from sea and soil; in this picture tinkers are crossing the ford between South Uist and neighbouring Benbecula.

Central Press.

The loch, the croft, barren moorland, and the majestic highlands of the Cuillins whose summits are well-nigh hidden in the clouds, contribute to this typical scene on Skye. The Cuillin Hills are not high, but they appear so because they rise sharply from sea level moorland or from deep glens.

the inner islands. The outer group consists of Lewis, North and South Uist, and several others.

People of the Islands

Perhaps you will be surprised to hear that there are about one hundred of these islands having people dwelling on them and hundreds more so small or barren that they give support only to seabirds and other wildlings. Many of the Hebrides have open moorlands studded with shepherd's huts or shielings, some of them so primitive that their roofs are formed of turves. Stornoway, on "the Long Island" (Lewis and Harris) is the chief town of the Outer Hebrides and has its own herring fleet.

It is at Harris that the crofters weave their renowned Harris tweed.

We can imagine how lonely life is on the remoter islands where the croft itself has to provide nearly everything needed by the crofters. School for the youngsters will be a problem, too: and there will be no question of going to the shops "down the road" for any day-to-day wants. The crofters will get what they need from day to day from the croft—materials for building or repairing the house, peat for the fires, vegetables, milk, and fish for food. Even their clothing may originate at the croft where the home produced wool will be spun and woven and skilfully dyed with the juices of certain plants.

But simple though the life of the crofters must be, it has its compensations. The lonely islands have produced a fine race of people, hardy, brave, patient, and hard-working; they are probably more contented and get greater

Copyright.

THE CAVE OF A WARRIOR HERO

Staffa, one of the smaller islands of the Inner Hebrides, has on its shores this majestic cave whose stony columns rear upwards like the pipes of a cathedral organ. Famous as Fingal's Cave, it is named after Finn MacCool, hero of the Gaels of the second and third centuries A.D. Because of the sound made at times by the wind its Gaelic name is the "cave of music."

Photochrom.

THE HOLY ISLAND OF IONA

Iona, an island of the Inner Hebrides, was once known as "the island of the Druids," but it is sacred to Christianity as the place where St. Columba built his church and monastery in the sixth century A.D. and which began the centre for missionary work in Scotland and northern England. The picture shows the ruins of the thirteenth-century cathedral of St. Mary, and also on the island are the tombs of the kings of long ago.

satisfaction from life than many a towns-man or city-dweller.

Orkneys and Shetlands

To visit the Orkneys and Shetlands is to visit islands rich in relics of the early history of Britain, from the burial cairns of the Orkneys' Bay of Skail to the traces of Saint Sunnifa's Chapel on Unst, the northernmost island of the Shetlands (and so, of Britain). But where are the Orkneys and the Shetlands?

To find the Orkneys on a map we must look to the extreme north of the sister country. Here we shall find, dotted about over an extensive area, a considerable number of islands, though fewer than thirty of them are large enough for human habitation. Nevertheless, the Orkneys have rich soil, are highly cultivated, and are one of the most prosperous agricultural regions in the British Isles. Kirkwall is by far the biggest township, ranking both as a city and a royal burgh, with an ancient cathedral. Stromness is another town in the Orkneys. Still farther north are the Shetlands, whose chief town is Lerwick, and whose chief products are fine woollen fabrics and the famous Shetland ponies.

Pentland Firth, with its wild waters, separates the Orkneys from the mainland; and, on the very point of north-east Scotland, hard by Duncansby Head, there once stood John o' Groats' House and stands to-day John o' Groats' Hotel. From Land's End to John o' Groats, a distance of 876 miles, would be the longest direct land journey we could undertake in the sister countries.

About John o' Groats

There are, of course, stories linked with the memory of John o' Groats. According to some legends, John de Groot was a Dutchman who, three hundred years and more ago, settled in this vicinity. The family grew and grew, as families did in those days,

until eventually there were eight brothers, and a dispute then arose as to which of them should sit at the head of the table, near the door.

To settle the quarrel once and for all John built a house that was octagonal, or eight-sided. It had eight doors and eight windows on the ground floor and the dining-table had eight sides to match. Thus each brother came into the main living-room by his own door, went straight to his place at the festive board, and so there was no excuse whatever for any argument.

Whether they are living in Scotland or are far from its lochs and glens, all true Scots take great pride in their national institutions. Their hearts gladden at the sound of the pipes; they staunchly uphold their national dishes, such as haggis; they cherish dearly the immortal poems of Robert Burns; and they still feel strongly the call of the clan and the power of the tartan.

Highland Dress

The tartan is the historic dress of the Highlander and its origins are lost in the mists of time. In the oldest form, kilt and plaid were one, and from very early times it was customary to make the cloth in distinctive stripes of different widths and colours. By these markings, which are the basis of the tartan, clan was distinguishable from clan. So, to the Scot of to-day, the tartan speaks of past glories and is an expression of his deep pride of race.

The National Trust for Scotland.

THE HIGHEST FALLS IN GREAT BRITAIN

Some of the finest scenery in the West Highlands can be seen at Kintail, Wester Ross. At Kintail are Beinn Fhada and the Five Sisters. Here, too, the Glomach plunges 370 feet in a sheer drop to form the beautiful Falls of Glomach, which are seen in this picture.

The Story
of the
World and
its Peoples

Northern Ireland
and the
Irish
Republic

J. Dixon-Scott.

THE HONEYCOMB, THE GIANT'S CAUSEWAY, COUNTY ANTRIM

Legend says that Finn MacCool, the warrior hero, built this strange causeway so that he could fight a Scottish giant who had challenged him, but who was afraid to swim the channel. Geologists explain these curious stone pillars as the result of freak cooling of lava during the earth's earliest times. The pillars mostly have three or five sides and are each from 15 to 20 inches in diameter.

BEAUTIFUL IRELAND

THE Green Isle of Erin is a little larger than Scotland, but has rather fewer people. It lies right in the track of the prevailing westerly winds of the Atlantic, which keep it ever fresh and verdant, so that it is known all the world over as " The Emerald Isle."

Ireland has two separate political divisions: (1) Northern Ireland, which is still part of the United Kingdom, and consists of the five counties around Lough Neagh and the county of Fermanagh; and (2) the Irish Republic, formerly known as Eire, which is the rest of Ireland, and is now a republic independent of the British Commonwealth of Nations. Of the two divisions, Northern Ireland, which has several flourishing manufactures, is the more densely populated; the Irish Republic is mainly a farming country, with a more evenly distributed population, whose great business is dairy-farming and the export of foodstuffs, largely to the sister island of Great Britain.

The Making of Erin

Ireland's mountains lie mainly in the great detached masses around its rim. The middle of the island is largely the great Central Plain through which flows the slow, deep Shannon, linked with Dublin by the Royal Canal and by the Grand Canal.

The Central Plain was once covered

by other layers of rock, among which were the coal measures ; but these have nearly all been planed off by the ancient ice and by the work of running water, leaving the old limestone floor with, here and there, steep isolated hills and mountains of millstone grit like that of the Pennines. Ireland has little coal, and this partly explains why she is not a manufacturing island. But in recent years the mighty Shannon has been harnessed to provide electricity at the great power houses of Ardnacrusha, above which is an eight-mile canal bringing water from the river. The Shannon Power Scheme has successfully brought electric light, heat and power not only to the large towns but even to country districts and has made possible the development of many manufacturing enterprises. The river Liffey, and the Erne in Donegal have also been harnessed, and the Lower Bann and river Mourne (both in Northern Ireland) may be used, before long, for the same purpose.

Peat Instead of Coal

Bogs are common on the Central Plain—soft, swampy and treacherous; others solid and full of the peat that is much more used than coal in Irish homes. The largest is the Bog of Allen. These bogs have been formed by the age-long decay of marsh plants and sphagnum moss in the water-filled

Topical Press.

THE SHANNON IS HARNESSED TO PROVIDE ELECTRICITY

The Shannon, the longest river in the British Isles, drains almost the entire plain of Ireland. Its waters are harnessed by the dam seen in this picture and produce electricity, not only for Dublin but for many parts of the Irish Republic, which has little coal. The rivers Liffey and Erne are also used for hydro-electric power.

J. R. Bainbridge.

WHERE NORTHERN IRELAND'S PARLIAMENT ASSEMBLES

Although Northern Ireland sends members to the House of Commons at Westminster, her six counties and two parliamentary boroughs have their own Parliament and Government. There is a House of Commons, a Senate, and a Governor who represents H.M. the Queen. The picture shows the fine Parliament Buildings at Stormont Castle, on the outskirts of Belfast.

hollows of the limestone, where boulder clay from the ancient glaciers has given them a waterproof bottom. There are bogs, too, in Connemara to the west, and in other low-lying spots among the Irish hills. They are by no means without natural beauty. As the year rolls on, " the bare brown bog turns gradually warmer in tone till it becomes a bright orange, a pale red, and then in October a vivid crimson as grass and bog-plants turn scarlet."

Colours, indeed, are nowhere brighter and fresher than in the clear rain-washed atmosphere of Erin. To appreciate this we have only to visit the lovely Wicklow Hills with their " sweet vale of Avoca," or the beautiful Lakes of Killarney amid their encircling peaks, or wild Connemara with its marble mountains and its deep lakes, Corrib and Mask.

Ireland's highest peak is Carrantuohill (3,414 feet) in Macgillycuddy's Reeks amid the mountainous region of south-western Ireland, whose coastline is cut up by long deep inlets called *rias.*

Northern Ireland has important manufacturing industries, the chief of which are the linen industry and shipbuilding. The headquarters of both are at Belfast, which contains about a third of all the people in Northern Ireland.

The linen industry grew up there because it is a flax-growing region, although to-day large quantities of flax from Belgium and Holland, Germany and the Baltic lands have to be imported to meet the needs of the linen mills of Belfast, Ballymena, Larne, Newtownards, Lurgan, Portadown, Armagh and Monaghan (though Monaghan is in the Irish Republic; Monaghan, Cavan and Donegal are the three Ulster Counties not included in Northern Ireland).

Ship building is mainly centred at Belfast at the head of the deep Belfast Lough, where are the famous shipyards of Harland & Wolff, which have launched many of our finest ocean liners. Although a little coal and iron can be got near Belfast, the main supplies come from Britain—coal from the Ayr coalfield and iron and steel plates from Northern England.

Belfast has also flourishing tobacco factories, the biggest rope works in the world, and food processing and mineral water factories. Her aircraft factories are building Canberra bombers and jet airliners. The historic city of Londonderry also—generally known as "Derry"—has a number of thriving industries, including shirt and collar manufacturing. During the last war it was an important naval base. It stands at the head of Lough Foyle.

Derry shirts are made in more than thirty modern factories in or about the city, and some 10,000 people are employed in making them and in the manufacture of collars and pyjamas as well. In the shirt factories you can see machines that can give 4,500 stitches per minute, and others which take 40,000 yards of thread and stitch at the rate of 8,000 stitches per minute. You can also see buttonholes made and buttons sewn on at amazing speed—to make one buttonhole and sew on the button takes three seconds!

Northern Ireland is a rich agricultural and stock-breeding country, too. Indeed, agriculture is the largest single industry, although most of the farms are small. The basin of the River Lagan is remarkably fertile and grows many kinds of crops; dairy-farming and pig-rearing being profitable occupations for many people.

Most farms in Northern Ireland are mixed farms; that is to say, they grow crops and raise livestock as well. Most of the crops grown are used by the farmers to feed their livestock and poultry, the sale of which provides much of their income. Northern Ireland has always had more farm produce than she

J. Dixon-Scott.

DONEGAL PLACE AND THE CITY HALL, BELFAST

First city of Northern Ireland, Belfast has important industries, the chief of which are linen and shipbuilding. Standing on the banks of the Lagan where it enters Belfast Lough, the city is also an important seaport. The City Hall shown in this picture stands on the site of the old Linen Hall and was opened in 1906.

BUILT IN A BELFAST SHIPYARD

Topical Press.

At the head of the deep Belfast Lough are the famous shipyards of Harland & Wolff from which many of our finest ocean liners have come. In this picture we see the launching of the " Edinburgh Castle," a fine ship built for the South African run and launched by Princess Margaret. Watched by the men who built her, she moves down the slipway to the water that is her natural element.

herself needs, and most of the surplus is sent across to Britain.

The Giant's Causeway

An interesting spot which every one who can makes a point of seeing is the Giant's Causeway, near Portrush, on the northern coast. It is built up of thousands of basaltic pillars, mostly five-sided or three-sided, standing up right out to sea, so that their tops form a rough platform. The cliffs near by have a similar formation. The famous " organ pipes " of Fingal's Cave in the island of Staffa are of the same structure, and are probably due to a similar great upheaval of ancient lava.

What are called textiles, *i.e.*, products that can be woven, always collect round them a vast industry, and Northern Ireland's textile interests find

employment for about 100,000 people. These interests centre round flax and linen, and few plants are more beautiful than flax, with its tapering leaves and tiny blue flowers. The stalk or straw is composed of a woody substance called the " boon," around which is a veritable network of fine, strong fibres. Seed is sown either in April or June, spring-sown flax being harvested in July and the later crop in September.

Harvesting the Flax

When it has grown sufficiently tall the flax plant is pulled up bodily by the roots, so that it does not have to be cut with scythe or machine like hay or grain. When a sheaf weighing about twenty pounds has been pulled it is carefully tied so that the root-ends are close together, and the bundles must next be put in a pond, roots downward

J. R. Bainbridge.

THE HARVEST OF FLAX

Flax, from the fibres of which linen thread is made, is not cut with a machine. Instead, the plants are pulled bodily from the ground and are then made into sheaves weighing 20 lb. The first step in the maturing of flax is to place the sheaves weighted down with stones in a pond to ensure that the sheaves remain below water.

J. *Dixon-Scott.*

LURIGEDAN'S MASSIVE BULK

The table-topped mountain of Lurigedan dominates Ulster's beautiful Vale of Cushendall whose pattern of rich fields laps the basalt foot of the mountain. Cushendall itself is a pleasant seaside place on the shores of Red Bay which is among the finest coastal scenery of Northern Ireland.

and covered first with rushes and straw to exclude the light, and then with stones to ensure that they remain below water. After about a fortnight of this treatment the bundles are spread out on grass and then placed in stooks in the field to mellow, much as one sees stooked sheaves in a cornfield.

The next step is called scutching. In the course of this process the flax straw is passed between heavy crushing rollers with intermeshing cogs on their surfaces, these cogs breaking the straw and partly separating it from the fibre. Scutched flax has now to be tied in bundles weighing fourteen pounds, known as a stone of flax, when it is ready for the market or the mills.

Long before cotton, silk or any other sewing material was discovered and put to man's use linen thread was in daily demand. In Bible times the vestments of the priests were made of embroidered fine linen, and to-day good linen thread is one of the strongest

fibres known. Many pages might be written on the making of linen yarn, how the first crude fibres are prepared and spun; how two or three strands are twisted together to make threads or twine; how it is reeled and made up into balls, cops, cards and skeins. Even then we should not have considered the weaving of linen cloth from the thread, spinning and weaving being distinct parts in the routine of all textile industries.

The Red Hand of Ulster

Ulster is another and older name sometimes used for Northern Ireland, and its badge is a red hand. Long years ago, so legend tells, a party of bold adventurers was approaching the coast of Ireland when the leader announced that whoever of his party first touched the shore should possess the territory he reached. Thereupon an ancestor of the O'Neills from whom descended the Kings of Ulster, finding another boat forging slowly ahead of his, struck off his left hand and flung it on to the land. Thus the hand of Ulster, red with O'Neill blood, still remains an emblem.

But remember that not all Ulster is in Northern Ireland. The Ulster counties of Cavan, Donegal and Monaghan are part of the Irish Republic.

The Parliament Houses of Northern Ireland are at Stormont Castle, on the outskirts of Belfast, one of the most modern and beautiful of all legislative buildings. The Ulster Parliament consists of a House of Commons of fifty-two members and a Senate, twelve members being still returned to the House of Commons at Westminster. There is also a Governor, who represents Her Majesty the Queen.

Regular services of mail steamers ply between Belfast and Liverpool, Heysham, Ardrossan and Glasgow and between Londonderry and Glasgow, and Larne and Stranraer. Inward-bound Belfast packets make their way through the broad lough with its entrancing views and berth in the very heart of the city. A regular B.E.A. air service connects Belfast with London and other great centres in Britain, the airport at Belfast being at Nutt's Corner.

In the Irish Republic

The Irish Republic is mainly a farming country whose real wealth lies in its dairy produce, and in its cattle and horses, pigs and poultry.

Potatoes, said to have been introduced from the Americas by Sir Walter Raleigh in the sixteenth century, grow well almost anywhere where there is soil enough, and to this day form the chief food of a large number of the Irish country folk. So much, in fact, have the Irish depended upon potatoes in past years, that the failure of the potato crop has meant widespread distress.

The dairy industry of the Republic has been greatly helped by the building of central creameries, run by co-operation among the farmers. The milk is brought to the creamery from farms great and small in all sorts of vehicles, from humble donkey carts to large motor lorries. Here the cream is separated from it by machinery to be made into the famous Irish butter, and the " skim milk " that is left is given back to the farmers to use at home or to feed the pigs. There are some hundreds of co-operative dairy societies worked in this way, which gives the big farmers and the poor people alike the chance of getting good prices for their cream in a ready market.

Bacon factories and ham factories are run on much the same lines. Poultry kept on the dairy farms yield additional income to their owners. Most of this dairy produce goes to the busy towns and manufacturing regions of Britain, through ports like Dublin, Wexford, Waterford and Cork.

Ireland exports cattle to the value of some £25 millions a year and in 1952 shipped 354,000 head—most of them beef cattle—for fattening in Britain. She is also developing a flourishing trade in meat, which is shipped to Britain in carcase form, slightly chilled, from such ports as Waterford. Canned beef is also exported.

Every true Irishman is a lover of fine horses, for some of the finest horses in the world are bred in the Emerald Isle.

Beautiful Connemara

Much of the Republic, however, is poor country for supporting the people who live upon it. In the far west—in Connemara, for instance, where the soil is poor and thin, and the climate wet and raw—the countryfolk, in their thatched and whitewashed homes, depend upon their small potato and cabbage patches and upon their pigs, if they are lucky enough to have them, for their living, adding to the scanty harvest of the land the inexhaustible harvest of lake and sea.

But Connemara is a beautiful region

CUTTING TURVES

Irish Tourist Association.

There are many bogs in Ireland, particularly on the Central Plain. Some are swampy and treacherous, but others are solid and full of peat, or " turf " as the Irish call it. Turf is the traditional Irish fuel. It is cut from the bog with a sharp spade-like implement called a slane in Ireland. The bogs have been formed by the slow decay of marsh plants and sphagnum moss, through the centuries, in water-filled limestone hollows waterproofed by boulder clay from ancient glaciers.

153

of lake and mountain, visited by more and more people every year for its scenery and its quiet, while its trout and salmon fishing attracts sportsmen from all quarters of the British Isles. The gate to it is Galway.

The eastern half of Southern Ireland is much more densely populated, and some manufactures are carried on in the towns and cities.

Dublin

Dublin (*Baile Atha Cliath*), the capital, shelters within its city boundaries almost a fifth of all the people in the Republic. Its port is Kingstown, which is now called *Dun Laoghaire*, and is in daily communication with Holyhead and Liverpool. The River Liffey cuts the city in two, and is lined with busy wharves and warehouses, for

Dublin is the main entrance into the Republic. Saint Patrick's Cathedral, founded in the twelfth century, and restored in 1865, and Christchurch Cathedral, stand not far from the Castle in the heart of the city. St. Patrick's Cathedral has a monument to Jonathan Swift, dear to schoolboys and schoolgirls as the author of " Gulliver's Travels." Collinstown, the airport of Dublin, is five miles from the capital and has links with London and the main services of the world.

A big town standing at the head of the Shannon Estuary is Limerick, capital of the county of the same name in the province of Munster. Though interested mainly in farm produce, Limerick is a centre for salmon fishing, and a certain amount of export trade is carried on from its docks.

GATHERING PEAT

Irish Tourist Association.

Most cottages in Ireland have their stacks of peat cut from the bogs, for peat is fuel which keeps them warm in winter and heats the ovens of the countryfolk who live there. Peat is cut from the bogs and loaded in pannier baskets on the backs of patient donkeys; other loads are carried in special baskets that fit one's back, as you can see from the picture.

In the south we find Cork, which ranks as the second port. Its name comes from the Gaelic word *corcaigh*, meaning "marsh." It has valuable imports, such as coal and grain, and sends away in substantial quantities livestock and dairy produce. It possesses a growing motor industry and stands on the River Lee, which is particularly beautiful where it winds through the city's outer suburbs. At the far end of Cork Harbour, on Great Island, is the port of Cobh (pronounced Cove) which was Queenstown in the old geography books and is still a port of call for Atlantic liners.

Ports of the South-East

Fifteen miles west of Limerick, on the Shannon river, is Shannon airport (Rineanna) whence services fly to all parts of Europe and—even more important—across the Atlantic to Canada and the United States. But in general there is not so much commercial activity on the western seaboard apart from fishing. On the other hand, the ports that give ready access to South Wales and Bristol are busy and prosperous. Waterford, on the River Suir, is one such place, and Wexford, on the River Slaney, another. From Rosslare there is a regular service of fine steamers to Fishguard, where express trains make a quick run to London through the Severn Tunnel.

As a result of its own Republic of Ireland Bill of 1948, the Republic ceased to be a member of the British Commonwealth of Nations. Commonwealth

Keystone.

NEAR THE MOUNTAINS OF MOURNE
The little harbour of Annalong, County Down, is overlooked by the two major peaks of the Mourne Mountains, Slieve Bingian and the 2,796-foot-high Slieve Donard. Slieve Donard is the highest of these lonely granite mountains which song, as well as their natural grandeur, has made famous.

links were first weakened in 1922 when the country became the Irish Free State. In 1937 it adopted the Gaelic name Eire, which means Ireland, and ranked as a free and self-governing state within the frame-work of the British Commonwealth of Nations, just as do Canada, Australia, New Zealand and the Union of South Africa. Thus, as well as its own national flag, a tricolour of green, white and orange, it had its own coins: its own Houses of Parliament—Dail Eireann (Commons) and Seanad Eireann (Senate). Now the Republic stands on her own, although Britain still gives her citizens full civil rights within the Commonwealth. English people will still find themselves at home in the Republic where English is the chief language spoken, though Erse is now taught by law in all the schools.

The Irish Countryside

We have now visited both town and countryside in the Emerald Isle, and of the two it is the latter—with its lovely hills, lakes, moors, and pastures—that is most characteristic of the island and its people. For although Ireland has her towns and cities, much of her area is countryside where thatched and white-washed farmsteads and newer two-storied houses are homes for the small farmers.

Here, and in the country towns and market centres, and along the roads leading to these towns and centres, we shall see things and people typical of the Emerald Isle. We shall meet perhaps the little carts, each with its pony or ass between the shafts: the shawled women carrying on their backs loads of turves to be added to the stack that is being laid in for the winter : and, by the roadside, the cottages with their gardens gay with flowers and flowering shrubs.

If you were to stop at one of these cottages, you might see Irish homespun being produced upon a cottage loom in the traditional manner. Such home-spun cloth, which is still produced in Donegal and elsewhere, is—like Harris tweed—famous the world over. Knitting and sprig embroidery are two other village crafts that you might see.

By the Peat Fire

Wherever you went, you would see the stacks of peat, or turves—even in such great cities as Dublin. These peat " mountains " are the fuel store for the cold winter months. Lacking coal supplies of her own, Ireland cuts the fuel for her homes from the peat bogs which cover a seventh of her land surface. In the course of a year not less than 7 million tons of peat will be cut.

But much is being done to bring the benefits of electricity to the Irish country-side. Since 1946, conditions of life in many country areas have become better as a result of the rural electrification scheme. It would be wrong to imagine that the Irish countryman cutting turves and loading them in his pony cart is the full story of how peat is used in the Irish Republic. Following the success of the new peat-fired generating station at Portarlington, County Kildare, peat is being used in increasing quantities as fuel for electricity generating plants. Speaking in the Dail in July, 1953, the Minister for Industry and Commerce stated that, by 1961, two out of every five generating stations in the Irish Republic would use turf as their fuel.

Turf for Electricity

Typical of this recent development is Bangor Erris, in the west of County Mayo, where a light railway runs across the vast and desolate expanse of bog that was once no more than the home of hares, snipe and other creatures of the wild. Here great excavators and other modern machines are at work, draining the bog and filling in the lakes and pools to make it fit for fuel production. Even so, it will be some years before the bog is ready to yield fuel.

When at last the peat has been taken, it is hoped to make the land fit for farm-ing or for foresty. Directed by a body called Bord na Mona, the project already includes experiments in the growing of grasses and clover, for crops of this kind help to make a fair depth of good soil. At the same time, country housing schemes are in hand and these, it is hoped, will check the move of people from western Ireland to the towns, or to Britain and the United States. Tomato-growing under glass, the grow-ing of sugar-beet, lace-making, weaving and other country industries and crafts are also being encouraged as part of the plan to make western Ireland more prosperous.

BY KILLARNEY'S LAKES

F. Deaville Walker.

Three hundred feet high, the famous Rock of Cashel in Tipperary has a twelfth-century fortified cathedral whose history is linked with the former kings of Munster. Notice (right) the Round Tower which was probably the bell tower of Cormac's Chapel, another building on this historic rock.

Photochrom.

The natural grandeur of the lakes of Killarney places them high among the many scenic beauties of the Emerald Isle. This picture shows the lovely Upper Lake where little islands, covered with magnificent shrubs and trees, rise intriguingly from the lake waters.

Reclaiming Peat Bogs

To see how peat bogs are being transformed into productive farmland, we must also travel to Gowla, which is in eastern Galway, about thirty miles from the town of Tuam with its sugar beet factory. The reclamation of Gowla Bog may not be complete until 1957; but it has been said that when the job is finished, it "may well rank with such works as the reclamation of the Pontine Marshes in Italy, or (on a smaller scale) with Vermuyden's draining of the fens of East Anglia."

Those fens of East Anglia now produce plenty of good sugar beet, as we have seen already, and it thus seems reasonable to expect the Gowla Bog to do likewise, when it has been fully reclaimed. And that is how it must have seemed to the Irish Sugar Company and its chief, Lieut.-Gen. M. J. Costello, who have taken the leading part in this great scheme. Their first experiments, at Kenmare in County Kerry, were highly successful and in 1951 a start was made on 1,000 acres of the Gowla Bog. That land, bought at a cost of about ten shillings an acre, was derelict; in fact, samples that were analysed contained 94 per cent. water!

Drainage was the first job and was done with the help of tractors, specially fitted so that they could travel over the boggy land, and with specially-equipped drainage ploughs. One result of drainage was the disappearance of two lakes which until then had been maintained by water from the bog. After drainage, turf cutting machines went to work, peat from the bog being used for fuel at the sugar beet factory in Tuam. Then

Topical Press.

HOME OF THE BLARNEY STONE

Fifteenth-century Blarney Castle, in County Cork, is the home of the famous Blarney Stone, the kissing of which is said to confer powers of persuasion and flattery. The Stone is let into the walls a short distance below the battlements of the tower which is 120 feet high. The castle was once a stronghold of the McCarthys.

the land was levelled, fertilizer was applied and worked in, and grass sown.

The results were so good that grass-drying machinery was obtained to deal with the crop and further areas of the bog were bought for reclamation. By 1953, the scheme embraced an area of 2,300 acres. Here, in time, grass crops and the grazing of cattle will produce the deep and fertile soil required for sugar beet. When large-scale beet growing becomes possible, there will be plenty of work for the small farmers of the district, whose own little holdings do not require all their time. And what is done at Gowla can be done elsewhere, for the Irish Republic has $2\frac{1}{2}$ million acres of peat. That is why Gowla is so important. Success there could transform the face of Ireland and bring a new prosperity to the country.

Central Press.

THE FASTNET ROCK LIGHTHOUSE

This lighthouse tells ships bound to Britain from America that they are nearing the end of their voyage. It stands on the Fastnet Rock, some four and a half miles off Cape Clear. The first lighthouse to be built here rose from the summit of the rock, but this dangerous site was forsaken when the new lighthouse was built.

The Puck Fair

You would not have a true picture of life in the Irish countryside, if you did not visit a cattle and horse fair. A great many fairs of this kind are held, sometimes weekly like the markets in the farming towns of Britain, sometimes monthly. Best of all are the great annual fairs, and the most interesting is probably the Puck Fair at Killorglin in County Kerry. For the three days that the fair lasts, a goat stands on a decorated platform high above the bustling market place. And bustling it is, with horses, foals, stalls, countryfolk and their carts, and gypsies, too. Above them all stands King Puck, the goat who has been put on his platform-throne on Gathering Day (the first day of the Fair) to remain tethered there until Scattering Day.

The reason why a goat should reign at the Puck Fair is lost in the mists of time. Some say that the custom sprang from some long-forgotten pagan rite of pre-Christian Ireland; others that it commemorates the warning given by goats to the Irish patriot, Patrick Sarsfield, when the troops of King William III were approaching his hide-out.

Ireland can show you many wonderful and often mysterious links with the past. No other country has such remarkable dolmens and similar relics of ancient times. At least 28,000 *raths* (early forts made of earth or stone) have been discovered; there are huge, overgrown cairns that were the burial-places of long-forgotten rulers, who were alive when Egypt's pyramids were still new; and there are the " beehive " buildings of rough stone, like the Oratory of Gallerus on the side of Mount Brandon, which were built by the early Christian missionaries and hermits. Other relics of the early Christians are the small, four-walled chapels, whose ruins can be seen in many places.

The Round Towers

There are the round towers as well, and these are almost uniquely Irish. Originally built as strongholds in which the local people could resist pirates and robbers, the round towers once existed in many parts of the country. Despite their strong construction, however, many of them are now no more than ruined stumps and not long ago it was calculated that there were only some eighty of them still in existence. One of the best preserved round towers is to be seen on Devenish Island, Lough Erne, in County Fermanagh. The tower here is more than eighty feet high and still has its stone conical roof. Another fine example stands on the Rock of Cashel in Tipperary.

Cashel was the fortress and sanctuary of the old Irish kings. The ancient ruins—walls, cathedral, chapel and round tower—stand upon a steep limestone rock on the Tipperary plain.

Independent Newspapers Ltd.

O'CONNELL STREET, DUBLIN

This is probably the most famous street in the capital of the Irish Republic. It is named after the Irish patriot Daniel O'Connell, sometimes known as " the Liberator." The street runs to the O'Connell Bridge which spans the River Liffey. The lofty column is the Nelson Pillar.

Topical Press.

ACROSS THE CHESHIRE PLAINS

One of Cheshire's famous landmarks, Alderley Edge, has been purchased by the County Council and vested in the National Trust. From the Edge wonderful views on every side can be seen and our photograph shows the scene looking across the broad Cheshire plain towards the high moors of Derbyshire.

BRITAIN'S HERITAGE

GREAT BRITAIN, an island which contains England, Wales and Scotland, is but a small country yet is wonderfully rich in buildings of historic interest and in the possession of some of the most beautiful landscape and coastal scenery in the world. There are no great lakes such as those of North America, but the English Lake District is famed throughout the world for its varied charms and poetic associations.

This small country is also a great industrial land and there have been many times when the coal-mines, factories and workshops have meant the destruction of pleasant countryside or when some building with an historic past has fallen into decay or been demolished to make way for modern manufacturing establishments.

During the latter half of the nineteenth century, when the industrialisation of Britain was most marked, a great deal of destruction was inevitable. Particularly in the North and in the Midlands, as well as in Wales and elsewhere, the pleasant centuries-old villages vanished and ugly factory towns rapidly took their place; the green valleys were buried beneath ever-growing slag-heaps, and the great houses and pleasant gardens which had for a time played their part in history were swept away to make way for steel works and foundries.

There are so many beautiful scenes and places in our countryside that are worth preserving. If you have been lucky enough to visit any of the English villages depicted in the next few pages, you will know how thatched cottage, ancient church, wayside inn and village green can combine with old oak and mellow hedgerow to form a landscape that brings visitors from all parts of Britain and from countries overseas. Perhaps you have followed one or other of our waterways as it winds like a silver ribbon across the countryside and come across beautiful reaches, like those of the upper Thames, or those peaceful stretches of calm water that may be found along certain of our canals. There are, too, those wonderful houses and mansions which, set in their green parklands, speak of the masons and master-builders of days gone by and were, perhaps, in their heyday, settings for some of the great events of our island history.

All these give our countryside its character. But with the passing of the years, there have inevitably been changes. As Britain developed her industries, places had to be found for the new factories and the teeming towns and cities to which they gave rise.

Safeguarding Our Countryside

Sentimental people might regret the passing of the old landmarks and beauty spots they had learned to love, but sentiment could not stand in the way of progress. In 1895, however, three public-spirited people, Miss Octavia Hill, Sir Robert Hunter and Canon Rawnsley, decided to do something about it. They had no desire to stop the building of factories or to halt the wheels of progress, but they felt there was need for discretion and that certain places should be preserved for the benefit and enjoyment of all. The outcome was the foundation of the National Trust for Places of Historic Interest or Natural Beauty.

The first practical step was to acquire a small property, Dinas Oleu, at Barmouth, North Wales, to save it from

Topical Press.

THE PEACEFUL CHARM OF OUR INLAND WATERWAYS

Although we usually connect canals with bustling factory towns, Britain has many stretches of inland waterways that are beautiful. This peaceful scene, for example, shows canal boats, and a hawthorn tree in full flower, near an old bridge over the Grand Union Canal near Uxbridge, Middlesex. The Grand Union Canal is the longest in Britain.

A DELIGHTFUL ENGLISH VILLAGE

England is justly famous for its old-world villages, where can still be seen humble dwelling-places built from local materials. Here can be found cottage homes, half-timbered, or of stone and thatch, that were new when Drake made his voyage round the world. Many a village of old has been swallowed up by urban growth. But others, such as the beautiful village of Selworthy, in Somerset, shown in this picture, remain to delight the eye and draw visitors from near and far.

ROOFS OF THATCH AND STONE

British Council.

The village of Compton Chamberlayne in Wiltshire provides these fine examples of the thatcher's craft. This charming village is but one of many scattered across the face of Britain which have become famous as places of quiet, unchanging beauty that has outlived the centuries.

Fox Photos.

With distinctive steep-pitched roofs and pointed gables, these cottages at Arlington Row in Bibury, Gloucestershire, have been standing for more than 200 years. Their quaint charm makes it easy to understand why Bibury has been called " one of the loveliest villages in England."

UNCHANGED BY TIME

Topical Press.

No modern " improvements " or signs of progress such as petrol pumps, advertisement hoardings, and telegraph poles disfigure the north Hertfordshire village of Westmill. Church, cottages, village green and parish pump remain much as they have always been.

Country Life.

Codiford St. Mary, in Wiltshire, is another village possessing quaintly-thatched cottages whose neatly-fashioned eaves overhang age-old walls of brick and timber. A thatched roof keeps the heat out in summer and the cold out in winter better than many a tiled roof does.

ON THE VILLAGE GREEN

At West Burton, a delightful village in the Yorkshire Dales, the old houses gather round a village green upon which stands a cross built to resemble the upper part of a church spire. Near the village, the becks (small streams) of Bishopdale and Walden flow together, and the valley of Waldendale, an offshoot of the famous Wensleydale, begins.

Photos: Leonard and Marjorie Gayton.

The pride of the Cotswold village of Northleach is its great church, which stands as a reminder of the days when the Cotswolds were the centre of a thriving wool industry. Within the church are many fine brasses, mostly bearing representations of sheep and woolpacks—the emblems of the Woolstapler.

LINKS WITH AMERICA

Miss D. I. Pullman.

Above the door of this old house at Stanton St. John, Oxfordshire, is this inscription: " The birth-place of John White, 1575–1648, fellow of New College, Oxford, and chief founder of the colony of Massachusetts in New England." He was rector of Holy Trinity at Dorchester, in Dorset, and in 1624 he sent " the Dorset colony " of people from his own town to Massachusetts.

Topical Press.

Jordans, the house seen in this picture, is an old Quaker meeting house in Buckinghamshire. William Penn, the founder of the state of Pennsylvania, was laid to rest in the small burial ground which can be seen to the left of the house.

HALL AND MANOR HOUSE

C. Hodgson.

This plain and rather stern old house may be seen in County Durham. It is Washington Old Hall, where the ancestors of the great George Washington lived before they moved to Sulgrave Manor in Northamptonshire.

L. E. A

The portrait in oils of George Washington hangs above the Tudor fireplace in the Great Hall of Sulgrave Manor. The window contains stained glass reproductions of the arms of members of the Washington family. On the far end of the Elizabethan refectory table stands a seventeenth-century wassail bowl.

AN EARLY COLONIAL GOVERNOR

John Winthrop, first Governor of the colony of Massachusetts, was born in 1588 at Groton, Suffolk. He and his family worshipped for many years at the parish church of St. Bartholomew. The church, seen in this picture, contains a stained glass window erected to his memory by his American descendants.

Photos: Topical Press.

At Groton, Suffolk, the old mulberry tree under which Winthrop played as a boy may still be seen. His father and grandfather were lords of the manor of Groton, and the parish registers contain many entries relating to the family. Winthrop himself emigrated to Massachusetts in 1630.

destruction. It was a beginning, and to-day the National Trust is so well known that it is often regarded as a Government body. Actually it is a non-profit-making organisation devoted to the preservation of lands and buildings for the benefit of the people. Its income is derived from membership subscriptions, private gifts and Trust property rents.

In rather more than half-a-century the National Trust has become the owner of about 120,000 acres, including over 1,000 properties, and in addition has control of another 50,000 acres by covenant with the owners. In the case of some of the great houses and places of historic interest a small charge is made for admission, and this money is, of course, devoted to the upkeep of the property.

To ramblers and holiday-makers the places of natural beauty which have been preserved for their use and pleasure may perhaps make an even greater appeal than some of the " stately homes of England " which have become famed in history and fiction. But the majority of these houses which have now been preserved for the nation belong very definitely to England's historic heritage.

There is that famous estate, Charlecote Park, four miles from Stratford-on-Avon. This has been the ancestral home of the Lucy family since the twelfth century, and even the rough oak palings which almost completely border the 200-acre Park are said to date from Elizabethan times. The records of the first house go back to 1189, but the old building was pulled down in 1558 and

Topical Press.

CLIVEDEN REACH ON THE THAMES

Cliveden in Buckinghamshire was the home of Lord and Lady Astor, who handed it to the National Trust. The gift included an endowment for the upkeep of the house, which can be seen on the hill to the left, and the famous woods with their mile-long frontage on the Thames.

Topical Press.

LACOCK ABBEY IN WILTSHIRE

It was early in the thirteenth century that Lacock Abbey came into existence as a nunnery, but in due course it became the residence of the Talbot family, who held it until recently, when Miss Matilda Talbot handed it to the National Trust, together with the village of Lacock itself. One of the pioneers of photography, Fox Talbot carried out his experimental work here.

the present Charlecote House was built by Sir Thomas Lucy.

When Shakespeare was Young

In his time Sir Thomas was a great man and entertained his Queen, Elizabeth I, at Charlecote when she was on her way to see the Earl of Leicester at Kenilworth. It was this Sir Thomas Lucy whose keepers captured a party of bright lads of the village in the act of poaching. They had shot a deer in the Park at night and were caught redhanded. Next morning in the Great Hall at Charlecote the poachers were lined up before Sir Thomas, a Justice of the Peace and a stern enemy of poachers. Their guilt was proved and swift punishment was duly meted out to the wrongdoers.

One of the poachers, a lad of nineteen, was a certain William Shakespeare, destined to achieve a far greater fame than the knight who sat in

judgment upon him that morning. There was more trouble later on between the two, and Will Shakespeare, then a young married man, ran away from his native town and eventually reached London. In the fullness of time he had his revenge on Sir Thomas, caricaturing him as Mr. Justice Shallow in *The Merry Wives of Windsor* and in *Henry IV* and even making fun of his coat-of-arms.

Among the records at Charlecote is a 1632 folio of Shakespeare's plays. There are, too, an autographed letter from Oliver Cromwell and other valuable documents. Charlecote was handed to the National Trust in 1946 by the descendants of Sir Thomas Lucy. In four months after it became part of the Nation's heritage more than 20,000 people visited the house and park.

For Gallantry at Crecy

Bodiam Castle in Sussex has been in

SHAKESPEARE AND THE BLACK PRINCE

"The Times."

The history of Charlecote, 4 miles from Stratford-on-Avon, goes back to 1189, but the house seen above was built around 1560 by Sir Thomas Lucy. It was owing to trouble with Sir Thomas over a poaching affair that Shakespeare left Stratford, but he returned in later years.

Topical Press

The lands on which Lyme Hall, near Stockport, Cheshire, has stood for centuries past were given as a reward for gallantry in the French wars to Sir Thomas Danyers by the Black Prince. His descendants have lived there until quite recently, but the house and grounds are now held by the National Trust and used for the public benefit.

WHERE KINGS HAVE WALKED

One of the " stately homes of England " which has now passed into the care of the National Trust is Polesden Lacey, near Bookham in Surrey. It was here that King George VI. and Queen Elizabeth, then Duke and Duchess of York, spent their honeymoon in 1923.

Twenty miles from London there is a meadow known as Runnymede, and here, or possibly on the island in the Thames just opposite the meadow, King John was forced to put his seal to Magna Carta on June 15th, 1215. The photograph above shows part of the meadow as well as Charter Island.

ruins for long years, but it still stands as a substantial link with those far-off days when Richard II prepared to defend this country against the French invaders. The enemy never came, but this moated castle remained ready for battle until the days when Oliver Cromwell became Lord Protector of the realm. It was then that Parliament " slighted " it, or, in more modern language, dismantled it, and it ceased to be a stronghold against invaders.

So Bodiam stands as a solid reminder of our past. Not all the great houses which have come into the hands of the National Trust are merely reminders of the past. There is Lyme Hall, not very far from Stockport in Cheshire. . The lands were given 600 years ago by Edward the Black Prince to Sir Thomas Danyers for the rescue of the English standard at Caen and the capture of the Constable of France at Crecy. Throughout those 600 years the descendants of Sir Thomas have lived at Lyme though the house was altered many times and then rebuilt in 1565.

Then in June, 1947, its last owner, Lord Newton, handed it over to the National Trust, together with its park lands. The Stockport Corporation joined hands with the Trust and Lyme Hall has become a residential horticultural school; it is also available to local societies, and meetings and dances can be held in the great rooms and galleries of "sweet Lyme, lovely Lyme." Every part of the park with its moorland and rhododendron dells is now open to the public.

There is much of the history of Cheshire bound up in Lyme. There are, too, carvings by Grinling Gibbons and wonderful woodwork and plaster scrolls in the great Elizabethan drawing-room. It is well for us at times to realise that there were wonderful artists and craftsmen in the slower-moving centuries when mass-production by machinery was unknown.

Not so very far from Lyme there is a

Country Life.

A FAMOUS BLACK-AND-WHITE CHESHIRE HOUSE

At Astbury, in Cheshire, is Little Moreton Hall, one of the finest black-and-white houses in the country. Here we see the gate-house which is almost a house in itself and which overlooks the moat. The house is thought to date from about 1520 and was added to by succeeding generations of the Moreton family.

Topical Press.

THE YORKSHIRE DALES NATIONAL PARK

An area of about 680 square miles in the West and North Ridings of Yorkshire has been designated as the Yorkshire Dales National Park. The picture shows some of the beautiful country within this area. It was taken above the village of Langcliffe and looks across upper Ribblesdale to Ingleborough. In the distance (extreme right) are the slopes of Whernside.

farm-house, Wibbersley Hall, which was the birthplace of John Bradshaw who became a judge and was the president of the Court that tried King Charles I. It was Bradshaw who pronounced the dread judgment upon the King.

This is not among the National Trust properties, but it has its links with that history in which Lyme played a greater part. Another Cheshire house, Little Moreton Hall, south of Congleton, is cared for by the Trust and is a fine example of the moated black and white timbered halls for which England was once famed. It dates from 1540 and is a delightful and picturesque residence from whatever angle it is viewed.

With the Men of Harlech

Going over the Cheshire border into Wales there stands a castle famed in song and story. There was a fortress at Harlech in Roman times, but the present building dates from the days of Edward I (1239–1307). In 1468 the Castle was taken by the Yorkists after a long siege, and it was this which inspired that famous Welsh song " March of the Men of Harlech." Nearly 200 years later it was again besieged and was one of the last places to hold out for King Charles I. When finally it fell to Cromwell's men the fortress was dismantled.

A place famous in English history is that meadow lying along the south bank of the Thames near Egham, some twenty miles from London. Runnymede is its name and here on June 15th, 1215, King John was forced to sign Magna Carta. Some say that the Great Charter was actually signed on the little island, now known as Charter Island, standing out in the stream, but no doubt both the King and his determined barons occupied the meadow and the island on that fateful day. More than seven centuries later they both came into the care of the National Trust to be preserved for the people whose liberties received their most important guarantee on that June day.

There is one stately mansion which is being preserved as an illustration of how a distinguished country house was furnished and equipped in the spacious days of long ago. Montacute House, near Yeovil in Somerset, a photograph of which you will find in the chapter " From Norman Times to Our Own Day," took over twelve years to complete. It expressed in stone the rise to power of an astute lawyer, Edward Phelips, who was the chief prosecutor of Guy Fawkes in 1606 and became both Speaker of the House of Commons and Master of the Rolls. For over 300 years his family held the estate.

Its magnificence and beauty belong to the great days of Queen Elizabeth I, and it remains to-day one of the most beautiful of all those stately homes of England which were once the pride of those who had risen to power and still remain a part of our national heritage.

The Gift of a Queen

There is Knole, too, photographs of which you will find in the pages following that of Montacute House. Knole was once the residence of the archbishops of Canterbury, but Henry VIII took it from Cranmer. Later, his daughter, Queen Elizabeth I, gave the great house and grounds to Thomas Sackville, afterwards Earl of Dorset. Early in the seventeenth century it was rebuilt and it has remained the home of the Sackville family ever since. It is they who have recently handed over Knole to the National Trust.

Other great houses have passed into the hands of the Trust. There is Polesden Lacey, near Bookham, Surrey,

Planet News.

IMMORTALISED BY AN ENGLISH PAINTER

John Constable, the famous East Anglian master painter, was born at East Bergholt, Suffolk, in 1776. To-day, we often speak of the district around East Bergholt and Flatford as " the Constable Country," for it is a countryside immortalised by Constable in his paintings. Here is Flatford Mill, the subject of one of his most famous pictures and a National Trust property now used by the Council for the Promotion of Field Studies.

THE GARDENS OF BODNANT

Country Life.

Near Llandudno is Bodnant, in Denbighshire, the beautiful estate which has been lovingly maintained and developed by the Aberconway family. This view from the house shows the terraced
gardens that fall away to the valley, delighting the eye with a great variety of flowering shrubs. At
one end of the lowest terrace (left) is a Georgian gazebo, or summer-house. In the distance, across
the valley, are the mountains of Snowdonia.

with its 1,000 acres, the house where King George VI and Queen Elizabeth spent their honeymoon. Then Cliveden, with its beautiful stretch of woods along the banks of the Thames, three miles beyond Maidenhead: it was the seat of Lord and Lady Astor and they have handed it to the Trust so that the lovely part of the river known as Cliveden Reach as well as the house and grounds have now become the property of the nation. Lord Astor, with Captain Rodd of Yelverton, supported by the Pilgrim Trust, all helped in 1947 to save Buckland Abbey and its tithe barn for the nation. The Abbey was remodelled by the famous Grenville of the *Revenge*, and became the home of Sir Francis Drake.

It is now cared for by the Trust and Plymouth Corporation will help in making it a Drake naval museum and using it for other purposes of public interest. A much smaller and more recently-built house is Cloud's Cottage at Bovington, Dorset, the home until his death of T. E. Lawrence, whose name is inscribed in Britain's roll of heroes as Lawrence of Arabia.

There are Lacock Abbey and its monastic remains in Wiltshire; and then, away to the North, Lindisfarne Castle, Holy Island, which takes us back over thirteen centuries of our history. St. Aidan founded a monastery here in 635 and the remains of its later Norman church still stand. In the sixteenth century a castle was built and is to-day a landmark for many miles.

Some of England's most picturesque villages now belong to the Nation. " The

E. O. Hoppé.

DERWENTWATER IN THE LAKE DISTRICT

Over 18,000 acres in the Lake District have been acquired by the National Trust. Here is a view of Derwentwater with its wooded islets as seen from the hills surrounding this three miles stretch of water. At the southern end of the Lake are the Falls of Lodore.

"The Times."

WHERE DUNKERY BEACON WAS LIGHTED

In *Lorna Doone* the lighting of the beacon on Dunkery Hill is described. About 5 miles from Porlock, in Somersetshire, Dunkery Beacon is the highest point on Exmoor, and, as will be seen in the photograph, its slopes are well wooded. Large tracts of country with several old-world villages which formed the Holnicote estate are now part of the nation's heritage.

old order changeth, yielding place to new," and in these days when a village of prefabricated houses can be put up in a very few weeks, and may perhaps vanish in due time almost as rapidly, it is well to preserve villages where the cottages have withstood the storms of centuries. On the 12,420 acres of the Holnicote estate, handed to the Trust by Sir Richard Acland, there are eight beautiful Somerset villages and hamlets, including Selworthy and Blackford, not very far from Minehead.

There are, too, four miles of coastland with wonderful views across Porlock Bay. Away to the South there is Dunkery Hill and Beacon. On one of the farms at Blackford is a stone-built dovecote which, they will tell you,

has stood there since about the time when William the Conqueror was making his Domesday Book.

In Lakeland and the Peak District

Other lovely country is now preserved for us. In Devon there is Watersmeet with its wonderful views. Away in the North, Derwentwater is but a part of the 18,000 acres in the Lake District over which the National Trust now holds guardianship. Farther south among the hills and dales of Derbyshire such pleasant stretches of country as Mill Dale and Dovedale belong to the nation and the Trust guards them from the hands of the despoilers. In Hertfordshire some 3,500 acres of Ashridge Forest have been taken over.

For All to Enjoy

In almost every county in England some place of beauty has been preserved so that all may enjoy its charms. In Surrey there is the Devil's Punch Bowl; Box Hill with its charm and its literary associations, and not so far away the delightful country in the neighbourhood of Dorking and Leith Hill. In Kent the house where the famous actress Ellen Terry lived, Smallhythe, near the ancient town of Tenterden, is now open to visitors. West Wycombe village in Buckinghamshire; Barras Head in Cornwall; Alderley Edge in Cheshire; Avebury in Wiltshire; Blickling Hall in Norfolk; Sugar Loaf Mountain in Monmouthshire: all these and many other places throughout the fair counties of England have become the property of the nation for the enjoyment of all who love beauty and the glories of the past.

In Scotland Too

In Scotland very much the same task is being carried out by a separate society, the National Trust for Scotland, founded in 1931.

Among the historic places and beauty spots of Scotland which are now preserved for the nation are some of the most beautiful areas of the West Highlands, including the rugged countryside around the beautiful Falls of Glomach, which are the highest falls in Great Britain; the historic Palace of Falkland, about sixteen miles from Perth, rich in its associations with the Kings of Scotland; and the shores of Loch Shiel, near Fort William, where the Glenfinnan Monument reminds us of Bonnie Prince Charlie and the '45. You will find pictures of these and other beautiful and historic places in Scotland in another section in this volume.

Two historic battlefields are among the properties of the National Trust for Scotland. Nearly six acres of the land where Bannockburn was fought in 1314 are owned by the Trust, which has also acquired part of the field of Culloden.

It was at Culloden that the '45 Rising was brought to an end in 1746 by the defeat of Prince Charles Edward and his army by the troops of George II under the Duke of Cumberland. The main road across the

Country Life.

THE TIMBER HALL AT RUFFORD

Rufford Old Hall, the house built by Thomas Hesketh about 1500 at Southport, Lancashire, contains this wonderfully preserved timber hall. Its hammer-beam roof, and the elaborately carved "spere" or movable screen, are typical of the early Tudor period.

IN CITY AND COUNTRYSIDE

In medieval times, this house near York Minster was the home of the Cathedral Treasurer. The present front, with its Dutch gables, was added about 1610. The Treasurer's House is beautifully decorated within and contains a fine collection of period furniture.

Photos: Country Life.

Dinton, in its setting of wooded parkland, looks out over the road from Salisbury to Wincanton. The house is in the Grecian style and was built for the Wyndham family in 1808–18 by Sir Jeffrey Wyatville. Wyatville was also responsible for much of the Gothic reconstruction work carried out at Windsor Castle.

moor is bordered by the Graves of the Clans. Here, also, can be seen the Cumberland Stone, from which the merciless Duke is said to have directed the battle, and Leanach Farmhouse, which it is said, was used by the Prince as his headquarters. The Memorial Cairn to commemorate the valour of Prince Charles and his Highlanders was erected in 1881.

But it is in the ever-growing industrial areas that the watchful eye of these guardians of our heritage must always be alert. A century or more ago the big movement from the countryside to the towns began and the vast majority of our population are now town-dwellers. Yet the urge to get back into the country for a breathing-space is still strong in the townsmen.

But this island of Britain is so small and there are so many living in it. As the demand for new factories and for big works for newly-developed industries continues to increase so the threat to the countryside grows.

Some of it does not matter; some of the changes are all to the good; but we should still keep some of the ancient beauty and have quiet places where only the song of the birds and the rustling of leaves in the breeze is heard.

Worth Preserving

It should still be possible for English people and visitors from the Commonwealth countries to look on the handiwork of craftsmen who had never heard of machine-tools or reflect upon those spacious days in our history when Drake sailed the seas and Shakespeare wrote his plays.

That is part of the purpose of the National Trusts in England and Scotland. All over the land these specially chosen tracts of lovely country, or those great houses which not only add to the beauty of our homeland but have played some part in the story of the days of long ago, are being preserved from the despoilers. These places of historic interest and of natural beauty are the heritage of all who are members of the British Commonwealth of Nations.

Country Life.

THE HOME OF RUDYARD KIPLING

This house is called Batemans and is to be found at Burwash, Sussex. For twenty years it was the home of Rudyard Kipling and is associated with his books *Puck of Pook's Hill* and *Rewards and Fairies*. The house was built in 1634, probably by a local iron-master, for Burwash was once the centre of a thriving smelting industry.

The Story
of the
World and
its Peoples

Countries
of the British
Commonwealth
of Nations

National Film Board.

LUMBERJACKS OF THE GATINEAU COUNTRY

Canada has more than a million square miles of timber land and is the world's third largest producer of wood. The logs are floated down to the mills. On rivers, the current carries them along, but when they reach lakes they must be towed. This picture, taken in the Gatineau country of Quebec, shows a boom being made ready for towing.

THE DOMINION OF CANADA

MORE than half the North American continent—from the northern frontier of the United States to the snow-and-ice islands within the Arctic Circle—is occupied by the great Dominion of Canada.

Many centuries ago, Leif Erikson, a Norse sea rover, probably voyaged here from Greenland in his "long dragon," but Canada remained largely unrevealed to Europe until John Cabot reached its shore in 1497. Even then the vast mainland was not penetrated, and western Europe rested content with the Newfoundland banks and mainland coasts as harvest grounds for her fishermen. In 1534, a French explorer named Jacques Cartier reached the Gulf of the St. Lawrence and travelled nearly a thousand miles up-river, marvelling at the vast forests and at the

red men who, he was convinced, were "Indians" and living proof that he had found the long-sought route across the Atlantic to the riches of the Orient.

With the Pioneers

Still no settlement was founded; that was left for Samuel de Champlain to attempt in 1604 at what is now Annapolis, Nova Scotia. Until his death in 1635, de Champlain went on exploring, journeying southwards to the magnificent lake that bears his name, and westward up the St. Lawrence and the Ottawa, searching, as Cartier had done before him, for the elusive route to the East. It was de Champlain who founded Quebec (1608).

The first settlements which he and others established were bases for French fur traders and for the missionaries brought out by the "Company of New

183

France " which Cardinal Richelieu had formed and to which he gave complete control of the St. Lawrence Valley. But its fortunes did not prosper. Trade was poor; the missionaries fell victims to the fierce Iroquois Indians, and in 1663 New France became a royal province.

Meanwhile, exploration went on, and two of the French colonists, Pierre Radisson and Medart Chouart (who also called himself *Sieur des Groseilliers*—the Squire of the Currant Bushes) voyaged to England with tales of the rich fur trade that could be built at Hudson Bay, where they had explored, and where they had established friendly relations with the local Indians. No less a person than King Charles II himself heard their story, the outcome of which was an English expedition to Hudson Bay and the setting up of the Hudson's Bay Company in 1670, with Charles' cousin, " his Deare and Entirely Beloved " Rupert, as its first Governor. Thus England returned to the bay on the fringes of the Arctic

Circle where gallant Henry Hudson's attempt to find the North-West Passage had ended in his tragic death at the hands of his mutinous crew. English settlements rose upon the shores of his bay and prospered : for, in 1713, defeated France had to admit England's claims upon Hudson Bay, Newfoundland and Nova Scotia.

Rivalry between British and French was inevitable. There was fighting between the rival nations in Canada, with the Indians taking part on both sides, even during times when France and Britain were nominally at peace. In vain, the French tried to safeguard their possessions by building a chain of forts along the great lakes. When the Seven Years' War began in 1756, the British fleet was all-powerful. Cut off from supplies and reinforcements, and outgeneralled by the young Wolfe, the French army in Canada surrendered at Montreal (1760) after Wolfe had led his men up the Quebec cliffs to win the battle fought upon the Plains of Abraham (1759).

British Columbia Government.

CAPITAL OF CANADA'S MOST WESTERN PROVINCE

Founded as Fort Camosun, the Indian name of the site, by the Hudson's Bay Company, in 1843, the present capital of British Columbia was renamed Victoria in honour of the young Queen in 1851. It became the capital when Vancouver Island and British Columbia were united as a Province in 1866. To-day it is mainly a residential and tourist centre, but it is also important industrially. Our photograph shows the inner harbour at Victoria.

THE DOMINION OF CANADA

E.N.A.

Canada is the largest country in the Western Hemisphere, the third largest country in the world, and its total area is approximately equal to that of all Europe. From its fertile plains to the icy Northern archipelago, or from its great cities to the lonely fastnesses of the Rocky Mountains, it has wide variations in temperature, scenery and products. Our photograph shows a scene near Banff, in the Province of Alberta. In the foreground a trooper of the Royal Canadian Mounted Police looks down the Bow River Valley with the Rockies in the background.

AMONG THE CANADIAN ROCKIES

The Rocky Mountains extend the whole length of North America, from Alaska to the South. Here we have a scene in the Canadian Rockies showing Emerald Lake, British Columbia.

This scene is in Alberta and again the Rockies are in the background. The photograph was taken from the grounds of a chateau situated on the shores of the picturesque Lake Louise.

This lofty peak in the Canadian Rockies is known as Mount Assiniboine, a name derived from the Assiniboines, one of the native tribes which formerly roamed in this part of Alberta.

Mount Brussels, seen in the centre background of this picture, is one of the most inaccessible peaks in the Canadian Rockies. It is in the Columbia icefield area of the Jasper National Park.

FOR SCENERY AND SPORT

H. Armstrong Roberts

Banff, in Alberta, is a district widely famed as one of the finest holiday resorts in Canada. Apart from its wonderful scenery a wide variety of sports, including hunting, fishing, and climbing are all at hand. This is a view showing Mount Rundle, near Banff, which is situated in one of the largest of Canada's great National Parks.

E.N.A.

From the vast forests of Canada come supplies of timber for building, paper-making, and many other purposes. Here we have a scene on the Montreal River as it runs through the Province of Ontario. Thousands of logs have been felled and trimmed farther upstream then carried down by the river itself. Probably the logs will presently be frozen in and will lie there till the spring thaws set in.

A COMMERCIAL CAPITAL AND ITS HISTORY

A Breton explorer, Jacques Cartier, made the first French exploration of Canada in 1534. Later, he discovered the river now known as the St. Lawrence, the gateway to Canada. Cartier made his way up the river to Hochelaga, which later became the site of Canada's largest city and commercial capital, Montreal, in the Province of Quebec. Our photograph, taken from Mount Royal, gives a general view of Montreal.

Photos: E.N.A.

The peninsula of Gaspé forms the eastern part of the Province of Quebec, and it was here that Cartier first landed. The photograph above shows a general view of Gaspé, with the Jacques Cartier Memorial in the foreground. After Cartier came Samuel de Champlain, explorer and trader, who sailed still farther up the St. Lawrence to found a settlement in 1608, and this grew into the city of Quebec.

National Film Board.

AT A HUDSON'S BAY COMPANY'S TRADING POST

It was in the reign of Charles II that the Hudson's Bay Company was founded for trading on the shores of Hudson Bay. To-day the Company still flourishes and carries on its fur trade as it has done through nearly three centuries. Their trading posts in modern times stock a wide variety of goods. Aluminium discs are given in exchange for furs brought in by the Eskimos who then use the discs to buy goods from the post. In this picture Eskimos are seen at the Chesterfield Bay Inlet as they wait for the supply ship to come in bringing new stock to the trading post.

At the time of the French surrender there were about 60,000 French in Canada. In 1951, there were more than 4,319,000 French-Canadians, most of them descendants of the early settlers. That they have so flourished is a remarkable tribute to wise and understanding rule in Canada where the defeat of 1760 might have produced lasting bitterness. French-Canadians to-day enjoy full rights and liberties in the Dominion and have their own cities, districts, newspapers, language, culture and traditions. It would be insulting to question their loyalty to the Dominion, and we have only to recall their contribution to the Allied cause in times of war to realise how much further that loyalty extends.

After the Seven Years' War, fresh colonists streamed into Canada, including 40,000 United Empire Loyalists from the breakaway colonies of America. Many of the new arrivals were Scots, as we might guess from the numerous Scottish names among Canadian people and upon the map of Canada.

The story of the inland exploration of Canada is bound up with the development of the Hudson's Bay Company.

Even in the early days, when French-Canadian *voyageurs* threatened the Company's outposts, there were such keen explorers as Henry Kelsey who, in the last decade of the seventeenth century, visited the Barren Lands, the Prairies, and the Eskimo people along the west coast of Hudson Bay. After the defeat of the French, one of the Company's greatest travellers—Samuel Hearne—made three expeditions into the Barren Lands, finding the copper deposits along the Coppermine river and looking out over the Arctic Ocean from the river's mouth. Under Hearne's leadership, the Company's forts extended to the Rocky Mountains and Lake Athabaska, competing with the Scots fur-traders from Montreal, who now menaced the supremacy of the Hudson's Bay Company, and continued to do so until the famous North-West joint Company was formed.

Great Trader-Colonists

There are many brave characters in the story of Canadian trade and exploration—the hard and powerful Simon McTavish : Alexander Mackenzie, an even greater explorer than he was fur trader, whose name has been given to the second largest river in North America : Lord Selkirk who, in 1811, founded the Red River Colony near where Winnipeg now stands : and Thomas Simpson, the greatest of the trader-colonists, called by his subordinates " the Little Emporor ": Donald Smith also, who in later years, as the Earl of Strathcona, was to represent the young Dominion in Britain.

In 1791, Canada had been divided into two parts, each with its own government: Lower Canada, which was predominantly French, and Upper Canada, where everything was British. In 1838, Lord Durham was sent to

Canadian Pacific.

GENERAL WOLFE'S HEADQUARTERS

This modest French-Canadian farmstead in Quebec was the headquarters of General Wolfe during his victorious campaign which led to the surrender of the French armies at Montreal in 1760. Wolfe himself was killed in the Battle of the Plains of Abraham, but lived long enough to receive news of his victory. " Now God be praised," he murmured. " I will die in peace."

Photographic Surveys.

THE LARGEST CITY IN CANADA

Where once there was only an Indian village, there now stands the city of Montreal, which has a population of about 1,140,000 and is the largest city in Canada. This aerial view shows part of the business section and port. The railway leads to the new Canadian National station. In the background (left) are the slopes of Mount Royal.

Canada, as a result of armed revolts against the administrations, to report on the situation there. His wise and conciliatory investigations led to the union of Upper and Lower Canada in 1840.

Twenty-seven years later, the provinces of Ontario, Quebec, New Brunswick and Nova Scotia federated in the new Dominion of Canada. British Columbia, where gold had been discovered, was later joined to the Dominion by the construction of the Canadian Pacific Railway—one of the greatest and most romantic engineering feats the world has seen. For nearly 3,000 miles across mountain barriers, through narrow gorges where angry rivers swirled and tumbled, over treacherous swamplands and across great plains where no man lived, the magnificent project took shape.

The route took many years to survey, and those who did the work suffered untold hardships in the mountain winters when avalanches continually threatened them and the temperature was often eighty degrees below freezing point. In 1875, the actual work of building began—causeways had to be built across the marshes, ways blasted out of the flint-hard rock, tortuous routes carved up the towering mountainsides. It was not until 1886 that this almost superhuman task was completed and workers from east and west met at Craigellachie, where the last spike was driven into place by the Earl of Strathcona.

The completion of the Canadian Pacific Railway was followed by other great railway schemes—the Canadian Pacific itself was extended : the Northern railway was carried on to Hudson Bay : and the Grand Trunk Pacific was planned. Meanwhile, prospectors were revealing the mineral wealth of the Dominion. Nickel was found at Sudbury: gold in the Yukon: gold, copper and silver in the mountains of British Columbia : coal at Crow's Nest Pass, British Columbia, and rich veins of silver and cobalt in northern Ontario. Canada, already prosperous, enriched herself from these discoveries : made her countless acres of forestland the core of a vast wood-pulp and paper industry : harnessed the power of her falls and rapids by hydro-electric schemes—all this with such success that she is to-day a mighty nation, proud of her achievements and of the independent spirit which is her legacy from the pioneers who laid her foundations so truly and so well.

Latest to join the great Dominion is Newfoundland which, with Labrador, became the tenth province of Canada in 1949. Newfoundland, territory of the first English colony in North America, founded its wealth and importance on its " Banks," long famous for cod fisheries, and on its forests and " white coal " It is, moreover, one of the finest hunting grounds in North America and has rich salmon and trout fisheries. Seal hunters, too, go out from Newfoundland to the coastal waters of Labrador. At such places as Grand Falls, Corner Brook and Lomond, there are timber, paper and pulp mills which are among the world's largest and which are worked by hydro-electric power from Newfoundland's rushing torrents and streams. From Bell Island, iron ore is shipped to Nova Scotian steelworks. Gander Airport is used by no less than ten airlines flying the North Atlantic route. But St. John's remains the only town of any considerable size in the new tenth province.

The Structure of Canada

The story of any country is, in the first instance, one of how its people conquered or were conquered by natural obstacles of land and climate that they encountered. A look at the structure of Canada shows, for example, why it was that there were no settlements on the great prairies of western Canada until the coming of the transcontinental railway.

Geologically, the oldest part of the North American continent is the " Canadian Shield," a wide expanse of old, hard rock spread horseshoe-wise round Hudson Bay whose streams, lakes and rugged forests penned in the early colonists and which is now the chief mining area of Canada. The " Canadian Shield " is part of the *Central Lowlands* of North America, south-east of which are the *Eastern Highlands*, with the Appalachian ridges and the plateau of the Alleghany. In the far west are the rugged ranges of the *Western Cordillera*, of which the Rocky Mountains are part. These ranges extend from Alaska in the north, through Canada and the United States, as far south as the Isthmus of Tehuantepec.

The Canadian Winter

Our great grandfathers used to think of Canada as a very cold land in which life was hard and full of adventure—chiefly because a famous poet called Canada " Our Lady of the Snows." There are even now some people who think that the greater part of the Dominion is a cold and barren land in which life is difficult and Nature cruel. Nothing could be farther from the truth.

It is a fact, of course, that most of Canada is much colder in winter than any part of Britain ; that the St. Lawrence and the Great Lakes are generally sealed by ice for five months in the year ; and that even in large and populous cities like Montreal and Toronto the thermometer in winter sinks to levels which startle us in our warm little Homeland, where even ten or twelve degrees of frost set us shivering unless we wrap up or snuggle down by the fire. But go to Canada and spend a winter there ; see how

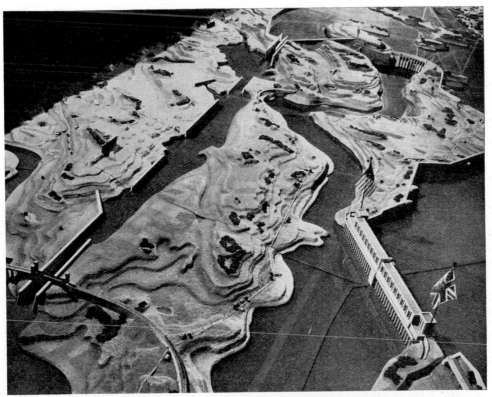

High Commissioner for Canada.

HOW THE ST. LAWRENCE SEAWAY MAY BE BUILT

This is a model of the St. Lawrence Seaway, the great new deep-water canal which will extend ocean navigation of the river to Toronto. At the top (right) we see the spillway dam at the foot of the Long Sault Rapids, between the north-western tip of Barnhart Island and the American mainland, and the power-houses (right foreground) which will span the river. To the left is seen part of the Seaway itself. As the flags show, both Canada and the United States are concerned in this great project.

boys and girls enjoy the snow and ice; find out for yourself how much cosier Canadian houses are than ours, and how little you yourself feel the cold, even when there are thirty, forty, or fifty degrees of frost, because the cold is a *dry* cold and not a damp chill like we often get in Britain!

The great gateway of Canada for most of us who visit the Dominion from Britain is the St. Lawrence, which with its five great lakes provides a waterway for at least 2,000 miles into the very heart of the North American continent. But if we were in a hurry we might travel all the way by air and reach Canada in a day via Gander airport, Newfoundland, and Montreal.

For seven months in the year, large ocean liners can steam up the St. Lawrence to the great Canadian city-ports of Quebec and Montreal, beyond which a series of rapids bars the way; although smaller ships, by using the canals which have been made to avoid the rapids, can pass up the river to the Great Lakes and on to the grain-shipping ports at the very head of Lake Superior.

At the Gateway of Canada

As a matter of actual fact, there are only about 120 miles of rapids between Prescott and Montreal that prevent ocean liners from reaching Toronto, and work is now going on to make the St. Lawrence Seaway, a great new deep-water canal, to improve this bad stretch of river, and to harness the rapids to power stations to earn the money to pay for it. When this scheme is completed, Toronto and not Montreal will be the head of ocean navigation, and Toronto will quite probably rapidly outstrip Montreal in size and importance.

Two great nations—the Canadians and the people of the United States—are concerned in this plan, for the international boundary at that spot passes down the middle of the St. Lawrence.

Power from the St. Lawrence

When we speak of the St. Lawrence Seaway, we must not forget the great increase that this project will bring in the amount of electricity available for large areas of Canada and the United States. The St. Lawrence project means more power, as well as an improved water-gate to this part of North America.

Work on the power part of the scheme began in August, 1954, when the Governor of New York set off a dynamite blast on Barnhart Island to turn the first earth of the project. This formed part of the opening ceremonies that took place on both the American and Canadian sides of the great river.

Winter Sea-Gates

The winter sea-gates of Canada are the "warm water" ports of Halifax in Nova Scotia and Saint John in New Brunswick; and of Portland, Boston and New York in the United States.

TORONTO SKYLINE
Canadian National Railways.

Toronto, the capital of Ontario, may owe its name to D'Arontal, an Indian chief of the days of Champlain. Some say that it comes from the original Huron name, meaning "a meeting place." The lofty, tower-like building in the centre of the picture is the Canadian Bank of Commerce which has been called "the highest building in the British Commonwealth."

DWELLERS IN THE NORTH

Will. F. Taylor.

FUR TRAPPING IN LABRADOR

In this wintry scene, the man is setting his trap to catch a mink. These animals live near rivers, where the ground is most likely to be an unbroken stretch of white snow. The trapper therefore builds a little house of tree boughs over this trap to keep out the snow. Once trappers could bring their furs south only in the summer, but to-day air transport carries them at any time of the year.

THE DOMINION OF CANADA extends in a tattered fringe of archipelago far towards the Pole. Its northern mainland is at the edge of the Arctic, and a wide strip of it lies well within the Arctic Circle. Here the long winters are severe, and the short summers often quite warm and pleasant, but on the barren islands of the Polar Sea climate conditions are much more difficult.

There are no trees, but a great deal of this tundra country is covered with coarse grasses, and in many places is brilliant with flowering plants during the brief summer. Berry-bearing bushes, too, are common, and at the end of summer give a pleasant change to the diet of the people who live in this scantily-populated land.

By the Air Mail

The northern islands are the home of the Eskimo, and the mainland tundra of both Eskimo and Indians, most of whom get their living by hunting and fishing. On the mainland these people are in touch with civilisation at the many trading posts, and have com- munication with the rest of Canada, not only by wireless, but also by the air mail, which can bring news and letters from the outside world every week, instead of once in two or three months, as was formerly often the case when the mails had to be carried by dog team in winter, or by canoe or coasting vessel in summer.

Air transport has, in fact, revolu- tionised life in Canada's Far North. Not only mails, but machinery and stores, medical and religious services, and police work now rely on air trans- port. Prospecting is done by air, and aircraft are used to help the seal-hunters find their prey. As early as 1937, Canadian airlines had regular services to such distant places as Goldfields, Coppermine, Great Bear Lake and Aklavik in the Mackenzie Delta.

Opening up the North West

Since then communications with the North West have been transformed. One of the greatest achievements was the Alaska Highway, built during the war by a huge force of United States soldiers, the work being undertaken in agreement

with the Canadian government. The
cost of this road to link the U.S.A. with
its outpost territory of Alaska was
quoted as £10,000,000.   Fifteen thousand miles long, it runs from Edmonton,
Alberta, to Grande Prairie, Fort Nelson,
Watson Lake, Whitehorse and Kluane
Lake in the Yukon, before crossing
the border beyond Snag to enter Alaska
and run on to Fairbanks.   Forming
a new North-West Passage to the east,
it marks the course of an important
air route and has opened up vast areas
of hitherto undeveloped country in
the coldest part of Canada.

Another important road, the all-
weather Mackenzie Highway, was opened
in 1948 to link Grimshaw, Alberta
with the Hay River Settlement on
Great Slave Lake in the Northwest
Territories.   And daily air services now
link Whitehorse in the Yukon with
Vancouver and Edmonton.   Other
services maintain contact with Aklavik,

Fort McPherson, Norman Wells and
Hay River, and with Port Radium,
Indin Lake, Yellowknife and other
places in the Northwest Territories.

Many Eskimo of the Canadian north
have their own schooners, some of
which are quite fine craft fitted with
auxiliary motors, and capable of almost
anything required of them in these
difficult waters.   Others have motor
boats or boats bought from ships
which call at various trading posts in
the summer when the sea is free enough
from ice.   Some have quite comfortable
huts of driftwood and turf in which
they live during the winter ; in summer
they prefer to use their tents and
kayaks, which are just the things for
the roving life they lead during the
better weather.

Those of us who do not realise how
much the world has changed during the
past ten or twenty years would be
astonished to find Eskimo at a northern

Polar Photos.

FOR WARMTH AND COMFORT IN WINTER

Canadian and American military authorities in Arctic Canada and Alaska are employing Eskimos
as instructors in the art of building igloos in the new military outposts in the Frozen North.   In a
well-constructed igloo, such as the house built of frozen snow seen above, the soldiers on duty at
these Arctic posts are able to keep as warm and comfortable as in a well-equipped Army hut.

Canadian Pacific.

A " MOUNTIE " IN THE WONDERLAND OF THE ROCKIES

The Royal Canadian Mounted Police are justly world-famous. Guardians of law and order in the remoter regions of the great Dominion, they also maintain " floating police detachments " along the desolate coasts of the Western Arctic. In 1940, the R.C.M.P. schooner *St. Roch* started on an historic voyage which made her the first ship to sail the Northwest Passage from west to east.

trading post listening to wireless programmes from the great American transmission centres, or sitting in their summer tents or in their winter huts enjoying the music of their gramophone, and perhaps even eating canned meat that has come from the more civilised lands of the south.

The Real Eskimo

But it is true. The Eskimo is not always buried away in his igloo, but, generally speaking, lives an active life to obtain the necessities of existence. Even far north among the great islands of the Polar Sea, where the Eskimo live to-day very much as their ancestors did 1,000 years ago, there is a short summer as well as the long and bitter winter; and during the summer these Eskimo take to the land with their hunting kit and their *tupic* or skin tent, as well as to the sea in their light and wonderfully-made kayaks, and gather what food they can from both. As winter comes down from the north, the Eskimo retire to their winter huts or *anis*, built of stones and turves, and often slightly underground, and perhaps built partly of drift-wood found on the summer beaches. Here they live snugly while the blizzards rage and howl outside, until the sea ice is strong enough to bear them on their winter hunting trips.

Each little Eskimo winter village is strung out over a considerable distance to give the people of every home a fairly wide area over which to hunt. *Igloos* or houses of hard blocks of frozen snow form the hunting and fishing headquarters of each family.

On the mainland, Eskimo hunters and Indian trappers collect furs and skins to exchange at the trading posts for things they need. But the big fur-trading is carried on in the great conifer forests, which lie to the south of the tundra lands. This forest belt stretches practically from ocean to ocean across Canada, and in parts is 600 or 700 miles in width. Its southern edges are fast being eaten into by the busy axes of the lumber-jacks, especially in Quebec, Ontario and Manitoba; but in the virgin depths of the forest and along its northern edges where it merges almost imperceptibly into the tundra, the trappers—Indians, half-breeds, and whites—set their traps, collect the furry pelts of the creatures they catch, and take or send them to barter at the Hudson's Bay posts for food, clothing, and other things.

Trappers and Fur Traders

The main trapping season is in winter when the fur-bearing animals are wearing their finest coats, and when the snow not only aids the trappers to conceal their traps, but enables them to

National Film Board.

INSPECTING HIS CATCH

In 1936, the Canadian Government built dams and canals to carry water into the dried swamps of Northern Manitoba so as to revive the conditions in which musk-rats like to live. Within 4 years, there were enough musk-rats for the trappers to start work again. This picture shows a trapper inspecting his catch, which he will take back to camp to prepare for marketing.

National Film Board.

GOLD-DREDGING IN THE KLONDIKE VALLEY

At the end of the last century the Klondike region in the Yukon basin was the scene of a famous gold rush and rich finds were made. In recent years there has been nothing spectacular but gold is steadily produced, and in this photograph is seen one of eight dredges used by the Yukon Consolidated Gold Corporation in the Klondike Valley. It can dredge the soil 63 feet below the surface of the water.

get about more easily by sleds, snow-shoes and skis.

As winter comes on, the trapper collects from the store of the fur trader the flour and bacon, the coffee and tobacco, the blankets and clothing, traps and snares, guns and ammunition, and whatever else he is likely to need during his lonely sojourn in the winter wilds. He may not be able to pay for all these goods, but the trader knows that the average trapper can be trusted to settle his debts in furs after the trapping season is over.

He sets out with his dog-team over lonely trails and arrives at last at his cabin, built of strong logs, with every crevice caulked to keep out the bitter cold. This hut is his winter head-quarters. He sets his traps and snares about three-quarters of a mile apart in a wide circle of perhaps thirty or forty miles, which he calls his "trap line." He has to be very cunning to deceive the wary, knowing creatures of the wild, whose sharp eyes and keener scent enable them quickly to detect the work of a "human." At times he may be absent from his cabin for several days—perhaps a fortnight—inspecting his traps, collecting his catch and resetting his traps for another.

The Trading Post

The skins or pelts of the creatures he catches—of the marten and beaver, fox and otter, wolf and ermine, musk-rat and other animals—he pegs out and dries, piling them in bundles ready for transport back to the trading-post. Here, as a rule, no money passes; for money is useless in such country as this. The trapper is credited with the value of his pelts, and against his credit he draws what goods he needs for his summer use; and later, when he once again sets out for his trapping ground, his stores for the long and lonely winter.

Air transport has made the trapper's life much easier. His furs can be sent south by air at any time of the year and he no longer has to wait for the spring thaw to unlock the streams and lakes that were his chief highways before the air lift came to put an end to strictly seasonal trapping. Canada also has fur ranches, particularly in Prince Edward Island, where such animals as the silver fox are specially reared for the fur trade.

A Gold Rush

What has drawn, not only Canadians, but men from all parts of the globe to the far north-west of Canada, is gold. In 1897 rich finds of gold were discovered in the Klondike region of the Yukon basin; a gold rush immediately set in, and in spite of the difficulties of reaching the Klondike in winter, swarms of gold-seekers attempted the perilous passage of the snowy passes from the North Pacific coast; and, when spring came, made their way in hastily-built scows down the roaring Yukon to the goldfields. Although the yield of gold from the Klondike has greatly decreased, mining (silver, lead and gold) is still the main occupation of the people. Gold remains the most economically-important mineral in the North. About twenty years ago new deposits were discovered in the Yellowknife River area of the Northwest Territories ; to-day, the Giant Yellowknife Gold Mine has some of the best mining buildings and equipment in the Dominion. Other natural resources are now being developed and as a result the population of the North is growing.

At Great Bear Lake, in the Northwest Territories, LaBine and Brintnell, who did their prospecting by air, discovered rich deposits of silver-radium ore. And at Port Radium, during the Second World War, the Eldorado Mine was worked to produce the pitchblende from which came the vital uranium component of the atom bomb. There are rich oil wells at Norman Wells on the lower Mackenzie river, and here also crude oil is refined.

The Changing North

The march of industry in the changing North is being helped by harnessing the water power of this vast region. The mining companies themselves have established hydro-electric plants: on the Klondike River, about 26 miles above Dawson in the Yukon, and at Bluefish Lake in the Northwest Territories. In 1948, the harnessing of the Snare River was completed; this scheme now supplies power for the Giant Yellowknife mine. A further hydro-electric scheme is proceeding at Mayo, in the Yukon.

But the riches of the North include more than furs and minerals. Great Slave Lake is the headquarters of a flourishing fishing industry, which in 1949 produced about 8 million lbs. of fish. The fisheries are worked on very modern lines, aircraft, snowmobiles and tractors being used. Wealth also lies in the rich grasses of the North on which animals like caribou and reindeer can be raised in large numbers. The caribou are already there in considerable herds —a herd may be 100,000 strong or more—that migrate north or south according to the season, in search of pasture. A recent count of caribou, made mainly by air survey as the animals made their spring migration north, showed that there were about 670,000 head.

Reindeer herding has also been introduced as a livelihood for the Eskimos and there are now some 7,500 reindeer —mostly maintained at the Reindeer Station east of Aklavik, at the mouth of

National Film Board.

THE SECRET OF PORT RADIUM

For a long time, activity at Port Radium on Great Bear Lake near the Arctic Circle was on the
" Top Secret " list, for it was concerned with the making of that terrible weapon the atomic
bomb. Here, 225 people worked the Eldorado Mine to produce the pitchblende from which
the vital uranium component of the bomb was obtained.

the Mackenzie River. Reindeer flourish there, for the Canadian tundra is no nearer the Pole than Lapland, where the chief wealth of the people is in their reindeer herds.

Arctic Outposts

In April, 1947, a small party of men were landed by aircraft on Slidre Fiord in Eureka Sound on Northern Ellesmere Island, which is only a few hundred miles from the North Pole. Despite the bitter cold—the temperature was forty degrees below freezing point—and the savage white wolves, the party set up their camp and installed their supplies, and their weather and radio equipment. A few months later, ships sailed from the American port of Boston to carry fresh supplies to these pioneer meteorologists and to set up other weather stations in the Canadian Arctic. Such was the beginning of the chain of Arctic weather stations established and maintained jointly by Canada and the United States.

The chief station is at Resolute Bay, Cornwallis Island. Others are maintained at Mould Bay (Prince Patrick Island), Isachsen (Ellef Ruignes Island), and Alert (Ellesmere Island). They are linked with civilisation by the spring and autumn flights of special Canadian and American aircraft and by the summer visits of coastguard and naval craft.

From these stations information is sent south by radio and is used to forecast the weather not only in North America, but in Europe as well. In addition, much scientific work is done from these bases; the behaviour of sea ice and of the tides is studied, and soil and snow observations made.

The meteorologists and other scientists who live and work at these desolate stations are " the important men of the Arctic." For it is quite true that " almost all other activities in this part of the world are designed to support the meteorological programme or are dependent upon the weather men."

LUMBER=JACKS AND FISHERMEN

H. J. Shepstone.

LUMBER-JACKS SORTING LOGS

These lumber-jacks stand confidently on the floating logs, which were once proud trees in the vast forests of Canada. These forests cover more than a million and a quarter square miles of which nearly 800,000 square miles are " productive " forests, providing work for many lumber-jacks and other workers.

CANADA has many millions of dollars' worth of valuable timber as yet untouched, although the eastern forests have been greatly cut into by the lumbermen, who have also made considerable inroads into the southern part of the forests in Quebec, Ontario and Manitoba.

Forest Rangers

As we have already seen, these great forests stretch in a wide and almost unbroken line from Atlantic to Pacific. The trees are mostly conifers like larch and spruce, whose soft woods are particularly valuable to the paper-maker and the manufacturer of artificial silk ; and tamarack and pine, with hemlock and birch and other trees. The great printing presses of the world, however, consume paper at such a rate that Canada is taking every possible step to conserve her forests, prevent waste, and arrange for new trees to be planted to take the place of those cut down.

Large areas have been set apart as National Forests to be strictly preserved and cut only when there is need. No lumber company can cut timber where, when and how it pleases. It is under more or less strict supervision every-where, so that young trees are not cut or damaged, and cutting is done in the most economical way.

Forest rangers are appointed to pre-vent waste and damage, to fight pests that damage trees, and, above all, to guard as far as possible against the worst peril there is—the danger of forest fires. Look-outs and other posts have been established whence the rangers can detect outbreaks of fire, and by means of the telephone and wireless can summon help and fire-fighting appli-ances to extinguish the blaze before it can spread over large areas. Hydro-planes, too, are used for fire detection and forest protection, for they can settle on the surfaces of the many lakes in summer. Like the planes used for carrying the Canadian air-mails, they are equipped with runners and skids in winter so that they can land on the snow-covered ice of the lakes and streams,

The following is part of a warning notice that appears in many of the Canadian railway time-tables:—

" Nine out of ten forest fires are let loose by human hands. An abandoned camp-fire, a glowing cigarette, a pipe-heel, or other innocent-looking cause ! Only a tiny point of flame which an hour hence becomes the fuse to a gigantic disaster."

Quebec province is the most important for wood-pulp and paper-making, but it is British Columbia that has the richest forests, for there the country is moister, and winters on the whole are much milder than in the central and eastern portions of the great Conifer Belt. Here grow the magnificent Douglas firs, whose feathery tips rise to a height sometimes of 300 feet: the splendid Sitka spruces, and the fine-grained red cedars whose timber is in great demand for building.

Lumber-jacks

Lumbering is carried on chiefly in winter over the greater part of Canada, for the heavy snowfall makes it easier to move the weighty logs by sledges or by slides to the nearest stream, there to await the break-up of the ice and the spring floods that will carry them down by the million to the saw-mills and the pulp-mills on the main rivers and the lakes.

This provides work for many men who otherwise would be idle because their ordinary jobs have been stopped by frost and snow and bitter weather. They move up-country from towns and villages and farms to the lumber camps, where they live strenuous lives, but earn good money. After the spring " runs " of logs on the rivers are over, many of the lumber-jacks go back to the warm weather work in town and village, farm and factory.

National Film Board.

MAKING A RAFT

These boom men in British Columbia are poling spruce logs to make a raft. Their sharp-shod shoes enable them to stand on the logs, which they jockey with their pike poles or " burl " with short forward or backward steps. The Canadian forests stretch in an almost unbroken belt, from six hundred to a thousand miles in depth, from the Atlantic to the Pacific.

E. N. A.

ON THEIR WAY TO THE SAW MILLS

Larch and spruce are known as soft woods and are particularly valuable to the paper-maker, the great printing presses of the world consuming an enormous amount of Canadian lumber. In this picture you are shown a riverful of logs, raw material for the saw mills or pulp plants, floating down the Mattagami River in Ontario.   It cheapens the product considerably when transport along a stream can be arranged.

In many parts of British Columbia, however, the lumbermen do not wait for winter before they begin their cutting, because the snows are not heavy enough to make it worth while. They fell the huge trees during the good weather, cut them into giant logs, and, by means of wire cables and donkey engines, lug them out of the forest and place them on lumber trains which convey them to the river, or very often to an arm of the sea—for the Pacific shores of Canada are in many parts indented by long deep inlets much like the fjords of Norway.

At these inlets, ships from all parts of the world load timber and wood-pulp:

but much timber is also shipped from such British Columbian ports as Vancouver, Victoria, and New Westminster.

East of Lake Winnipeg, and south of the St. Lawrence Gulf, are the hardwood forests of Southern Canada, where woodsmen work on such trees as yellow birch, red maple, sugar maple, basswood, and trees more familiar to us like oak, elm, and beech.

Great Fisheries of North America

Newfoundland's Grand Bank is still the most renowned of the world's cod fisheries.   From Newfoundland and Nova Scotia, fleets of auxiliary schooners set out to bring in the rich

THE GREAT SALMON INDUSTRY

Canada's salmon fisheries and canneries form one of her most important industries. The salmon are caught as they return from the sea to lay their eggs in the lakes and rivers. Great care is taken to ensure that only the best salmon is put on the market, and here we see cooked salmon being tested for texture by microscope.

Photos : National Film Board.

Nearly 25,000 workers are needed to cope with British Columbia's mid-summer salmon harvest. The world's largest salmon fleet keeps the canneries constantly supplied, and each fish passes through careful processes of cutting, cleaning, washing, and inspection before it is finally canned, cooked, and packed. This picture shows Indian girls working in the canning department

COOKING AND CANNING SALMON

Cut, cleaned and scraped by an ingenious machine called an " Iron Chink," the salmon is then washed and inspected and put into tins by a machine which fills more than 100 tins a minute. In this picture a truck loaded with freshly-filled tins is being pushed into the cooking retort.

Here, Indian girls are taking the tins from their trucks and packing them in boxes ready to be sent away. Canadian salmon goes to all parts of the world, and besides the fish, the industry has waste products which are useful in providing such things as fish-oil and fertilizer.

TIMBER FROM CANADA'S FORESTS

Canada sends large quantities of timber and salmon to other countries. One of the chief ports from which these products are sent is Vancouver. This picture shows us a wharf in the docks at Vancouver, with timber awaiting shipment. Vancouver is second only to Montreal in the amount of cargo handled during a year.

Photos : National Film Board.

Canada's great timber industry makes a major contribution to the world supply of wood pulp for paper. From her vast forests comes the cellulose for Britain's rayon industries and the paper-pulp which makes your daily newspaper possible. This picture shows the chip conveyor belt in a pulp mill taking chips to the digester building for making sulphite pulp.

harvests of cod, halibut, haddock, and hake.

No less famous are the great salmon fisheries of British Columbia and Alaska. The salmon are caught as they return from the sea to lay their eggs in the lakes and rivers. Traps, salmon-wheels, curtain-like gill-nets and purse seine nets are used to catch them, and some are caught by trolling. But the most common equipment used is the pound-net made so intricately of wire netting that once fish have entered it they cannot escape. Tenders from fish canneries collect the catch in flat-bottomed barges called scows. From these an endless belt system carries the fish into the cannery where they are sorted and then cut, cleaned and scraped by an ingenious machine called an " Iron Chink " (it was given this name because it does work formerly done by Chinese labour). Inspectors wash and examine the fish which then pass on to cutting and filling machines which can fill more than one hundred tins a minute. The sealed tins are then loaded in trays on small trucks which are put into the cooking retort. Cooked, and then cleansed and cooled, the tins are labelled and packed ready to be sent off to Europe or other parts of the world; some of them, perhaps, will come to the shelves of your own grocery shop.

National Film Board.

CANADIAN FORESTS SUPPLY THE WORLD'S NEWSPAPERS

All our newspapers and many books are to-day printed on paper made from wood pulp, and it is in countries with vast forests, such as Canada, that the manufacture of " newsprint " has become a great industry. To-day there is still not enough paper to supply world demands. In this photo-graph the finished rolls of newsprint are seen as they are being carried by narrow gauge railway from the Powell River mills in British Columbia down to the wharves for shipment by sea.

THE PRAIRIES AND WHEAT

A WHEATFIELD OF THE PRAIRIES

Before the white man came, this large wheatfield near Edmonton, the capital of Alberta, was part of the vast natural grasslands frequented only by bison and the Indians who hunted them. To-day, the prairies yield rich harvests of wheat, and the " Prairie Provinces " (Alberta, Saskatchewan and Manitoba) contain nearly three-quarters of the occupied farm land of Canada.

THE CANADIAN PRAIRIES lie south of the forest belt, and between the Rocky Mountains foot-hills and the Lake of the Woods east of Winnipeg. The name means " meadows " or natural grass-land. The prairies are by no means level ; they rise gently in three broad steps or very wide terraces from Winnipeg westward to the Rocky Mountain foot-hills; and the top of the easternmost of those three gigantic " steps " is gently undulating country, with few trees and open horizons.

The " prairie provinces " are Manitoba, Saskatchewan and Alberta, although it should be remembered that all three stretch far north from the prairie lands into the great belt of conifer forests. Manitoba, indeed, stretches from the international boundary of the forty-ninth parallel to the shores of Hudson Bay, where she has built her port of Churchill.

The soil of the prairies is extra-ordinarily fertile, and in many places will grow grain for several years before the farmer finds it necessary to restore its fertility by scientific manuring.

Although grain—especially wheat—is the chief prairie product, there are regions where the rainfall is hardly enough for grain, but where large numbers of cattle, sheep and horses can be reared, as they are on the eastern foot-hills of the Rockies. Grain farmers, too, do not lock up all their capital and spend all their energy in grain-growing; they grow other crops as well, and rear farm animals too. It is true that when a man first takes over his land, and breaks it up for farming, he generally grows wheat first, because wheat is pretty certain of making him a return of ready money. But after that, he begins to lay out his farm so that he can grow other crops too, and rear animals. One of the main reasons for this is that if the farmer grew wheat continuously, his soil would soon become exhausted—to such an extent that in time, fertile land might become barren desert. Moreover, as the prairie settlements developed into towns the need for the products of mixed farming increased. Many of the prairie towns are now manufacturing centres for agricultural machinery, clothing, and all those things that the prairie farmer had once to import from the east, or even from Britain and Europe.

The prairies, however, are the real "golden lands" of the West, and rich hard wheat sown in spring and reaped the following autumn is the main crop. But we must think of them also as great stock-breeding lands and we must bear in mind that although a farmer's mainstay may be wheat on the richer and moister lands, he also goes in for a good deal of mixed farming.

The Bison

Before the coming of the white men, the Indians roamed the prairies, hunting the bison (or "buffalo"), and following the great bison herds as they migrated in their millions yearly across these vast natural grazing grounds. When white men came, and the Indians found a ready market with them for hides and "buffalo robes," both whites and Indians (now armed with guns capable of far swifter execution than their bows and arrows) carried on a campaign of ruthless slaughter, bringing down the bison in uncountable thousands, stripping them of their hides, and leaving their carcases to the coyotes and the buzzards. The greed that prompted this wholesale extermination of the bison herds soon brought its retribution, and in a comparatively few years the bison was in danger of becoming as extinct as the prehistoric monsters whose remains we find in the rocks.

The magnitude of the slaughter may be realised when we read records which tell how, in the middle of the nine-

National Film Board.

THRESHING THE PRAIRIE HARVEST

The prairie farmers sow their wheat in spring and reap the golden harvest in the autumn. Although large, modern combine harvesters are used to reap and thresh the grain in the field, horses still play a part in the work of the harvest on some prairie farms.

National Film Board.

NO ROOM IN THE ELEVATOR

In seasons when the crop is particularly heavy the granaries are filled to overflowing. This photograph shows what happens when for the time being the elevators are full and the grain has to be temporarily piled in one corner of a vast Saskatchewan wheatfield until the elevators can take more thousands of bushels to be shipped later to some country depending on Canadian wheat for its daily bread.

teenth century, travellers saw the plains covered with grazing bison from horizon to horizon. Yet the day soon arrived when only a few hundreds were left. Luckily, some of these were captured and at last preserved in the great National Parks of Canada and the United States, where they could live and multiply unmolested. Wood Buffalo National Park, between the Athabaska River of Alberta and the Slave River, which runs partly in the Northwest Territories, is the home of the largest remaining herd of bison in North America.

Where the bison herds formerly roamed in yearly migration over the prairies are now broad lands of golden grain. More and more land is being taken up by the wheat farmers, who now grow wheat, especially in Alberta, much farther north than was formerly thought possible. On these northern wheat-lands, the great length of day amply compensates for the shorter summer, and the long hours of continuous sunlight ripen the grain more quickly. In Alberta, too, and Saskatchewan, the warm Chinook winds come down from the west, licking up the winter snow as if by magic, and giving the farmers the chance of early spring sowing.

How Wheat goes to Market

It is one thing to grow wheat and quite a different thing to market it. Were it not for the amazing network of railways serving the prairie lands and the wonderful organisation that permits growers to despatch, store and export their crops, the business of wheat-growing on this gigantic scale would be unprofitable.

Co-operation among the farmers has led to the creation of what are known as wheat "pools"—the collection and storage of the grain at one or two great central points which are most convenient for storage and for transport to tide-water. The threshed grain is stored in giant buildings called elevators, some of which can hold as much as six millions of bushels.

Smaller elevators are set up at central points on the railroads all over the grain-lands; and it is to these that farmers bring their harvest by wagon and lorry. From these the grain is sent to monster elevators, at Winnipeg for example, whence a comparatively short haul by railroad delivers it to other great elevators at Port Arthur and Fort William at the head of Lake Superior, whence the wheat can be loaded into specially constructed lake-steamers for transport as required, to the ocean ports of Montreal, the world's greatest grain port, and New York. In the summer months, grain also goes from Winnipeg to the Hudson Bay port of Churchill which provides the shortest sea link between Britain and the prairies.

Grain Export

More and more grain nowadays is being sent westwards to the Pacific ports, instead of eastward. The Alberta wheat " pool " has constructed giant elevators at Prince Rupert, one of the Pacific terminals of the Canadian National Railways ; there are others, too, at Vancouver, which is the Pacific terminal of both the Canadian Pacific and the Canadian National. From

National Film Board.

TOWERING GRAIN ELEVATORS NEAR SASKATOON

These are among the largest grain elevators in the world. Many such elevators have been built along the railways in the prairie country to hold the grain until it is taken to such centres as Winnipeg, Edmonton, and Calgary, whence it goes to ports on Lake Superior or direct to the shipping ports.

these ports grain is shipped to Britain and Western Europe by way of the Panama Canal—a long sea voyage of six weeks or so, it is true, but cheaper in the long run, because of the shorter railroad haul to the sea, and because of the fewer changes from land transport to water transport by the western route.

The Wheat Pool

Grain going east from the Winnipeg " pool " must change from rail to lake steamer at Lake Superior, and very often from lake steamer to rail again at Georgian Bay on Lake Huron, and from rail to ocean steamer at Montreal. All these changes add to the cost of transport and greatly increase the price at which the wheat can be sold. The sum paid to the farmer for his wheat is usually less than half the price charged for it when it is exported from Montreal to Liverpool.

The wheat " pool " has other advantages than those we have already mentioned. First of all, the wheat can be held back in the big elevators until the price is good enough for it to be released ; and secondly, the " pool " arranges for the farmer to receive his money in three parts if he chooses— one on receipt of the grain, one when he sows his spring crop, and a third to help pay for harvesting it. This means that farmers need not borrow money to keep themselves going, nor be practically a year behind with their profits.

Queen City of the Prairies

The transport of grain on the Great Lakes is carried on in specially-built " lake freighters " with engine-rooms at their sterns and navigating bridges and living quarters at their bows—all the rest being cargo space. The need for many of these freighters is easily seen when we read in some recent Canadian official records that 380,000,000 bushels of grain had to be shipped

National Film Board.

GRAIN FROM THE GOLDEN PLAINS
Much of Canada's great wheat harvest is exported. Here we see grain being tested for quality on arrival at Winnipeg.

from Fort William and Port Arthur during the season. This partly explains why Ontario and Quebec, both inland provinces of the Dominion, have so many thousands of tons of shipping on their registers.

The great centre of all this business is *Winnipeg*, the " Queen City " of the prairies, which has grown from a small prairie town of wooden shacks to a splendid city with fine buildings and all the requirements of civilisation in a remarkably short time—and is still growing fast. It is often called the " Keystone of Canada," because all traffic across Canada east and west must pass through this central point. A glance at the map of Canada reveals the reason.

First of all, it is almost midway between the Atlantic and Pacific Oceans; second, it is in the " bottleneck " between Lake Winnipeg and the international border, at the confluence of the Red River and the

National Film Board.

ROUNDING UP THE CATTLE

This is a common enough scene in springtime in western Canada, where there are many large cattle ranches, and where sheep and horses are also reared.   Most ranches lie along the eastern foothills of the Rockies, where there is less rainfall than on the wheat prairies.   But cattle-rearing is not restricted to the west.   Some parts of Ontario raise large numbers of beef cattle.

Assiniboine River, forty miles south of the lake and sixty miles from the boundary between Canada and the United States.   And to this " bottle-neck," commanded by Winnipeg, traffic must converge; the C.P.R., the C.N.R., the Midland Railway of Manitoba and the Northern Pacific of the U.S.A. all meet there.   The Winnipeg railway sidings are astonishingly large, to accommodate the huge movements of grain, cattle and other products from the west, and of manufactured foods from the east.   Winnipeg has flour-mills, meat-packing, clothing, food products and sheet metal industries; and with its suburbs a population which, in 1951, was over 233,000.

Other Prairie Cities

Other prairie cities are much smaller, but are fast growing, as more and more lands are brought under yield. *Calgary*, the centre of the stock-raising and agricultural region of Southern Alberta, has important oil wells nearby with their own refinery, and the town has 150 different industries.   Both C.P.R. and C.N.R. serve the area.   Another large town is *Edmonton*, the capital of Alberta, near good coal, on the N. Saskatchewan river, and the gateway to the famous Peace River country to the north, now being rapidly settled and developed.   Oil wells have been bored at Wainwright, 100 miles from the city, at Turner Valley, and at the

GRAIN LOADING

Harvested grain is stored in wheat elevators whence it goes by rail or special lake-steamer to ports in British Columbia, Eastern Canada, and Hudson Bay. As the picture shows, lake-steamers come right alongside the elevators at such places as Fort William and Port Arthur and load cargoes for Buffalo, New York, and Montreal.

14—2

important new fields of Leduc and Red-water. More will be said presently about this valuable " black gold."

The E.P. ranch once owned by H.R.H. the Duke of Windsor, is in the neighbourhood, and has oil wells near it; it probably has oil beneath it too. Natural gas (50,000,000 cubic feet daily) is brought in pipes to the city from the oil regions. Both C.P.R. and C.N.R. serve Edmonton; the city has the first municipal aerodrome constructed in Canada, and its industries include engineering, meat-packing, flour-milling, coal-mining, timber-working and butter and cheese-making. It is a great fur-trading centre for the north-west.

Farming in Eastern Canada is rather different from farming on the prairies. Wheat-growing and mixed farming are the chief businesses in the prairie provinces; but in the east dairy-farming, stock-breeding and fruit-growing are the most important branches of the farming industry. The fruit and dairy farms of Eastern Canada lie in the St. Lawrence valley and in the peninsula formed by lakes Huron, Erie, and Ontario. Dairy produce and bacon are the main products, and large crops of hay and oats are grown to feed the cattle and pigs from which these products come. Fruit crops are mainly apples, pears, cherries, and plums: and in the Niagara peninsula the climate is warm enough for choice grapes and peaches to be grown.

But other parts of Canada yield this kind of farm produce. The apple orchards of Annapolis Valley, Nova Scotia, are far more important than those of the St. Lawrence valley, as are the fruit valleys of British Columbia where apricots and peaches are grown as well as the more usual fruits.

Canada's Great Cities

Conditions in the east are different from those of the western prairies. The climate is different, and the soil is

National Film Board.

APPLE PICKING IN NOVA SCOTIA

The Annapolis-Cornwallis region of Nova Scotia contains the largest apple orchard acreage in the British Commonwealth and has been called " the apple barrel of eastern Canada." Most of Nova Scotia's average annual crop of over 2 million barrels comes to British markets.

National Film Board.

THE PRAIRIE PROVINCE OF ALBERTA ALSO HAS RICH OILFIELDS

Besides her fertile grainlands, Alberta has valuable oilfields, which provide more than ninety per cent. of the oil produced in Canada. This picture shows part of Turner Valley, one of the older centres of the oil industry. Recently, pipelines have been built to carry oil east and west from the newer Leduc and Redwater fields near Edmonton, the Albertan capital.

different too. The needs of the east for farm produce are greater than those of the west, for the valley of the St. Lawrence and the Lake Peninsula of Ontario have the densest population in the Dominion ; all Canada's great cities, except two, are there, and Canada's biggest manufacturing industries have their homes there. It is more profitable from the point of view of the ready market in this populous region of the Dominion for farmers to go in for dairy-farming, poultry-rearing, raising stock for meat, and fruit-growing ; and it is fortunate that the moister climate favours these businesses to a far greater extent than the drier climate of the prairies.

Across the St. Lawrence

A glance at the map will show the marked difference between the east and west of the Dominion. Nearest to Britain comes Newfoundland. Then we see the huge Province of Quebec, bounded on the north-east by Labrador. This vast tract has the sea on three sides, for Quebec's western extremity is bounded by Hudson Bay. South of Quebec, across the St. Lawrence, are New Brunswick and Nova Scotia ; whilst the section containing Ottawa comes between the frontier of the United States of America and the Great Lakes.

The prairie wheatbelt is therefore mainly in the centre of the continent. Here it has a purely inland climate, unaffected by the sea summer or winter. To the south of Alberta, Saskatchewan and Manitoba, is the boundary of the U.S.A., with the Missouri River not far away.

The prairie climate is one of extremes, with hot summers and very cold winters. The rain of late spring and early summer helps along the wheat which ripens in the dry summer months that last over the autumn harvest period.

Scientists have helped the prairie farmers by developing special " breeds " of wheat which are ideally suited to the soil and climate of the prairies.

THE BUSIEST PARTS OF CANADA

MONTREAL, CANADA'S LARGEST CITY

Canadian National Railways.

Of Canada's cities the largest is Montreal with a population of over one million people. Here is a view of the city, which contains the Cathedral of St. James and the McGill University, and is itself a vast seaport. The aeroplane is the express between Montreal and points west of Vancouver flying on one of the Trans-Canada Air Lines.

THREE-FIFTHS of Canada's population of more than fifteen millions live in Ontario and Quebec, and the greater number of these dwell in the lowland of the St. Lawrence, where all Canada's cities of over 100,000 people are situated, except two, and where we find the only cities with populations of more than half a million—Montreal and Toronto.

Canada's Largest City

Montreal is the largest city in Canada, with a population (including its suburbs) of more than a million people. It is at the head of an ocean navigation on the St. Lawrence, and is therefore a great seaport, with routes converging in it from the Lakes and the Canadian west, and from New York and the busiest regions of the north-eastern United States. It has abundant hydro-electric power from the Lachine Rapids close by, and can therefore carry on a large variety of manufactures independently of coal. Nearly 2,000 factories of various kinds have been erected in the city or in its immediate neighbourhood.

It is amazing to think that this vast business metropolis of the Dominion has grown up from the tiny settlement founded on the island of Mont Real in 1642 by the Sieur de Maisonneuve. You can see his statue to-day in the old Place d'Armes in the heart of the city. The French element still predominates; newspapers in French are as common as those in English, and four out of every five inhabitants can speak French.

Montreal's great cathedral of St. James is a reproduction on a smaller scale of St. Peter's, Rome. Near Mount Royal Park, on the lower and eastern slope, is the famous McGill University. The French University of Laval is in the French quarter of the city.

Canada's two great railway systems have monster stations there; the bigger is the C.N.R. New Central Terminal, Dorchester Street, which was opened in July, 1943. Montreal has thirty miles of water-front, with dock and wharfage accommodation for vessels up to 25,000 tons; a huge network of rail connections; and giant grain elevators (some capable of storing nearly 3,000,000 bushels), which can handle a million bushels of wheat a day.

The great disadvantage from which the port suffers is that it is closed by ice from November till March.

The St. Lawrence river, on which Montreal stands, and the Great Lakes provide a water highway nearly two thousand miles long. At places along its course, the river has wild rapids and these have been avoided by building such canals as the famous Lachine Canal, on which work began as long ago as 1700: the Welland Ship Canal, which bypasses the Niagara Falls: and the Rideau Canal. From Lake Erie, the Erie Canal runs, via Buffalo, to Albany on the Hudson river, and so to New York. On these great inland waterways, you will see shipping of all kinds, including " lake carriers," a special sort of craft for transporting bulk cargoes across the lake waters.

Toronto

Toronto, the capital of Ontario, bids fair to outstrip Montreal; when the St. Lawrence is rendered navigable to ocean liners between Montreal and Lake Ontario by the great new Seaway, Toronto is bound in time to usurp Montreal's position as Canada's leading port, and to grow proportionately in population and importance.

In its business quarter, Toronto's skyscraper buildings remind one somewhat of New York; and, seen from a high viewpoint, its principal thoroughfare, Yonge Street, looks like a road ribbon at the bottom of a deep canyon of

Canadian National Railways.

WHERE CANADA'S PARLIAMENT MEETS

Ottawa is the capital of Canada and stands on the river of the same name which is of Indian origin. This picture shows the imposing Parliament Buildings, which occupy a lofty bluff overlooking the river. The tower is called the " Tower of Peace " and is a memorial to the 60,000 Canadian soldiers who gave their lives in the war of 1914-18.

masonry. Its fine harbour on the lake is protected by a low sandy island, where people amuse themselves much as New Yorkers do on Coney Island. Power from Niagara has made Toronto one of Canada's leading manufacturing centres.

Niagara Falls

A favourite excursion from Toronto is, of course, to the famous *Falls* themselves.

They occur where the whole of the Niagara River plunges headlong over a great ledge of limestone into the pool below, to gather speed rapidly as it enters the Niagara gorge, through which it foams and leaps and boils in raging whirlpools. By the time the flood has reached Queenston it has calmed down, and makes exit to Lake Ontario with a quiet that strangely belies its mad energy a few miles up-stream.

Ages ago, geologists tell us, the Falls were seven miles or so down-stream, but since that time they have gradually cut their way back—a process that is still going on. What will happen when they have receded to Lake Erie no man can tell; it is not likely to concern the present generation, at any rate !

The Falls are divided by Goat Island into the Canadian or Horseshoe Fall (158 feet high, 3,100 feet wide), and the American Fall (167 feet high, 1,080 feet wide). You can go to the foot of the Falls in a tiny steamer and view the great rushing torrent at close quarters; you can even pass behind the American Fall, clad in oil-skins ; and led by a guide through the onslaught of wind and spray, amid the noise of thundering waters, you may dare to open your frightened eyes to see the fall rushing in sheets of light and darkness in a great curve that seems within reach of your outstretched hands.

The rapids in the Niagara Gorge are even more terrifying than the Falls themselves. The falls are liquid moving translucent Majesty ; the whirlpools in the gorge are howling demoniac Force that threatens.

No wonder Niagara is a sort of Mecca for the

National Film Board.

TO THE MEMORY OF FRENCH PIONEERS

The Evangeline Monument and Church at Grand Pré recall the days when Nova Scotia was called Acadia. The tragic expulsion of the first settlers by the British in 1755 is told in Longfellow's poem *Evangeline*. The bronze figure shown in the picture is the work of a direct descendant of one of the pioneer families.

VANCOUVER AND NIAGARA

British Columbia Government.

Vancouver is the commercial centre of British Columbia and Canada's chief Pacific seaport. It has a fine harbour and is the western terminus of the Canadian Pacific and Canadian National Railways and northern terminus of two U.S.A. railways. In addition there is a large airport with daily services to the chief cities of North America. Our photograph shows Brockton Point, Stanley Park.

Central News Press.

Many thousands of tourists visit each year the famous Falls at Niagara. In actual volume they are the greatest falls in the world. As seen in this picture there are two distinct waterfalls, side by side : the American Fall and the Horseshoe Fall on the Canadian side. It has been estimated that the water coming over the Horseshoe Fall is at least 20 feet in thickness.

tourists of all the globe. Hundreds of thousands visit it every year; for despite the great power-houses built to steal some of the energy of the rushing river, there has been no visible diminution in its resistless flood, and no detraction from the marvellous beauty of the Falls—unless you cannot shut your eyes to the hotels, the trams, and the establishments and activities of those who cater for tourists who must have amusements, and souvenirs, and picture postcards and other things to make them really happy !

Two other famous Canadian beauty spots are Rocky Mountains Park and the Jasper National Park, which contain some of the finest Rocky Mountain scenery. Jasper National Park is " one third the size of Switzerland and is the greatest game sanctuary in the world." Visitors to the Jasper Park make a point of seeing Mount Robson, highest peak in the Rockies, and the vast Columbia icefield.

Ottawa, the Dominion Capital

Ottawa is the beautiful capital of the Dominion on the Ottawa River, opposite the busy lumber and pulp-mills of Hull, which, like its regal sister across the river, derives power, light and heat from the Chaudière Falls. Its fine Parliament Buildings and Government Offices stand on a high bluff overlooking the river. Its wide and shady streets, and its lovely houses with fine lawns and beautiful gardens, make Ottawa a city of wonderful homes.

There are other cities, too, in this busy region of the lower Lakes and the St. Lawrence. There is *Hamilton*, west of Toronto, with its great steel and iron works, its electrical workshops, its textile mills, its chewing gum and confectionery businesses, and the famous works that send out vacuum cleaners to eat up the dust of a million homes in Europe and America. There is *Trois Rivières* (Three Rivers) on the St. Lawrence

Canadian National Railways

WHERE THE SCHOOL COMES TO THE CHILDREN

Travelling schools, like the one shown above, provide thoroughly modern education for boys and girls in the scattered communities of Northern Ontario. School cars travel in circuits, spending about a week with each group of children—and leaving behind enough homework to keep everyone busy until the next visit.

IN CANADA'S NATIONAL PARKS

These canoeists on Vermillion Lake, Banff National Park, Alberta, get a fine view of Mount Rundle, whose strange slab-like structure was brought about by a great shifting of the earth's surface about 60 million years ago.

Photos : National Film Board.

This is the Athabaska Glacier seen from Icefields Highway, Jasper National Park, Alberta. A million years ago western Canada was covered by an ice mass whose traces can be seen to-day in the famous Columbia Icefield, of which Athabaska Glacier is one of the main flows. Athabaska is an Indian word meaning " where there are reeds."

ON THE GREAT LAKES

This picture shows the type of craft you will see on the Great Lakes. The ship pictured is the *Lemoyne*, the queen of the Great Lakes fleet, here shown going through one of the locks of the Welland Canal. The Canal, linking Lakes Ontario and Erie, is one of the greatest engineering feats of the kind and took 17 years to build.

Photos : National Film Board.

These miners are working on the biggest salt deposits in the British Commonwealth—those of the Malagash Salt Mine, Nova Scotia. They shovel the salt into a tunnel whence a scraper will drag and collect it to be dumped. The Malagash salt deposits are 100 miles long and 400 ft. wide, and are thought to be 27 million years old.

THE ALUMINIUM INDUSTRY

National Film Board.

Arvida, Quebec, is the home of the Aluminium Company of Canada and produces enough aluminium to supply the whole British Commonwealth and nearly 50 per cent. of United States' needs as well.   Here we see bauxite from British Guiana being reclaimed.

Canadian Pacific Air Lines.

The power stations of the great Shipshaw Dam on the Saguenay River produce hydro-electric power for the largest aluminium plant in the British Commonwealth.   This aerial view shows the No. 2 Power House which contains 12 generators.

about half-way between Quebec and Montreal that draws its power from the great Shawinigan Falls on the St. Maurice River and runs one of the biggest paper and pulp plants in the Dominion, as well as cotton factories and shoe factories.

Canada To-day

The Canada of to-day is a very different Canada from that of even twenty or thirty years ago. She no longer imports most of her manufactured goods from Britain and other lands; she has become a manufacturer herself, and is beginning to penetrate into the markets of the world in competition with those very countries to which she formerly looked for manufactured goods.

Canada's busiest industrial region is far from her sources of coal in Nova Scotia, the Rockies, and British Columbia. But coal is imported from the United States across the lakes, and Canada has, in addition, " white coal " from such hydro-electric plants as Niagara, Shawinigan Falls, and Gatineau River. " White coal " from the Shipshaw dam and power station on the Saguenay is used at the nearby works at Arvida of the Aluminium Company of Canada which produces about a quarter of the world's aluminium. The Shipshaw development and the new Beauharnois Power Development on the shores of Lake St. Louis, east of Montreal, are the two largest hydro-electric plants in the Dominion.

One of the directions in which Canada has forged ahead in recent years is in the manufacture of iron and steel. This has led on to shipbuilding, and the Dominion has come in a very short space of time to hold a prominent position in this field of industry, having more than a score of major shipyards of her own.

In addition to the ships, Canada can make all the great array of fitments needed for ocean-going vessels. In Vancouver, for example, there is a

plant, probably the only one of its kind within the Commonwealth, which turns out massive anchor chains each of them weighing 50,000 lbs. and being almost a quarter of a mile in length. These chains are forged on mass production lines, operatives welding links with the latest electric appliances as the chains pass in front of them on an endless band.

Canada also makes her own textiles, machinery, aeroplanes, cars, and leather goods, as well as food and timber products, metal goods and other manufactures.

Recently vast iron ore deposits were discovered extending across the Quebec-Labrador boundary in the area where Burnt Creek, the main development centre, now stands. It is known that there are over 400 million tons of good ore here, and it is thought that the total amount available may be no less than 2 billion tons—so vast a supply that it can hardly be imagined. Working together, Canada and the United States have just built a 360-mile railway from Burnt Creek to Seven Islands, on the St. Lawrence, where a port is being built to handle the ore which will serve the steel mills of both countries.

The time may soon come when Labrador's mighty Hamilton River is harnessed for power. 560 miles long, this river has falls that are second only to Niagara, yet few people have seen them, for the river flows through a part of Canada that is hard to reach. Iron ore and water power may alter this. Grand Falls and Muskrat Falls on the Hamilton may become hydro-electric centres.

Canadian Oil

Canadian oil production has increased rapidly during the last few years as a result of the discovery in 1947 of the Leduc field, near Edmonton, Alberta, and subsequently of other fields. Turner Valley, in the same province, is now much less important than the fields at Leduc and Redwater, both

THE MAJESTIC BEAUTY OF BANFF

Canadian Pacific.

Some of the most magnificent scenery in the world is to be found in Canada's National Parks in the Rockies. This picture shows the Banff Springs Hotel where King George VI and Queen Elizabeth stayed during their tour of the Dominion in 1939. Behind lies the grandeur of the mountains, while round the hotel cluster the feathery-topped trees of the Bow River Valley. Equally famous is the Jasper National Park, north of Banff, whose 4,200 square miles make it the largest national park in the world. Wild life in these parks—deer, bears, mountain goats and sheep—is protected.

near Edmonton. An important new oil-field was discovered early in 1954 about a hundred and twenty miles south-east of Regina, Saskatchewan, not far from the United States border.

The Interprovincial Pipe Line now carries crude oil from Edmonton, by way of Regina, to Superior, Wisconsin, in the United States. From Superior, lake tankers take the oil to the refinery at Sarnia, Ontario. Covering a distance of 1,127 miles, the new pipeline is an amazing feat of construction—and it took less than 150 days to complete ! A second pipeline, the TransMountain Pipe Line, has been driven through the Rockies to carry oil from Edmonton to Burnaby near Vancouver, in British Columbia.

Other new pipelines include the Trans-Northern (from Montreal refineries to the Toronto-Hamilton area, with a branch to Ottawa) and the line from Sarnia to Toronto. Before many years have passed, Toronto may also receive natural gas from Alberta by pipeline.

The story of how Canada is developing her natural treasures does not end with iron and oil. In 1946, titanium ore was discovered in vast quantities on the shores of Lake Allard, near Havre St. Pierre, Quebec. Once used mainly in making paint, titanium can now be produced in metal form. It is much heavier, but much stronger than aluminium: and about half as light, but just as strong as steel. In the Lynn

Aluminium Company of Canada.

KITIMAT, A GREAT NEW PROJECT THAT MEANS MORE ALUMINIUM

Kitimat, about four hundred miles north of Vancouver in British Columbia, is the heart of the newest and largest project undertaken by the Canadian aluminium industry. The construction work of this huge scheme has included the cutting of a 10-mile tunnel through Mount Dubose and the building of a hydro-electric generating station to power the aluminium smelter at Kitimat. This picture shows us the Kemano Camp, where the power house has been built into the base of the mountain (right). Sufficient power will be generated to produce half a million tons of aluminium every year.

Canadian Pacific Railways.

CANADA'S "GATEWAY TO THE PACIFIC"

This name is often given to Vancouver, the largest city in British Columbia and the third largest in Canada. This picture shows us part of the long waterfront of Vancouver, which is the principal western seaport of the great Dominion. The berths and wharves of the busy harbour handle most of Canada's trade with the Orient, as well as cargoes for Britain and Europe. The city stands on the shores of Burrard Inlet and English Bay, bounded in the south by the Straits of Georgia and in the south-east by the northern arm of the Fraser River. Its metropolitan area has a population of over half a million.

ON THE SHORES OF LAKE LOUISE

In western Alberta, on the eastern slope of the Rockies, are the two largest and most famous scenic National Parks in Canada—Jasper and Banff. The smaller of these is Banff National Park, which has an area of 2,564 square miles, and it was here that this picture of beautiful Lake Louise was taken. Dominating the scene is the majestic face of Victoria Glacier. The National Parks are maintained by the Federal Government. Many are scenic in character, but others have been established to protect wild life or to preserve historic sites.

N.P.K. III, p. 225.

Aluminium Company of Canada.

THE TUNNELS OF THE KITIMAT PROJECT

By building the Kenney Dam, the engineers of the Kitimat aluminium project created a huge reservoir from which water could be carried by tunnel to the new power house generating electricity for the smelter at Kitimat. The main diversion tunnel, ten miles long and 25 ft. in diameter, was drilled from three points, one of which was the Horetsky adit (opening), which is shown in this picture.

Lake district of northern Manitoba, great deposits of nickel are being developed and a railway is being built to bring the metal out. Already Canada is producing over three-quarters of the world's supply of nickel.

One of the most remarkable feats of construction is the Nechako-Kitimat project, about four hundred miles to the north of Vancouver, in British Columbia. This great work, which will enable aluminium to be produced at Kitimat at the rate of half a million tons each year, has required (i) the building of the Kenney Dam on the River Nechako ; (ii) the construction of ten miles of tunnels through the mountains and of nearly 3,000 feet of penstocks ; (iii) the building of a power station at Kemano to provide power for the aluminium smelter at Kitimat, fifteen miles distant over a high mountain pass. Such projects support the claim that Canada " is witnessing the greatest wave of mineral resources development in its history."

Even without such developments, Canada would have impressive mineral wealth. Her province of Ontario produces gold at such centres as Porcupine,

Red Lake and Kirkland : silver and cobalt at Cobalt : nickel and copper at Sudbury : and iron ore near Fort William, at the western end of Lake Superior. In western Quebec such centres as Rouyn-Noranda produce gold, copper and other metals. The Thetford Mines district of the same province contains fabulously rich deposits of asbestos. Lead, zinc, gold, silver and copper come from British Columbia, where typical centres are Rossland, Copper Mountain and Kimberley. Near Rossland is Traill, with its large ore smelters. Most of the mineral output of Manitoba and Saskatchewan comes from Flin Flon, whose great copper-gold-silver-zinc mine straddles the boundary of these provinces.

Travelling about Canada

All these activities in the Dominion demand good communications and, as we have seen, air, rail and road transport is taking an important part in making it easier for people to travel to the remoter regions where lie the new riches. But even in the south, Canada seeks to improve ways of transport and travel. The St. Lawrence Seaway is being built by Canada and the United States. And in December, 1949, an Act was passed which approved the building of the Trans-Canada Highway. When complete, this great national road will cover a distance of some 4,580 miles, linking province with province and coast with coast. By April, 1952, about 4,260 miles of the Highway had been made, but only about 2,000 miles had been surfaced.

Crossways of the Air

Canada is a crossways for many of the aerial services of the world. It is situated centrally between east and west and is on the All-Red route from Great Britain to the Pacific. Further, parts of Canada sit almost on the top of the world and it is obviously a shorter journey to fly high across Polar regions between, say, Russia and the U.S.A. than to make the aerial voyage round the earth where its circumference is considerably greater.

The Dominion is a key to the airways of the universe when vast distances will be covered in a few hours as commonplace routine, quite apart from its trans-Canada routes and the international routes for air mail. Neither deep water nor the rigours of the Pole will affect the efforts of man to fly by the nearest way from point to point much as does the proverbial crow.

But in the field of aviation, the most revolutionary developments have taken place—as we have already seen—in the opening up of the Canadian North-West, where air travel has done more than anything else to " discover " hitherto desolate and difficult regions of country. To-day, Canadian Pacific Air Lines serving the Far North and the North-West link up with such great world services as T.C.A. (Trans-Canada Air Lines) which not only operates from Pacific to Atlantic, but has trans-Atlantic services to airports in the British Isles.

National Film Board.

LEARNING HIS TRADE

This student at an Ottawa technical school is learning a useful trade for civilian life or a career in one of the services. Canada's modern schools and colleges give expert cultural, scientific and technical instruction, building first-class citizens of the future.

The Story
of the
World and
its Peoples

Countries
of the British
Commonwealth
of Nations

THE FEDERAL PARLIAMENT HOUSE, CANBERRA

Pictorial Press.

Canberra, the capital of the Commonwealth of Australia, stands in its own " Federal Capital Terri-
tory." The capital city has been carefully planned so that there shall be nothing to spoil its beauty.
When finished, it will be one of the most imposing capital cities in the world. The Federal Parliament
House was opened by the late King George VI when Duke of York.

AUSTRALIA, THE ISLAND CONTINENT

TO see the Australian Commonwealth to-day, with its great
cities, its rich rolling farmlands,
and its important manufacturing and
industrial centres, makes it hard to
realise that this vast continent " down
under " was little more than an
unknown wilderness just over 150
years ago.

Terra Australis Incognita, the
Unknown Land of the South, was a
vision that haunted the explorers and
map-makers of the western world for
two thousand years before it became a
reality.

The first Englishman to give a
detailed account of those parts of
Australia that he saw was William
Dampier, a man of many talents. He
was scholar, planter, explorer, and
buccaneer; and he made two voyages
to Australia which he called " the
most barren spot on the face of the
earth." It was left for another Englishman to discover, explore, and chart the
East Coast of Australia and to see the
best of the continent. This man was
Captain James Cook, the greatest
navigator-explorer the world has ever
seen, whose story you can read elsewhere
in these volumes. Cook's report was
much more favourable than the one
Dampier had made nearly a century
earlier. The story of his voyages and the

account he gave of his discoveries roused interest in Australia as a place for colonisation, and in 1788 the first thousand British settlers, under Captain Arthur Phillip, landed to found the township of Sydney on the shores of one of the greatest natural harbours in the world.

Captain Arthur Phillip, the first Governor of New South Wales—for that is all Australia was in the early years—was " the first man to believe in the future of Australia as a white nation at a time when it was unreasonable to believe." Food shortage and rebellion were among the many difficulties that Captain Phillip had to face, and though his Governorship ended in 1792, he left behind an influence and example that are remembered to this day.

The earliest British settlements in Australia were naturally coastal, and coastal exploration had been done by Bass and Flinders seven years after Captain Phillip had founded Australia's chief city, Sydney.

It was not long before men began to wonder what the interior of this new continent contained. The settlement round Sydney was hemmed in by the range of the Blue Mountains across which none found a way for twenty-seven years.

The conquest of the Blue Mountains and the exploration of the continent is a tale of great human endeavour, of wonder and success, of suffering and tragedy. It contains the story of Charles Sturt, one of the earliest and bravest of Australian explorers and discoverer of the great Murray river; of Eyre who, with Wylie, failed in a gallant attempt to penetrate the barren heart of the continent; of Leichhardt, the German botanist who crossed bush and grasslands to the north and gave his life in the cause of

By courtesy of " The Navy."

THE FIRST SETTLEMENT

It was in 1788 that the first real settlement was made in Australia at Sydney Cove, later known as Port Jackson. From this grew the township of Sydney, now a great city of 1½ million people, the capital of New South Wales, and possessing the finest harbour in the world. This picture shows Sydney, with the Governor's House in the background as it was in 1802. Compare this with the picture on p. 232.

Fox Photos.

WHERE GOVERNOR PHILLIP ONCE FARMED

The Botanic Gardens at Sydney occupy the original site of a farm established by Captain Phillip to provide more food for the early colonists. The Gardens look out over Farm Cove and contain a splendid collection of Australian and overseas trees, shrubs and plants.

exploration; of Mitchell, who explored the south; and of Burke and Wills whose expedition to the interior brought them to their death. These are only some of the names in the long list of those who worked to reveal all the mysteries of the great continent. In northern Australia, in Arnhem land which is one of the last strongholds of the Australian aborigines, exploration continues to-day, for there are still small stretches of the continent where white men have yet to tread.

The Early Settlers

With New South Wales as the mother colony, new settlements sprang up: at Hobart, Tasmania, in 1803, to forestall colonisation by the French: at the old convict settlement of Moreton Bay (Queensland), where free settlers came from 1840 onwards to rear sheep and cattle and to develop the town on Moreton Bay into the modern city of Brisbane: in

Western Australia, where French penetration was also feared, and where Captain Fremantle founded the city of Perth in 1829: in what is now Victoria, where John Batman sited a village in 1835, little dreaming that this was the seed of the fine modern city of Melbourne: and in South Australia, where in 1836 the name of the British Queen was taken for the new town of Adelaide at the foot of the Lofty Mountain Ranges.

In 1851, Edward Hargraves discovered gold at Summerhill Creek about 20 miles north of Bathurst. The search which his discovery began revealed gold at Anderson's Creek, near Melbourne, and on the Yarrowee river at a place that was to become world famous as Ballarat. The news flashed across the world bringing emigrants from all parts to Melbourne. Soon the new gold areas of the continent were as rough and roistering as the American California where Hargraves had first noticed the similarity between the gold-bearing soil there and the soil of his native Australia. Other rich goldfields were found at Bendigo, Clunes, Castlemaine and Maryborough, and later at Coolgardie and Kalgoorlie in Western Australia whose rich fields became known as the " Golden Mile."

As the separate colonies of the continent developed so they took up the right to self-government which had been granted them in 1850. By 1860, five of the present States had their own representative assemblies, and

L. T. Sardone.

THIS MEMORIAL COMMEMORATES THE DUTCH DISCOVERER OF STREAKY BAY

Almost a hundred and fifty years before Captain Cook's famous voyage of discovery, Pieter Nuyts, an official of the Dutch East India Company, sailed along the shore of the Great Australian Bight as far as the islands of St. Francis and St. Peter. This monument commemorating his voyage of 1627 in the *Gulden Zeepaert* was erected in 1927 in the main street of Streaky Bay (Flinders).

Western Australia followed in 1890. The establishment of self-government was accompanied by the growth of a national, of an Australian, spirit. It was realised that there were many matters affecting, not only the individual States, but the continent as a whole. Federation had been suggested by Earl Grey in 1850, but it was not until 1899 that representatives from various colonies received the approval by general vote of the Australian people of the scheme they had prepared.

In 1901, a new nation was born —the Commonwealth of Australia, and the first Federal Parliament was opened in May of the same year. The administrative ties that had bound Australia to Great Britain were severed, but their place was taken by the stronger, worthier, and more enduring links of sentiment and friendship. Of her own free will, Australia acknowledges ties of blood and affection to our own country which Australians still call " Home."

A Land of Many Climates

Australia is twenty-five times the size of the British Isles, and nearly as big as the whole of Europe. At present it has fewer people than Greater London, but there is room for millions more.

So great a land has many climates. Nearly half of Australia lies within the Tropics, and the rest lies in warm, temperate regions. The northern parts, where there are hot, wet forests and mangrove swamp, are as near the Equator as Ceylon and Southern India ; the southern parts lie in the same latitudes as the Cape Province of South Africa and have much the same kind of climate. On the Queensland coast the climate is wet and hot enough for planters to grow sugar-cane, bananas, cotton and rubber, and to cultivate coconut palms in great groves facing the sea ; for this is the region where the South-east Trades sing their eternal song and bring moisture from the wide Pacific. In many of the southern parts the climate is not unlike that of the Mediterranean with its long, hot dry summers and its mild, wet winters—ideal country for the cultivation of oranges, grapes, olives, coconuts and other fruits, or for growing grain. It is fortunate that in these regions artesian wells can be sunk to fetch up water from great depths ; water from these wells or from large reservoirs among the hills can be led to fields and orchards in myriads of channels during the dry weather.

Other parts of Australia are great natural grass-lands, especially in the interior of New South Wales and Queensland, where sheep are reared in enormous numbers and where cattle can be fed on the moister lands.

Australian News and Information Service.

WHERE THE DOG SITS ON THE TUCKER BOX

This memorial to the early pioneers in Australia has been set up five miles from Gundagai in New South Wales where the bullock teams were often stuck on the track and where sometimes they halted for the night. The statue was unveiled in 1932 by Mr. J. A. Lyons, then Prime Minister of Australia.

Australia's Riches

Australia has forests, too, of splendid timber and rich deposits of coal and metal ore ; so that Australians who speak in praise of their homeland, as all real Australians do, make no vain boast when they say they have the finest climate in the world and one of the richest countries on the globe in which to live.

But although Australia is a land of splendid opportunities for those who love a free life in the open air, we shall make a great mistake if we suppose that most Australians live active lives on the sheep stations and cattle sta-

tions, the farms and the orchards, and the plantations. At present two-thirds of the Australian population of over 8½ millions live in the six State capitals and large inland towns—they are townsmen and city folk, and get their living much as people of that kind do throughout the civilised world, except perhaps that the splendid Australian climate tempts them to live a freer and more enjoyable life in the open air. Sydney and Melbourne alone contain nearly one-third of the total population of the Australian Commonwealth.

The Australians

A famous Australian writer says:

GOVERNMENT HOUSE, SYDNEY

Pictorial Press.

It is said that the first " Government House " at Sydney was a portable canvas building, bought in London at a cost of £125. The present Government House, which is the residence of the Governor of New South Wales, is a mansion built in the Tudor style. It stands in its own grounds overlooking the Harbour at Farm Cove.

" Probably not two out of every 200 Australians have ever seen a wild kangaroo, although there are thousands of them in the distant ' bush '. Many Australians have never set eyes on a flock of sheep or a herd of cattle larger than one which might be seen within twenty miles of London; yet on some of the large sheep stations out-back, over 100,000 sheep are shorn annually, and herds of 50,000 cattle are not uncommon."

The kind of people Australia needs are not only men and women with good industrial trade or professional qualifications, but especially those who will make use of the rich farming and stock-breeding lands. Speaking in London in 1948, the Lord Mayor of Melbourne said, " We all realise that there are 70 or 80 or 90 million white British people in the world and we want 10 million of them."

The Australian Interior

There are parts of Australia which can never support many people; some of them, indeed, will never provide homes for settlers, for they are desert lands, dry and waterless, where not even goats and camels could find a living ; but even among these desert patches there are areas of good pasture with prosperous little townships here and there.

People once believed that the whole of the Australian interior was a great desert—perhaps because of the unfortunate experiences of the early explorers who made their way into the interior at times of great drought. It is a fact, however, that many parts which their discoveries condemned as arid, barren lands quite unfit for human habitation are now among the richest and most fertile regions of the Australian continent. Irrigation has brought about this wonderful transformation, by leading water in canals and channels from thousands of deep artesian bores, or from reservoirs created by building

IN CUMBERLAND VALLEY, VICTORIA

Planet News Ltd.

These forest giants are some of Australia's tallest trees. They are White Mountain Ash trees growing on Victoria Forests Commission land in the Cumberland Valley. Although on an average only 13½ feet in girth, most of the trees are more than 260 feet high, and the tallest actually tops 300 feet. They are described by the Forests Commission as " the tallest trees in the Southern Hemisphere and the tallest hardwood species in the world." Jarrah and karri are the most famous of the Australian hardwoods ; at one time karri wood was used for paving streets.

dams across the river valleys among the hills where there is generally plenty of rain.

Conquering Drought

Irrigation, too, has done much to rob drought of its terrors—the terrible drought that in past years dried up all the springs and made rivers mere chains of muddy water-holes ; that withered all green and growing things, and brought the torture of death by thirst to the squatter's sheep, the stockmen's cattle and even the wild creatures of the bush; the drought that brought misery and ruin to men and to all other living creatures.

Drought is still a thing to be reckoned with, especially in the wheat districts and in the great pastoral lands where lack of rain at the proper season may do untold damage. For example, in the drought of 1944, no less than 15 million sheep died.

Drought and desert have made water more precious than gold in many parts of Australia, where only engineering and

scientific skill have kept fertile the barren desert lands or protected wheat and pastoral districts from the drought that spells disaster.

It is not only the farmlands that are endangered by drought. An Australian writer has recorded that the great city of Sydney was " on the verge of a water famine " after several dry seasons. " If the ' dry ' had lasted much longer partial evacuation would have been inevitable." It is to safeguard the city's water supply that a big new dam is being built across the Warragamba River, west of Sydney, to hold back 445,000,000,000 gallons of water.

Pioneers of Irrigation

Australia's first large-scale attempts at irrigation began with the great Murray river, at Mildura in Victoria and Renmark in South Australia. Here the pioneers of irrigation were the Chaffey brothers, George and William, who received encouragement from Alfred Deakin, a Victorian Premier who afterwards

Australian News and Information Bureau

IN THE HEART OF AUSTRALIA

These two travellers are looking across a stretch of country near Aynes Rock, south-west of Alice Springs in the heart of the Australian continent. The earth is red and sandy, and supports hardy mulga trees and small plants.

PICKING SULTANA GRAPES IN MILDURA

Mildura, in Victoria, was one of the two pioneer settlements established by the Chaffey brothers, the other being Renmark in South Australia. To-day, there are many such irrigation settlements along the Murray River. Mildura, Renmark, and Berri (South Australia) are particularly noted for their grapes for drying (sultanas and raisins).

became Prime Minister of Australia. The Chaffeys were Canadians who had settled in California and there successfully irrigated poor land. George Chaffey came to Australia in 1886, bought derelict land at Mildura and Renmark and, with his brother, founded a company to transform this land into fertile acres. They had many disappointments and setbacks, and George returned to America when all seemed lost at Mildura and Renmark. But William Chaffey stayed and brought success out of disaster.

The Murray river is now controlled by a Federal Commission, on which New South Wales, Victoria and South Australia are represented. Its precious waters are now regulated by such fine works as the Hume Dam, near Albury. The wall of the dam is over a mile long and the reservoir is the largest in the Southern Hemisphere, with an area of about seventy square miles. This area will presently be increased and the water power used to generate electricity. The Lake Victoria storage, near the South Australian border, is another important feature of the Murray river scheme. In all there are some twenty-six locks and weirs, and money spent so far is in the region of £A.12,000,000.

In addition to the work of the River Murray Commission, much has been done by the various State authorities on the tributaries of the Murray. New South Wales has built the Burrinjuck Dam on the Murrumbidgee and the Wyangala Dam on the Lachlan, and Victoria has the Eildon Dam on the Goulburn, and the Warranga Basin, associated with the same river.

Thanks to works of this kind, vineyards and orchards, and poultry, dairy and market garden farms flourish in the Murray basin, yielding produce to the value of some £A.19,000,000 each year. It has been estimated that without irrigation, the yield could not be more than £A.2,000,000 each year.

Paul Popper.

A BUSH TRACK IN SOUTH AUSTRALIA

This picture of a track through the bush in South Australia conveys to us something of the vastness and solitude of the " outback." In terms of trees and other vegetation, the bush means mulga, dwarf mallee, saltbush and many varieties of eucalyptus, or gum tree. It reminds us that Australia is a continent of many contrasts, with tropical jungles and snow-capped mountains, great cities and vast uninhabited areas, and many varieties of soil and climate.

The Snowy River Scheme

Another full-scale project which was recently undertaken is the Snowy River scheme, which involves seven main dams and between eighty and a hundred miles of tunnels through the Australian Alps. The first stage of the scheme, involving the diversion of much of the Upper Snowy River into the Murrumbidgee, requires four main dams, forty-two miles of tunnel and seven power stations. It is estimated that this stage will take eight years to complete. The water thus harnessed is to be used for both irrigation and generating electric power. The Snowy River scheme is the largest hydro-electric and irrigation scheme in Australia.

It might almost be said that whatever State you visit, you will find projects of this kind already in being or in course of construction. In 1951, Victoria had nearly 750,000,000 acres under irrigation

—as much as in all the other Australian States put together. But this is not enough and work in hand includes the Rocklands Dam, on the Glenelg River, and the Cairn-Curran Reservoir on the Loddon. The biggest project of all is to increase the capacity of the Eildon Dam on the Goulburn River, making it the greatest water storage installation in Australia.

It is Victoria, too, that is carrying out an important hydro-electric project in the Australian Alps, on the Kiewa River, which is a tributary of the Murray. When complete, the scheme will include seven reservoirs, five main dams and six power stations.

In Western Australia millions of pounds are being spent on water supply schemes, which include enlarging the Mundaring Weir whose 430 miles of steel pipe-line supply mixed farmlands and the distant, waterless goldfields.

THE SNOWY RIVER SCHEME

The Snowy River is now the scene of Australia's greatest hydro-electric and irrigation scheme.   This great engineering project requires dams, racelines and tunnels.   Among the latter is the Guthega-Munyang tunnel, on the construction of which these men and their tunnel loader are working.

Photos : Copyright.

The building taking shape in this picture is the Munyang Power Station, which was planned to produce the first Snowy River power in 1954.   Water from the Guthega-Munyang tunnel will reach the Power Station through large pipes and after passing through the turbines, will be returned to the river.

TWO IMPORTANT DAMS

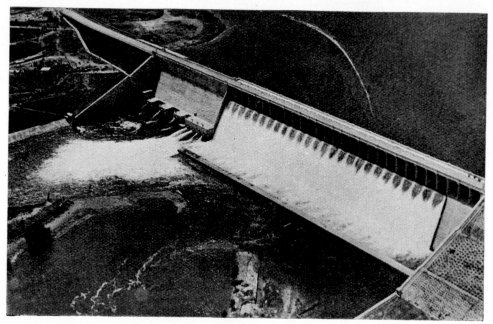

The Hume Dam, near Albury, New South Wales, is one of the great works built to control the waters of the River Murray.   The wall of the dam is more than a mile long.   The reservoir has an area of about seventy square miles and is the largest in the Southern Hemisphere.

One of the more recent Tasmanian power stations is Butler's Gorge, which was completed in October, 1951.   It stands at the foot of the 200-feet-high Clark Dam and uses water from the upper Derwent River.   This picture was taken during the building of the Dam, which is now finished and has created a large artificial lake.

CATTLE AND CORN

Here we see a cattle round-up, " mustering " as it is called in Australia, where fine herds of beef and dairy cattle are the source of a great meat and dairy products industry. The calves in this herd, perhaps, are wanted for branding, or maybe some of the herd is to be sent to market. Whatever the reason, " mustering " is part of the everyday work of an Australian stockman

Photos : Planet News.

These men at Melbourne, Victoria, are at work on a 132,000-bag stack of wheat for export. During 1951–52 season, over 10 million acres of the Commonwealth's fertile land were devoted to wheat production, the largest acreages being in New South Wales and Victoria.

ORANGES AND PINEAPPLES

Camera Press.

Western Australia has about 4,000 acres of citrus orchards, most of which are devoted to oranges. In Western Australia, oranges are grown chiefly in the hills near Perth; most of the crop is consumed within the State, very little being exported.

By courtesy of Rotary Hoes Ltd.

This picture was taken on a mixed farm near Brisbane, Queensland, and shows the farmer cultivating his young pineapple plants with a rotary cultivator. Practically all the Australian pineapple crop comes from Queensland. Pineapples and bananas are grown chiefly in the Moreton and Maryborough districts. Among other tropical fruits grown in Queensland are papaws, custard apples and mangoes.

From the picture by Francis Wheatley.   *Reproduced by courtesy of the Trustees of the National Gallery.*

THE FOUNDER OF AUSTRALIA

The Commonwealth of Australia, made up now of great and important States, was actually founded by Captain Arthur Phillip, R.N., later Vice-Admiral and Governor of New South Wales. It was he who, in January, 1788, instituted a tiny settlement on the shores of Port Jackson, where now stands the great metropolis of Sydney. Captain Phillip was born in London and a national memorial on the wall of St. Mildred's Church, Bread Street, unveiled in 1932, commemorates the fact that he laid the foundation of the colony which became the Commonwealth of Australia.

Australian News and Information Bureau.

SYDNEY HARBOUR BRIDGE FROM THE CITY

The famous harbour at Sydney, capital of New South Wales, Australia, extends for twenty miles inland and is the finest in the world, being surrounded by scenery of surpassing beauty. Sydney Harbour Bridge, opened for traffic in 1932, is the largest arch bridge in existence, its great steel arch having a span of 1,650 feet. With roadway, footways, rail and tram tracks, it is 160 feet wide and at high tide is 170 feet above the water below. The picture above shows the bridge as seen from the entrance to the botanic gardens.

ON A SHEEP STATION

Here we see sheep being mustered on a " station " in New South Wales, the most important wool-producing state in Australia.   Mustering, *i.e.*, rounding up the sheep, is work for the stockmen and takes place, for example, when the sheep are to be sheared.   August and September are the main shearing months.

Photos : Australian News and Information Bureau.

When they have been shorn, sheep are sprayed with " dip," a chemical solution, to protect them from parasites.   From the pens on the right of the picture, the sheep pass through the spraying enclosure, where they are sprayed with " dip " for eight minutes or so.

Once Perth itself was supplied by Mundaring, but the city's water is now supplied by the Canning Dam. In Tasmania, the waters of the Great Lake are harnessed by the Waddamana and Shannon power stations, while the Tarraleah power station generates electricity from the water power of Lake St. Clair. Clark Dam at Butler's Gorge on the River Derwent now helps to increase the output of the Tarraleah power station.

There is not space to mention all that Australia has done and is doing to use her water supplies for irrigation and electric power, or to discuss the various plans that have been put forward to irrigate the desert lands of the continent. More water and more power are vital for future development. As one writer has put it recently: "Australia is the driest continent and water is the key to national prosperity."

Australia and the World

If you look at a map of the world, you will find it easy to understand why Australia was the last continent, except for Antarctica, to be discovered. Australia stood apart from the rest of the world and did not lie on any of the old-established trade routes. Her isolation remains to-day, to some extent; she is two thousand miles from the mainland of Asia and six thousand miles from the United States.

But these great distances have very little meaning now. The fast aircraft of modern times have made a very small place of the entire world. Within little more than three days, we could fly from London to Sydney. Australia herself discovered how little distance counts these days when Japan came so near to invading her during the Second World War.

Thus it is that the growing nation of Australia plays an increasingly important part in world affairs. She takes her full share in British Commonwealth matters and, at the same time, works closely with other Western Powers interested in the Pacific area.

Sunday Times.

PRIMITIVE YOUTH AND MODERN PROGRESS

These aboriginal boys belong to one of the world's most primitive human groups. There are some 47,000 Aborigines in Australia and these three boys were playing at "warriors" near an "outback" airfield in Central Australia when the fortnightly mail plane landed. This photograph by Douglas Glass shows the youthful "blackfellows" gazing in wonder but no longer with fear at this example of modern civilisation.

AUSTRALIA AT WORK

Australian News and Information Bureau.

TRANSPORTING PRIZE RAMS BY AIR

Australians are very air-minded, and Sydney is probably the greatest air centre in the Common-wealth, for from Sydney there are air links with all parts of the world as well as with the capital cities of Australia. Nowadays, even livestock may be carried by air. The rams in this picture made a 340-mile flight from their sheep station to Sydney recently to be exhibited in the Sydney Sheep Show.

IN 1805, when Captain MacArthur brought eight sheep from the Royal flocks in England to New South Wales, he could not have guessed that this was the beginning of Australia's most important primary industry. But to-day Australia has more than 123 million sheep and wool is her most valuable export. During the season 1950–51 over 1,000 million lbs. of wool were produced and the value of wool exports was over £A.633 million.

Most of the sheep are found on the great grasslands of the island continent, which form a broad belt around the dry lands at the heart. The moister parts of these grasslands are used for cattle-rearing. Sheep are reared on the drier parts where there is not too much rain to bring foot-rot and other diseases. Where the sheeplands border on the desert heart, the grass is thin and a shrub called salt-bush provides food for the sheep. Some sheeplands, particularly those in the hotter and wetter areas, have trees growing here and there and so resemble broad, open parks. This type of country is known to geographers as Savannah, and often supports both sheep and cattle.

Every State in Australia has some sheep, but nearly half the total number are found in New South Wales. The sheeplands of New South Wales lie to the west of the Great Dividing Range and in the basin of the Darling-Murray river, which is the chief river system of Australia.

The Sheep Station

If you visit a typical Australian sheep farm you will quickly learn that it is not called a farm; "station" is the correct term. You will also learn that the owner or manager is called the "boss" and the men who work for

16—2

him, " stockmen." The land where the
sheep roam is referred to as the " run."
A large station will probably be divided
into what you will be tempted to call
" fields," but the proper Australian
name is " paddocks." Each paddock
is large enough for about 5,000 sheep.

Most sheep stations have an area of
about 1,000 to 5,000 acres, but quite
a number have more than 50,000 acres,
and some 100,000 acres or more. A
station will probably be forty or fifty
miles from its neighbour and very
much farther from the post-office and
railway. A sheep station has therefore
often to be a little world of its own,
holding all the stores and equipment
it needs. It may well have more people
working on it than live in many small
English towns. Aircraft, as well as
cars and lorries, are used for transport
and the wealthy grazier may well have

his private aerodrome and plane. If
the doctor is wanted in an emergency
he, too, may come by air, and when
the time of the great sheep shows
comes round, animals for show may
travel by air from the station.

There are sure to be horses on the
station. They are needed by the boundary riders, who patrol the fences of
the vast paddocks, mending any breaks
and reporting any which need materials
or special labour from the head station.
They are needed, too, by the stockmen
for such work as mustering ; that is,
rounding up the sheep.

August and September are the main
shearing months. Nowadays most
Australian sheep-shearing is done with
shears fixed to a power-shaft by flexible
metal tubing, so that shearers can use
them at any angle. One man can
satisfactorily shear two hundred sheep

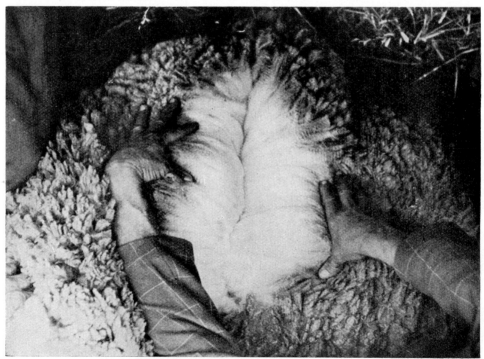

Australian News and Information Bureau.

SHOWING THE " CRIMP " IN THE WOOL

Well crimped or frilled wool is crisp, elastic and most satisfactory from the point of view of spinning.
The Corriedale ram hidden by the fine fleece shown here was sold for 1,000 guineas after a recent
Melbourne sheep show. This breed was originally evolved in New Zealand by crossing British breeds
with merinos and is a dual purpose type, yielding both excellent wool and mutton.

Pictorial Press.

EXPERT SHEARERS HANDLING A CLIP

A good shearer can handle from 180 to 200 sheep in a day. In the large shearing sheds as many as 4,000 sheep may be shorn in a day. The yield per sheep averages 8½ lb. greasy weight, but some of the heaviest wool-producing sheep will yield 15 lb., perhaps more. Some rams have produced as much as 40 lb. within a year.

a day, but the Australian record is 321 in 7 hours 41 minutes.

Australian Wheat

Among the people brought out by the First Fleet in 1788 there was only one farmer. The land they came to had never before been farmed and the first wheat farm, established by Captain Phillip where the Botanical Gardens of Sydney now stand, was a failure. To-day wheat is the most important Australian crop. During 1950–51 over 11½ million acres were sown to wheat and yielded over 184 million bushels. Wheat exports for this period amounted to more than 2¼ million tons valued at over £A.74 million. It may well be that the bread in a British larder had its beginnings on a farm in Australia, for much Australian wheat comes to Britain.

The wheatlands run in a belt about 150 miles wide, from the Darling Downs in Queensland, through New South Wales and Victoria and well into South Australia. Another smaller belt runs from around Geraldton on the west coast of Western Australia to just north of Albany on the southern coast of the same State. April and May are the usual sowing months and the crop is harvested in November and December.

Beef and Dairy Cattle

Australia is also the home of fine dairy produce. Dairy farming is an important industry along the coasts of Queensland and New South Wales ; in the Gippsland region of Victoria, where are some of the world's finest dairy cattle; and on the irrigated south-western coastal plain of Western Australia. During 1950–51 Victoria led the way in the production of butter and cheese, making over 58,000 tons of butter and more than 22,700 tons of cheese.

Central Press.

CATTLE CROSSING A NEW SOUTH WALES RIVER

Rivers are no obstacle to the Australian stockmen and their herds, as this picture shows. The vastness of the Commonwealth and the enormous size of its sheep and cattle stations are realised from the fact that a herd like this may travel 1,000 miles or more along pioneer stock routes.

Already a great beef-cattle country, Australia may before long take the place of Argentina as a leading meat producer. Her cattle lands run in a broad arc from the Kimberley district of north Western Australia, across the northern part of the Northern Territory and then across much of Queensland. Queensland, indeed, is the chief beef-producing and beef-exporting State of the Commonwealth of Australia. During 1950–51, she had nearly $6\frac{3}{4}$ millions of the $15\frac{1}{4}$ million cattle in Australia.

Like the sheep stations, Australian cattle stations cover vast tracts of territory. The cattle runs of the Northern Territory are said to be the largest in the world ; the Alexandria station, which spreads across the Barkly Table-land, covers 11,262 square miles and has a herd of over 80,000 cattle. At such places you may see the tough, wiry stockmen with their long, hide whips rounding up beasts for market.

" Air Beef "

Getting a " mob " of cattle to market is often a dangerous and anxious operation, involving a long trek over one or other of the great stock routes, where, in bad times, water may be scarce and where a stampede at night might scatter the cattle and leave the hands in unknown country to die of thirst. Life is often lonely and hazardous for the station hands ; even a visit to a neighbour may mean a journey of a hundred and fifty miles, perhaps more.

As we have seen, air travel plays an important part in linking up station

MUTTON, LAMB AND BEEF

Planet News.

Once sheep were raised only for their wool; but with the coming of refrigeration, sheep were reared for mutton and lamb for sale overseas, especially in Victoria, New South Wales, and South Australia; it was in New South Wales that this picture of sheep entering the pen of a meat works was taken.

Australian News and Information Bureau.

During the summer large herds of cattle pasture on the Dargo High Plains in the Australian Alps, and when the winter snow comes drovers, dogs, and horses bring the cattle down to paddocks in the lowlands. The cattle in this picture have just completed their journey over the high mountains.

A SHAFT HEAD ON " THE GOLDEN MILE "

This modern, steel fabricated structure is the poppet head, or shaft head, of the Perseverance Mine at Kalgoorlie, whose " Golden Mile " is the richest goldfield in Australia. The field has been in continuous production since 1893 and now employs about six thousand men. More than $55\frac{1}{4}$ million fine oz. of gold, worth more than £A.344 million, have been won from " The Golden Mile," which is still providing rich yields.

with station and homestead with home-stead. In the Kimberley district of the North-west it has also been proved a sure and better way of getting carcass meat from the stations " out back " to the coast. Thanks to the air freight planes of Australian National Airways, the Glenroy cattle killing and chilling plant now stands on the Mount House station in the central Kimberleys, whence the chilled meat is flown to the freezing works at Wyndham for shipment. Instead of travelling three hundred miles along the stock-routes—a journey that only older cattle were strong enough to make—cattle are now handled at Glenroy and flown as carcass meat to Wyndham, a mere 160 miles by air. The perils of the stock-route

are avoided, cattle is in prime condition when it is killed and younger beasts can be handled—all of which means more profit for the station and so more money for development. The value of this system was shown in the drought year of 1952, when conditions on the stock-routes were so bad that few of the cattle stations of the Kimberleys would have sent beef to market, had it not been for Glenroy and the freight planes.

Fruit, Vines and Sugar Cane

It is said that Captain Bligh (of *Bounty* fame), who was an early Gover-nor of New South Wales, planted the first apple trees in Tasmania. To-day the island State of the Commonwealth

FELLING A GUM TREE

Australian News and Information Bureau.

To be an efficient axeman you need strong muscles, a keen eye, and perfect balance. To fell this lofty gum, the axemen stand on springboards about 15 feet above the ground. The tree into which their keen axes bite is a Flooded, or Rose, Gum, which bushmen sometimes call the Sydney Blue Gum, or Woollybutt. The specimen seen in this picture is typical; it reaches a height of 145 feet, has a 12-foot butt, and weighs about 11 tons. The wood is particularly suitable for building work.

249

is the chief source of the Australian crop and Tasmanian apples are world famous. The most important orchards are along the Huon Valley, near Hobart, but another important apple-growing area is near Launceston, in north Tasmania.

Fruit-growing generally is an important part of Australian primary production, and as we have already seen, much of it flourishes because great rivers like the Murray and Murrumbidgee are used to irrigate the farms and orchards of the south-eastern States. Apples, pears, peaches and plums are among the fruits grown in Victoria and New South Wales, and the latter State also provides large crops of citrus fruits. The orchards and farms of South Australia provide apples, oranges, apricots and other fruit, also almonds and olives, but this State is particularly noted for its vineyards. Approximately 22 million gallons of wine are produced each year in South Australia and there are some 28,500 vineyards on irrigated land, the total land area allotted to vineyards averaging about 125,000 acres.

Queensland is famous for the tropical crops which grow in the coastal regions. Because most of Queensland lies within the Tropics, her farmers on the north-east Pacific shore can grow bananas, pineapples and similar tropical crops. Queensland is the only sugar-producing area in the world where the cane is cut and processed entirely by white labour before it is shipped from such ports as Cairns, Mackay, Bundaberg and Brisbane. Some sugar cane is also grown in New South Wales, along the coast northwards from the Clarence River.

Mineral Riches

It would be very wrong to imagine that Australia's wealth lies almost entirely in her pastoral lands, agriculture, orchards and vineyards. The Commonwealth has great mineral riches; indeed, it was the discovery of gold near Bathurst in New South Wales, by Edward Hargraves in 1851, that first brought settlers to Australia in really large numbers. Since then much other mineral wealth, including uranium, has been discovered and mining has become a major industry, the output of which in 1951 was valued at over £A.119 million.

The chief gold-producing area is the *Kalgoorlie* field in Western Australia, chanced upon by Pat Hannan and Tom Flanigan in 1893, a year after Bayley and Ford had discovered gold at Coolgardie, a short distance to the south-west. There was gold, indeed, but there was little or no water. How, then, could men remain in the desert to mine the precious deposits? The answer came from John Forrest (later Lord Forrest), explorer and State Premier, and C. Y. O'Connor, an Irish engineer, who together planned the piping of water across the desert to Kalgoorlie, which still obtains its supplies in this way.

In 1950 Western Australia produced nearly £A.9½ million worth of gold. Other important sources are *Mt. Morgan* in Queensland; the *Bendigo* and *Ballarat* districts of Victoria; and *Broken Hill*, New South Wales. Gold is also produced at *Tennant Creek*, a township in the Northern Territory on the Stuart Highway linking the northern railhead of Birdum with that of Alice Springs in the south.

But gold is not the greatest mineral product in value or quantity. Of the figure of £A.119 million already mentioned, 31 per cent. was earned by the lead-zinc-silver mines, 27 per cent. by the coal industry. Lead, zinc and silver (and some gold and other metals) are all produced at *Broken Hill*, New South Wales, which is Australia's largest single mining field. The smelter and refinery for Broken Hill's lead is at *Port Pirie*, South Australia, while the zinc is either shipped untreated or first treated in South Australia and then shipped to

SILVER AND GOLD

Australian News and Information Service.

Broken Hill stands near the South Australian border, about 700 miles west of Sydney. Its deposits of silver-lead-zinc ores are among the richest in the world. The picture shows us part of the Albert Morris Park, part of a great improvement scheme in and around " The Hill," and (background) the vast Open Cut.

Australian News and Information Service.

The Golden Mile of Kalgoorlie, Western Australia, is the richest goldfield in Australia and it has been producing gold continuously since 1893. The picture shows a miner drilling a lode for blasting out the gold-bearing ore. This ore is colourless and contains gold in a finely divided state.

NEWCASTLE SKYLINE

This picture of part of the huge Broken Hill Pty. Steel Works at Newcastle, New South Wales, reminds us that this important city is often described as "the industrial capital of Australia." Newcastle stands on the fringe of Australia's largest coalfields and is a centre for mining, iron and steel, and other industries.

Risdon, Tasmania, for smelting. Other sources of lead and zinc include *Mt. Isa* in Queensland; *Captain's Flat* in New South Wales ; and *Read-Roseberry* in Tasmania. Copper is produced at *Mt. Morgan*, Queensland, and *Mt. Lyell*, Tasmania.

Coal and Iron

But industry relies upon coal and iron, and these are found in plenty in Australia. The richest coalfield is the New South Wales Coal Basin, which extends from *Newcastle* and *Maitland* in the north to *Wollongong* in the south, and as far west as *Lithgow*. Other coalfields include *Ipswich*, south-west of Brisbane ; *Collie* and *Geraldton*, in Western Australia; and *Fingal*, Tasmania. Brown coal is produced at *Leigh Creek*, South Australia, and at *Yallourn* and *Bacchus Marsh* in Victoria. Extensive near-surface deposits of black coal are being worked by open-cast methods at *Blair Athol*, near Clermont in the north Queensland coastal region. They are said to be the largest known deposits of their kind in the southern hemisphere.

Australia has two major sources of iron ore : the Middleback Ranges in South Australia, where there are literally hills of the ore, the chief being *Iron Monarch* and *Iron Knob ;* and *Yampi Sound*, off Western Australia, where vast deposits are now being worked. These sources supply the iron and steel mills of *Newcastle* and *Port Kembla* in New South Wales, and *Whyalla* in South Australia.

Geologists think that the supplies of ore at Iron Monarch and Iron Knob may not last more than fifty years. This is one of the reasons why the vast deposits at Yampi Sound are being rapidly exploited. Most of the iron ore is on two islands—Cockatoo and Koolan. It is on the former that the deposits are being worked, and it is estimated that there are 20 million tons above, and a further 20 million tons just below, high water level.

Picture Cockatoo Island, washed by the waters of Yampi Sound on the south and by the Timor Sea on the north. The island is a little under four miles in length and just over a mile across at its widest point. Seven million Australian pounds are being spent on the development of this rugged isle, where a forbidding 400 ft. high cliff of iron ore is now being worked.

Machinery for working the ore had to be brought entirely by sea and included giant electric shovels, heavy American trucks (each capable of taking a load of 26 tons), and elaborate equipment for crushing the ore and loading it from the specially-built jetty. "Specially-built" is the phrase which summarises most of the activity on Cockatoo Island. Roads have been built, homes for the work-people and a school for their children. Special ships have been built to carry the ore on its 3,000-mile voyage to the blast furnaces of Newcastle and Port Kembla, the first shipment being made on the *Iron Yampi* in July, 1951. These vessels are also used to bring essential supplies to the island, including water.

The company responsible for this

Planet News.

THE HUGE OIL RIG AT EXMOUTH GULF, WESTERN AUSTRALIA

On December 4th, 1953, it was announced that high grade crude oil had been struck in the Exmouth Gulf district of Western Australia. Prospecting and drilling were the work of a joint Australian and American company, which erected this huge oil rig at the test site near Learmonth. The drill is about 140 feet high and is one of the largest in the world. The pipes can be seen within the derrick. Under the canopy at the base of the rig are powerful diesel engines.

great project, Australian Iron and Steel Ltd., is doing everything possible to make life pleasant for the pioneers of Yampi Sound. Life can be uncomfortable in these parts during the humid wet season, and the houses have therefore been built on piles to give the best ventilation. A canteen, mess-room, medical room and a tennis court are all to be found on this remarkable island which promises to yield a million tons of ore and more each year. As the Australian magazine *National Development* said recently : " The Yampi development takes its place with other notable pioneer ventures and is very much in the Australian tradition. . . . The success of this venture, which is now beyond question, gives tangible evidence of what can be done in those regions given resource, energy, technical skill and financial strength."

Uranium and Oil

Australia's natural resources also include tin, tungsten, mica and titanium. Particularly important are the recent discoveries of uranium at *Radium Hill* in South Australia, *Rum Jungle* in the Northern Territory, and other places.

For many years, Australian geologists searched for oil without real success. Some was found, but not in worthwhile quantities. Then, in 1949, it was announced that one of the world's largest potential oilfields had been discovered in the Exmouth Gulf area of Western Australia. By the end of 1953 drilling at Learmonth had confirmed the presence of a rich field of high-grade oil.

Oil is responsible for two other important developments in Australia.

Pictorial Press.

STACKING COPPER BLISTER BARS

The Mount Morgan Mine in Queensland yields valuable copper-gold ore. These copper bars contain gold recovered from the ore.

South of Fremantle, Western Australia, on the shores of Cockburn Sound, the new township of Medina and Kwinana oil refinery are being built. At Geelong and Altona, in Victoria, there are also new oil refineries, and a pipeline, the first of its kind in Australia, has been constructed to carry refined spirit into Melbourne, the State capital. These new refineries were not the result of the Exmouth Gulf discoveries, but were planned to handle imported crude oil.

To complete our picture of Australia at work we must now look at her great manufactures, her secondary industries, as they are sometimes called. It is amazing how they have forged ahead in recent years: indeed, some writers have described the process as " a revolution." As might be expected, the Second World War spurred Australians to produce for themselves the goods and commodities which they could no longer get from elsewhere; but even before the war began, the steady increase in Australian secondary industries was gathering speed. During the period 1950–51, the output of manufacturing industries was worth more than £A.2,000 million ! Manufacturing is now Australia's biggest single economic activity, employing almost double the number of persons engaged in the agricultural, pastoral and mining industries put together !

Manufactured Goods

Within a century, the country " has reached the stage where, with a population of but 8½ million people, it is producing motor cars and trucks, tractors, front line aircraft, ships, newsprint, lifesaving drugs, heavy earthmoving equipment and, in fact, almost the whole range of products necessary to a modern society. It is, indeed, easier to list those few fields in which Australian manufacturers do not participate than to list their achievements." By September, 1952, the manufacturing industry was employing nearly a million people, in other words, about 28 per

MAKING POWER FROM WATER

By harnessing her lakes and rivers, Tasmania has become one of the most highly electrified states in the world. Among her many great hydro-electric power stations are those of Waddamana, which are seen in this picture. Like the Shannon station, Waddamana " A " and " B " use water from the Great Lake catchment and from the Ouse River. Waddamana " A," which was first put into commission in 1916, is the oldest of the major stations in Tasmania. Waddamana " B " was not completed until 1949.

cent. of the total working population of Australia.

Power for Industry

Any manufacturer wanting to establish a new factory will like to have readily available power for his machinery, work-people to operate his machines, good transport to take his products from the factory and markets within easy reach where his products can be sold. It is not surprising, therefore, to find that New South Wales and Victoria are the main manufacturing States, with South Australia coming next.

In New South Wales, factory development at such places as Wollongong, Newcastle and Sydney has been helped by the nearness of the coalfields. This is also true of Ipswich, Queensland, which is one of the main centres for the construction of railway rolling stock. Yallourn power station in Victoria, the second largest in Australia (the largest is Bunnerong in Sydney), provides cheap electric power for the factories of Melbourne, Ballarat and Geelong. In Tasmania there is abundant hydro-electric power, and industry embraces paper mills, food products and newsprint.

Many Manufactures

During the war practically all the clothing required by the Allied forces in the Pacific was produced by the textile mills of New South Wales and Victoria. Factories in Western Australia make food products, tobacco, clothing and paper; in Queensland, sugar, leather goods and food products. There are also in the Commonwealth some two hundred agricultural engineering concerns which produce much of the machinery used by Australian farmers and also provide some for export. Machinery and equipment made in Australia are helping in the Colombo Plan.

Agent-General for Western Australia.

MINING IRON ORE IN WESTERN AUSTRALIA

This is Arbitration Cove on Koolan Island, one of the rich iron ore islands of Yampi Sound. Activity is greatest on neighbouring Cockatoo Island whence specially built ships take ore to Newcastle and Port Kembla in New South Wales.

SEEING AUSTRALIA

Keystone.

Canberra, the national capital of Australia, stands in its own territory a hundred and forty-five miles south-west of Sydney. The city is based upon plans submitted by W. B. Griffin in an international competition in 1911. This aerial view shows part of the suburbs.

AUSTRALIA, then, is a busy progressive continent, rich in natural resources and powerful in industry, where a good and full life awaits anyone who is prepared to take a hand in building the Commonwealth's prosperity. But Australia is more than a bustling workshop building for the future. She possesses some of the finest cities in the world, where life is as comfortable as it is in London or New York. Her various States are graced with wonderful scenic beauties, and with unique animal and plant life that is described elsewhere in these volumes.

Western Australia

Many people get their first glimpse of Australia at *Fremantle*, the out-port of Perth named after Captain (afterwards Sir) Charles Fremantle, who landed here in 1829 from his ship, the *Challenger*. Fremantle is the chief port of Western Australia and stands but twelve miles from *Perth*, the State capital on the Swan River. Perth is a city of splendid streets and lovely gardens. Its University buildings are among the finest in the Commonwealth; its thousand acres of King's Park provide many travellers with their first taste of the beauties and aroma of the Australian bush. Amid noble trees and brilliantly coloured vegetation, it is hard to believe that you are still within walking distance of the heart of the city.

Another favourite pleasure haunt not far from Perth is the Yanchep National Park. Here you can sail, swim, canoe and play tennis amid 6,000 acres of natural bushland; and when these pleasures are exhausted, there are the famous limestone caves to be explored.

Perth, with Fremantle, has a population of some 351,000, which is more than half the total population of the State. For although Western Australia is the largest State in the Commonwealth, much of her land is dry country and her population of 622,000 is smaller than that of any State except Tasmania. Although Western Australia is sometimes spoken of as the loneliest of Australian States (because she is separated from the eastern States by the desert, and by the Great Australian Bight), she makes important contributions to the wealth of the continent, as we have already seen.

The most thickly populated and active part of the State is the south-west. Here, stretching south-eastwards from Northampton along the line of the Darling Range, as far east as Merredin and as far south as Ongerup, are the State's rich wheatlands; here, too, are the sheeplands of Western Australia. In the extreme south-west, in the Bridgetown and Mount Barker districts, are the orchards whence come the famous red-case apples. Dairy cattle flourish on the coastal plains between Perth and Albany. Jarrahdale, Pemberton and other centres have timber mills to handle the fine hardwoods—those great karri and jarrah trees that tower to heights of over 200 feet. In the Perth-Fremantle-Northam district grapes are grown for wine-making. The south-west, too, has its industry—*Collie* is the coal-mining centre of Western Australia.

The northern parts of the State are virtually isolated from the south by the barren " Ninety-mile Beach " and "Sandy Desert." The Kimberley district is noted for its beef cattle, for which Wyndham, with its meat works, is the chief outlet.

Travelling eastwards from Western Australia, we might prefer to avoid the Great Australian Bight, whose weather is often unpleasant enough to daunt the hardiest seafarer. We might go by air, of course, for the Commonwealth has one of the most highly-developed airway systems in the world, with all the main centres linked by the services of such companies as Australian National Airways, Trans-Australia Airways and Ansett Airways. During 1949–50 internal air services in Australia flew over 36½ million

Pictorial Press.

THE UNIVERSITY OF WESTERN AUSTRALIA

This beautiful building is part of the University of Western Australia at Perth, the State capital. The University was founded in 1911 and owes much to Sir Winthrop Hackett, who left his fortune to the foundation. The oldest University in Australia is that of Sydney, which was founded more than a century ago. In 1946, an Australian National University was established at Canberra, the Federal capital, for post-graduate scholars and research workers.

CITY OF SUNSHINE

Pictorial Press.

From King's Park, we can look across a stretch of the Swan River known as Perth Water to the harbour and city of Perth, the capital of Western Australia. The Park, which covers a thousand acres, is actually within the city and displays all the beauty and colour of natural bush.

Keystone.

This picture of St. George's Terrace, Perth, shows what spacious avenues and fine buildings there are in this beautiful city. Perth is often called the " City of Sunshine " because it has more hours of sunshine than any other State capital in Australia.

17—2

miles and carried nearly $1\frac{1}{2}$ million passengers, over 44,000 tons of freight and more than 2,500 tons of mail. But as we want to see as much of this great country as we can, we will make the 1,617-mile desert journey from Perth to Adelaide by rail across the great Nullarbor Plain. Travelling this way we go by the Trans-Australian Railway, which links Kalgoorlie in Western Australia with Port Augusta in South Australia.

The railways connecting the capital cities of Australia suffer from the great disadvantage of being constructed on three different gauges, which prevents long " through " journeys from west to east or vice versa. For example, to travel from Fremantle to Brisbane by way of Adelaide and Melbourne would involve us in no less than six changes of trains and three or four of gauge. As a result of the Railway Standardization Agreement Act of 1949, however, plans are now in hand for converting the railways of the Commonwealth to a standard gauge.

South Australia

Adelaide, the capital of South Australia, is a beautiful city of spacious boulevards, lovely parks and pleasant open spaces, nestling at the foot of the Lofty Mountain Ranges which are the city's playground. Names in the Lofty Mountain countryside would surprise and interest us. How did such pleasant country places come to be called " Aldgate " and " Piccadilly " ?

Adelaide was founded by Colonel William Light, a talented officer with a very colourful career. Before becoming Surveyor-General of South Australia, he saw service in the Royal Navy and the Army, and then in the Egyptian Navy. He was, we are told, " artist, musician, mechanic, seaman, soldier, surveyor and town-planner." From him Adelaide got its long streets, straight as Roman roads, and its delightful open spaces. His statue can be seen there to-day. The population of the city he founded was 459,000 in 1952, and in this same year the total population of South Australia numbered 751,500.

Wheat is the most important of South Australia's crops. The State is also noted for its vineyards and for its orchards, which lie mostly in the irrigated areas of the Murray River. Along Spencer Gulf are industrial outlets like Whyalla, which handles ore from Iron Knob and Iron Monarch; and Port Pirie, with its large lead smelter and refinery, and plant for treating uranium ore.

From Adelaide we can cross the Commonwealth from south to north, using the railway that follows the route of the Overland Telegraph and goes up through the salt lakes to Alice Springs, and the Stuart Highway. Those lakes (including Eyre, Frome, Torrens and Gairdner) are coloured blue on some maps, but they are little more than huge salt pans; only for a little time after the rains are they covered by shallow but salty water.

Well to the west of us as we travel north from Port Augusta, not so far from Pimba on the railway across the Nullarbor Plain, is the main centre of the long-range weapons (rockets) range. A good name was chosen for this place. It is called *Woomera*, which is the aboriginal name for the wooden stick by which a throwing spear is launched. On an isolated part of this range, too, atomic weapons have been tested. But Australia's first experience of atomic tests was in October, 1952, when Britain and Australia together carried out a successful atomic explosion at the Monte Bello Islands off the coast of Western Australia.

The railway will take us to Alice Springs, a Northern Territory township in the desert heart of the continent. Here, in the interior, there are some stock-bearing lands, but there is also the terrible desert, where thirst and heat will kill the unwary traveller.

The Northern Territory

In the Northern Territory, and particularly in Arnhem Land, are Aboriginal

Central Press.

ADELAIDE FROM THE AIR

This picture of the capital of South Australia shows many of the fine buildings which contribute to the beauty of this noble city. In the foreground we see part of the University buildings. The trees and lawns in the centre of the picture surround Government House, to the right of which is Parliament House.

Reserves, the home of the " blackfellows " who are all that remain of the original primitive inhabitants of the continent. In the days of Captain Phillip there were about 300,000 blackfellows in Australia; now their total is estimated at about 52,000. Blackfellows can be seen elsewhere in the Commonwealth, but Arnhem Land is the only part where they have still been known to resist the approach of the white man. They live in much the same way as men did in the Stone Age. They hunt and track with a skill that has long been lost to modern man; they use stone knives and axes, spears which they hurl, and cunningly shaped *boomerangs* and throwing sticks.

The railway ends at Alice Springs, but from here we can travel by the Stuart Highway, the Great North Road of Australia, which links the railhead at *Alice Springs* with the railhead at *Birdum*, whence a train will take us to Darwin. The Highway runs all the way from Alice Springs to Darwin via Newcastle Waters and Birdum. It is over 950 miles long and was completed in December, 1940, as a military supply route. Another important road built during the war years links the Northern Territory with Mount Isa, in Queensland.

The fine airfield at *Darwin* is the first Australian port of call for practically all aircraft coming from Europe and Asia. Darwin is also the headquarters of the Administrator of the Northern Territory.

Queensland

Queensland is the second largest State of the Commonwealth and has a popula-

Central Press.

AT THE CENTRE OF AUSTRALIA

Alice Springs is actually the geographical centre of the island continent of Australia. This Northern Territory township, however, even if it is isolated from the great centres of population, has a fine school equipped with fluorescent lighting and modern equipment as this picture shows.

tion of over 1,247,000, of which some 464,000 live in *Brisbane*, the State capital. Seen from the summit of Mount Coot-tha, Brisbane shows itself to be a busy city set astride the Brisbane River about twenty miles from Moreton Bay, where the river enters the sea. The city is different from all other State capitals because it is in sub-tropical latitudes. Its streets are coloured by exotic trees and shrubs—among them jacaranda, poinsettia, hibiscus and bougainvillea. Within fifty miles of the city are Southport, Brisbane's holiday resort, and Mount Tambourine, where flying foxes cluster on the fruit trees in splendid woods of tropical palms. Another show place for visitors is " Australia's Lost World "—the 4,800-acre reserve of Lamington National Park, which is the natural home of thousands of white cockatoos.

Queensland's Pacific coast is fringed by one of the most amazing natural wonders of the world—the Great Barrier Reef. There are 1,250 miles of the Reef, which is thought to be the largest single mass of coral in the world. Running from Torres Strait in the north to Lady Elliot Island, off Sandy Cape, in the south, the Reef was built—and is still being built—by countless numbers of tiny sea creatures called polyps. Its fantastic beauty embraces all the colours in the rainbow, and it is almost impossible to describe the castles, grottoes and other coral formations which can be seen in this fairyland of wonder and loveliness.

The pools and channels of the Reef are the home of many fish and other sea creatures. Here dwells the loathsome stonefish, whose thirteen poisonous spines bring slow and painful death to any living thing that touches them. Here also can be found the beautiful butterfly cod, and the mudskipper, which likes to climb the roots of mangrove trees. Turtles, bêche-de-mer (sea slug) and pearlshell also come from the Reef. But the headquarters of Queensland's pearling and sea-slug fisheries are Thursday Island, in Torres Strait, north-west of Cape York. Bêche-de-mer is considered a great delicacy in some parts of the world, particularly China.

If you look at a map of Australia you will notice how the Great Dividing Range extends from Tasmania to the Cape York peninsula, dividing the broad inland plains from the narrow coastal plain. The shorelands of Queensland are hot and wet and produce many tropical crops such as sugar, bananas, pineapples, oranges and papaws, all of which are raised by white labour. Along the coast are a number of important centres such as *Bundaberg, Rockhampton, Townsville* and *Cairns*. From several of these ports there is good road and rail communication with the rich cattle and sheep lands of the interior.

Probably the most fertile region of Queensland lies in the south of the State, on the Darling Downs, on the western slopes of the Great Dividing Range, where stands *Toowoomba*, the second city of Queensland and the home of 40,000 people. Here are rich dairy herds and golden wheat-lands. It is said that the average yearly yield of wheat from this rich district is " well over one million bushels," and it is not surprising that the Darling Downs are sometimes described as " the richest agricultural region in the whole of Australia."

Queensland's mineral wealth has already been described. In 1950 the products of her mines were valued at more than £A.16¼ million. Her forests of gum, pine, cedar and other woods are important.

E.N.A.

QUEENSLAND'S CAPITAL FROM THE AIR

Brisbane straddles the Brisbane River about eighteen miles from the sea. This aerial view of the city where the sun seems always to shine shows us the Victoria Bridge, and the City Hall, whose tower is 320 feet high and whose clock face is 16 feet in diameter. The black dome covers an assembly hall that will seat 2,500 people. Beyond, leading to the Victoria Bridge, is Queen Street, the chief business centre of the city.

New South Wales

New South Wales has the largest city in the Commonwealth as her capital. This is *Sydney* which, like Melbourne, has a population of some 1½ millions. Sydney stands on one of the finest harbours in the world, where large liners can come right up into the very heart of the city and berth at Circular Quay.

The streets of Sydney are lined with many splendid buildings, which include huge department stores of the kind common in America, where goods of every kind can be bought. Some of these stores have over thirty departments and employ hundreds of assistants.

Sydney's beautiful suburbs where business men have their homes are on the many arms of the great harbour; one of the most important is Mosman Bay, which has pretty houses embowered in trees at the edge of the blue waters. Ferry boats ply constantly between the suburbs and the city. Sydney is also served by an underground railway, electric trains to the suburbs and extensive tram and omnibus services.

ON THE GREAT BARRIER REEF　*Paul Popper.*

If you look carefully at this picture of a coral formation, you will see a giant clam. The clam can be found on the right-hand side of the picture, where the zigzag shape of its open shell is seen. Giant clams are often as much as 3 feet in length and are the largest shellfish in the world.

Sydney's Giant Bridge

Sydney is justly proud of her mighty steel bridge that was built by a famous Middlesbrough firm across the harbour. Its main span is 1,650 feet long; with its approaches, the bridge is 3,770 feet from terminal pier to terminal pier. It carries two electric railway and two tramway tracks, a four-line traffic roadway and two footways across the harbour at a height of 172 feet above high-tide level. The steel for the bridge was all fabricated in Australia and the granite and cement were local products. The total capital cost of building this, the largest arch bridge in the world, was £9,743,252.

Another great engineering achievement to be seen in Sydney is the graving dock, called "Captain Cook Dock," which was opened by the Duke of Gloucester, as Governor-General of Australia, in 1945. Over 30 acres of land had to be reclaimed from the harbour waters before work on the dock could begin; 700,000 tons of concrete were used and 3,500 men employed to build the dock, which is capable of taking an 80,000-ton liner for overhaul.

Bathing Beaches

Sydney's bathing beaches are immensely popular. Thanks to their delightful climate, practically all Australians are great sportsmen and lovers of the open air; bathing is one of the greatest summer attractions. Bondi, Manly Beach, Freshwater, Collaroy, Avalon, Palm Beach and other spots are the week-end haunt of thousands. At one bathing beach as many as 10,000 people may be in the water at the same time.

At these beaches the joy of bathing is sometimes interrupted by the clang of an alarm bell, and those who

AUSTRALIA

Australian News and Information Bureau

Although the development of heavy industries has made rapid progress in recent years, Australia is still largely concerned with pastoral and agricultural products. Today her wool production easily surpasses that of any other country in the world. There are about 120 million sheep on the farms and the value of the wool clip has been over £600,000,000 in a single year. Here we see a drover with some of his charges on a sheep station in the State of Victoria.

Captain Phillip, first Governor of New South Wales, was the real discoverer of Sydney Harbour in 1788, and he described it as "the finest natural harbour in the world," a statement no one would contradict. Phillip founded and named the city after Lord Sydney. Today it is the largest city of Australia and capital of New South Wales. The view above is of Sydney Harbour from Macquarie Street.

Photos: Australian News and Information Bureau

Perth, a photograph of which is shown above, is the capital of Australia's largest but least populated State, Western Australia. The city is built on both shores of a broad reach of the Swan River, some twelve miles from its mouth, and its founders in 1829 had a wonderful eye for the preservation of its natural beauty. Behind the city are the Darling Ranges and a national park and bird sanctuary.

TASMANIA—AUSTRALIA'S ISLAND STATE

It was a Dutchman, Tasman, who in 1642 first discovered the island that bears his name, but he named it Van Diemen's Land. Nor did he know that it was an island and no one troubled much about it until 1802. In that year the Governor in Sydney sent a party across to take formal possession and settlement began in 1803. Our photograph is of Eaglehawk Neck, Tasman Peninsula.

Photos: The Agent General for Tasmania

Tasmania is separated from the mainland of Australia by the Bass Strait, 140 miles wide, and the island itself is mountainous, some of them being clothed almost to their summits with wonderful forests as may be seen in this picture, taken on the River Derwent at New Norfolk, Tasmania. Hobart, the capital, on the south side of the island, stands on the Derwent, some twelve miles from its mouth.

AWAITING THEIR TURN WITH THE SHEARER

The vast numbers of sheep on the Australian continent have been of inestimable value to the peoples of Europe and Asia in the years following the war. The average wool clip each year exceeds a thousand million lb., and each sheep produces, on an average, rather more than 9 lb. Here we have a typical scene on an Australian station with the sheep penned near the shearing shed, waiting to be shorn.

Australian News and Information Bureau

Cattle raising is another great Australian industry and our photograph shows a herd of cows against the background of Mount Kosciusko, New South Wales.

Here are seen two Australian axemen in the coach-wood forests of New South Wales. They are mounted on boards, felling the tree for timber which will be made into plywood.

do not know what it means are astonished to see the whole vast mass of bathers rush to the shore as quickly as possible. The bell is sounded from one of the towers by the watchman on the look-out for sharks!

About fifty miles from Sydney are the beautiful Blue Mountains. They are rugged ranges whose slopes are thickly forested and they take their name from the fairy-like blue mist which veils them. Katoomba is a popular mountain centre, but many prefer to explore the remoter parts of the ranges where they can be alone with the natural beauties of the peaks and crags.

The loftiest mountains of New South Wales, however, are in the south towards the Victoria border. Here is found the grandeur of Australia's Switzerland: great peaks, some of them more than 7,000 feet high, and mighty Kosciusko (7,328 feet), the highest mountain in the continent, whose summit is snow-covered for seven months of the year. In summer-time you can ride the trails in these mountains and fish the mountain streams for trout; in winter, snow makes this region a fine place for ski-ing and other winter sports.

With an area of 309,433 square miles, New South Wales is almost as large as the United Kingdom. In 1952 her total population was estimated at nearly 3½ millions, of whom more than 1½ million were living in Sydney and its suburbs. *Newcastle* is the second largest city in the State.

Dorien Leigh.

A GIANT GROPER FROM BARRIER REEF WATERS

Queensland gropers are among the largest of bony fishes and often weigh several hundredweights. Indeed, some specimens have been known to weigh as much as seven hundred pounds. Because it is more cunning and less easily frightened than a shark, this bottom-dwelling monster is greatly feared by divers.

New South Wales is a great agricultural State, the home of millions of cattle and sheep, with such variety of climate and soil that all kinds of crops can be grown—from the sugar-cane and tropical fruits of the northern coastal plain to the wheat of the Riverina and other areas west of the Dividing Range. "Riverina" is the name given to the fertile region between the Murray and Lachlan Rivers.

Industry is scarcely less important and covers any number of flourishing centres, from the vast lead-silver-zinc mines at *Broken Hill*, in the Barrier Range, on the South Australia border, to the mighty coal, iron and steel industry of such growing cities and towns as *Newcastle* and *Port Kembla*.

Victoria

Melbourne is the State capital of Victoria. In 1952 its population was estimated at over 1,300,000, that is, nearly 60 per cent. of the total population of Victoria, which then numbered over 2¼ millions.

Melbourne is a splendid city, standing at the head of Port Phillip Bay. It has wide, straight streets at right-angles to one another, fine shops, imposing buildings in the modern style like the Royal Melbourne Hospital, electric railways, and—on the outskirts—beautiful parks. The best-known street is Collins Street, tree-lined like the boulevards of Paris and flanked by many handsome buildings. It is difficult to realise that all this began when Edward Henty settled at Port Phillip in 1834 with twenty-two cattle, six dogs, two turkeys and two guinea-fowl.

Another and less welcome settler was the rabbit. Rabbits reached Australia with the "First Fleet," but they did not become a serious menace until after 1859, when twenty-four wild rabbits arrived in Hobson's Bay on the clipper *Lightning*. Within six years these two dozen had multiplied to over 30,000 and were overrunning Victoria, crossing the Murray and doing untold damage. To-day the rabbit is as much an outlaw in Australia as the bush-ranger was and is rated as a "noxious animal."

Keystone.

MACQUARIE STREET, SYDNEY

Macquarie Street is the eastern boundary of Sydney city proper and is one of the show streets of the capital of New South Wales. It is almost entirely occupied by Government buildings and the medical profession. It is named after Governor Macquarie, who administered the colony from 1809 until 1821.

SURFING AND SAILING

Surfing is an exciting sport which requires great skill when surf-boards are used. These boards are about 8 or 10 feet long and are shaped rather like an ironing board. This picture shows experts displaying their skill at one of Sydney's many beaches.

Photos : Pictorial Press.

Sailing is another popular sport at Sydney, where the green headlands and blue waters of the great harbour make a perfect setting for the white sails of the yachts. This aerial view takes our gaze across " The Spit " and down Middle Harbour towards The Head.

Fighting the Rabbit Pest

In 1951, the rabbit population of Australia was estimated at 400 millions! Not only does the pest cause grave damage to fertile land, eating away the grass and laying bare the soil to erosion; the rabbit means a considerable cost in time, labour and money in attempts to keep the pest under control. Thousands of miles of rabbit-proof fences have been built, special equipment designed to destroy the burrows and laws made to compel farmers to take action against the pest.

Australia recently took up the large-scale use of myxomatosis virus, which has destroyed 80 per cent. of the rabbits in Victoria in less than two and a half years. But it is not yet suggested that this is the final answer to the problem, for the danger is that in time the rabbits may become immune to the virus, which would then cease to have any effect on them. Some time must pass before the scientists can give a definite opinion on this point.

Animal Sanctuaries and Parks

While in Melbourne we should certainly visit the large animal sanctuary on Phillip Island, the home of koala bears, seals, mutton birds and penguins, and the Botanical Gardens for which Melbourne is famous. Even more remarkable is the animal sanctuary at Healesville, the Sir Colin Mackenzie Fauna Sanctuary, where all kinds of Australian animals live under natural conditions. Healesville was the home of " Splash," the famous tame platypus, and at Healesville the first platypus to be born in captivity was successfully reared.

A favourite place near Melbourne for

Pictorial Press.

RIDERS ON " THE ROOF OF AUSTRALIA "

These riders are at a height of 7,000 feet above sea level, in the high country near Mount Kosciusko—a district which is sometimes called " the roof of Australia." The countryside around them is deeply covered with snow during the winter months. It forms part of the catchment area for the great Snowy River hydro-electric and irrigation scheme. " Catchment " is the word used to describe an area which feeds a river or reservoir with its water.

hikes and picnics is the Dandenong Mountain Range. The Dandenongs are also a good hunting ground for anyone wishing to see Australia's fascinating bird life—the kookaburra or laughing jackass, bell birds and lyre birds, and colourful lories and parrots.

But Victoria's great peaks lie in the north-east of the State, where Mount Buffalo, Mount Hotham, Mount Buller and other centres are popular with winter sports enthusiasts.

It is often said that Victoria is the most fertile State in Australia. In the period 1950–51 her production of wheat was higher than that of any other State, in wool production she was second only to New South Wales, and in dairy produce she led the way. Victoria, too, has many large and important towns and cities, the largest (after Melbourne) being *Geelong*, a port and important industrial centre, with a population of over 47,000. The new refinery at Geelong is one terminal of the forty-five miles long pipeline which takes diesel oil and petrol to Melbourne at the rate of 28,500 gallons an hour.

Two other cities, *Bendigo* and *Ballarat*, have more than 30,000 inhabitants. Both rose to fame as centres for the gold-mining which made them famous. Bendigo is still important for its gold; at Ballarat, where gold-mining has de-

Pictorial Press.

COLLINS STREET, MELBOURNE

Melbourne, the capital of Victoria and Australia's second city, is a busy commercial and industrial centre. Collins Street, which crosses the heart of the city from east to west, is largely occupied by banks and insurance, shipping, stock-broking and other commercial firms. In Collins Street, too, are found many Melbourne doctors.

clined, there are now factories of many kinds producing goods for the rich farming area surrounding the city.

Tasmania

Tasmania, the island State of Australia, is the smallest in the Commonwealth. Her population numbers over 311,000 (1953) and the population of *Hobart*, the State capital, is more than 93,000. *Launceston*, the second city of the State, has a population of some 50,000.

Called " Tassy " by Australians, Tasmania is a favourite tourist centre. The climate is like that of Britain, and the fruits for which Tasmania is famous are much like those grown in Britain.

Hobart is on the deep estuary of the Derwent, with Mount Wellington behind it. Like Sydney, Hobart can receive large vessels into its very heart. Once Hobart's land was covered by dense forests; tracts of these still remain at such beauty spots as Hobart's National Park, with its magnificent Russell Falls, and in the Lake St. Clair Reserve. Lake St. Clair, with an area of some fifteen square miles, plays an important part in Tasmania's industry, for it is an important source of hydro-electric power. But the largest lake in the island is the Great Lake, which has an area of sixty square miles and is noted for its trout-fishing. The waters of the Great Lake, too, are used to provide electricity.

Tasmania has mineral wealth, including copper, tin, lead and zinc. *Risdon*, near Hobart, is important for its electrolytic-zinc works ; *Bell Bay*, on the Tamar River, for its new aluminium works.

The Commonwealth Capital

The honour of being the capital of the Australian Commonwealth falls upon *Canberra,* which stands in its own " Federal Capital Territory," whose beautiful scenery includes several peaks over 5,000 feet high. The site was selected in 1908 and the plan for the Federal capital chosen by international competition, the winning plan being submitted by W. Burley Griffin, of Chicago. The Commonwealth Parliament moved to Canberra in 1927.

Canberra is thus a planned city where nothing is allowed that is not in keeping with the plan, and it has still to be completed. Its streets radiate from a magnificent Capitol and from other points in its austere geometrical layout. Everything is being done to make the capital the most beautiful in the world. It is estimated that the spacious streets and avenues are already lined by more than 2½ million flowering shrubs and

trees. More than eight million trees and shrubs have been planted in the Federal Capital Territory, which was once no more than a sheep run. When complete, Canberra will be a fitting jewel to the rich setting of the Commonwealth.

Australian Territories

North of Cape York, across the Torres Strait, lies New Guinea, where there are still large tracts of unexplored territory. About half of this island is now administered by the Australian Government, and it was due to Australian enterprise that such gold-fields as Edie and Bulolo were opened up.

Papua, the south-eastern part of the vast island of New Guinea, may one day be an enormously rich territory. There is mineral wealth, rich soil and good rainfall, useful timber and pearl fisheries. The Papuans themselves are a primitive people, who once opposed the white man's penetration of their land with bow and arrow, stone club and spear. Many of their villages are organised on a communal basis, the men living apart from the women and children in their own houses.

Tribal practices which are bad and inhuman are, of course, suppressed by the Australian administrators, but in other respects the native people are allowed to continue with their tribal customs and way of life. The countryside is very mountainous, with dense jungles, and travel is difficult. There are literally hundreds of different languages and dialects spoken by the native people, and the administrators therefore have no easy task. Indeed, there are still some regions where the tribes live out of touch with the civilising influence of the administrative officers and where the witch-doctors still hold sway over the credulous and superstitious villagers.

Papua and New Guinea are difficult territories to develop. For many years, gold and copra have been the chief commercial products, but recent experiments with tea, coffee and fibre crops (e.g., sisal) have been successful

BEAUTIFUL TASMANIA

Keystone.

One of the most beautiful parts of Australia is the Cradle Mountain-Lake St. Clair National Park of Tasmania. Lake St. Clair, seen from Mount Rufus in this picture, is but one of many lakes in this delightful region. The Park also contains at least fifteen mountains over 4,000 feet high, and many lovely waterfalls and fern gullies.

E.N.A.

Hobart, the capital of Tasmania, has a harbour that for depth and beauty rivals that of Sydney. Ocean Pier, at which the largest ships berth, is actually in the heart of the city. Beyond Hobart looms majestic Mount Wellington, seen in this picture with clouds dusting its summit.

in many areas. It is also hoped to grow rice, and to replant and extend the areas devoted to rubber trees. At the Hallstrom Trust Station in the central highlands, trials are being carried out to discover whether sheep can be profitably raised, and investigations are also going on to find a breed of cattle that can flourish under local conditions. Timber has become more important ; a modern timber factory was opened at Bulolo early in 1954.

Port Moresby is the headquarters of the administration of Papua and New Guinea. It is linked with Australia by a regular air service and, like Rabaul, Lae and other places, by regular shipping services.

Besides Papua and New Guinea, Australia has about half of the great Antarctic continent with which we at once link such names as Scott, Shackleton, Mawson and Wilkins. In these desolate regions research stations are maintained by the Australian Government, and one day, perhaps, a way will

be found to extract the coal and plutonium which are known to exist beneath the ice and snow. For the present, investigation lies in the hands of the Australian Antarctic Research Expedition, which in 1948 set up the first permanent outpost on lonely Heard Island.

In the Antarctic

A second permanent base was established on Macquarie Island, and in January, 1954, an expedition left Melbourne to set up yet another base, this time on the Antarctic Continent itself. The new weather station came into being on February 13th, 1954, when Mr. P. G. Law, the leader of the expedition, hoisted the Australian flag on the Antarctic mainland. The station has been called Mawson, after Sir Douglas Mawson, the great Australian explorer. Its position is 67½ deg. south and 65 deg. east, and it is the nearest permanent habitation to the South Pole. A point for stamp collectors is that Mawson has its own post office—the first to be established on the Antarctic Circle.

The scientific observations and records made at these outposts will add to present knowledge of Australian weather and climate, and make possible more accurate long-range weather forecasts for the island continent.

Apart from these territories, Australia has the responsibility for appointing the Administrator of the Pacific island of Nauru, which is jointly held under United Nations' trusteeship by Great Britain, Australia and New Zealand. Nauru is an important source of phosphates. About a million tons of phosphates are mined each year on the plateau that forms the greater part of the island.

The money earned makes life pleasant and prosperous for the Nauruans. But the deposits will last only about another seventy years, and it may then be necessary to transfer the people of Nauru to another part of the Pacific.

Tasmanian Government Photographic Laboratory.

A BEAUTIFUL FERN GULLY

Among the many scenic wonders of Tasmania are fern gullies. Here, for example, is the Notley Fern Gorge in northern Tasmania.

OCEAN-GOING VESSELS AND FERRY-BOATS USE SYDNEY'S FAMOUS CIRCULAR QUAY

Every visitor to Sydney, the largest city and leading port of Australia, knows Circular Quay. The ocean-going ship which brought him to the Common-wealth may well have berthed here, in the very heart of the city. To see more of the beautiful Harbour, he may take a trip on one of the many ferries that run from Circular Quay—to Kirribilli, Mosman, Taronga Park with its famous Zoo, Cremorne and Hunters Hill. This picture of the Quay also shows us (left) part of the Botanic Gardens and, rising out of the trees, the State Conservatorium of Music. It was at Circular Quay that Captain Phillip landed in 1788.

The High Commissioner for New Zealand.

AMID THE BEAUTIES OF NEW ZEALAND'S SHEEP FARMS

Two-thirds of the area of New Zealand is under farming occupation and nowhere in the world is this great open-air industry carried on more efficiently. The soil is fertile and the climate allows stock to be kept out of doors all the year round. More than thirty million sheep graze on the farms such as the one seen in the picture above of an early morning scene on a station in the picturesque country of the Hawkes Bay district on the East coast of North Island.

The Story
of the
World and
its Peoples

Countries
of the British
Commonwealth
of Nations

The High Commissioner for New Zealand.

A MAORI WAR DANCE

Present-day Maoris are descended from the original inhabitants of New Zealand, the fierce and warlike natives who lived there when Captain Cook first sailed round the islands. To-day there are over 123,000 Maoris in the Dominion. You see some of them above in traditional kilt-like costume giving an exhibition " haka " or war dance.

NEW ZEALAND

THE Dominion of New Zealand is often called " the Britain of the South," not only because it is the home of nearly two million people of British race, but also because, like the British Isles, New Zealand consists of an island group on the edge of a great ocean, and largely in the west-wind belt.

Early Explorers

But New Zealand is not *exactly* at the opposite point of the globe to Britain, as we can easily discover if we look at the latitudes within which it lies. North Island is in similar latitudes to those of middle and Southern Spain, and South (or Middle) Island is in latitudes corresponding to those of Northern Spain and Southern France. This is important, because it largely

explains why the climate of New Zealand is, on the whole, warmer and sunnier than ours.

Again, Britain is on the eastern side of a great ocean; but New Zealand is on the western side of the Pacific, and is 1,200 miles or so from the nearest continent, instead of being only about 21, as is the case with Britain and Europe.

Tasman, who had charted much of the southern shores of Australia, discovered and mapped a small part of the great northern peninsula of North Island about the middle of the seventeenth century and gave New Zealand her name. One hundred and thirty seven years later Captain Cook sighted the eastern shores of New Zealand, and conjectured that it must be part of the great southern continent which the geographers of his day believed to exist. He sailed north round the cape which Tasman had named after the daughter of Anthony van Diemen, Governor of the Dutch East Indies, and then voyaged south along the western coast of North Island until he found a wide passage leading east again. This was Cook Strait.

Cook and the Maoris

So the land he had seen was a large island, and not part of a great southern continent, for he had sailed round it. Cook then circumnavigated South Island (1770) and passed on to explore the eastern shores of Australia. But he had learned enough about New Zealand to astonish people at home with his descriptions of the native people, the plants and the creatures of the new islands far away on the other side of the world.

He found the islands inhabited by the fierce and warlike Maoris, who lived in " pahs " or villages surrounded by high, strong palisades. " They are a strong, rawboned, well-made, active people rather above the common size," he wrote in his journal; " they are of a dark brown colour with strong white teeth. Both men and women paint their faces and bodies with red ochre mixed with fish oil. They wear ornaments of stone, bone and spills at their ears, and about their necks, and the men generally wear long white feathers stuck upright in their hair."

To-day over 123,000 of the Maoris still live in New Zealand, principally in North Island. They have their own land, their own schools, and their own representatives in the Dominion Parliament. Many are wealthy, progressive and influential citizens of the British Commonwealth.

A Treaty with the Chiefs

Captain Cook actually annexed New

The High Commissioner for New Zealand.

THE " HONGI," A MAORI GREETING

When Maori friends meet they may perform the " Hongi," pressing their noses together and murmuring sounds of pleasure at the meeting. The Maoris are descended from people of the Polynesian islands who voyaged to New Zealand in sea-going canoes some centuries ago. Their modern descendants are Christians and a happy and contented people.

MAORI GAMES AND DANCES

These Maori children at the Native School, Whakarewarewa, are playing a hand game. Cultured and charming, the Maoris have a splendid soldiering record. They have their own representatives in the Dominion Parliament and some of them have become important and affluent Dominion citizens.

The High Commissioner for New Zealand.

These Maori women are performing the romantic " poi " dance. The dance tells the story of the voyage from Polynesia to New Zealand. Starting with the launching of a long canoe, it goes on to show in actions the buffeting of the canoe in a storm, how the canoe was saved from wreck, and the eventual landing on the beach of a new country.

18—2

IN THE SOUTHERN ALPS

New Zealand's Southern Alps are well-named, for their towering snow peaks, deep valleys, huge glaciers and dark forests are very like those of the Swiss Alps. The finest glacier, the Tasman glacier, is seen in this picture; it is eighteen miles long, two miles wide in places, and up to 1,000 feet deep. Huts and hostels for climbers and trappers have been set up in the Southern Alps.

Zealand, but the British government of his time had no interest in his discovery. Other explorers and navigators, French, Spanish, Russian and American, came to New Zealand: and whaling ships, and merchantmen after flax and timber, before Samuel Marsden and a group of English missionaries landed in 1814. It was not until 1840 that Captain Hobson was sent to annex the country to the British Empire—a move made to forestall a French colonising company which planned to take possession of New Zealand.

The Treaty of Waitangi

Captain Hobson made the Treaty of Waitangi with the native chiefs who accepted British sovereignty in return for the guarantee of their rights and lands. The first British settlers, a shipload sent by Wakefield's New Zealand Company, arrived almost as soon as Hobson did.

New Zealand was granted self-government in 1852 and four years later had its own parliamentary system with Auckland as the seat of government (Wellington did not become the capital until 1864).

There were bitter conflicts between the settlers and the Maoris, who fought fiercely under such leaders as Rewi and Te Kooti. By 1871, both sides had become weary of the struggle. The Maoris were exhausted and virtually defeated. The colonists wanted nothing more than peace in which to develop their country. Much progress had already been made. Sheep farming was spreading across the rich natural pastures of the country, and in North Island cleared forest land was being planted with English grasses. In South Island grain crops were almost as important as sheep rearing. Gold, too, was discovered in Auckland province and in the south and west of South Island, and New Zealand went

THE "CLOUD-PIERCER"

The High Commissioner for New Zealand.

The Maoris call Mount Cook *Aorangi*, which means "Cloud-Piercer." The great mountain, which rears up to 12,349 feet, is the highest in New Zealand. It forms part of the main chain of the Southern Alps, which form the rugged backbone of South Island and which divide the fertile eastern plains from the narrow west coast. In the main alpine chain there are more than two hundred peaks with a height of over 7,500 feet.

through hectic gold-rush times. But her true wealth lay not in mineral deposits, but in the fields and pastures of her farms. All that is New Zealand to-day has come about through the industry of her farmers and the world markets which their meat, wool, cheese, and butter command.

New Zealand remained a colony until 1907, when the young and energetic country achieved Dominion status. Modern New Zealand is an independent and self-governing country of the British Commonwealth, built from mountain and forest and raised to prosperity through the skill of her sheep and dairy farmers. But though their achievements entitled New Zealanders to a just national pride, they have not forgotten the island group on the other side of the world whence their pioneer ancestors came. The New Zealanders are among the most "intensely and patriotically British" peoples in the Commonwealth of Nations, loyal members of a great

The High Commissioner for New Zealand.

THE FRANZ JOSEF GLACIER

This is one of the most low-lying glaciers in the world. Its terminal face is only 690 feet above sea level. Its length is 8½ miles.

family whose welfare is ever dear in their hearts.

Splendid Mountain Scenery

New Zealand is a very beautiful country, and much of its fine scenery is mountainous. South Island has the great mountain backbone of the Southern Alps, whose highest peak, Mount Cook, rises to an altitude of over 12,000 feet. The Maori name for it is Aorangi, the "Cloud-Piercer." This mountain backbone, which lies nearer the west coast than the east, is difficult to cross, but a railway links up the prosperous cities of the east coast with those of the west. There is a road by way of Arthur's Pass, whose general direction is followed by the railway which goes through the Otira Gorge in a series of cuttings and tunnels, linking up Christchurch on the east with Hokitika, Greymouth, Westport and other centres on the west.

The Southern Alps are well named, for their towering snow-peaks, deep valleys, huge glaciers, and dark forests are very like those of the Swiss Alps; and every year those who love the mountains or seek the risk and thrill of hazardous climbing, go there for holidays, just as people flock to Switzerland. The finest glacier is the great Tasman glacier, which challenges comparison with any other in the world.

New Zealand's Fjords

In the south-west the mountains come steeply to the sea much as they do in Norway; and, as in Norway, the coast has undergone glacial action there in past ages, allowing the sea to invade the long deep-cut valleys and turn them into tortuous and narrow inlets like the Norwegian fjords—steepwalled, profound and still. The best-known of these New Zealand fjords is Milford Sound. Some of them have the tongue-like ends of great glaciers within 600 feet of the sea, and yet with graceful tree-ferns spreading their curling fronds within sight of the glacier ice—a sight to be seen nowhere else in the world.

Natural Grass-lands

The Southern Alps lie across the track of the prevalent westerly winds, so that the western side of South Island has very much more rain than the long slopes and the coastal plains on the eastern side. Forests clothe the wetter western slopes, but the drier eastern plains are natural grass-lands, ideal for sheep-rearing. These are the famous Canterbury Plains, whose name is associated all the world over with the finest New Zealand lamb and mutton. Much dairy-farming is carried on there, too, especially in the moister parts; the real dairy country of South Island is the rich pasture land all down its eastern side, but most dairying is carried on in North Island, especially in the Auckland peninsula and Wanganui Plains.

North Island

North Island is very different in structure from South Island. The mountain backbone in North Island is nearer the *east* coast; it is broken into several ranges which nowhere exceed 7,000 feet. To the west of it lies one of the most remarkable volcanic regions in the world. It is a great volcanic plateau, pitted with geysers, mud volcanoes, and hot springs, with Lake Taupo in its midst, from which issues the Waikato River to run many miles north to the Sea. Lake Taupo covers an area of 250 square miles, and is fed by thirty rivers.

Above the plateau three great volcanoes raise their triple cones; Ngauru-

International Wool Secretariat.

A SHEPHERD TO THE RESCUE

When winter comes to the high hill-country farms of South Island, the sheep are sometimes caught by the heavy snowfalls. Then the shepherd has to trudge through the deep snow to rescue as many as he can of the flock. But usually, the Merino sheep climb to the highest peak and feed systematically to the lower levels before the snow comes. Merinos are the only breed which can really stand up to the hard conditions of the highlands.

hoe, mightiest of all, is still active, but his brothers, Ruapehu and Tongariro, were thought to be quiescent or extinct until 1945 when Mt. Ruapehu erupted. As for Tongariro—who can say? There is certainly no telling when such sleepers may waken into life.

Hot Springs and Geysers

This thermal region of North Island is visited by thousands of people every year; fine hotels have been built for their accommodation, and Maori guides make good money during the tourist season. Rotorua is the principal

NGAURUHOE BELCHING MOLTEN ROCK

Normally the 7,515-feet high cone of Ngauruhoe only gives forth a thin wisp of steam, but from time to time it stirs itself into full activity and belches forth smoke and molten rock. The two brothers of this formidable peak, Tongariro and Ruapehu, are no longer active and it is possible that they have become extinct—though none can say as much with certainty.

The High Commissioner for New Zealand.

The cave here shown is to be seen at Waitomo, between Rotorua and the western coast. The visitor is taken by his guide through an insignificant opening in the mountain side and then passes from cavern to cavern, each with wonderful stalactites hanging from the roofs and strange limestone formations. The cave depicted is picturesquely called " The Bride's Jewels."

A GEYSER IN ACTION

The High Commissioner for New Zealand.

This picture gives you a " close-up " view of the largest and most famous of the geysers of Whakarewarewa Valley. The great column of scalding water that you see has been thrown up by the geyser called Pohutu. On rare occasions, these geysers burst forth, throwing their scalding water anything up to 1,500 feet in the air and spewing forth black mud and stones; but for the most part, they are safe enough, if treated with respect, and in the very heart of this amazing region the Maoris have built villages, often on the very edge of steaming crevices or boiling pools.

centre. There you can see great jets of boiling water spouting into the air, driven by giant forces that lie beneath the ground, and can watch the mud pools seethe and bubble and swirl like the dark contents of a witch's cauldron. The sulphur springs of Rotorua fill the marble baths of a wonderful sanatorium built there to give new life and vigour to those who come from afar to seek health.

You can smell sulphur in the air as you approach Rotorua, but this is not nearly as astonishing as the sights you see. From green valleys and hills rise mysterious puffs of steam, and by the very roadside are mud-holes that seethe and bubble like boiling porridge, and hot lakes of yellow, or blue, or green or pink.

In the valley of Tikitere, ten miles from Rotorua, " the earth is hot beneath your feet, the country gapes with steaming cracks, and if a cane is thrust a few inches into the soil a jet of steam or a spout of boiling water reminds you that, just beneath, the very bowels of the earth are seething towards the surface."

Geyser Valley

Go to Wairakei and see the marvels of the Thermal Valley, where geysers with strange names, like the Champagne Cauldron, the Dragon's Mouth, the Prince of Wales's Feathers and the Donkey Engine, throb and boil and spout aloft in giant columns of boiling water, only to gurgle and hiss back again into their craters. You can almost set your watch by some of them, they are so regular. The Paddle Wheel performs with unfailing regularity every ten minutes; the Twins every four minutes and a half. Te Reke Reke takes rather

The High Commissioner for New Zealand.
" THE CHAMPAGNE CAULDRON " AT WAIRAKEI

The remarkable Wairakei Thermal Valley lies between Rotorua and Taupo in the heart of North Island, New Zealand. Here can be seen nearly every kind of boiling spring, geyser and fumarole. Among the wonders of nature which Maori guides show to visitors is the boiling, bubbling " Champagne Cauldron." Experts say that to maintain such a pool artificially would require electric power amounting to 7,000 kilowatts.

The High Commissioner for New Zealand.

A MUD VOLCANO IN WAIRAKEI VALLEY

Wairakei Thermal Valley, North Island, can show you nearly every kind of thermal activity for which New Zealand's Rotorua district is world-famous, including boiling springs, geysers, fumaroles, blow-holes, and mud volcanoes. Here, where the ground quivers beneath you as you stop to marvel, nature is at her most violent and her most wonderful.

longer to make up his mind; he spouts once every 4½ hours.

Tarawera is a mountain of grim memories; its appalling eruption in 1886 altered the whole countryside and spread ruin and death for many miles around. Large areas of fertile land and numerous happy villages were destroyed, and the famous Pink and White terraces of Rotomahana were utterly wiped out.

Maori Villages

The giant geyser of Waimangu, the greatest in the world, burst forth near this spot, spouting its 1,500-feet column of scalding water, black mud and stones from a quiet pool which no one had dreamed capable of such astonishing activity, but it has not been in action since 1917.

It is difficult to imagine human settlement in country like this, yet the Maoris have built some of their villages in the very midst of it. Not far from

Rotorua is the old Maori village of Whakarewarewa, with houses perched like match-boxes often at the very edge of boiling springs and fumaroles (steam holes). The Maoris regard these terrifying things as advantages, and make use of them as "fireless cookers" and "free hot baths." Over a fumarole they place a small box with its bottom of laths, and in it they put food wrapped in green leaves to be cooked. Washing day presents no problems; it is done out of doors in the grim wash-tubs which Nature has provided, and there is never a queue for the bath, no matter how big the family.

In this thermal region the Maoris not only act as guides, but, attired in the native dress, often perform some of their ancient dances and sing the old, old songs that have come down to the present from the far-distant past when the Maoris came in their long canoes from over the sea to the " Long White

Cloud," which to-day we know as New Zealand.

Maori Dances

This ancient Maori tradition is told in action and in song in the dances performed by the women. The launch of the long canoe, its swaying rhythm, its buffeting in storm, its overthrow and quick righting again, and its landing on the beach are shown in rhythmic pantomime. The paddle-stroke is heard in the *poi* dance in the flick of two balls tied with flaxen cord and wielded by the dancers, and the swish of the water is suggested by the rustling skirts of stiff flaxen fibres.

More vigorous still is the *haka* or war

The High Commissioner for New Zealand.

A DINNER COOKED IN NATURAL HOT WATER

So hot is the earth in the neighbourhood of Rotorua that the Maori women can actually stew meat and cook their dinners in a "stewpan" provided by Nature. Fireless cookers and warm baths, not to mention the laundry affairs, are simple matters when one lives in such an area.

dance performed by the men, each clad in a kind of kilt of striped flax, and brandishing his *tewhatewha* or long-handled fighting axe.

But Maori boys and girls who have of course been to school, and have become as interested in " going to the pictures " and dancing as any other young modern folk, are not very intrigued by the old tales and songs and dances, which may quite possibly soon die out.

People who visit the thermal regions of North Island usually find time to inspect the famous caves of Waitomo, between Rotorua and the western coast. Through an insignificant opening in the mountain side, the visitor passes through cavern after cavern with wonderful stalactites pendent from their roofs, and with strange limestone formations that resemble fantastic turrets, or cathedral aisles, or perhaps fine shawls marvellously carved in old ivory.

The Glow-worm Cave

Presently he is led steeply down to the brink of a subterranean river whose waters gleam blackly in the gloom. There he steps into a boat and pushes off into the darkness—a little apprehensive and perhaps afraid, until his eyes become accustomed to the place and he sees above him a myriad of tiny stars of blue and green and opalescent sheen twinkling from the roof, flickering, fading and twinkling again as if alive.

And they certainly *are* alive, for the guide tells how multitudes of curious glow-worms have made their home in the roof of this strange cavern, turning it into an Aladdin's Cave of jewelled splendour. No one who has ever seen it can forget the

Standing on the southernmost beach of North Island and looking across Cook Strait to South Island you get this fine view of the Kaikoura Range, whose highest peak is 9,467 feet high Tapuaenuku. Cook Strait is about twenty miles wide at its narrowest point.

The High Commissioner for New Zealand.

Some of the finest scenery in New Zealand is along the fjordland stretch of the west coast of South Island, particularly around Milford Sound. The picture shows us Pembroke Peak and The Lion, impressive heights which proudly rear their heads from verdant lakeland beauty-spots that are a paradise for those who love the beauties of nature.

Fox Photos.

A DAY'S CATCH FOR BIG GAME FISHERMEN

Swordfish, mako shark and other big game fish are caught chiefly off the east coast of the Auckland Provincial District. One of the chief centres is Tauranga, where this picture was taken. Specially equipped launches are used by the fishermen. Notice the stout rods, which are fixed to the stern of the vessel. No launch is permitted to catch more than four fish per day. The season lasts from December until May.

mysterious beauty of the Glow-worm Cave of Waitomo.

Wild Life

New Zealand has no truly *wild* animals, although she has animal colonists that have since run wild such as pigs, goats, and rabbits which are now pests to be shot, and hedgehogs and Australian 'possums. But New Zealand is very rich in bird life, and the kiwi shares with the fern-leaf the honour of being a national emblem. Kiwis are found only in New Zealand, and bear the name given them by the Maoris. The kiwi has no apparent wings, and though it does not fly, it can run very rapidly. It is about the size of a large

chicken, and usually sleeps by day and feeds by night.

Another strange and rare inhabitant of New Zealand is the tuatara, a harmless lizard-like reptile which has survived from ancient times and has a rudimentary third eye. Years ago, New Zealand had another remarkable survival from the world's earliest times— the moa, a huge bird about eleven feet tall, which can now only be seen as a specimen in New Zealand museums.

The huia, a bird whose feathers were greatly prized by the Maoris, was also thought to be extinct. But in December, 1953, a forester and two other travellers through the thickly-wooded ranges of the Auckland province claimed to have seen a pair of birds belonging to this species.

THE NEW ZEALAND COUNTRYSIDE

The High Commissioner for New Zealand.

These drovers and their dog are taking sheep along the Wairoa-Mohaka road in North Island. The first sheep to reach New Zealand were landed by Captain Cook in 1773, but sheep were not permanently established until 1834. In 1952, the Dominion had more than 35¼ million sheep.

Aerofilms.

This is Rangiora, near Christchurch, the largest city in South Island. We are looking towards Port Hills and Banks Peninsula. In the foreground are ranks of tall trees, which act as wind-breaks. Christchurch is the chief city of the Canterbury Plains which, like the Southland Plains in Otago, are noted for their sheep and general farming.

Deer and other game can be hunted not far from most towns and cities in New Zealand, and one does not have to be wealthy to engage in this sort of sport. Practically everyone can enjoy all forms of sport, from ski-ing and yachting to cricket and football.

Big-Game Fishing

Big-game fishing is an exciting pastime. The main fishing grounds for striped and black marlin swordfish, mako shark and other game fish are off the east coast of Auckland Provincial District. Whangaroa, Russell (Bay of Islands), Whitianga (Mercury Bay) and Tauranga are the chief centres for the specially built and equipped launches hired by the fisher-men. The game-fishing season runs from December to May, but February and March are the best months. The number of fish which may be caught each day from a launch is limited to four.

Much could be written of the trees, shrubs and plants which make the New Zealand countryside so beautiful. In the sub-tropical land of North Auckland are forest giants such as the kauri, one of the finest timber trees in the world. Characteristic of New Zealand is the tea-tree, whose white, pink, or red blossoms can be seen everywhere and whose aromatic leaves were used by the early settlers as a substitute for tea.

The Christmas Tree

Another beautiful New Zealand tree is the pohutu-kawa, or Christmas tree. Not that it resembles the small conifers we have in our homes and decorate at Christmas time. It is a spacious, friendly tree providing plenty of shade and bearing, in summer, crimson flowers. In the mountain country, you will find the New Zealand buttercup, its centre gold in colour and its petals white or yellow; here, also, can be seen the celmisia, or mountain daisy.

But it is the fern which New Zealand has adopted as its national flower. There are ferns everywhere in the open country, from the small varieties to the graceful tree ferns whose slender trunks may be anything from ten to forty feet high. The tree fern can be seen, not only in the country-side, but in many New Zealand parks and gardens.

The High Commissioner for New Zealand.

POPLARS IN SOUTH ISLAND

What could be more charming than this poplar-lined road at Lawrence, Central Otago, in New Zealand's South Island? The Dominion has many fine trees, including such forest giants as the kauri and such lovely trees as the crimson-flowered pohutukawa or Christmas tree.

THE VICTORIA FALLS IN SOUTHERN RHODESIA

First discovered by David Livingstone in 1855, the Victoria Falls on the Zambezi River are on the border of Southern and Northern Rhodesia. Livingstone's black followers called them Mosi-oa-Tunya, which means " the smoke that thunders." The Falls are about a mile long and some 357 feet deep. What makes the Falls so remarkable is that the level of the country is the same above and below them, the water falling into a huge fissure.

THE LOVELY TAJ MAHAL, BUILT IN MEMORY OF A MOGHUL QUEEN

The Taj Mahal at Agra, in the Union of India, has been described as "the most splendidly poetic building in the world." It was built by order of the Moghul emperor, Shah Jehan, as a mausoleum for his beloved Queen, Mumtaz Mahal, after her death in 1631. The emperor himself is also buried in this wonderful sepulchre. The Taj Mahal is built entirely of white marble and many parts of it are ornamented with agates, jaspers and other precious stones, set in the stonework in the form of intricate designs. It has probably been painted and photographed more often than any other building in the world.

NEW ZEALANDERS AT WORK

The High Commissioner for New Zealand.

A CO-OPERATIVE DAIRY FACTORY AT TIRAU, AUCKLAND

This huge churn produces in one churning enough butter to fill one hundred 56-lb. boxes. Three such churns and one 64-box churn are in use at this factory. Churning usually takes from half to three-quarters of an hour. During the 1951–52 season, butter, cheese and other milk products of New Zealand were worth nearly £78 million.

NEW ZEALANDERS make the most of their fertile country and its genial climate both in their work and their play. They get their living mainly by using the opportunities offered them by the great stretches of natural grasslands in both islands, where very large numbers both of sheep and cattle are reared, and by farming in the rich soil.

Produce of the Dairy Farms

New Zealand's prosperity comes from farming and from processed farm produce. Wool, frozen meat, dairy produce, skins and hides are all exported from the Dominion which is the greatest exporter of butter, cheese, lamb and mutton in the world. In 1952, butter and cheese alone were exported to the value of over £N.Z.71,900,000. The total value of these pastoral products runs into millions and millions of pounds; it is as great as New Zealand's population is small.

New Zealand butter, cheese and lamb are always in demand, because their high quality is maintained by a careful system of Government inspection. Large freezing plants have been set up at many centres, especially at or near the meat-exporting ports of Lyttelton, Dunedin and Invercargill in South Island, and Wellington, Auckland and Napier in North Island. Co-operative dairies have done much to make dairy-farming successful, and at Hamilton, in the Waikato valley of North Island, one of the largest dairy companies in the British Commonwealth has its headquarters.

Most dairy farms are small and average a herd of 50 milking cows each; but mixed farms are larger; sheep and cattle runs larger still; along the East Coast there are sheep farms of 20,000 acres or more.

Farming is the backbone of New Zealand's life, and it is therefore natural for the government Department of Agriculture to take an active interest in farmers' problems and in increasing the quantity and raising the quality of farm produce. The Government, too, helps farmers through its Marketing department, and by loans and the control of land values.

New Zealand's farming industry is run on the most modern lines. It is mechanized, and much of its machinery is driven by power from hydro-electric stations driven by the many mountain streams and waterfalls. Water is electrically pumped; milking, processing and packing machines are electrically driven. Cream is extracted at the farms and taken to the butter factory for the district where it is processed by power operated machinery. Mechanization of the dairy industry and the use of modern refrigeration plant (in which New Zealand has led the world) have rightly been described as "milestones in the industrial history of New Zealand."

In the Rotorua area, thousands of

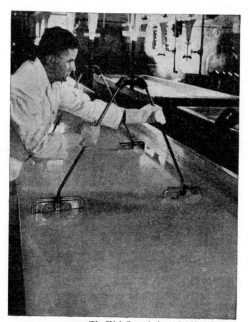

The High Commissioner for New Zealand.

CHEESE IN THE MAKING

Mechanical agitators being put into a vat of milk. The vat contains 900 gallons and will produce about 1,000 lbs. of cheese.

acres are being cleared of scrub and brought into cultivation. Big tractors are used to draw the rollers and ploughs which deal with the dense undergrowth. "Farming from the air" also plays its part; special air-strips have been built so that fertilizers can be sprayed from aircraft. This scheme is the largest of the kind ever undertaken in New Zealand; it will eventually bring into being two thousand new farms.

Coalfields and Water Power

New Zealand has comparatively little heavy industry. But her miners can supply all the coal she needs, and this comes mainly from the large coal field on the north-western shores of South Island, where *Westport* and *Greymouth* are the chief outlets. Good coal is also mined in the *Waikato district* of North Island. But New Zealand also has abundant "white coal" in her water power which is harnessed at such hydro-electric stations as the one at *Arapuni* on the Waikato river, forty miles west of Rotorua in the geyser country. The Waikato river is the chief source of water power in North Island and is to be harnessed by ten power stations in all. One of the most recent is Maraetai, which is also the largest. The others will include Whakamaru, Maipapa, Atiamuri and Ohakuri. In South Island power is obtained from the Lake Coleridge scheme and the Waitaki river. The Clutha river is to be harnessed under the Roxburgh project. The Dominion has gold mines in Otago and other districts of South Island. But these are not nearly as important as the gold mines of Australia, over 1,200 miles away.

Geothermal Bores

Another source of power which may soon be tapped is at Wairakei, in North Island, where the underground heat and steam tapped in geothermal bores could produce enough power to operate

CITIES AND PORTS

The largest city in New Zealand is Auckland, seen here from the east. It has a population of 350,500. To the right are St. Helier's and Kohimarama and Mission Bay. Beyond them is the main part of the city and (right) the main port installations.

Photos : The High Commissioner for New Zealand.

Standing on Cook Strait and spreading into the surrounding hills is Wellington, the capital and first port of New Zealand. Its population of more than 137,600 makes Wellington the third largest city in the Dominion, the second largest being Christchurch (population 182,800). The picture shows the harbour and city as seen from Mount Victoria.

19—2

The High Commissioner for New Zealand.

HARNESSING THE WATERS OF THE WAIKATO

Ten new large hydro-electric stations are being built to harness the waters of the Waikato river, North Island. This picture shows the first of the ten at Karapiro, a place about six miles from Cambridge. Such hydro-electric plants provide cheap electric power for New Zealand homes, factories, and farms.

the Main Trunk railway from Auckland to Wellington. Heavy water, which is important in the development of atomic energy, is also to be produced from geothermal bores at Wairakei with the help of equipment designed in Great Britain.

If New Zealand has little heavy industry, she has very many factories making products for her home market. For in common with Canada, Australia, and South Africa, New Zealand has—partly as a result of two world wars—greatly expanded her secondary industries. New Zealanders can now buy clothing, carpets, furniture, pottery, toys, crockery, wireless sets, and many other things made in their own factories. Except for tea and sugar, almost all the food required is produced and processed in New Zealand. Since the war, plans have been completed for textile and aircraft factories, paper mills, and many other similar projects. A Glasgow linen

company has opened a factory in New Zealand to make linen threads from local flax, and a famous British firm has built a rubber factory near Wellington, and already has another at Christchurch.

New Zealand Cities

All the big towns in the Dominion are either on the coast or near it. The largest city is *Auckland*, the former capital, which with its suburbs has a total population of 350,500. *Wellington*, the capital, has 137,600 people in city and suburbs, while *Christchurch* has more than 182,000.

Wellington, on the splendid natural harbour of Port Nicholson, which could accommodate the whole of the British Navy if necessary, has a central situation in the Dominion which fits it admirably for its position as capital and chief distributing centre of New Zealand. It exports butter, cheese, fruit, hemp, frozen meat and wool, and

SIGHTS AND SCENES IN NEW ZEALAND

The Dominion is rich in timber, a very valuable tree being the kauri pine. Here one of the big logs is being sawn into convenient lengths for transport.

Here is a mustering of sheep from the outlying parts of an extensive farm in the neighbourhood of Auckland. Whenever sheep are on the move there is a light dust haze.

This a cameo of the famous Sutherland Falls, in which the cascading water makes a total drop of 1,904 feet. The Falls are found in the neighbourhood of Milford Sound.

The High Commissioner for New Zealand.

In the middle distance is seen the silvery streak that is formed by the great Franz Josef glacier. There is a considerable glacier system in the South Island.

CHRISTCHURCH CATHEDRAL

Christchurch is the city of the Canterbury Plains from which comes the best lamb. Here everything is as English as possible, as the Cathedral and other buildings show.

the bulk of its trade is with Britain, Australia and Canada.

Auckland, on Waitemata Harbour, at the head of Hauraki Gulf, is the great port of call for vessels using the Panama route to New Zealand. At the entrance to the harbour is the island of Rangitoto with its single-coned volcano, now extinct. The water is deep enough to allow large ships to berth within a few yards of the main thoroughfare of the city. For its beauty, Auckland has been called "The Naples of the South."

Auckland's increasing size and importance have made vital the construction of a bridge across Waitemata Harbour. Described by a prominent New Zealander as "the most ambitious engineering project yet planned for New Zealand," the bridge is to be built by two famous English firms whose contract for the task is worth more than £4 million. The Auckland Harbour Bridge will be 3,345 feet long and of the

cantilever type with seven spans. Its weight will be approximately 10,000 tons and it will carry a 55-feet wide roadway as well as wide footways. The bridge will take four years to build.

Another great engineering project is the railway tunnel which is being driven under the Rimutaka Hills near Wellington. Five and a half miles in length, the tunnel will be one of the longest in the British Commonwealth. It will bring the town of Featherston "within an hour's travelling of Wellington—nearer than many of the city's tramway-served suburbs."

The Canterbury Plains

Christchurch is the city of the Canterbury Plains. Its harbour is Port Lyttelton. From it the railway to the west coast crosses the Southern Alps by the famous Otira tunnel, which is, like the Rimutaka tunnel, five and a half miles long.

The High Commissioner for New Zealand.

AUCKLAND UNIVERSITY

This view of the University is taken from Albert Park, whose exotic trees are a contrast to the architecture. Auckland is the largest city in the Dominion.

A NEW ZEALAND FARMSTEAD

Hard work, good land, and a friendly climate provide a good living for the farmers of New Zealand, and most of them can afford a comfortable home with a car and a telephone. New Zealanders are proud of their homes and, having plenty of space in which to build, do not erect row upon row of terrace houses such as may be seen in Britain. There are pleasant farmsteads like the one shown in this picture, but bungalows are the more usual form of residence.

Dunedin got its name from its Scottish founders, who gave it the ancient name of Edinburgh. It is a port as is Port Chalmers, near the mouth of Otago Harbour.

New Zealand has nothing comparable to the prairies of Canada or the pampas of South America, though there are fine open plains in the Canterbury region. Most of this sheep-rearing area has, however, been cleared by settlers, for the country in the main is a land of rich forests, and timber had invariably to be swept away before a farm could be firmly established. To-day there is a State Forest Service with control of many millions of acres, whilst some of the forests are just as primeval as they were before the coming of the white man.

Digging Kauri Gum

Of all the timber trees in the Dominion, the kauri pine is outstanding, but there are rigid laws against cutting specimens below a fixed diameter, whilst exceptionally large, noble trees are preserved as national monuments. Where there have been long-standing plantations of the kauri a kind of resin forms in conjunction with the vast root system, and this kauri gum as it is called is much used in the manufacture of linoleum and for other purposes. Gangs of men dig for it among the soil crust of the decaying forest and make a good living, though the work is tough. In 1952 gum to the value of £81,517 was exported.

One of the great forestry problems is efficient fire control, and look-out stations are provided in most of the tree-covered areas. Radio has been developed to a wonderful degree for the rapid assembly of fire-fighting units, and even aeroplanes are freely employed for directing this vital work.

In the towns, on the farms, and even round the homesteads trees are very freely planted and help a great deal to make life in New Zealand so delightful. Though there is such a wealth of native trees, many varieties have been imported from Britain and found to thrive. Indeed, the people of the Dominion do everything possible to preserve the ideals that mean so much to us at home. For example, the architecture and planning of Christchurch are typically English, while Dunedin recalls the style and buildings of Scotland. English, Scottish and Irish names, as well as those of Wales, are found everywhere on the map of the Dominion, but many places still retain the names given them by the Maoris.

Life in New Zealand

If you were living in New Zealand your home might be like the typical farmhouse shown in one of the pictures; but more probably it would be a bungalow. For bungalows, built for comfort and equipped with all sorts of labour-saving devices, are homes for most New Zealanders. Not that there is a drab sameness about New Zealand homes. Her bungalows are trim and individual, with modern timber and brickwork, and roofs of cheerfully coloured tiles. The New Zealand government itself is now the biggest home builder in the Dominion. Its

The High Commissioner for New Zealand.

BUILT IN NEW ZEALAND

Once dependent on such distant places as Britain for her needs n heavy industry, New Zealand now produces for herself many of the things she wants. This " K " type locomotive was built in New Zealand and specially designed for conditions in the Dominion.

NEW ZEALAND SCENES

High Commissioner for New Zealand

The Rotorua district in the North Island of New Zealand is world-famed for its hot springs and geysers. There are, too, volcanoes, one of which, the snow-capped Mount Ruapehu, is 9,175 ft. high and has at its summit a crater lake of warm water which boils and is heaved into the air and splashes the surrounding ice cliffs. In the photograph above, the climber is resting on a rocky prominence on the slopes of Mount Ruapehu, gazing across the valley to the summit of another volcano, Mount Ngauruhoe, which is in eruption.

FROM VOLCANOES TO THE SOUTHERN ALPS

It is mainly in the North Island that volcanoes are found. In the South Island there are hot springs and, by way of contrast, glaciers and Alpine lakes. Our photograph shows the cone of Mount Egmont, an extinct volcano in North Island, standing in isolated grandeur above the waters of Lake Mangahao and the wooded slopes of lesser hills.

Photos: E.N.A.

In the South Island of New Zealand there is a district which will bear favourable comparison with Switzerland, for those who are enthusiasts for snow sports. Ski-ing on superb snowfields, skating and mountain climbing, are all to be found as well as splendid holiday accommodation. Our photograph gives a beautiful view of Mounts Sefton and Cook in New Zealand's Southern Alps.

CAPITAL OF A DOMINION

Wellington in North Island is the capital of the Dominion of New Zealand and stands on Cook Strait. It was founded in 1840 by pioneer settlers under an emigration scheme and has grown steadily in size and importance. As the photograph shows it is built in terraces on the hillside running down to the Bay. The picture gives a general view of the capital, taken from Tinakori Hill.

Photos: E.N.A.

New Zealand is rich in natural beauty as this photograph shows. It is of the magnificent Bowen Falls which from a height of 540 ft. tumble into Milford Sound, South Island.

Here is a companion picture, taken in North Island. In this we have a view of the Wanganui River and a Maori and his wife are in their canoe paddling themselves back to their riverside home.

THE MAORIS PRESERVE THEIR OWN CUSTOMS

Photos: High Commissioner for New Zealand

The native people, who were in New Zealand long before the European settlers, are the Maoris. Our photograph shows the carved top of a Maori Meeting House in the Rotorua district, North Island.

The Maoris are aristocrats among the native races. Valiant soldiers and skilled craftsmen, they have responded to education, yet have preserved their own character, as this photograph indicates.

E.N.A.

On September 15, 1882, the 1,200-ton ship *Dunedin* sailed from New Zealand with the first shipment of meat and butter, preserved in the freezing chambers science had devised. It was a big success and today New Zealand is one of Britain's main sources of food, while sheep farming has developed into a great industry. Our photograph was taken near Te Kooti in North Island.

The High Commissioner for New Zealand.

WITH BEAUTY ON THE DOORSTEP

These attractive bungalows at New Plymouth, North Island, are typical New Zealand homes. In the distance you can see the snow-tipped 8,260 feet high Mt. Egmont, " one of the world's most symmetrical mountains." The Dominion Government is the biggest home builder in New Zealand, whose modern houses are equipped with all sorts of labour-saving devices.

Housing Construction Branch, set up in 1937, has erected thousands of homes in attractively planned " State suburbs."

New Zealand has plenty of good schools—from free kindergarten schools to high schools, secondary and technical schools, and universities. Maoris attend schools in the ordinary way—there is no question of any " colour bar " as in some other parts of the world, although in some districts there are special Maori village schools. In remote parts of the country, children may even receive their lessons by post because they are too far away from any school.

The New Zealander, like the Australian, is a good sportsman as well as a hard worker. Rugby football is even more of a national sport than cricket, and as well as these sports there are yachting, tramping, hunting, and fishing for all to enjoy. At Christmas time, in the height of the summer, New Zealanders throng the many fine bathing beaches. The climate

is ideal for work and play in the open, and it is small wonder that the New Zealanders are natural lovers of outdoor life.

Though some parts of the Dominion —Christchurch, for example—resemble Britain, life there is very different from life in our own islands. What differences would you notice? The towns would probably be the first, for once you get away from the four " main centres " (Auckland, Wellington, Christchurch, and Dunedin), the New Zealand country towns have a strange air of newness. In some ways, they are more like the small, new towns of certain parts of America than any towns in Britain. Their streets are straight and wide, flanked mostly by wooden buildings.

Another difference to be noticed is that the major centres of population in New Zealand are along the coast. There are no inland cities as we know them. You would find, too, that the Dominion lacks the ugliness of the industrial centres of Britain and Europe,

FROM ORCHARD AND PASTURE

In an average year more than a million cases of apples are exported from New Zealand, and there are orchards such as the one shown in this picture in both North and South Islands. Citrus fruits—oranges, lemons, and grape-fruit—are also grown.

Photos : The High Commissioner for New Zealand.

New Zealand's dairy industry, dependent upon fine herds and pastures, is the most important. At such factories as the one seen above, cream from the herds is churned into butter. A typical factory like this will make more than six thousand tons of butter in a season.

SCENES FROM SOUTH ISLAND

Christchurch, on the Canterbury Plains in South Island, is the third largest city in the Dominion with a population of over 182,000. The city has many fine public buildings. Here, for example, is the Nurses' Home of the Christchurch Public Hospital.

Photos : The High Commissioner for New Zealand.

St. James' Church, Waiho Gorge, South Island, claims to possess the most beautiful reredos in the world. It consists of a window which reveals a glorious view of Franz Josef Glacier, the mighty ice river of the district known as the South Westland

Factories are operated on hydro-electric power in the main, and this " white coal " leaves the atmosphere refreshingly free from smoke and grime.

And what if you lived on a farm ? Most farmers in New Zealand have to work hard, but reap good rewards for their industry. The farmer's home will be comfortable and he will usually be able to have a car and a telephone.

Travel by Air

With such airports as Whenupai and Mechanics Bay at Auckland, Paraparamu and Rongotai at Wellington, and many others, New Zealand caters widely for commercial aviation, not only for internal services between the islands of the Dominion, but for services from all parts of the world. At *Rongotai*, a new airport for Wellington is to be built. From Auckland air routes stretch to London (via Sydney), to Honolulu, Los Angeles and San Fran-cisco, and to Vancouver. Internal services are operated by the New Zealand National Airways Corporation.

Stewart Island

So far, we have considered only the two main islands, the North and the South. South of these is Stewart Island, which is also part of the Dominion. It is very mountainous and rich in timber and one is not surprised to find it quite a holiday centre. It is divided from South Island by Foveaux Strait, but is sparsely peopled.

Other and more remote islands for which New Zealand is responsible are Kermadec, Chatham, Three Kings, Auckland, Cook and other islands of the South Pacific. New Zealand also holds the mandate for former German islands of the Samoa group, and is responsible for that vast stretch of the Antarctic called the Ross Dependency.

Photos : The High Commissioner for New Zealand.

NEW ZEALAND'S LARGEST CITY

Auckland's population of 350,500 makes it New Zealand's largest city. This picture shows the busy shopping centre, Queen Street. Standing on the isthmus formed by the Waitemata estuary to the east and the Manukau to the west, North Island's great city port of Auckland is New Zealand's gateway to the Pacific.

The Story
of the
World and
its Peoples

Countries
of the British
Commonwealth
of Nations

South African Railways.

KRAALS OF THE BANTU

Kraal is a word of Dutch origin meaning either a complete village, or an encampment of the Bantu people who are natives of South Africa, or a single hut of the kind shown above. The huts are ingeniously made of mud, which bakes hard in the fierce sun rays, and are strongly thatched with reeds and grasses over an umbrella-like frame.

UNION OF SOUTH AFRICA

WHEN, in 1487–8, Bartholomew Diaz discovered a sea route round the southern tip of the African continent, he told the Portuguese King of the terrible storms he had encountered rounding *Cabo tormentoso,* "the Cape of storms." The King, however, rejected this name, saying, "Rather let it be called *Cabo da Bona Esperanza,* Cape of Good Hope"—and Cape of Good Hope it has remained.

But the Portuguese made no attempts to colonise the Cape, which to them was no more than a milestone on the route to India and a sheltered anchorage (at Table Bay) for refitting. It was left for the Dutch to found Cape Colony, and the fine old Dutch houses that can still be seen in Cape Town and its neighbourhood remind us of sturdy Johann van Riebeeck who founded the first settlement in 1652. French Huguenots, victims of the revocation of the Edict of Nantes in 1685, also settled in the Cape where they were absorbed into the Dutch colony.

For a long time the nations of Europe were too preoccupied with their own wars and politics to give much attention to Africa which was almost a forgotten continent. This was an age, as Jonathan Swift puts it, when—

Geographers, in Afric maps
With savage pictures filled their gaps,
And o'er unhabitable downs
Placed elephants for want of towns.

But towards the end of the eighteenth century, public indignation against the slave trade revived interest in "the Dark Continent" and explorers began

301

to push into the interior—men like James Bruce, Mungo Park, a Portuguese doctor named Lacerda, and Pedro Baptista and his fellow trader José who together crossed Africa from Angola to the Zambezi.

On the Great Trek

War with Napoleon led Britain to seize the Dutch colony of the Cape which, in 1814, was formally ceded to Britain. In 1820, the Albany Settlers, over 5,000 of them, were landed where Port Elizabeth now stands to form the first living link between Britain and the Cape. But the Dutch farmers, or Boers, as they are called in their own language, were many more in number. Ruggedly independent and jealous of their liberties—particularly as regards treatment of the Native peoples—they soon became dissatisfied with British rule.

A year after the cession of the Colony, the Boers had revolted, and in the thirties of the nineteenth century there took place a wholesale emigration of Dutch farmers and their families known in history as the Great Trek. In numbers running into thousands the Boers packed their homes on their stoutly-built trek wagons and trekked across the Orange river to make new homes where they would be free from British rule. A few earlier settlers had already gone this way, but it was from the Great Trek of the Voortrekkers, as the emigrants were called, that sprang the Orange Free State and the Transvaal—developments which heralded the opening up of the whole continent and the extension of British rule from the Cape to the Zambezi.

It needed great courage and bravery to go out thus into the veld wilderness and build new states; for in addition to the natural dangers of the trek, the hostility of the native Africans had to be faced. A year before the great Trek began, 12,000 Kaffirs had raided the Cape Colony, murdering, plundering and pillaging. The story of South

South African Railways.

CAPE TOWN AND TABLE MOUNTAIN FROM THE AIR

Cape Town is the sea gate to the Union of South Africa and the capital of Cape Province. Here, spread out before us, are the busy docks and noble city with Table Mountain towering majestically behind. Table Mountain is often enshrouded in mist whose white cloud is termed " the tablecloth." At one point, Table Mountain is 3,549 feet high; its horizontal front is two miles long.

South African Railways.

CAPE TOWN'S CENTRE OF LEARNING

Magnificently set amidst lofty mountains and spacious parkland, the University of Cape Town marks the realisation of one of Cecil Rhodes' most cherished dreams. He had always wished to see a University on the Groote Schuur Estate, and this wish was respected when the foundation stone of this fine building was laid in 1925. The University has over 200 teachers and an average of more than 1,800 students.

Africa contains accounts of many wars —against the Hottentots, the Xosas, and the formidable Zulus. In 1877, the same year as the Transvaal was annexed, a peace of twenty years was broken by the Galeka-Kaffir War; and two years later, a British army over 22,000 strong was needed to break the power of the Zulus under their king, Cetewayo.

Stormy years still lay ahead. In 1880 there was the Basuto War—and in the same year the rising of the Transvaal Boers against British rule. Much more

South African Railways.

NATIVE WOMEN AT A DOMESTIC TASK

In this picture we see Native women of Bavenda stamping mealies, that is to say, making a form of flour from the grain of Indian corn. In South Africa there are five times as many non-European people as there are whites. Most of the Bantu live in kraals or villages, growing maize and other foodstuff crops and tending their cattle. Maize, Indian corn and mealies are names given in different parts of the world to the same crop.

serious was the Second Boer War of 1899 in which the Orange Free State and the Transvaal joined issue with the British forces in South Africa. But if the Boers lost the battles of the war, and if for a time they felt themselves to be an isolated and defeated people, they have now come into their own again. The Union of South Africa is now as independent as any member of the Commonwealth can be and includes Cape Province, Natal, the Orange Free State, the Transvaal and the mandated territory of South-West Africa. The

LIKE A HUMAN BEE-HIVE

The kraals or huts in which Natives make their homes are well adapted to the climate of South Africa, and we see above the Swazi method of construction. First of all, men set up a strong wickerwork frame, supported internally by upright poles and rafters. Women then assist in covering the structure and cording over the grass. There are no windows.

Photos : South African Railways.

The roof of this hut is supported by growing trees from which the branches have been stripped. The entrances to some huts may be so low that the occupants have to crawl inside. Notice the orderly assembly of the pots and utensils and the complete absence of furniture.

305

latter territory is now represented in the Union House of Assembly. Over 60 per cent. of the Union's white population is of Dutch descent. In addition to English, the Union has Afrikaans (South African Dutch) as an official language. Men like Botha and Smuts led the Boers to make their peace with the British; their goal—a united nation in South Africa—confronts us to-day as a tribute to their success. And while there might still be cause for resentment of Britain and things British, South Africa has shown that this is not so by her loyalty to Britain and her service to the Commonwealth cause in two world wars.

Cape Town

For many people, their visit to South Africa begins when they step off the ship at Cape Town. Cape Town is built round a beautiful bay some distance north of the famous Cape off which sailormen still believe old Vanderdecken, "the Flying Dutchman," cruises in his ghostly ship in unending efforts to weather the Cape. Over the city towers Table Mountain which, at certain times of the year, has its flat top shrouded in mists that overhang it and form what is popularly known as "the Tablecloth." To one side of Table Mountain is the Devil's Peak, and to the other Lion's Head—so called for reasons that are perfectly obvious the moment you see the mountain.

Cape Town is a city of splendid buildings and wide streets of which the finest is Adderley Street. From Cape Town runs the great railway northwards for many hundreds of miles to the Victoria Falls of the Zambezi, and on into the copper-mining country of the Belgian Congo, forming the southern part of the "Cape-to-Cairo" railway

South African Railways.

THE SNAKE PARK AT PORT ELIZABETH

Port Elizabeth, the second city and port of Cape Province, stands on the shores of Algoa Bay. Its famous Snake Park in Bird Street is known to all visitors, who will have living specimens of the snakes to be found in South Africa held up to their gaze by the attendants. Also at Port Elizabeth is Fort Frederick, which was built in 1799 and is thought to be the oldest British building in Africa south of the Equator.

South African Railways.

BUILT IN THE DUTCH STYLE

This is the Homestead of Groot Constantia, built by Governor van der Stel in 1685. Constantia is a famous wine centre, and the Groot Constantia wine farm contains about 140,000 vines. The early Dutch colonists introduced vines into South Africa to make brandy, and in 1688 Huguenots began to make wine there. To-day the vineyards of South Africa produce more than 7 million gallons of wine and 4 million gallons of brandy each year.

that was the cherished dream of Cecil Rhodes, the most famous of South African colonial pioneers.

The Native Peoples of South Africa

Land at Cape Town and you at once realise that Africa is the native continent of coloured peoples. In 1951 there were more than $8\frac{1}{2}$ million Native Africans in the Union, practically all of them members of the great Bantu race of Negroes. There were also some 365,000 people of Asiatic stock and more than a million of mixed or coloured origin. In contrast, there were only 2,643,187 Europeans.

Many of the workers on the waterfront and in the streets are Natives who do most of the labour in South Africa, both in town and in country. Large numbers of the Natives still live in their kraals or villages, growing maize and other crops, or keeping cattle. In the old days they fought, tribe against tribe; raids were common, and life was held cheaply by the great Bantu kings who swept as conquerors over wide areas. To-day, far from civilisation, the Natives live in peace and lead healthy lives in the open air. But in the towns they too often drift into bad habits, and live in what we should call slum conditions, learning only the evils and neglecting the good things of European civilisation.

How the Natives Live

The Natives no longer roam about in armed bands as they did before the rule of the white settlers; many live in Native Reserves where they can have their own farms; still others live among the white population, but keep to their own " locations." The Native Affairs Department of the Union government is responsible for many successful Native settlement schemes by which Native tribes are persuaded to permit

BOTH GOLD AND PRECIOUS STONES

This picture shows one of Kimberley's diamond mines, the Dutoitspan, with its surface plant and headgear frame. The first South African diamond was discovered in 1866 by a farmer named Schalk van Niekerk and sold for five hundred pounds.

Photos : South African Railways.

As this picture shows, the thoroughly up-to-date equipment of South African gold mines includes pneumatic drills. Workers like the Bantu shown in this picture drill out the valuable ore, their work yielding more than a hundred million pounds' worth of gold each year.

IN A VALLEY OF DIAMONDS

Not far from Pretoria, in the Transvaal, is the Premier Diamond Mine. It is a typical example of the older method of diamond-mining by means of an open shaft. This system has been discontinued, but it seems wonderful that man should burrow after precious stones so much as completely to change the surface of the earth over a wide tract. This famous mine is the one which yielded the great Cullinan diamond, one of the largest ever discovered. In 1946, over ten million pounds' worth of South African diamonds were sold.

their land to be classed as a Betterment Area in which old tribal practices give way to modern beliefs and methods. The government has also granted land to the Native Trust and is at present working on a 12-year scheme costing £10,000,000 for the betterment of the life of the Native peoples. Native health has recently been described as "a major national objective," and the memorial for South African soldiers who fell in the war has taken the form of a Health Foundation which supplements the work of the many existing fine hospitals available to Natives, as well as of the hospitals for the white population.

Native education is being extended and the National Housing Board is speeding up the production of homes for Natives and tackling the slum areas which tend to form when the Natives move into the towns.

Native Africans are in great demand as labourers on the farms and in the gold and diamond mines ; they are also employed as domestic servants in town and country. But always in the towns they live in parts set aside for them, where they have their own churches, schools and colleges. If they travel by train they must ride in the carriages that are specially reserved for them. Many are well educated and speak English quite well : large numbers, indeed, speak no other language nowadays. Perhaps the finest of them all are the Zulus, some of whom you are sure to see when you visit Natal.

In Natal, too, you will find large numbers of East Indians and you might wonder what these Asiatic people are doing in South Africa. They came originally to work on the sugar plantations, bringing their families and their own civilisation with them. Many have since become market gardeners and merchants.

South African Railways.

A SCENE IN THE "CITY OF GOLD"

Johannesburg has been rightly named the "city of gold," for it is the centre of the Witwatersrand goldfields, the richest in the world. Here we have a view of one of the principal streets in this prosperous city.

The Build of South Africa

What is the country itself like ? The map

AT CAPE TOWN AND PRETORIA

The Parliament of the Union of South Africa sits at Cape Town in the Houses of Parliament shown in this picture. The buildings are constructed of Paarl granite and red brick and have blue skies, brilliant sunshine, stately oak trees and the vast bulk of Table Mountain as their lovely setting.

Photos : South African Railways.

Though Parliament meets at Cape Town, Pretoria is the administrative capital of the Union. Here we see the stately Union Buildings which overlook the city from half-way up the Meintjeskop and are set in beautiful gardens.

tells us that most of South Africa is a series of great table-lands, whose average height above sea level is from 3,000 feet to 4,000 feet. This fact is very important, for it means that South Africa is not so hot as it would be if it were lower, and is one of the reasons why South Africa has the sunniest climate in all the world. Wherever you enter it from the sea, South Africa rises steeply and suddenly a little way from the coast. If you leave the sea at the shore of the Cape Province, you climb up a giant " step " to the plateau of the Little Karroo; cross this plateau and climb another " step," and you are on a still higher table-land called the Great Karroo; go farther north still and up another " step " and you reach the High Veld—the rich grass-land country of the Orange Free State and the Transvaal.

The Great Rivers

The southern African plateaux are crossed by three great rivers: the *Zambezi*, which divides Northern from Southern Rhodesia; the *Limpopo*, whose monster bend forms the northern boundary of the Union; and the *Orange*, whose tributary, the *Vaal*, divides the Orange Free State from the Transvaal. All three of them have falls and rapids where they cut through the table-land edges; on the Zambezi are the famous Victoria Falls, discovered by Livingstone in 1855; and on the Orange are the high Aughrabies Falls. The Orange flows west down to the sea through dry and desert country and has no port at its mouth; but the Zambezi and Limpopo flow east and down to hot, wet shorelands on the edge of the Indian Ocean.

Railways, Roads and Airways

A map of South African railways is an astonishing thing. If we take the great main Cape-Cairo route as a dividing line, we see to the east of it a network of railways serving busy towns, prosperous farms and rich mining areas; but to the west of it there are very few towns and hardly any railways at all. The reason is a simple one. The eastern part of South Africa is not only sunny, but it has plenty of rain brought by the onshore wet winds from the Indian Ocean; while the western part becomes drier and drier the farther west you go, until you come to real hot desert—the Kalahari, " land of the Great Thirst," where only a few Hottentots and Bushmen can exist. The western half is no home for human beings; the eastern half is rich in all things that make human life happy and prosperous.

As late as 1860, South Africa had but one railway, and that a very short line. To-day she has well over 12,000 miles of 3 feet 6 inches gauge line, and nearly another thousand miles with a somewhat narrower gauge. The railway system of the Union has more extensive main line electrification than any other similar undertaking in the British Commonwealth.

Apart from railways, South Africa has a maze of good roads along which heavy goods are often transported by " trains " of coupled vehicles. The Union also has highly developed commercial aviation, and air services— apart from local " air taxis "—have been under government control since 1934. Every large town has its airport or landing ground. *Palmietfontein* and the smaller *Germiston* airport are focal points for air routes to Durban, Port Elizabeth, Windhoek, Kisum on Lake Victoria, and Nairobi. The new £2,000,000 international Jan Smuts airport at *Kempton Park* is the most modern air terminus in the South. It is about twenty-seven miles from Pretoria and eighteen miles from Johannesburg. New airports are also being built at Durban and Cape Town.

Vines and Fruits

The region to the north of Cape Town is a land of vineyards and fruit farms, yielding wine, grapes, raisins,

THE UNION OF SOUTH AFRICA

Planet News

Cape Town is the Mother City of South Africa, an important world seaport, and the legislative capital of the Union of South Africa. It lies in an amphitheatre between Table Bay and the steep sides of Table Mountain, which rises to a height of about 3,500 ft. Part of Cape Town is built on the slopes and there is a cable-way up Table Mountain. Green Point, almost at the top of this photograph and about two inches from the right-hand side, is a bathing beach and residential area. Part of the city can be seen stretching away below the two climbers making the ascent of Table Mountain.

ROARING WATERS AND A SILENT BELL

E.N.A.

Here is a distant view of the famous Victoria Falls, on the Zambezi River in Southern Rhodesia. It was taken from the eastern end of the gorge into which the Zambezi drops.

Dorien Leigh

Most old Dutch homesteads have these slave bells, mementoes of the days when they called the slaves to work. The photograph shows the slave bell preserved in the Cape Town Municipal Gardens.

E.N.A.

The name of Cecil Rhodes is closely associated with the development of South Africa towards the end of the nineteenth century. This was Rhodes' house, Groote Schuur, in Cape of Good Hope Province.

E.N.A.

The Transvaal is famed throughout the world for its gold mines. In this photograph we have the headgear of a Rand gold mine with native workers coming from the mine at the end of the day.

WITH THE ZULUS OF TODAY

E.N.A.

Zululand is a division of Natal but was formerly ruled by Zulu kings. The Zulus include various tribes of Bantu speech. In these days most of them are engaged in peaceful pastoral and agricultural occupations and live in kraals under their own chiefs. A certain number migrate to the towns or to work in the mines. A typical Zulu kraal is seen in the photograph above.

Topical Press

Great warriors were the Zulus at one time and early in the nineteenth century they had developed an autocratic military organisation. Under their King Cetewayo they came into conflict with the British and fierce battles took place. Today their military attire is not greatly in evidence except on special occasions. Our photograph shows four Zulu warriors in full dress, carrying shields, assegais and knobkerries.

THE LAND OF THE OSTRICH AND ZEBRA

Central Press

Largest living bird in the world is the Ostrich, and in South Africa ostrich farming is quite an important industry, as the plumes of the birds have a high value. These plumes are taken three times in two years, the feathers being cut two inches from their sockets. These sockets are without nerves and the birds feel nothing when the plumes are cut. Our photograph was taken on an ostrich farm at Outsdoorn, South Africa.

More than sixty years ago, there was great danger that the wild life of South Africa was vanishing before the guns and snares of white and native hunters. A great national park was planned but it was not until 1902 that the Kruger National Park became really established. Today, the animals for which South Africa is famed, such as the zebra, the giraffe and others, can roam unmolested in this great park.

SCENES IN A NATIVE COLLEGE

In many parts of the Union, modern ways and beliefs are taking the place of the old tribal practices of the Bantu people. Native education is being extended and this picture shows us students of Bacteriology at the Fort Hare Native College at Alice in Cape Province.

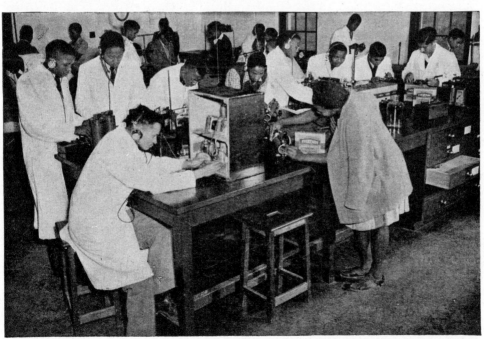

Photos : South Africa State Information Office.

Christian missions did fine work in the cause of Native education, and at Fort Hare Native College there are Anglican, Presbyterian, and Methodist hostels. As you can see from this picture of students in the physics laboratory, the old days of primitive life in a kraal are passing.

peaches and other fruits that adorn our shop windows when such fruits are not in season in the northern hemisphere. For South Africa is on the other side of the world and has seasons opposite to ours. This fruit-growing business is much like that of the Mediterranean lands and of California; for this part of the Cape Province has rain chiefly in winter, and the long, dry sunny summers that favour fruit-growing if only enough water can be supplied.

At Cape Town and other places can be seen fruit canneries, and " pre-cooling plants " where fruit is " cooled " before it is exported in ships specially equipped with " cool chambers " in which the fruit will not over-ripen on the long voyage.

A great contrast to these South African fruit-lands are those of Natal, where the climate is hotter, and where rain is much more abundant and spread more evenly over the year. In Natal grow pineapples, bananas and other fruits, as well as sugar-cane and a little tea—just as they do in the hot wet coast-lands of Queensland, Australia.

The Veld

Farther away from the sea are great stretches of natural grass-land, known generally as the Veld, and in many ways like the grass-lands of Australia or the Argentine. Millions of sheep are raised on these splendid pastures, and wool is one of South Africa's chief exports as a result. In the drier areas such as are to be found on the Karroos, sheep, too, as well as goats and ostriches are reared; but since feathers went out of fashion, fewer ostriches are kept. The wetter grass-lands of the Transvaal and the south-east are fine cattle country, for cattle need much more water than sheep, which flourish best on the richer parts of the Great Karroo. In the cattle-lands dairy-farming is a very profitable business.

South African Railways.

This could be a school in Britain, but it is actually the Roedean Girls' School at Johannesburg, named after the famous girls' school at Brighton, England. Education in the Union has reached very high standards and about 92 per cent. of the European children in the Union go to state schools. Native and non-European children go to schools mainly provided by missionary and other private societies.

South African Railways.

A SKYMASTER OVER JOHANNESBURG

The Union's state-owned Airlines use Douglas Skymasters for their share in the air service which links Johannesburg with Britain. South Africa is very air-conscious and her airways are a vital part of her internal and world communications. The Jan Smuts International Airport at Kempton Park, 14 miles from Johannesburg, is one of the finest of its kind.

But rich as South Africa is, in fruits and grain, in sheep and cattle, we think of it first and foremost as the land of diamonds and gold; for its fortunes were largely built on these two valuable minerals, and diamonds and gold are still very important among its products to-day.

The " Valley of Diamonds "

A railway journey from Cape Town to *Kimberley*, in the " Valley of Diamonds," and then from Kimberley to *Johannesburg*, the " city of gold," will give us a very good idea of what the Union of South Africa is like. From Cape Town we steam for many hours through a rich fruit-growing region, past towns with beautiful old Dutch houses, and with sparkling streams of water running down the sides of their shady avenues. We are over 100 miles from Cape Town before the train begins to make the steep ascent to the Karroo by many rising bends and tunnels. Up and up we go, but it is not until the morning of the second day of our journey that we are really on the Karroo, rolling across the dry lonely plains, past kopjes that stand out like high islands of steep red stone above the general level. At evening the drab plain becomes almost wonderful— it takes on new colours; the scent of thyme and bush-herbs fills the air. Camp fires flicker in the dusk, and noises of cattle come from a distant farm, snug amongst its clumps of gums and willows.

The Cross-roads of South Africa

At *De Aar* junction we pass the cross-roads of South Africa, where a line of railway branches off north-westwards to cross the Orange and link up with the railway system of South-West Africa, and another runs south-east across the Karroo to the coastal plain and the seaports of *East London* and *Port Elizabeth*.

South-West Africa is mainly stock-

ON THE FRUIT FARMS

The climate of South Africa is ideal for the growing of luscious fruits of many kinds, the most famous of which is the orange. Citrus fruits such as oranges, grapefruit, and lemons form the second most important of South Africa's exports of farm primary products, and we see here Native orange-pickers bringing in baskets of fruit to a Northern Transvaal Farm.

Photos : South Africa State Information Office.

These Native girls are picking papaws on a Native Trust farm in Northern Transvaal. The papaw is a melon-like, semi-tropical fruit, with honey-golden flesh and myriads of tiny seeds in the centre. Papaws contain *papain* which has valuable medicinal uses, and though they are native to Central America they are grown extensively in the Transvaal.

SCENIC BEAUTIES OF THE UNION

Eighteen miles from Oudtshoorn, Cape Province, are the wonderful Congo Caves of whose subterranean wonderland only two miles have been explored.   Rider Haggard visited the caves and is
said to have been inspired by them to write *King Solomon's Mines*.

Photos : South Africa State Information Office.

When Sir Francis Drake sailed round the Cape of Good Hope in 1580, he described it as " the most
stately thing and the fairest Cape we saw in the whole circumference of the earth." This description
might well apply to the whole Cape Peninsula whose grandeur is revealed by this aerial picture.

BANTU LIFE AND WAYS

These Shangaan women, who live on a Native location in the Letaba district of the Transvaal, are using a maize " mortar " for pounding their maize into meal.

Wearing pale blue blankets and adorned with many necklaces, bracelets and anklets, two Pondo housewives pause by the roadside for a friendly chat.

This shows us the inside of a typical Zulu home in one of the more backward areas where tribal customs, witchcraft, and the witch doctor still influence the lives of the Natives. Such homes are visited by Health Assistants, under the Family Welfare Service scheme.

'NEATH AFRICA'S AZURE SKIES

South African Railways.

Fruit grows as well in South Africa as it does in California, for both are lands where sunshine never fails. Here we see the harvesters at work on a typical farm in Western Cape Province where some of the best grapes in the world are grown.

South Africa State Information Office.

South Africa has an important canning and preserving industry which, as far as fruit is concerned, has most of its factories in the Western Cape Province near the chief fruit-growing districts. This picture shows us fruit being prepared for jam-making at Worcester in Cape Province.

raising country. Cattle and sheep are supplied to the Union proper and meat is exported from *Walvis Bay*, where there is cold storage plant. Diamonds are an important export. They are found along an extensive coastal stretch extending northwards from the Orange river. *Windhoek* is the capital of South-West Africa.

But as we are bound for Kimberley, we branch neither right nor left at De Aar junction. Our journey continues northward, and 470 miles from Cape Town we cross the Orange and arrive at Kimberley, 547 miles from our starting-point, where fortunes were won in a day when the diggings were first opened up. Since then many great stones have been found—one, the Porter-Rhodes diamond, discovered near the centre of the Kimberley mine, was valued at £60,000.

Diamond-mining has given Kimberley the "greatest man-made hole in the world." This "Big Hole," as it is called, is the Kimberley Open Mine, and it is practically within the city. During the forty-four years in which it was worked, the Open Mine produced three tons of diamonds.

Near Warrenton, north of Kimberley, the railway crosses the Vaal river and divides, one line going via *Vryburg* to *Mafeking* (famous for its siege during the Boer War) and thence to Bulawayo in Southern Rhodesia; and the other line going via Christiana, Klerksdorp and Potchefstroom to our next stopping place, Johannesburg.

Riches of the Mines

Johannesburg is the "city of gold," for near it is the richest goldfield on the globe—the Witwatersrand ("white waters ridge"), or, as it is popularly called, "The Rand." The Rand stands on a high plateau nearly 6,000 feet above sea-level and stretches 70 miles from *Randfontein* and *Krugersdorp* in the west, through *Johannesburg* and *Germiston*, to *Springs* in the east. The rock in which the gold is found is now got from deep mines by expensive and up-to-date mining machinery, to be treated by scientific methods to make it yield its golden treasure.

Fewer than forty years ago the total area covered by Johannesburg was but nine square miles; to-day its municipal boundaries enclose an area of about ninety square miles, with nearly a thousand miles of streets and roads.

Johannesburg of To-day

South of the Equator, Jo'burg is the largest city in Africa, its Commissioner Street and other business centres being comparable to those of any place in the world. Looking at a picture of Commissioner Street, it amazes one to realise that well within the span of a single human life this vast metropolis of gold has grown to its present proportions and that precious metal to the value of over fifteen hundred millions of pounds has been won from the reef on which it stands. Although the Rand spreads across a high plateau, toil in some of the gold mines is actually carried on below sea-level and at a depth of one and a half miles under the earth's surface. South of Johannesburg is the Village Deep Mine, which goes down to 7,700 feet.

Quite recently, new gold deposits were discovered in the Orange Free State, in an area centring round *Odendaalsrus*, about 150 miles from Johannesburg. The gold here does not lie close to the surface and prospecting the new field has meant deep drilling.

The new fields are about thirty miles long, and ten miles across at the widest point. Thirteen mines are being developed to work the £3,350,000,000 worth of gold which the fields are said to contain. Once a small village, Odendaalsrus is on the way to becoming a town of 40,000 people. Three other towns will also serve the new fields: *Welkom*, *Virginia* and *Allanridge*.

An interesting point about South African gold ores is that they contain "one of the largest known sources of uranium." In 1950 an agreement was

South Africa State Information Office.

HOFFMAN SQUARE, BLOEMFONTEIN

Bloemfontein is the capital of the Orange Free State and has a total population of about 90,000, of which some 41,000 are Europeans. Here are the lovely gardens of Hoffman Square set around a memorial to those who fell in the World War of 1914–18. Bloemfontein is also the judicial capital for the Union, the Court of Appeal being set up here in 1910.

made by the Union Government for the sale of its uranium to the United Kingdom and the U.S.A.

The Jacaranda City

About thirty miles from Johannesburg is *Pretoria*, the administrative capital of the Union of South Africa. It is a city made particularly beautiful by its famous jacaranda trees, which are planted along 250 miles of streets and avenues. In October and November, when the trees bloom, they are ablaze with lovely mauve flowers.

There are many interesting places to visit around Pretoria, among them the famous Premier Diamond Mine, where the Cullinan diamond, which is now among the Crown Jewels, was found; the Wonderboom Nature Reserve and

Bird Sanctuary, with its remarkable, 300-years-old wild fig tree; and the recently completed Voortrekker Monument. Built in granite, the Monument tells the story of the pioneers in the marble frieze which runs round its Hero's Hall, and also has massive figures of the leaders of the Great Trek.

Kruger National Park

But to many visitors the most fascinating part of the Transvaal lies along its eastern border. For here is the Kruger National Park, one of the most impressive wild animal reserves.

This park has an area of about 8,000 square miles and is the home of almost every species of African wildling from the elephant and the lion to the smallest of antelopes.

NATAL AND THE ZULUS

South African Railways.

THE RICKSHA "BOY"

A favourite form of transport in Natal is the ricksha, which may be said to take the place of taxi cabs for short distances. These vehicles are drawn by Zulus picturesquely garbed and wearing strange headgear. Many of these ricksha "boys" are upwards of 6 feet in height, and can pull their loaded carriages at a rapid pace mile after mile without tiring. Owing to the nature of their work, however, these men are said to be short-lived.

IT was Vasco da Gama who gave Natal its name. When, in 1497, he "doubled" the Cape and began feeling his way carefully along the shores of South Africa, he came on Christmas Day to a dim coast-line which he called in honour of the day the "Land of Natal."

The Terraces

To-day Natal is one of the most prosperous provinces of the Union of South Africa. She is different from all the rest. The long slope from the high ridges of the mighty Drakensberg down to the Indian Ocean looks towards the sea and the warm trade-winds which bring abundant rains to all the province. Natal is warmer and wetter than the rest of the Union; the land rises from the coast in three wide terraces or belts, each of which offers its own special advantages to farmers and planters.

Nearest the sea is the subtropical belt, moist and warm, where planters grow sugar-cane and tea, subtropical fruits like bananas and pineapples, mangoes and papaws. Many of the workers on the sugar plantations are not African Natives, but Asiatics, who have come from India, bringing with them their families, their priests, their shops and their amusements. You can see them at work in the green cane, the bright dresses of the women giving gay spots of colour here and there; at night you can hear the beat of their

THE VALLEY OF A THOUSAND HILLS

South Africa State Information Office.

Half-way between Durban and Pietermaritzburg is "The Valley of a Thousand Hills," one of the most famous beauty spots in Natal province. The picture shows us the hotel to which tourists come for magnificent views of the surrounding countryside.

South African Railways.

Though Durban is not the capital of Natal province, it is the chief commercial centre. The city has a population of over 475,000 (more than 150,000 Europeans and 324,000 non-Europeans). This picture shows the shopping centre and City Hall.

South African Railways.

IN THE DRAKENSBERG MOUNTAINS

The beautiful and rugged Drakensberg Mountains form a giant rampart dividing Basutoland from Natal. They are the " Himalayas of South Africa " and their jagged peaks rise in places to over 11,000 feet. In few parts of the world can untamed nature be seen in such magnificence.

drums and the thin pipe of the Hindu flute;   you may come upon a small Mohammedan mosque or perhaps a white plaster Jain temple in the heart of the sugar-cane country;   and you meet in your walk home in the cool of the evening veiled Moslem women, slender Hindus, and quiet Tamils— of different religions but all from India.

The Higher Belts

Beyond the coastal belt there is another and higher terrace where maize, millet, Kaffir corn and other grains are grown, and where cattle, sheep and horses are reared. It is chiefly in this " midland " belt that the wattle grows, whose bark is of great value in tanning, and is used not only to cure South African leather, but also in the tanneries of other countries.

Above this belt rises the third—the " upland " belt, which is cooler than the others because it is much higher above sea-level.   This is a land of cattle and sheep, of wheat and barley, of potatoes and garden vegetables.

Up in the Drakensberg

Behind all three belts rise the slopes of the Drakensberg Mountains, a giant rampart 600 miles long, separating Basutoland from Natal. The highest peaks are Champagne Castle (11,500 feet) and Mont aux Sources (10,800 feet). You can go up to these grim heights from the coast at Durban, the busiest port in the Union of South Africa, taking the train to Bergville, where you leave the railway for a mountain hotel near the deep gorge of the Tugela river.

Very early in the morning you start out with the guide, breakfast at " Breakfast Rock " before 8 a.m., and go up and up through woods of wild elder and tree-ferns to the magic colour of the lower rocks of Mont aux Sources in the sunlight. It is cold up there, especially to those who have come from the lazy warm lands by the sea;

THE MEN OF ZULULAND

Here is a Zulu chief in full war kit standing keen and alert outside his hut in the native kraal or village. The Zulus are a splendid race of African Natives.

This elderly Zulu is sitting in solemn contemplation, wearing his ceremonial blanket. At one time, Zululand was a powerful kingdom.

Photos : South African Railways.

The word Bantu is used to describe the various languages, numbering nearly 400, of the African Natives; it is also used as a racial description and includes many types of African from the pygmies to the tall Zulus. Our picture shows a typical Zulu craftsman engaged in making clay models of animals and heads outside his native hut.

SOME ZULULAND TYPES

The Zulus are a splendid race of Africans, tall and well-built, and once formidable warriors. To-day they live a peaceful farming life in their own country of Zululand, ruled by their chiefs under official supervision. The picture shows two Zulu wives and (right) an unmarried girl.

Photos : South Africa State Information Office.

Here, in the finery of their ceremonial dress, are three members of the Mandhlakazi tribe of Zulus. We can imagine from this picture how fearsome and imposing the Zulu *impis* must have appeared in the times before peace came to Zululand. Older Zulus will still tell tales of those distant days when such kings as Chaka, " that great one," ruled.

WONDERFUL HOWICK FALLS

South Africa State Information Office.

Fifteen miles from Pietermaritzburg, Natal Province, the Umgeni river plunges over a sheer precipice into a dark basin 365 feet below, forming these beautiful Howick Falls. The distance is double that of Niagara; and when rain swells the river waters, the falls become one of the most impressive in the world. Part of the power of the falls is used to generate electricity, but their scenic beauty has not been spoilt.

but the view is one of the world's wonders.

There is a famous pass in the Drakensberg at the head of the Goodoo Gorge, over which the dignified Basuto farmers stalk beside their shaggy ponies loaded with bags of grain or rough bales of wool from their farms in the valleys of Basutoland to sell in Natal. There are places, too, where you can see the rock paintings of the first people who lived among these mountains—the Bushmen, who dwelt in this part of Africa long before the

advance southwards of bigger, stronger and more intelligent people from the north.

The Natives who lived in Natal when first the Dutch and then the British began to make their homes in the country were the Zulus, who live to-day mainly in their own country of Zululand, ruled by their chiefs under the supervision of officials.

A Race of Warriors

The Zulus are a splendid race of Africans, tall and well-built, living in their neat huts of beehive shape in their kraals or villages, sometimes on the hilltops, sometimes on the slopes just above the bottom of a valley. Their homes are marvellously constructed of pliant twigs and poles bent over and plaited with smaller ones, and then covered with long grass thatch. The furniture is of the simplest—a few mats, vessels for cooking and storing food, a kaross (skin) or two, and that is all. Around the kraal are the mealie patches in which maize is cultivated; a cattle enclosure is close by, for the Zulus rear many cattle.

When the white men first made treaties with the Zulus, the terrible Chaka was lord of the land ; he was slain by his brother Dingaan, another powerful Zulu king whose *impis* (regiments) " ate up " all the smaller peoples who dared to resist him. Cetewayo, a later king, fought the Zulu War with the British, but was defeated after a brave struggle, and Zululand was taken over at last in 1897 by Britain, forming now part of the Union of South Africa.

In the towns, especially in Durban, you will see Zulus most wonderfully decorated with ostrich feathers or horns on their heads and ornaments and bangles on their arms, drawing the rickshas that are commonly used by people for short journeys.

South Africa State Information Office.

A ZULU CONSTABLE

This Zulu constable typifies the proud warrior tradition of his race. His name is Baile and he is the great-grandson of a Zulu king. Like the other members of his Force, he is a dependable and trustworthy policeman.

The Zulu of To-day

It is only in remote Zululand that

South African Railways.

ON AN OSTRICH FARM

Of all the birds in existence in our time the ostrich is the largest. To the top of its back and not counting its neck, the creature may be 5 feet in height. In parts of South Africa are large farms devoted to the breeding of flocks of ostriches, whose value lies chiefly in the wonderful plume feathers. The feathers are cut about once in eight months and the bird feels no more pain than you do when trimming your finger nails. About 60,000 lbs. of feathers are exported from the Union each year.

you will see Zulus as they were when Chaka, "the great elephant whose tread shakes the earth," ruled with a rod of iron; and that only on special occasions—tall warriors with their karosses about them, white tails of gnus at their knees, with hide shield and assegais. To-day the Zulus are peaceful farmers growing mealies, Kaffir corn from which their favourite drink, *tshwala*, is made, pumpkins, beans and sweet potatoes. Cattle, sheep and goats are looked after by the boys. Gardening near the kraal is done chiefly by the women and girls. Men set up the framework of the huts, but women always do the grass-thatching.

Not so long ago the real power in the Zulu kraal was the witch doctor whose command over the spirits of the forest, bush, and water was respected and feared by all. Witch doctors are now

forbidden by law, but in the kraals you may still hear tales of their charms and of the "spirits" they controlled; and older Zulus will tell how the spirit of Chaka, "that great one," wanders at night with his ghostly *indunas* and *impis* over such old battlefields as Rorke's Drift, Isandhlwana, and Ulundi.

One of the sights for visitors to Zulu-land is the Hluhluwe Game Reserve, nearly 200 miles from Durban, which is famous for its Black and White Rhinoceros. Accompanied by Native Game Guards, you can wander freely in the Reserve, staying overnight at one of the rest huts where everything—including hot and cold water and servants—is provided at a remarkably low cost. The Reserve has the appropriate telegraphic address of "Rhino."

British South Africa

Three Native protectorates, which are

not part of the Union of South Africa, form British South Africa. They are Basutoland, Bechuanaland and Swaziland, and they are administered by a High Commissioner appointed by the Queen. The largest of the three is Bechuanaland, which is the home of over 292,000 Africans. The most important tribe in Bechuanaland is the Bamangwato, once ruled by the famous Native king, Khama, who died not long ago at the great age of ninety-three. *Serowe*, their capital, is probably the biggest Native town in southern Africa.

The Kalahari Desert

Much of the Bechuanaland Protectorate forms part of the waterless area of the Kalahari Desert, the " thirstland " as the Boers called it. The only true inhabitants of the Kalahari, and there are comparatively few of them, are the small, yellow-skinned Bushmen, who live on roots and small animals that they find, with an occasional large animal (springbok, perhaps, or giraffe) killed with the help of a poisoned arrow.

The Bushmen are expert trackers. When they have hit an animal with one of their arrows, they will follow its trail for hours, or even days until the poison has taken effect. Then they will camp by the carcase until they have eaten every part of it. They get water from " sip-wells "; these are hollow reeds placed in holes in the sand at places where certain plant life shows that water is present. Water sucked up the reed is carefully stored in ostrich-egg shells, which are then sealed with clay and buried in caches in the hunting grounds to be used when the dry season comes.

Basutoland is much smaller, but has a population of over half a million. *Maseru* is the chief centre. Swaziland has a population of some 184,000. The chief centre is *Mbabane*.

South African Railways.

AN OX-WAGON AT THE FORD

Though the Union of South Africa has State-owned air services, good roads, and steam and electric railways, almost every country district has its traditional ox-wagons. To-day, the patient beasts haul heavy loads for the South African farmer as their kind did for his pioneer ancestors.

The Story
of the
World and
Its Peoples

Countries
of the British
Commonwealth
of Nations

Paul Popper.

"WHO DESERVED WELL OF THEIR COUNTRY"

From this granite height in the Matopo Hills can be seen the wonderful panorama known as " The World's View." This spot was named by Rhodes as a resting-place for those " who deserved well of their country." Cecil Rhodes himself lies buried here and his grave is seen in this picture. On this same summit are the graves of Sir Starr Jameson and Sir Charles Coghlan.

RHODESIA AND NYASALAND

ON July 14th, 1953, the Royal Assent was given to the Rhodesia and Nyasaland Federation Bill, which thus became law. In this way the path was prepared to bring together in a Central African Federation three important parts of the British Commonwealth— the self-governing territory of Southern Rhodesia, Northern Rhodesia and the Nyasaland Protectorate. For the present, the Federation will be called the "Federation of Rhodesia and Nyasaland," and *Salisbury* has been named as its capital.

The Rhodesias take their name from Cecil John Rhodes, who did so much to develop this vast part of Africa. A large bronze statue of him stands in *Bulawayo*,

the second city of Southern Rhodesia, whose Government House was built where Lobengula, King of the Matabele, had his kraal until his downfall in 1893. The statue does not bear Rhodes' name, for everyone here knows of the great Empire Builder and his achievements.

Visitors to Bulawayo make a point of going to the Matopo Hills, south of the city, to see the last resting-place of Cecil Rhodes. It stands at the top of a rounded granite hill, known as " The World's View " because the surrounding scenery is so wonderful. Chosen by Rhodes himself as a burial ground for those " who deserved well of their country," the hill top is also a resting-place for Sir Starr (Dr.) Jameson and Sir Charles Coghlan.

In both the Rhodesias and Nyasaland, the Europeans are very much outnumbered by the Africans. For example, in 1951, it was estimated that there were nearly 2 million Africans and about 136,000 Europeans in Southern Rhodesia; in 1952, Nyasaland had nearly 2½ million Africans and only 4,000 Europeans.

The Rhodesias are part of the savannah region of the African plateau. Cattle and other animals are reared in large numbers by the Africans, who grow food crops (especially maize) in their fields. Maize, wheat and tobacco are important crops for European farmers in the Rhodesias. In Southern Rhodesia cotton is also grown, and there are large fruit orchards and important dairy farms.

Southern Rhodesia

The capital of the Federation is *Salisbury*, which has a European population of over 40,000 and is the centre of an important gold-mining area. At Salisbury, too, are tobacco factories and many other industries. A still more important centre for the mineral wealth in which Southern Rhodesia abounds is *Gwelo*. Within seventy-five miles of the town are: *Que Que*, an important gold-mining centre, near which are large deposits of ironstone and lime, and the important *Riscom* steel works ; *Selukwe*, where chrome ore and gold are mined ; and *Shabani*, with its asbestos and gold-mines.

From Selukwe we might travel to Fort Victoria, twelve miles from which are the remarkable ruins of Great Zimbabwe.

There has probably been more argument about Great Zimbabwe than there has been about the Pyramids. Nobody really knows who built this city stronghold, although all sorts of stories have been told to explain it. Its origin is hidden in the mists of the past, but it is evidently the work of a forgotten people

AFRICANS PERFORM A TRIBAL DANCE

Paul Popper.

Wearing the skins of wild animals and carrying knobkerries, these Africans of the Charter District, Southern Rhodesia, execute a tribal dance to the hand-beaten rhythms of a drum. A delighted audience of Africans and Europeans watches the steps and gestures that have probably been handed down through the ages.

Paul Popper.

AN AFRICAN COMPOUND AT SELUKWE, SOUTHERN RHODESIA

At the Wanderer Gold Mine near Selukwe, the thatched huts of the African Compound are dotted over the hillside. The Gwelo District, which includes Selukwe, contains several of the most important gold mines in Southern Rhodesia, among them being the Wanderer and Tebakwe Mines, which are the most productive mines of the district.

who knew that gold was to be got in large quantities in the neighbourhood, for abundant traces of their workings have been discovered. For a long time it was thought that this was the city whence the Queen of Sheba procured gold to present to King Solomon when she paid him the State visit recorded in the Old Testament, but this has been proved to be only a romantic tale.

Zimbabwe

Zimbabwe ruins lie in three great groups, which all at one time probably formed parts of a well-populated city, of which the so-called citadel formed the central point. The Zimbabwe people had wonderful systems of irrigation for their fields, carrying water for hundreds of miles along the hillsides. The stones of which the temples, forts, walls and palaces are built are set in place without mortar. One of the strangest buildings is a mysterious conical tower in front of the court of the temple. Yet the

people who inhabit the region to-day are the simple Makalanga tribesmen—Natives whose best efforts at architecture are their little huts of wattle-and-daub.

Bushman Paintings

Great Zimbabwe, once a king's capital, a great trading centre, with its fortress and temple, its gold-mines, craftsmen, builders and skilful farmers, is now nothing more than heaps of ruins for learned men to dispute over while the Makalanga squat at their hut doors and wonder in their simple minds what all the fuss is about.

If we explore the Matopo Hills carefully, we shall find things far older than Zimbabwe that are the works of men. On the rocks are strange paintings in colour done by the prehistoric bushmen—hunter-artists who lived there long ages ago. More than one such rock painting shows the Victoria Falls as five streams of white water falling over red cliffs, with a cloud of white vapour rising high above all.

Did the race of men who built Zimbabwe come from far-away Arabia? No one can say, but the Arabs have always been wonderful traveller-traders.

Some claim that Southern Rhodesia was the land mentioned in the book of Genesis as "the whole land of Havilah where there is gold," and that the people who built Zimbabwe were Sabaeans from the distant Yemen. But proof of such theories has yet to be found. The ancient builders left neither burial grounds nor inscriptions, although statuettes and trinkets have been found and can be seen in the museums at Bulawayo and Cape Town.

The Victoria Falls

Southern Rhodesia is extremely rich in coal. The main field is in the north-west, at *Wankie*, and is said to contain more than 4,000 million tons. Some $3\frac{1}{2}$ million tons are mined each year—

enough to supply the whole of south central Africa.

About sixty-eight miles by rail from Wankie is Victoria Falls Station, which is about a mile from the famous Falls and not so far from the Victoria Falls Hotel, which we can make our centre for the trips to the chief points of interest.

The Victoria Falls are even more astonishing than Niagara. The Zambezi River, here rather more than a mile in width, plunges bodily into a chasm over 300 feet deep, to rush madly through a narrow zig-zag gorge that straightens out eventually; and after forty-five miles of pent-up energy in this long cleft, the Zambezi recovers its normal width and its stately progress to the sea.

The Smoke that Thunders

David Livingstone discovered these famous Falls in November, 1855. In his account of this discovery he tells

Paul Popper.

A MODERN STREET IN BULAWAYO

The city of Bulawayo in Southern Rhodesia was founded in 1893 and has grown rapidly. To-day, its population numbers over 40,000. Its name comes from the Zulu word *ubuluwayo*, meaning "killed." Among its modern thoroughfares is 8th Avenue. The statue in the background is a bronze memorial to Cecil Rhodes.

Paul Popper.

GOING TO SCHOOL IN SALISBURY

These children are about to enter the David Livingstone primary school at Salisbury, the capital of the Federation of Rhodesia and Nyasaland. Salisbury was formerly the capital of Southern Rhodesia, but was named as the first city of the Central African Federation in 1953.

how he saw in the distance five tall columns of vapour, white below and dark above, as if vast areas of grass were on fire, and thus accounts for the native name given to the Falls by his followers—Mosi-oa-Tunya, " the smoke that thunders." He describes his canoe journey to the island, which hangs perilously over the lips of the Falls (now called after him " Livingstone Island "). " Creeping with awe to the verge," he says, " I peered into a large rent which had been made from bank to bank of the broad Zambezi. . . . On looking down into the fissure on the right of the island, one sees nothing but a dense white cloud, which at the time we visited it, had two bright rainbows in it. From this cloud rushed up a great jet of vapour exactly like steam, which condensing, came back in a constant shower, which soon wetted us to the skin. This shower falls chiefly on the opposite side of the fissure, and a few yards from the lip there stands a straight hedge of evergreen trees, whose leaves are always wet."

The Rain Forest

This " hedge " is the dense Rain Forest fringing the shore opposite the southern lips of the Falls, and divided by the chasm known as the Boiling Pot, through which the imprisoned Zambezi makes its escape from the Palm Grove opposite the south-eastern rim of the Falls. The railway from Cape Town skirts the edge of the Rain Forest, crossing the gorge at a point about 200 yards below the Boiling Pot in one magnificent arched span of 500 feet, at a height of 400 feet above low-water level. Trains cross this bridge at only about five miles an hour, and when the river is high, in the month of April, the spray from the Falls washes the carriage windows. You can cross this bridge on foot, if you pay the usual toll of 1s. " return." You may even descend by iron ladders fixed in the side of the gorge to the left of the bridge, into the gorge itself and view at close quarters the terrifying rush of waters.

The Rain Forest is a tangle of great trees linked by festoons of creeping vines, amid which fairy rainbows continually dance in the spray. Sometimes you may see a troop of baboons busy amidst the greenery, and if you hunt among the tree roots and the stones you will find hundreds of *crabs* of all sorts, sizes and colours—land crabs, of course.

The most beautiful of the cataracts into which the Falls are divided are the Rainbow Falls, which can be best viewed from Danger Point; but the most awe-inspiring are the Main Falls, by the side of Livingstone Island. There is nothing on the African continent more calculated to inspire awe, and you may be sure that no one with nerves stands too near the edge of any of the numerous vantage points. At the Falls is an excellent hotel which offers the best civilisation has to give actually in the realms of the primitive and in a setting that has been termed the Taj Mahal of Nature.

Victoria Falls and Niagara

A comparison between the Victoria Falls and Niagara is very startling—the Victoria Falls are over 300 feet high, while Niagara at its highest is only about 167; and Victoria Falls discharge 100 million gallons of water a minute, while Niagara discharges about 84 millions. For a long time there has been talk of harnessing the Victoria Falls to power-stations, and of sending electrical power by transmission lines to the great gold-fields of the south, just as the Canadians and Americans have harnessed Niagara. A small hydro-electric station does actually exist and generates enough power for Livingstone and the Victoria Falls Hotel. Apart from this the Falls remain unharnessed, although the possibilities of a great hydro-electric station at Kariba Gorge, east of the Falls, are still being considered. Early in 1953 it was decided to build hydro-electric stations on the Kafue River, which is a tributary of the Zambezi. These will probably be at Kafue Gorge and in the Keshya Ravine and will serve, in the first place, the needs of Northern Rhodesia's copper belt as well as industry in Southern Rhodesia.

Another sign of progress in this part of Africa is the new importance of *Livingstone*. The airport opened there in 1950 is considered the largest and most modern in southern Africa and is used regularly by the London-Johannesburg services.

Northern Rhodesia

From Livingstone we can continue the journey by rail to *Lusaka*, capital of Northern Rhodesia, and on to *Broken Hill*, a rich lead, zinc and vanadium mining centre. (Vanadium is used for toughening steel). Cobalt, used for making high-grade steel, and copper are obtained from Northern Rhodesia's *Nkana* mine.

Northern Rhodesia is one of the four greatest copper producers in the world. Her copper area adjoins the rich Katanga copper area of the Belgian Congo and has such centres as the *Kansanshi* mine, the *Nchanga* copper mine, the *Roan Antelope Mine* and several others. In some of the larger mines gold as well as copper is obtained. Iron ore deposits are being investigated near Lusaka, and coal was recently discovered at Neganega, south of Kafue.

People sometimes speak of the native Africans as if they were all much of a muchness. In fact, there are often many differences in a comparatively small area, and an excellent example of this is provided by Northern Rhodesia. Its African population numbers less than two millions, but is made up of no fewer than sixty tribes speaking more than thirty languages.

There are Native Reserves and large areas of Native Trust Land. Among the former is Barotseland, which occupies the westerly part of Northern Rhodesia.

TWO VIEWS OF THE VICTORIA FALLS

The Victoria Falls on the Zambezi River in that part of Africa now known as Southern Rhodesia were first discovered by the famous missionary, David Livingstone, in 1855, and are about a mile wide and more than 300 feet deep.   This photograph was taken from the air.

South African Railways.

Livingstone's black followers called the Falls Mosi-oa-Tunya, which means " the smoke that thunders."   After the Falls the river runs through gorges and ravines till it reaches the Kebrabasa Rapids after which it becomes navigable for 400 miles to its mouth.

These Reserves, and similar areas in Southern Rhodesia, are set aside for the native Africans, who can there live the peasant-farming tribal life that has been theirs for many centuries.

But in some parts of Central Africa, particularly in Southern Rhodesia, this way of life is changing; and the change is expected to become sharper as time passes. It has been estimated that in about twenty-five years' time the number of Africans living in towns, with their old tribal links severed, will have risen from a few thousand to some two million in Southern Rhodesia alone. Housing these new town-dwellers and establishing industries which will provide employment for them are but two of the problems that will have to be solved when the African population becomes too large for areas set aside for it.

Nyasaland

Between Northern Rhodesia and Lake Nyasa lies the Nyasaland Protectorate. Its soil is very fertile ; tobacco, cotton, tea and other crops are exported.

Zomba is the headquarters of the government, but *Blantyre* and *Limbe* are the chief towns, and both stand on the railway that runs from *Salima*, near Nyasa, to the port of *Beira* in Portuguese East Africa. This railway crosses the longest bridge in the world—the Zambezi Bridge, which spans the great river between Sena and Dona Ana. Built by a Darlington engineering firm, the bridge is 12,064 feet long and is supported by thirty-five main piers sunk 120 feet down in the river bed.

A. J. Shipley.

A TOWERING CITY OF THE ANTS

Even in England we can find quite large ant-hills, but none to compare in size with the Rhodesian ant-hill shown in this picture. More than a dozen sturdy Natives are needed to overthrow the giant hill which has been reared above the ant-city.

The Story
of the
World and
its Peoples

India and Pakistan:
Two Members
of the
Commonwealth

Paul Popper.

THE ESPLANADE AT BOMBAY

Modern blocks of flats look out over the calm waters of the bay, but not far away can be found the docks and cotton mills which explain the importance of Bombay. More than 2,800,000 people now live in the city ("greater Bombay"), which in size is second only to Calcutta. This great port on the western seaboard is a gateway to the whole of India.

TWO COMMONWEALTH REPUBLICS

THE vast sub-continent which is often still called "India" by geographers is now divided into two separate nations. They are the Union of India and the Dominion of Pakistan. Both are republics, which have chosen to remain members of the British Commonwealth.

The sub-continent is the home of many peoples. About 222 languages, apart from many dialects, are used and there are many different religions and customs. Of the total population of more than $432\frac{1}{2}$ millions, over 65 per cent. are Hindus, living chiefly in their own Union of India. The Moslems form more than 23 per cent. and live chiefly in their own country of Pakistan. In the Union of India, fourteen languages are officially recognised and, although English is at present used for all official purposes, its place will in time be taken by Hindi. The national language of Pakistan is Urdu.

To understand why the sub-continent has had to be divided we must know a little of its history. The beginnings of that history are in the distant past; the oldest books are believed to date from about 1500 B.C. and are written in Sanskrit, which is not unlike Persian. But the first real landmark was the invasion in 326 B.C. by Alexander the Great.

There had been many and varied chapters in the long story before the East India Company was founded in 1600 to carry on trade in the subcontinent. The first settlement of the East India Company in time grew into the great city now known as Calcutta. By 1758, when Clive became the Governor of Bengal under the East India Company, British influence had become dominant. Just a hundred years later the British Government took over control of all the territory administered by the Company. Later, on January 1st, 1877, Queen Victoria was proclaimed Empress of India.

The British Raj (rule) largely brought to an end the quarrels among the different races. There was firm rule and progress. Great and beneficial changes were brought about by education, and the spread of medical science and industrial organisation. British advice and assistance was given to the Indian princes who, as a result of treaties they made with the British, continued to rule their own territories. At one time there were actually over 560 separate States in India, some large like Hyderabad, others so small that they contained but a few thousand people. Practically all the princes' States have now joined either Pakistan or India, but the future of some areas (e.g., Kashmir) was not decided immediately.

During the present century there were various changes in the government of the country, while much was done to improve education, carry out public works and build railways. The wish of the different peoples to govern themselves grew stronger steadily, and several British commissions tried to arrange a system of government that would be fair to all peoples and parties and avoid the dangers of civil war.

At last Britain decided that the sub-continent should become self-governing and Lord Mountbatten was appointed Viceroy to help in bringing this about. The hope, of course, was that the different peoples would agree to work together and that the whole sub-continent would become a single self-governing nation of the British Commonwealth. But the differences were too great, and

E. N. A.

THE LEGISLATIVE ASSEMBLY BUILDING AT NEW DELHI

New Delhi has arisen at Raisina, some three or four miles from the walls of the old city. Most of its buildings are white, but the Secretariat, Government House and some of the other structures are of red sandstone. Above is depicted the Legislative Assembly Building at New Delhi, the city which is the headquarters of the Government of India.

Pictorial Press.

KARACHI, CAPITAL OF THE DOMINION OF PAKISTAN

Karachi is a comparatively modern seaport and city of the Province of Sind. Founded in 1843 it became the capital of Pakistan in 1947. It has a fine harbour and airport and is the main gateway for the trade of the Punjab. In this photograph is seen Bunder Road, one of the main shopping districts of the city.

as a result two separate nations were created—India and Pakistan—as from August, 1947. This was the best that could be done, for the Hindu and Moslem points of view could not be reconciled. Lord Mountbatten ceased to be Viceroy but was appointed Governor-General of the Dominion of India in order to complete his task during the period of transition. He retired when the two new nations had become fully established and the Prime Minister, Pandit Nehru, appointed a member of the new Dominion government to succeed him. In 1950 India became a Republic but remained a member of the British Commonwealth of Nations.

A tragedy that threatened serious outbreaks of violence was the assassination of the great Hindu leader, Mahatma Gandhi, in January 1948. Fortunately, the worst fears were not borne out by events. Pakistan also had its own tragic loss within some eight months after Gandhi's death.

Mohammed Ali Jinnah, who had led the Moslems of India in the struggle to maintain their own independent state of Pakistan, died suddenly at the capital of the new Dominion, Karachi.

It was a serious loss to Pakistan at a time when the leadership of Mr. Jinnah was most needed. He had himself taken on the post of Governor-General at the beginning of the new era. The formation of two new and separate nations created tremendous problems which needed the combined wisdom of both Hindu and Moslem to overcome successfully. These problems are being slowly solved.

Mountain, Forest and Plain

Taken together, India and Pakistan can be divided into three main geographical regions.

Firstly, there is *Himalayan India and the North-West*. Here the climate ranges from the icy snows of Everest and other mountain giants to the humid heat of the tropical jungles at the foot of the great ranges. Below the snow line there are mountain pastures, and then dense forests with valuable stands of timber. Sheltered valleys are farmed by the Gurkhas of Nepal, the Bhutanese of Bhutan and similar peoples. Kashmir, in the far North-West, also has fertile lands where fruit, grain and vegetables are grown.

But the North-West generally is drier and comparatively barren. The soil is poor, the climate harsh, and people there find it hard to get a living from the land, although such areas as the valley of Peshawar are fertile, and goats, camels and cattle are raised on the dry plateau of Baluchistan.

The second region is the *Indus-Ganges Plain*, formed by the middle and lower basins of the rivers Indus and Ganges. The Punjab region of the Indus basin is an important farming area whose fertility has been brought about by irrigation canals. The dry area of the Sind also depends on irrigation works. It is the controlled use of water that makes possible the large crops of grain, cotton and fruits. In the basin of the Ganges grain, cotton, jute and sugar-cane are grown; on the hillsides, particularly in Assam, there are tea plantations.

The third region is the *Deccan*, whose plateau forms the peninsular part of the sub-continent. In the north-west Deccan cotton is grown for the mills of Bombay, Ahmedabad and other centres. Rice, sugar-cane and gourds are also crops of the Deccan, and there are rich forests of teak and sandalwood.

Visiting India and Pakistan

For a visit to India and Pakistan we should require clothing for both cold and hot weather. The sub-continent is so large that, while it is pleasantly warm in the south, it may be unpleasantly cold in the north. The best time to go would be during the cool season. This lasts from October until the end of February; there is little rain and travel will be comfortable. From March until June there is the hot season, when the ground is parched and it is very dusty. In June the south-west monsoon brings the rainy season, which continues until October.

If we had plenty of time for our visit, we might travel to the sub-continent by ship. But there would be so much to see that we would probably prefer to get there as quickly as possible, in which case we would travel by air. Our B.O.A.C. jet air liner will speed us comfortably from London to Karachi, the capital of Pakistan, via Rome, Beirut and Bahrein. We would leave London Airport at 9 a.m. and be in Karachi, more than 4,400 miles away, by 11.20 p.m. the same day! The next day, the same service would take us on to Delhi or Calcutta before continuing its journey to Tokyo.

Once in India or Pakistan we could make use of the many internal air services operated by Indian companies such as Air India, Indian National Airways, and Air Services of India; and by Pakistan companies such as Orient Airways and Pak Air. There are also the roads and railways.

The major roads follow the routes of the old trunk roads, the greatest of which was known as the Grand Trunk Road; it ran from Peshawar in the north-west to Calcutta, a distance of some 1,500 miles.

But as far as the past is concerned it was the railways which opened up the sub-continent. The first railway was opened to traffic in 1853, and since then such expansion has taken place that India and Pakistan have the third largest railway system in the world. It was not an easy system to build; in the mountainous north, for example, engineers had to cut over a hundred tunnels to carry the line up to Simla. To-day the railways mostly belong to the two Governments and are known respectively as Indian and Pakistan State Railways. They carry 600 to 700 million passengers every year.

THE UNION OF INDIA

Col. F. D. Fayrer.

A WONDERFUL BUILDING AT RAGNAGAR

Ragnagar is a remote place in Rajasthan, a Union of twenty-two States, and here we see a structure of singular beauty whose pillars and ceiling give evidence of most exquisite carving and workmanship. This building is of great antiquity, but so far from the beaten track that few people can visit it.

WHEN partition took place in 1947, much the richer and greater part of the sub-continent became the Union of India. It was only in the production of certain food-stuffs that Pakistan found herself the wealthier of the two new nations. According to the census of 1951, India has a population of more than $356\frac{3}{4}$ millions, of which more than 241 millions get their living from agriculture.

Farming, then, is the chief industry of India. But, although such concerns as the big sugar mills may farm large acreages, Indian farmers are mostly of the peasant kind, living in countless small villages scattered across the country. Only $61\frac{3}{4}$ millions of India's population live in towns. Of her cities, only Calcutta and Bombay have populations of over a million, and there are not more than fifty towns in all whose populations exceed 100,000.

The most common centre of life is the village, with its simple crafts and industries. Some villages are lucky in having rail and road links with the towns. But in those parts remote from train and bus travel there will be small communities whose only contact with the towns is through any inhabitant who has been on a pilgrimage, perhaps, or has served in the army. This isolation has not made it any easier to spread education and knowledge of ways and methods that will raise the standard of life.

Water for Dry Lands

Improving life in the villages is the object of the Community Development Programme which forms part of India's First Five-Year Plan. This plan was approved by the Indian Parliament in December, 1952, and is intended to provide more food for India's millions, not only by introducing better ways of farming to the villagers but by increasing the fertility of the land by more irrigation. The experts say that only by bringing more land under irrigation can India grow enough food to feed her people properly.

Many new dams and canals are therefore to be built; indeed, many have already been constructed, including the Nangal Dam in the Punjab. This dam

343

THE TATA STEEL WORKS AT JAMSHEDPUR

For many years India had to import steel, but she now has her own flourishing steel industry with its headquarters at Jamshedpur. Part of the great Tata plant there is seen in this picture of electric magnets loading shipyard plates into trucks.

is part of the Bhakra-Nangal scheme, by which water will be taken from the upper Sutlej to irrigate nearly 3½ millions acres and at the same time generate electricity for Delhi, the capital of India. Bihar and West Bengal will benefit from the Damodar Valley Scheme, which is to be carried out by the Damodar Valley Corporation, a newly established body very like America's famous Tennessee Valley Authority and responsible for much the same type of work. The first works of this scheme, the Tilaiya Dam and Bokaro Power Station, were opened by the Indian Prime Minister, Mr. Nehru, in February, 1953. What he then said shows how important these projects are to India's future: "The people in the villages need no longer be afraid of famine and drought. They are assured of an ample water supply throughout the year. Cheap electricity will not only illuminate their houses but will go a long way towards the industrialisation of an important area. Mills and factories will grow and flourish and help in solving unemployment in the country."

In the Damodar Valley

India is already one of the leading industrial countries of the world. For many years she had to import steel, but now she makes not only enough for her own needs but a surplus for export. Her centres of iron and steel production are *Jamshedpur* (Bihar), *Bhadravati* (Mysore), and *Hirapur* and *Kulti* (Bengal). Of these the most important is Jamshedpur, which is the headquarters of the Tata Iron and Steel Company and produces some 800,000 tons of finished steel every year.

The raw materials for this Indian "Sheffield" are found within the sub-continent. Half India's coal (and India

OLD AND NEW WAYS IN INDIA

Indian Official Photograph.

Ploughs of this kind were in use in Bible times and are still used in some parts of the world. Britain now has an important share in providing modern ploughs, tractors and other implements for farmers in the more backward lands where up-to-date ways of cultivation are being practised for the first time.

By courtesy of Rotary Hoes Ltd.

Once this Indian rice farmer had no better tools than the oxen and wooden plough seen in the top picture. But to-day he finds it better to use a British tractor and rotavator for the cultivation of his flooded rice fields.

is among the eight leading coal producers in the world) comes from Bihar. About three million tons of iron ore are mined each year in India, and about half of this comes from the Singbhum district of Bihar. If we except Soviet Russia, India is the largest producer of manganese in the world, and this comes mainly from the Central Provinces. It is thus easy to understand how something approaching an industrial revolution has taken place in India in recent years and how the centre of this revolution has been Bihar where the raw materials of heavy industry are so easily accessible. India now makes her own aircraft, her own motor vehicles: and what is more, has shown in the success of the Jamshedpur plant that no matter what their caste, religion, or tongue, her many different peoples can work in hamony side by side. For the workers at Jamshedpur are among the best paid and best housed in India. What is most interesting about them is that they include Brahmins, Mohammedans, Buddhists, Christians, and Untouch-

ables: that is to say, peoples of different ways and beliefs who do not always get along well together in other parts of the sub-continent; at Jamshedpur, however, they work together amicably, so pointing the way which all the peoples of both India and Pakistan must tread.

Changing India

New industries, new towns and cities, new irrigation and land improvement schemes—all these are naturally to be expected in India as part of the rapid growth of this new nation. An example of these developments is Chandigarh, the new capital of the East Punjab. This entirely new city is being built on the plains south-west of Simla to take the place of the old Punjab capital, Lahore, which went with western Punjab to Pakistan. European and Indian architects are working together on the new capital and by early 1954 some of the Government departments had already moved into the city.

But the fact remains that the villages are still the homes of most of the people.

Photos : Crown Copyright.

OFF TO THE SMELTING HOUSE

This is another part of the Tata works. Metal pours from one of the runners of the blast furnace into a giant ladle which will take it to the smelting house.

IN A BOMBAY COTTON MILL

Bombay is the centre of the important Indian cotton industry. This picture shows the reeling department in one of the most modern mills in the city.

THE SIGHTS OF SOUTHERN INDIA

E. N. A.

THE ELEPHANT TEMPLE AT MADURA

Madura is one of the most wonderful old cities of Southern India, and here we see the famous Elephant Temple. Elephants were often carved out of solid rock, and we should remember that Ganesh is the elephant-headed god of wisdom and good fortune—one of the sons of Siva the Destroyer. Visitors to some of the temples of Madura have bestowed upon them garlands of marigolds at the time of the Hindu festival held at the January full moon.

THE traveller entering India from Ceylon lands at Danuskodi. From this port among the sands the train runs across a low-lying country with clumps of cabbage palms and clusters of mud huts, thatched with palm leaf, to the richer land where peasant farmers clad only in waist cloths are busy in the paddy fields, watering the land by the ancient method of raising water from the wells and pouring it into little channels of the fields.

At the Well

Patient bullocks work all day long up and down the little slopes by the wells, lowering the big hide buckets into the water and lifting them filled. The buckets are emptied by the peasants with a pleasant gurgling as the cool water slips down the conduits.

Our first stop is at Madura, one of the most wonderful old cities of Southern India, containing a great temple which is reckoned to be the finest of its kind in the sub-continent. It covers twenty-five acres. Like most temples of Southern India, it stands within a number of squared walled enclosures, pierced by magnificent tall gateways called *gopurams*, which rise storey upon storey on a rectangular base to a high crowning ridge.

Gods and Heroes

Each storey is carved into thousands of sculptured figures of gods and heroes, with an effect that is staggering to the Western mind bewildered by the over-richness of detail. To understand the meaning of the figures one must be well-versed in the Hindu religion, and know at least the chief of the hundreds of shapes and forms assumed by the two great gods—Vishnu the Preserver, and Shiva or Siva the Destroyer and Re-creator. The most important of the three principal gods is Brahma, the Supreme Being, or Universal Soul. These three, Brahma, Vishnu and Siva, form the Trimurti, on which Hinduism is based.

A Hindu Festival

Within the walled enclosures are the priests' dwellings, and the temple itself, which rises tier upon tier, each crowded with sculptures. Within the temple is the sacred place where the figure of the god is kept. At Madura there is the image of Ganesh, the elephant-headed god of wisdom and good fortune—one of the sons of Siva the Destroyer. We give a present of money to the priests and go into the

temple to wander for an hour or so through its mysterious interior and among its thousands of carven pillars.

As we come out a priest bestows upon each of us a garland of marigolds, for this is the time of the Hindu festival that is held at Madura at the January full moon. The streets of the city are thronged with pilgrims gathered together from all parts for this solemn occasion. The chief ceremony will be the passage of the gods on richly-ornamented rafts round the sacred tank, which is a vast sheet of water two miles in circumference.

Millions of fairy lamps will glow from the terraces round the tank, and the procession of the gods will be illuminated with coloured fires and heralded by the booming of gongs and the beat of drums. Elephants will clear

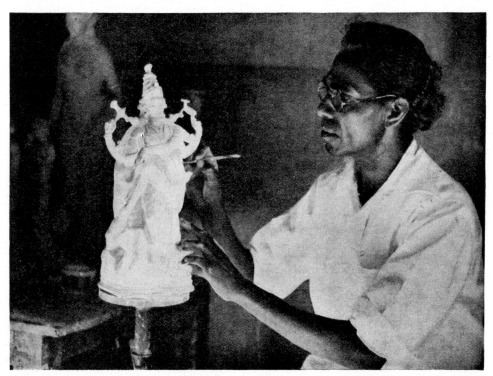

The High Commissioner for India.

IN A TRAVANCORE CERAMIC FACTORY

Recent excavations in various parts of India have revealed that a highly advanced knowledge of pottery making as well as other branches of art and architecture existed as early as 3,000 B.C. In more modern times the artist has been employed in designs for factory-made goods. In this picture the modeller is giving the finishing touches to a figure before the mould is made in a factory at Travancore.

the road round the tank so that the priests and their helpers, pulling on the huge hawsers, will have clear space in which to manœuvre their unwieldy rafts to the landing-place whence the gods will be borne high to the temple from which they were brought, there to rest until next year's festival.

Hindu Castes

This visit to Madura brings us into contact with Hinduism, one of the great Indian religions. We cannot pretend to understand it, and we are far too wise to smile at what we do not understand. What to us is a meaningless jumble of gods and goddesses, and a number of festivals attended by crowds of excited people, is a very different thing to the Hindus themselves.

We learn, for the first time, that

The High Commissioner for India.

A DANDI SADHU

India has always been noted as a land of religious tolerance. For thousands of years various religions have existed side by side. In this picture is seen a Dandi Sadhu, one of the ascetic sects which practise self-denial.

The High Commissioner for India.

A BENGALI GIRL IN SARI

The *sari* is a garment of great antiquity in the East and India has long been famed for the beauty and quality of this type of product. In this photograph a Bengali girl is seen with the *sari* draped from the shoulder as this garment is usually worn in India.

the coloured marks we notice on the foreheads of many Indians are marks that indicate the particular religious sects to which they belong. These marks are not caste-marks, as some people suppose.

Caste, again, is another matter which we find difficult to understand. The Hindus are divided into many castes or " classes," each of which keeps strictly to itself ; a man of one caste may not marry a woman of another—he may not eat with people of another ; even the shadow of a lower caste person falling upon his food will prevent a high-caste man partaking of it. Long ago the castes were only four — the Brahmins, of priestly descent ; the Kshattruyas, of military descent; the Vaishiyas, or merchant class ; and the Sudras or workers, builders, farmers and labourers. Later, there were many divisions and subdivisions of these, as

E. N. A.

BOULDER-PERCHED TEMPLE AND FORTRESS

At Trichinopoly is a great rock-fortress which towers above the town roofs from its high perch
on the rock that heaves its shoulders above the palm trees. The rocks are picturesquely sculptured by nature, and on the very summit is a temple. This is one of the most impressive sights
of Southern India, and the rock-mass rises to a height of more than 270 feet.

well as the "untouchables." Many
influences are at work to-day, however,
which tend to break down the caste
system.

From Madura we take train again for
Trichinopoly, not forgetting to buy a
bunch of small plantains to give to the
monkeys that come down from their
playgrounds on the roofs of wayside
stations to beg at the carriage windows.

Trichinopoly and the Carnatic

The sight to see at Trichinopoly is the
great rock-fortress, which towers above
the town roofs from its high perch on
the rock that heaves its shoulders above
the palm trees. Facing it is the
sacred tank, in the midst of which is a
small shrine; the temple itself is
carved out of the rock. The great
plain which stretches around Trichinopoly in a sea of chequered tints of

growing crops is the part of the
Carnatic about which we read in our
history books at those pages which tell
of the exploits of Clive in the early
days of British interest in India. The
Fort of Arcot is only 140 miles away to
the north.

Madras

Madras is our next objective. Like
all India's great sea gates, it has a
part that is distinctly European, with
fine modern buildings, and a portion
that is even more distinctly Indian.
The bazaars interest us more than the
European quarters of the city; but
we find the splendid Law Courts worth
a special visit. The great banyan tree
—a tree which we see in Madras for
the first time in reality—commands our
attention; its branches drop to the
ground suckers which take root and

MADURA'S GREAT TEMPLE

E. N. A.

If you were travelling in Southern India you could see this wonderful Great Temple of Madura which rears its stone head to a height exceeding 150 feet. The Temple Gate is shown on the left. Amidst what looks to be a maze of sculpture are figures of gods, heroes, bulls, elephants and many other gilded or brightly-coloured forms. There are thousands of these sculptured figures, some of them representing Vishnu the Preserver and Siva the Destroyer in hundreds of shapes and styles.

become new trunks, so that a single tree looks like a grove of trees.

In the hot weather, the Europeans who can afford it forsake Madras for Ootacamund—" Ooty " they call it— a hill station in the midst of the beautiful Nilgiri Hills, where the tea estates and cinchona plantations flourish, and where tiger as well as sambhur and other deer roam in the thick forests that clothe the wetter slopes. These forests are the homes of the primitive Toda people, who speak their strange language that has never been written down, and live their lives in the same way as their forefathers did 2,000 years ago and more.

The High Commissioner for India.

STUDENTS AT AN ADULT NIGHT SCHOOL

India's universities are well-known, but as in Britain there are also other institutions where older students can pursue their studies after they have spent the day in normal work. Students at a night school for adults in the Morabad District of Sahaspur are seen at their studies in this picture. One advantage of India's warmer climate is that many of the classes can be held in the open air.

Specially painted for this work.

AT THE CHAR MINAR IN HYDERABAD

Hyderabad, the fourth largest city in India, is the capital of the great Indian State of the same name. Among its famous buildings is the Jama Masjid, a copy of the Mosque at Mecca. Another, equally well known, is the Char Minar, seen in the picture above, which stands in the heart of the city where the four principal streets all meet. With four minarets, built upon four huge arches, the Char Minar was erected in 1549 and was formerly used as a college. It is 180 feet high and each side is 100 feet wide.

Paul Popper.

THE ROOFLESS SHRINE OF THE STANDING BUDDHA

Time and the elements have eaten away much of the statue of the Standing Buddha in the Lankatilaka Shrine at Polonnaruwa. Many centuries ago this sacred ruin was one of the splendours of a royal city, for Polonnaruwa was the residence of kings and the capital of Ceylon. Then came the abandoning of the city. Its strong walls and rich temples were swallowed up by the jungle, which held them in thrall until recent times. Among the many remarkable ruins to be seen at this ancient place are the palace of King Parakama I and the imposing Jetawanarama temple.

H. J. Shepstone.

THE CAVE-TEMPLES OF ELLORA

The temples of Ellora, believed to date from the eighth century, have been carved out of the solid hillside—great pillars, images of gods and goddesses, life-size elephants and a profusion of intricate ornamentation all cut with patient perfection from the rock itself. Above we see the Kailas Temple, and there are in the same neighbourhood caves of great antiquity hewn in the rock.

RAILWAY travel in India is very different from a journey by rail in Britain. The distances, to begin with, are much greater, and the trains are specially adapted to give passengers as much comfort as possible over long journeys in a climate which is distinctly hot for the greater part of the year.

Every traveller who intends to see more of India than he can from the windows of his express train will engage an Indian servant or "bearer" to take a good many of his little worries from his shoulders and to smooth out the way, so that everything runs without a hitch. If he plans to go any distance from the main routes, the

traveller also takes care that a "cook" goes too.

As long as you are in one of the fine trains of the Indian State Railways, or located at one of the many excellent hotels in the cities, you are quite able to fend for yourself; but directly you strike out into less beaten tracks, you will be sadly at a disadvantage without your "boy" or bearer. For it is he who books your seat in the trains, packs and looks after your luggage; he sees that your meals are forthcoming at the proper time, whether you are on the train or staying for the night at one of the "rest-houses" provided at convenient places along the roads away from the towns; he makes your bed for you, valets you, tips the right people (with *your* coins, of course) and sees that you get your money's worth everywhere.

Indian Trains

The carriages on the Indian express trains are so arranged that the seats, which lie in line with the length of the train, can be converted into comfortable beds for the night—a job which your bearer does for you. The carriages are fitted with electric fans and dustproof windows; and there is a comfortable restaurant car as well as a bath-room. You can, if you wish, have one of the splendidly-equipped tourist cars, with your own private dining-room, sitting-room and bed-room, and with your own kitchen and

your own servants' quarters; but that is for wealthy people who like to travel in luxury!

Suppose you have landed at Bombay, the great port on India's western seaboard that is the gateway to the whole of India. You have your choice of at least five mail trains and three main line expresses a day on the old G.I.P. (Great Indian Peninsula) route—to the Punjab by way of Delhi and Lahore; to Calcutta *via* Jubbulpore and *via* Nagpur; to Cawnpore, Lucknow and the cities of the Ganges; or to Madras and the wonderful city-temples of Southern India, by way of Poona and Raichur.

Railway Routes from Calcutta

If, however, you have made Calcutta

The High Commissioner for India.

AN INDIAN ORCHESTRA GIVES A BROADCAST

Radio entertainment has become as popular in India as in most other parts of the world, and India's musicians have taken to broadcasting with enthusiasm. The instruments are different from those seen in a similar British orchestra, though some of the stringed instruments bear a certain resemblance. This photograph was taken at the Dehra Dun broadcasting station which forms part of the Indian Government's rural development scheme.

your starting-point, you have the choice of an even greater variety of routes and fast trains. From Howrah terminus two mail trains and seven expresses run daily to Benares, Cawnpore, Lucknow, Agra, Delhi, the Punjab and Bombay. From Sealdah terminus you can travel to Darjeeling, the beautiful hill station which is the refuge of many Europeans during the hot season, to the tea estates of Assam, and to Chittagong in East Pakistan.

Using the railways alone, it is possible to visit all India's finest cities and to learn a great deal of the country without departing very far from the beaten track. But if you want to see the real India, you must forsake the tourist routes, strike out into less-known highways, and live in India long enough to understand her people and their ways.

Let us take such a journey, starting from Victoria Station at Bombay, and climbing over the Western Ghats on to the Deccan by the pass. Four hours' journey brings us to the sacred city of Nasik, which is the holiest of all Indian cities, save Benares. It stands at an altitude of nearly 2,000 feet above sea level, near the source of the sacred Godavari, by whose waters

Associated Press.

THE MUNICIPAL BUILDING, BOMBAY

Bombay, on India's western seaboard, is the gateway to the whole of the Indian sub-continent; and besides being a great seaport, the city is the centre of India's cotton industry. From the harbour, the city's stately buildings form an impressive sight. Here is the Municipal Building, one of the features of the city.

gather millions of pilgrims from all parts of India to perform the one essential duty which ensures them salvation. Nasik is a city of Hindu temples where, at certain times of the year, great religious festivals are held.

The Ellora Caves

Stranger still are the cave-temples of Ellora. These we can visit by car from Aurangabad, which is not on the main line, but on a narrow-gauge railway from Manmad. If we elect to stay at

23—2

Ellora for the night, there is a good rest-house or dak bungalow where we can put up. The temples of Ellora have been carved out of the solid hillside—great pillars, images of gods and goddesses, life-size elephants, and a profusion of intricate ornament all cut with patient perfection from the rock itself.

Monasteries, too, with numerous rooms and windows and staircases for the monks of old, have been similarly excavated from the solid rock with infinite care and labour. At least three religions have played a part in the work: Buddhist, Hindu and Jain. The Buddhist temple has great seated figures of Buddha, and a marvellously-carven roof ; the Jain caves are filled with perfect statues, each in its niche, storey upon storey. The Jains have their finest temples at Mount Abu, which is visited by many tourists during the season ; their faith is very much like that of the Buddhists, for they believe that after this life a man's soul may pass into the body of an animal, and they therefore look upon ill-treatment and slaughter of animals as utterly hateful.

Ellora is in the State of Hyderabad, the largest and most populous in the Indian Republic. It is as large as England and Scotland combined and has a population of over 18½ millions. In *Hyderabad* city, the capital of the State, are the Osmania University, which was the first to teach entirely in Urdu ; the Falaknuma Palace, which is considered a fine example of modern Indian architecture ; and the Char Minar, a graceful sixteenth-century arch crowned by four minarets.

Cotton on the Deccan

Up here on the Deccan is the wonderful black soil in which cotton grows best. It was formed by the breaking up of the lava which covers the north-western part of the Deccan. It does not powder into dust as most other soils do in the hot season, but re-

tains a great deal of moisture, although it cracks widely. The cotton seed is sown when the big rains are over, and the tenacious lava soil forms a sort of clod round the roots of the growing plant, so that it flourishes without irrigation and without much rain, and the cotton is ready to pick when the hot season begins in March. Cotton is grown also in the Upper Ganges basin and in the Punjab, but under very different conditions.

We saw at Bombay how the people of India engage in the cotton manufacture themselves, employing the most up-to-date machinery in large cotton mills that bear comparison with those of Lancashire. We shall see the same thing at Delhi, Lucknow, Cawnpore, and other cities, where the tall fingers of factory chimneys break the beautiful skyline of ancient temples and palaces. The people of India, however, also use cotton in the ancient way, weaving it on their primitive looms and dyeing it perhaps with the old vegetable dyes, producing really fine fabrics.

Famous Strongholds

Back at Aurangabad, we are reminded of the great Moghul Emperor, Aurangzeb, who gave his name to the city, for we can go to see the stronghold of Daulatabad which he built for himself long years ago. Farther north, another stronghold perched bravely on a great hill overlooks the city and the palaces and gardens. From Bhopal, visitors go to see the strange domelike monuments on the hill at Sanchi. They are called stupas or topes, which the ancient Buddhists erected over sacred relics or holy spots. The most wonderful things at Sanchi, however, are the beautifully-carved gateways, stone rails and steps, which are covered with elaborate sculptures that tell the story of the life of Buddha. They are the Buddhist scriptures written in stone by the sculptor-artists of the sixth century before Christ, at the command of the great Indian Emperor, Asoka. Some of the stupas

"CROWN OF THE PALACE"

E. N. A.

The Taj Mahal near Agra is known throughout the world as the loveliest specimen of Indian architecture. It was built by the Shah Jehan in memory of his beloved queen, Mumtaz Mahal, whose sepulchre it forms. Twenty thousand men worked upon this beautiful building.

have been opened and found to contain the bones of famous disciples of the great teacher, Gautama Buddha.

Gwalior's Castled Crag

Going north, the train takes us to Gwalior, dominated by the " castled crag of Gwalior," flat-topped, with steep sides that actually overhang in places, and approached by a single road guarded by six great gates. Here the mutineers of 1857 took refuge, and held out until two young British officers with a small force, including a clever blacksmith among its number, crept up and picked the locks of the first five gates before they were discovered by the defenders.

Now we are on the way to Agra and Delhi, the two great Indian cities that recall most vividly the splendour of the Moghul Emperors who, from the time of our good Queen Bess to the days of Queen Anne, ruled over the greater part of India—sometimes from Agra, sometimes from Delhi. Their names are more than memories, for they stand also for mosques, palaces and monuments that to this day are among the wonders of the world— the Emperors Humayan and Akbar, Jehangir, Shah Jehan and Aurangzeb.

The Great Moghuls

It was Babar, descendant of the great Mongol conqueror, Genghiz Khan, who swept down into the plains of the Ganges and Jumna with his twelve thousand wild hillmen and desert warriors, met Lodi, the last of the Afghan kings of Agra, and completely routed his hundred thousand men and their thousand armoured elephants, in 1526.

Both Agra and Delhi became the prizes of the conqueror, whose son, Humayan, was the second of the Moghuls to rule an empire in India. It was Humayan who began to build Agra's great fortress of red sandstone that still sprawls along the banks of the Jumna, at which people of to-day may marvel. Its walls were 70 feet high and

a mile and a half long ; within them still remains enough of the palaces, mosques, marble baths and terraces to testify to the splendours of the place when Humayan and his successors lived there. There are the balconies and balustrades of exquisitely-carved stone built by Akbar, and the Pearl Mosque built by his grandson, Shah Jehan.

At this fortress the Great Moghul received envoys from the kings and princes of lands near and far. Among those who came to his court was an ambassador from King James I of England. Moghul, incidentally, comes from the word " Mongol." The emperor was called the Great Moghul because his people had come from Central Asia.

The Taj Mahal

Most marvellous of all Agra's monuments is the peerless Taj, which is known throughout the world as the loveliest specimen of Indian architecture—some say the most beautiful the world has ever seen. It was built by the Shah Jehan in memory of his beloved Queen, Mumtaz Mahal, whose sepulchre it forms. Taj Mahal is a modern corruption of her name.

Mumtaz Mahal—" Crown of the Palace "—was famous throughout the land for her charity and wisdom as well as for her beauty. She was married to Shah Jehan in 1622, and died in 1631, four years after her lord became Emperor. Shah Jehan's grief was so poignant that he wished to give up his throne. He was persuaded to remain, however, and resolved to erect for his beloved the most beautiful building in all the world. Twenty thousand men worked upon it for twenty-two years ; twenty precious kinds of stone were used in its fabric, and its design was chosen from among those submitted by all the master architects in the Moghul Empire.

The Taj Mahal stands on its marble terrace by the Jumna, with a beautiful mosque at each side, the whole set in wonderful gardens.

DELHI AND THE NORTH=WEST

The Kashmir Gate of Delhi. In the crowded streets of this city you may meet representatives of other nations of the East. Many motors as well as carts and bullock wagons now pass through this ancient gateway.

FOUR hours from Agra by train is Delhi, the capital of the Indian Union. Seven cities, all capitals at one time or another, have arisen on or near this spot since the eleventh century, although the name "Delhi" is as old as the first century before Christ. The present city is a strange medley of old and new, of the tawdry and the magnificent. There are the high-balconied houses and the crooked narrow streets of its bazaars ; there are the great fort and its halls, its wonderful palaces, and its mosques that tell of the vanished splendour of the Great Moghuls.

Delhi proper is known as Shah-jehanabad—the city of Shah Jehan. It is surrounded by a great wall of red sandstone pierced by seven glorious gates. In the centre of the city stand the beautiful Jama Masjid (great mosque) and the palace built by Shah Jehan in 1638. The palace is mainly of white marble with inside work of mosaic in beautiful stones of many colours, and its ceilings were once covered with paintings and ornamented with gold.

Visitors to the great Hall of Public Audience (the *Diwan-i-Am*) are shown the recess in which once stood the famous "Peacock Throne" of Aurangzeb, made of solid gold, encrusted with diamonds, rubies and emeralds, and ornamented at the back with two peacocks ablaze with gems. Between the peacocks was a parrot carved from a single magnificent emerald. Above all rose a golden canopy upheld by twelve pillars rich with jewels and fringed with precious pearls.

The Wonders of the East

This wonder of the East was carried off by Persian invaders in 1739. It is said that it was worth nearly seven million pounds sterling.

The innermost court of the palace

is the Hall of Private Audience (*Diwan-i-Khas*), which bears over its outer arches a Persian text which runs : " If there be a Paradise upon the face of the earth, it is this, oh ! it is this! "

Within the precincts of this marvellous palace-fort there are also beautiful gardens, and the three domes of the perfect Moti Masjid, the Pearl Mosque built by Aurangzeb of marble. The Jama Masjid is built of red sandstone and flanked by two tall minars or towers 130 feet high, ornamented with vertical stripes of white marble and red sandstone. It is one of the largest mosques in the world, and is regarded as particularly sacred because it contains precious relics of the Prophet—one of them a hair from his beard.

Leave Delhi by the Delhi Gate or by the Ajmer Gate and you come to old Delhi—Firozabad ; and beyond that the ruins of six former Delhis stretching over a distance of some twelve miles.

Among the most interesting of these ancient monuments are the Tomb of Emperor Humayan, beneath whose marble dome repose the bones of the Moghul in their coffin of pure white marble ; and the Kutb Minar that points its tall tower of red and cream-coloured stone 238 feet in the air. Close by is the famous iron pillar—a solid shaft of plain wrought iron, at whose base is the inscription : " Whilst I stand, shall the Hindu Kingdom endure."

On the northern side of modern Delhi a new Delhi has arisen at Raisina, some three or four miles from the city walls. Most of the buildings are white, but the Secretariat, Government House, and the Rotunda are built of the same red sandstone which the architects of the Moghul emperors used for much of their finest work. New Delhi was the centre of the old Indian Government and remains the capital of the new India.

What is there about this spot that

F. Deaville Walker.

IN THE PALACE OF SHAH JEHAN

The interior of the innermost court of the Palace at Delhi is here illustrated. It is known as the Hall of Private Audience, and bears over its outer arches a Persian text which runs: " If there be a Paradise upon the face of the earth, it is this, oh! it is this! "

H. J. Shepstone.

In Old Delhi you may see the Kutb Minar, here illustrated. This tall tower of red and cream-coloured stone rears its head 238 feet into the air. Close by is the famous iron pillar—a solid shaft of plain wrought iron, at whose base is the inscription: " Whilst I stand, shall the Hindu Kingdom endure."

has made it the site of seven Delhis—and of the new one that has been created in recent years? The choice of the ancient rulers of a suitable spot for their seven capitals was endorsed by the British and confirmed by the Hindus as the best that can be made. A glance at a good map of India will answer this question for us.

Delhi stands between the ridge that is the north-easternmost spur of the Aravalli Hills and the Jumna, and in the narrowing of the gap between the Himalayas and the Deccan; so that it is ideally placed for commanding both the Ganges and the Indus Basins. This central position has always made Delhi the meeting place of many peoples, and to this day you will see in its crowded streets representatives not only of most of the people of India, but of other nations of the East. Where the tall houses lean towards each other across the narrow ways, buffalo carts, ekkas drawn by sleek bullocks, camels with bulging loads, tall narrow camel carts, asses bearing incredible burdens, and mules with tails like frayed-out steel rope dispute the passage with a crowd of people dressed in many colours—and all apparently with time to spare. Indeed, there is not such a thing as " time " in the East—or if there is, it is quite unimportant.

The Holi-puja

Visit the bazaar during a festival—the Holi-puja, for example, which comes in spring at the time of full moon in the month of Phalgoon. That is the time when the mango trees are loaded with blossom, and the sweet-scented flowers cover the asoka trees. All the world is abroad, enjoying the festival. Boys and girls bombard passers-by with powder which stains the white garments with red that looks like blood. They will tell you it is the sand of the Jumna stained with the gore of the evil spirits and demons whom Krishna slew.

Within the bazaar you find each trade in its own particular quarter, where it has been established from the beginning of Delhi. The vegetable sellers squat cross-legged by their heaps of produce, some of which we recognise and some of which are new and strange; the rice-seller, not far away, has his stall in the same old spot, where he sits, balance in hand, and with his image of Ganesh near by to bring him luck in the days of trading. Ganesh is the elephant-headed god—benign, and the bringer of good fortune.

In the Bazaar

The *haloai* and his wife sell strange and sticky sweetmeats, or fry over an absurdly tiny charcoal fire the twisted rings of *jelabi* which all Indian boys and girls love. Over there, down another alley, is the fishwives' quarter, as you can hear by their shrill cries. They sit by their baskets of plaited bamboo, in which are the fish caught by husbands and brothers. Strong women they are, and tremendous talkers. They are keen bargainers, and eye you with reproach if you offer too little, following this up by proving volubly that the fish they sell are the best in the world.

Coppersmiths, goldsmiths, silver-smiths—all have their corners in the bazaar. So do the perfumers, whose attar of roses, musk and sandalwood fill their quarter with fragrant odours.

The barber shaves the heads of his patrons, telling all the latest news to an interested group of hangers-on and prospective customers. The story-teller sits cross-legged on his box-like platform holding his audience spell-bound with his tales of the old heroes and their adventures. The letter-writer plies his trade in public. A holy man or *yogi* plucks plaintively at his one-stringed instrument, and gives advice and comfort to those who seek his aid.

News travels fast in the bazaars. What the newspapers do not tell, you can always hear from your servant if you have won his heart—for he has heard it in the bazaar.

THE SIKHS AND THE RAJPUTS

E. N. A.

A MAHARANA'S WATER PALACE

In this captivating picture one sees the beautiful Lake Pichola at Udaipur in Rajasthan. Mirrored in the silvery waters is the island palace of the prince. The princely Rajput families are the most ancient dynasties in India.

THE hill station for Delhi is Simla, where, before partition, the Government of India had its headquarters during the hot weather. Although Simla is only about 7,000 feet above sea level, there is a great difference between its genial climate and the baking heat of the plains.

You go up to Kalka by the single-line 5 feet 6 inches gauge railway, and there you take the narrow-gauge Kalka-Simla line which winds up and up through deep cuttings and round perilous-looking loops and bends to the forested hills, among which stands Simla, with magnificent views of the far-distant snowy ranges of Tibet.

Our next journey, however, is in a different direction, through the country of the Sikhs towards the far north-western gateway of the Khyber, through which wave after wave of invasion has, in past ages, descended to the fertile plains and rich cities of India.

Amritsar, some 300 miles from Delhi, is the most holy city of the Sikhs, and a great market and caravan centre for the whole of central Asia. Here, in the caravanserais, you may see merchants from Persia and Bokhara, slant-eyed Tibetans and Mongols from the interior plateaux, Kashmiris and Afghans, Baluchis and Turkomans, and sturdy Gurkhas and lean tribesmen from the frontiers.

The Golden Temple

Its chief glory is the Golden Temple —the " Darbar Sahib "—whose white marble walls, adorned with patterns in precious stones and surmounted by a roof of gilded copper, rise from a stone platform that rests island-like in the Pool of Immortality, whose glassy mirror reflects every tiny detail of this holy of holies of the Sikh religion. Around the Pool the *bungahs* of great chiefs are built. The temple is approached by a beautiful causeway and gate of marble; within, beneath a canopy lies the holy Granth, the Sikh "bible," in which are recorded the wisdom and teaching of the Gurus, the first of whom, and the founder of the Sikh religion, was Nanak, who was born in 1469. This great book is wrapped in rich silk coverings, and is constantly guarded by an official of the temple. Pilgrims from afar make offerings of flowers and grain, as well as things that appear strangely tawdry to European eyes, but which must have meant much work and self-denial on the part of those who bestow them.

Visitors to the temple must remove their shoes as a mark of respect; and when they go up to the roof to view the city they must, above all things, avoid the holy circle that has been drawn above the spot where the Granth—the holy book—lies on its silken cushions in the temple below.

Among the Sikhs

The Sikhs themselves, bearded and handsome, are men of splendid physique. Their religion forbids the cutting of hair and beard; their hair is curled up under the conical peak in the midst of their voluminous turbans, set off by quoit-like steel ornaments. The women-folk plait their hair into a peak at the back of the head and load their ears with rings and precious stones.

The chief industry of Amritsar is the weaving of fine carpets on the primitive looms, some of which have done duty for centuries. At each is the master weaver with six or eight boy workers who weave in the colours as their master calls out the patterns.

The Warrior Rajputs

In the middle of North-western India is the land of the Rajputs, "sons of princes" and a warrior race who held sway over most of the upper Ganges until the Moghul conquerors came down into the plains from the Khyber. Their country, Rajputana, once consisting of several states, is now the United State of Rajasthan which, with its capital at *Jaipur*, is the largest single unit in the Indian Union—a dry region, but with wonderfully fertile spots here and there, and with beautiful cities containing palaces and strongholds. A large part of it is the Thar or Indian Desert, which for ages protected the Rajputs from attack by way of the north-west.

Col. F. D. Fayrer.

A RAJPUT SERGEANT

This tanned and bearded non-commissioned officer was photographed at Udaipur. The word "Rajput" means "a prince's son," and members of this race are great warriors. They have fought with the British Army in the two World Wars.

THE GOLDEN TEMPLE OF AMRITSAR

Will F. Taylor.

Amritsar, some 300 miles from Delhi, is the most holy city of the Sikhs, and its chief glory, the Golden Temple, is illustrated above, with some fakirs and the sacred pool. This impressive building has white marble doors, adorned with patterns in precious stones and surmounted by a roof of gilded copper. Visitors to the temple must remove their shoes as a mark of respect.

Rajput history is full of heroic stories that are equal in their romance and fineness to the best we know of the days of chivalry in Western Europe. Many of them deal with the exploits of Rajput heroes in the stirring times of the Moslem invasions. The very names of the cities recall great deeds of heroism and sacrifice. There is *Chitor*, whose ruined fortress and towers remind us of the three times it was taken and sacked by the invaders, despite the brave resistance of its defenders, and of the devoted self-sacrifice of the people of the city who made a vast funeral pyre in the caverns beneath the rock and threw themselves upon it—clad in their finest garments and singing as they did so. When the city was taken—but only when its defenders had been slaughtered to a man—the conquerors entered it to find its streets and houses deserted. It was in very truth a city of the dead.

The City of Sunrise

Udaipur, the " City of Sunrise " and chief town of Mewar, is one of India's most lovely cities, with its palaces and ghats mirrored in its beautiful lake Pichola, amid which, like a fairy palace floating upon the water, is an island bearing the Jag Mandir (" World Minster ") of the reigning Prince. This lovely water palace was built in the first quarter of the seventeenth century by the Maharana Karasinghji. During the Indian Mutiny the Maharana supported the British and lent his water palace as a home for Mutiny refugees who sought shelter in Udaipur.

The water palace of the Maharana is hardly less wonderful than his great high palace with its three-arched gateway and its domes and spires, that stands on a ridge above the lake.

In the city, tall men of fine physique and martial bearing, with black beards parted in the middle and drawn aside to curled ends, and the graceful women closely veiled against the curious eyes of strangers, decked with ornaments of silver or gold, and clad in robes of every hue, tell plainly that here are people of a splendid race—the descendants of warriors who 700 years ago were masters of Upper India.

Jaipur

Jaipur is another fine city—the capital of the new Rajasthan—with wide streets and a busy market. You can see here the ancient observatory of the Indian astronomers; the instruments are of stone. One of them is a giant sundial—Samrat Yantra—whose gnomon is nearly 80 feet high. The old capital of Jaipur State was Amber, whose ruins lie some few miles from the present capital.

If we wish to visit the drier part of Rajasthan we cannot do better than go to *Bikanir*, which stands in its oasis in the Thar Desert. Here camels are as common as are elephants in the cities farther east, and the water carrier is one of the most welcome of all the traders in the city.

Another ancient city and stronghold of the Thar region is Jaisalmer, whose towers and walls seem to hold at bay the menacing sands of the desert.

Here and there in this dry, barren country are small villages of cone-shaped straw huts, or of houses made of stones loosely piled together. Life in such oasis communities is a constant struggle ; the lean and hungry appearance of the camels, cattle and goats kept by the villagers tells plainly of its hardships.

Mount Abu

In the south, the Thar Desert is bounded by the mountains of the Aravalli Range, which runs from south-west to north-east across this part of Rajasthan. At the south-western end of the range is Mount Abu—a granite island set in an ocean of sand, with forests and beautiful lakes upon it, and a town that to-day is the headquarters of the government in this part of India. Over 4,000 feet above sea level, Mount Abu is a pleasant place

THE PUNJAB'S NEW CAPITAL

Chandigarh, the new capital of East Punjab, is now rising in the plains south-west of Simla and north of Ambala. Within little more than two years, miles of road were laid and hundreds of houses built, and by early 1954 some of the Government departments had already moved into the city. This picture shows the office of the Chief Engineer.

Photos: Press Information Bureau, Government of India.

Nine thousand acres have been taken for the new city, which is being built mostly with local materials, equipment and labour. The city has been planned by a famous French architect, Le Corbusier, and a number of other European and Indian architects. This picture of newly-completed living quarters shows how modern Chandigarh will be.

in the hot weather, and is a favourite spot for many Europeans.

People come to Mount Abu especially to see the famous temples built by the Jains at about the same time as William of Normandy was setting about his conquest of England. These are at Dilwara among the green hills. Their multitudes of marble columns, their lovely arches linking the columns together, and their marvellously carved shrines, roofs and pillars make the Dilwara temples a sight to astonish the beholder. Strange legends arrest his ear—he hears how Siva in the days of the gods thrust his foot through the earth from his shrine at Benares to steady Mount Abu when it quaked, and how the mark of Siva's toes is still to be seen in a hole, whose depth has never been plumbed. "It goes down," say those who tell the tale, "even unto Patal," which everyone knows is the very lowest part of the earth.

Why a Throne was Lost

There was a prince who doubted this tale and swore that he would fill the hole with water. He gave orders to his masons to build a great aqueduct, through which water was allowed to flow for six months, but without avail. The anger of Siva at his unbelief cost the prince his throne, for his people revolted and cast him forth.

The Jains who built these marvellous temples were members of a religious sect that arose 500 years before the birth of Christ, and was founded by men who did not agree with all the beliefs and ceremonies of the Hindu religion. In many ways the teaching of the Jain *tirthankars* (holy teachers) was like that of Gautama Buddha.

Paul Popper.

JODHPUR, A CITY OF THE RAJASTHAN UNION

The Union of Rajasthan is made up of eighteen of the former Indian states and forms part of the republic of India. The city of Jodhpur was founded in 1459 and has a present-day population of 54,000. Surrounding it is a wall nearly six miles in length protecting the many fine residences and temples of the city.

Paul Popper.

MERCHANTS IN THE WALLED CITY OF KANO IN NORTHERN NIGERIA

Protected from the sun by bamboo shelters, their wares displayed on low and roughly-made tables, these merchants await their customers. The white caps they wear are very popular in this part of West Africa. What a bewildering variety of goods there is for sale! Mirrors, beads, charcoal, peppers, thread, kohl, cotton manufactures—these and many other things are bought and sold in Kano, the largest trading centre in the whole of West Africa. Here, too, cloth and yarn are dyed, and—at harvest time—the groundnut crop is collected.

IN THE GRAND HARBOUR AT VALLETTA, MALTA

Since 1814, when it became British, Malta has been our chief naval base in the Mediterranean and a leading port of call for merchant ships. The Phœnicians had a trading station here in the sixteenth century B.C. and it was the scene of St. Paul's shipwreck in A.D. 58. In recent times the story of the Malta convoys and the magnificent resistance of the islanders to enemy attacks have added fresh chapters to the island's great history.

CALCUTTA, DARJEELING AND THE SNOWS

Indian State Railways.

THE VICTORIA MEMORIAL, CALCUTTA

In 1698 the East India Company purchased three villages on the banks of the Hooghli, most westerly mouth of the Ganges, and in 1702 Fort William was built. It was from this that the great city of Calcutta grew. Within this city East meets West and some 400 nationalities, races and castes are numbered among its population. One of the finest of its many splendid buildings is the Victoria Memorial, seen above.

THOSE who enter India by the Calcutta sea-gate are following the old way of the East Indiamen, who in the days of "John Company" thronged the Hooghli and made Calcutta the chief seaport and the capital of India. For as long as British interests in India had to be backed by a show of armed force, the capital was bound to be a sea-gate, since Britain's lines of communication with India in those days were sea-ways.

The Treacherous Hooghli

The Hooghli (or Hugli) is one of the many mouths of the Ganges. Among sailors it has an evil reputation; its swift and dangerous currents and its shifting mud-banks make it extremely difficult to navigate, and the job of a Hooghli pilot is one not to be envied. He must be more than a knowledgeable man; he has to be ever on the alert, ever learning the new positions of the shifting banks, and very resourceful. If the ship but touches the tail end of one of the banks, the current may quickly swing her broadside on, heeling her on to the bank and at the same time scooping out a steep hollow on the downstream side of her, with the inevitable result that she tumbles sideways. The tons of silt swept down upon her by the currents soon bury her in the graveyard that holds the bones of the ships of all the centuries since the navigation of the Hooghli began.

Sundarbans of the Ganges

The lowlands of the Ganges delta are known as the Sundarbans. They are covered with low and malaria-smitten jungle, and are the haunts of that log-like reptile, the crocodile.

The tiger, too, inhabits the drier

parts of these jungle lands, although he is very seldom seen by those who pass up and down the waterway in the ships.

Man disputes with the tiger and the crocodile the right of living in the delta lowlands, for he has planted jute in the rich wet soil, and toils amid fever-haunted waterways to reap his jute harvest and to prepare it for sale to the jute factories.

All about Jute

Jute grows to a height of 11 feet or 12 feet. If you penetrate up one of the narrow creeks to the jute plantations you may see thin, brown men clad only in waist-cloths, cutting down the tall jute stems, trimming them and making them into bundles to be carted away by buffalo wagons or taken off in square-ended punts to the pools, where the stems will be steeped for many days in order that their juicy, fleshy parts may rot. Later you may see men standing up to the waist in murky brown water beating the stems with flat-ended mallets to get rid of the waste material, while on the higher ground other workers are hanging up the long silky, pliant fibres to dry in the hot sunshine.

The sequel to all this you may see at the great jute mills of Howrah, across the Hooghli from Calcutta, where the jute is made into bags and sacks, rope and mats. Jute, indeed, is a flourishing crop in the north-east, where

Bourne & Shepherd.

BALING JUTE IN THE INTENSE HEAT

At Howrah, which faces Calcutta across the river, are the great mills where jute is made into bags and sacks, rope and mats. Here you see this useful commodity being baled under tremendous pressure and in terrific heat for transport overseas. Jute is a plant used after the manner of flax, but its fibres are tougher than those of flax. Near Calcutta jute grows to a height of 11 feet or more, the moist heat favouring its rapid development.

The High Commissioner for India.

A VIEW IN ONE OF CALCUTTA'S STREETS

With its suburbs Calcutta has a population of over four and a half millions and is the largest city of India. It is the gateway and market-place of the rich valleys of the Ganges and Brahmaputra rivers and one of the greatest commercial centres of the East. The street seen in this photograph was known until recently as Clive Street but has been re-named Netaji Subhash Bose. Calcutta University, established in 1857, is numerically the largest in the world.

plenty of heat and moisture favour its tall growth. Bengal, Bihar and Orissa, and Assam all grow it, but 75 per cent. of it is produced in the Bengal delta lowlands of Eastern Pakistan. Jute is the cheapest fibre in the world ; it is cultivated on a large scale only where abundant rain and moist heat favour its quick growth. All over the world where grain, seeds, and other dry foodstuffs and raw materials are produced there is a demand for the " gunny bags " made from jute, which to-day forms an important part of the exports of Pakistan and India.

Calcutta

Eighty miles up the Hooghli is Calcutta, long the capital and still the leading seaport of India. Mills and factories announce to the new arrival by sea that industry is carried on here on a European scale, and ships of all the seafaring nations in the world testify to the city's greatness as a port. You can still see old Fort William on the eastern bank of the river, where the British built it in 1702, and on three sides of it—north, east and south—stretches the wide plain of the Maidan, east of which is the European part of the city with fine hotels, public buildings and houses that tell of the British people who live and work there. The old city lies away to the north, with its crowded bazaars, its narrow streets and its jostling crowds buying and selling, gossiping and gaping at shows and sights, as crowds do all the world over.

Nothing in Calcutta is more wonderful than the crowd which flows endlessly across the great new Howrah Bridge from dawn to dusk—a moving throng which seems to have in it representatives of every nation under the sun. This structure, opened in 1943, is the third largest cantilever bridge in the world and has a span of 1,500 feet. Across the bridge is Howrah with its great jute mills and steel works.

Up to Darjeeling

Calcutta people who can afford it go up to beautiful Darjeeling during the hot weather, a lovely spot with pretty villas and bungalows among the forests of pines and firs seven thousand feet above the bed of the Testa River, and with the grandest mountain scenery in all the world as a background.

Lofty peaks crowned with eternal snows occupy two-thirds of Darjeeling's horizon. Everest, the giant that overtops all others, can be seen from Darjeeling itself, and all who long for a glimpse of this peak that until recently defied every effort to scale it, can see it on a fine day from Tiger's Hill, which can be reached on pony back, by rickshaw, or by *palki*—a chair carried by four sturdy bearers. Kinchinjunga, as well, can be seen from Darjeeling, and so can other mighty peaks over 22,000 feet in height.

The journey from Calcutta to Darjeeling is made by one of the most wonderful railways in the world, and one of the most costly ever constructed. The first stage is across the lowlands of the Ganges plain dotted with many villages amid rice fields and jute fields, waving palm and big-leaved plantains, and clumps of feathery bamboos. The Ganges is crossed by the great Hardinge or Sara Bridge; it is nearly a mile and a quarter in length, and cost over two and a half million pounds.

The next stage takes us into the tea country of the Dooars, and on to Sukna, where the real difficulties which the railway builders had to face begin to show themselves. The train suddenly enters dense forest of tall sal and giant bamboo, and other quick-growing vegetation which seems woven into an impenetrable mass by great creepers that throw curtains of blossom sunwards. This is the jungle of the Terai, the home of the tiger and the Indian rhinoceros, the sambhur and the wild buffalo, where even experienced *shikaris* go with caution.

In Sight of the Himalayas

Up and up the line twists and turns, boring into tunnels, skirting giddy precipices, crossing deep gorges by slender bridges, and now and again stopping to reverse because of the impossibility of negotiating the steep gradient by loops or hairpin bends. Soon the increased altitude begins to be evident in the change of vegetation —oaks and mulberries, peach trees and almonds are common at 4,000 feet; another thousand feet takes the traveller

High Commissioner for India.
IN THE HILL COUNTRY
Transport in the hill country may present difficulties, and here we see an Indian coolie using a basket chair to carry the youngster on an awkward journey over rough ground.

A TEMPLE OF THE JAINS

E. N. A.

The Jains form a very ancient religious sect in India, and this is a picture of the famous Badri Das Temple which they built in Calcutta. The Jains number to-day about a million followers. They will never kill an animal, however insignificant, because they believe that after death human beings enter the kingdom of four-footed creatures.

to the region of tree ferns; then come the pine forests and glimpses of the far-away Himalayan snow peaks; and at last Darjeeling, which means " the place of the thunderbolt."

The Himalayas, which lie partly beyond the frontiers, form the natural northern boundary of India. This vast mountain range, which includes the highest peaks in the world, runs from North-west to South-east for some 1,500 miles, varying in width from 150 to 200 miles, and with a general height of 20,000 feet. The perpetual snow-line is about 16,000 feet. From the melting snows of the great rampart spring the rivers Ganges, Indus, Jumna, Sutlej and Brahmaputra.

Heroes of Everest

No man with British blood in his veins can arrive at Darjeeling without a proud memory of those heroes of his race who gave their lives in the attempt to scale the highest mountain on earth —of Mallory and Irvine, who were last seen by anxious watchers from Camp VI, within 800 feet of Everest's snowy summit.

> " Climbing in air too thin for mortal breath
> These men stood poised on the world's parapet;
> Watched by the stars, on the last height they met,
> Content in Victory, the Kiss of Death."—*Douglas Freshfield.*

From Darjeeling the first seven Everest expeditions set forth. All were British. These and later attempts failed, and at least sixteen lives were lost in efforts to climb the mighty peak. It seemed that the old gods painted on the walls of the Rongbuk Monastery—guardians of sacred Everest—were defending their charge all too well. Then, in 1953, came another British expedition, led by Col. H. C. J. Hunt, C.B.E., D.S.O. The story of its triumph and of the climb of Hillary and Tensing to the very summit

Paul Popper.

IN THE " LAND OF THE LAMAS "

Tibet is known as " the land of the lamas," the lamas being the priests who to a large extent rule the people. A boy intended for the priesthood enters the lamasery about the age of four. In this picture lamas at a Tibetan monastery are blowing ceremonial trumpets, some of which are 12 feet long. They make a loud rasping noise which is accompanied by the wailing note from the smaller trumpets.

CROWNED WITH ETERNAL SNOWS

Darjeeling is the hot-weather capital of the district of the same name and the favourite summer resort of Bengal. It is also a centre of the tea industry, over 20 million pounds being grown in the neighbourhood annually. Magnificent mountain views are obtained and both Everest and Kinchinjunga are visible. A general view of the town, taken from the Mackenzie Road, is seen here.

Photos: E. N. A.

Another view of the great Kinchinjunga range, which forms part of the Himalayas, is shown here, taken from the Mall at Darjeeling. Monsoon clouds can be seen in the foreground. The town of Darjeeling is approximately 7,400 feet above sea level and is some 300 miles from Calcutta with which it is connected by railway.

is told elsewhere in these volumes.

It is at Darjeeling that the traveller meets for the first time the hill people who are in every way different from the inhabitants of the plains. Darjeeling stands at the gate of Sikkim, and between Nepal, the mountain land of the sturdy Gurkhas, and Bhutan, the home of the Bhutia mountaineers; and it is near enough to the Tibetan frontier to have many people of Tibetan stock in its neighbourhood. Buddhist temples, like those of Tibet, can be visited from Darjeeling; there are several monasteries where the strange Tibetan "Devil Dances" are performed by the lamas, dressed in their frightful masks and gorgeous costumes, and gyrating to the horrific music of gongs and cymbals, and the blare of mighty trumpets ten or twelve feet long. Great prayer wheels turn, reiterating the mystic Buddhist text, "Om Mane Padme Hum"; fluttering prayer-flags from little forests of poles carry on them other prayers and symbols.

The High Commissioner for India.

AT THE GATE OF A BUDDHIST TEMPLE

Architecture in India was in a fairly advanced state so long ago as 3000 B.C. and has been cultivated through long centuries as many remarkable and imposing buildings still testify. In the building of temples it is seen in its highest form and some of the carvings and elaborate decorative work are marvels of the sculptor's craft. This photograph of the East Gate of the Buddhist Temple at Sanchi Tope is a typical example.

MOTHER GANGES

Hedda Morrison.

THE HOLY CITY OF BENARES

Benares, or Banaras, as it is more commonly called nowadays, is built along one bank of the Ganges only. On the populated side the city slopes steeply down to the river and the banks are covered with temples, religious hostels and other foundations. The city is the religious capital of India and is also an important commercial and administrative centre. It also has a famous University as well as other educational institutions.

MOTHER GANGES is the greatest river of India, and the most sacred. Her waters from their sources to the sea are holy to the Hindus, and her banks are lined with wonderful temples and stately cities which have arisen through the ages to bear witness to the might of Hinduism and the sacredness of the Ganges flood.

For 1,500 miles Ganga Mai traverses the most densely-peopled plain in the world spreading abroad her great fan of tributaries and their associated networks of irrigation canals. She comes down from the cold Himalayan snows to holy Hardwar and the plains, and flows on to the jungles and marshes of the Sundarbans to empty her waters into the sea. On her bosom she bears craft strange to European eyes—rice-boats, boats laden with pilgrims journeying to one of her many shrines, and hosts of smaller craft with wide curved awnings of matting amidships to give shelter from the hot sun.

Benares, a Holy City

The most holy of her cities is *Benares*, whose proper name is Varanasi—" bright-robed daughter of Ganga." This city is visited by hundreds of thousands of pilgrims every year from all parts of India. Nowadays, Benares is commonly called Banaras.

Benares can be reached from Calcutta by following the main Calcutta-Bombay railway route as far as Moghal Serai junction, whence a short run of ten miles takes us across the Dufferin Bridge over the Ganges to the Holy City, whose splendid temples and

377

palaces are mirrored in the face of
" Ganga Mai " herself—Ganga Mai who
appeared at the god Siva's wedding,
they say, clad in many-coloured robes,
" when the rivers and the Seven Seas,
as well as the Sacred places of Pilgrimage assembled together, with the
Sun and the Moon and many other
notabilities."

For four miles the high northern
bank of the Ganges at Benares is
crowded with palaces and temples,
most of them built of reddish-yellow
sandstone, looking across the river to
a low and sparsely-inhabited shore.
Leading from the temples on this
high bank to the river are the
great flights of stone steps known as
the " ghats," from which the Ganges
is worshipped every day by her
followers, who bring offerings of rice,
milk and flowers, and bathe in the
holy waters.

The Ghats

At the Dasasanedh Ghat—" the ghat
of the Ten Horse sacrifice "—all the
chief roads of Benares meet. It is one
of the five sacred places to be visited by
the Hindus who come to the city to take
part in the great religious festivals.
Crowds of bathers throng the steps;
processions of men, women and children
swell the number as the day wears on,
bearing the brass or copper vessels used
in pouring the sacred water over their
bodies and garlands of flowers and sacred
leaves to cast into the stream. Men
pilgrims throw off their outer garments
before entering the river, but the women,
clad in their brightly-coloured *saris*,
wade in slowly until they can dip their
heads below the surface. Thrice im-
mersing themselves in the sacred flood,
the pilgrims emerge, dry themselves,
and go to the *yogis* or wise elders seated
beneath the shade of great mushroom-like

The High Commissioner for India.

AT THE BATHING GHATS OF HARDWAR

In the Hindu language the word " ghat " means a path of descent and is used particularly to
describe the steps upon a river bank. These steps, used for bathing, drinking and other ritual
acts, are found along the Ganges at every city from Calcutta to Hardwar. Our picture shows
the bathing ghats at Hardwar, a city of great antiquity. It is one of the holy places of India
and a centre for pilgrims who bathe in the waters of their great river, Ganges.

TRACTORS AND TEA CROPPERS

The High Commissioner for India.

Following the creation of two separate nations, India and Pakistan, in 1947, a grave problem arose owing to the migration of thousands of families. The Indian Government created a separate Ministry under which various agencies were set up to deal with resettlement schemes. In this picture, the Prime Minister, Pandit Nehru, is seated in a tractor during his visit to one of these new farming colonies.

Tea Bureau.

Picking the tea leaves has always been done by hand until quite recently, when the first experiments with mechanical croppers were made. In this picture a generating set is seen on the right at work on a tea estate in Assam. Two croppers, electrically operated, but guided by workers, are picking the leaves. This method is still in the experimental stage.

umbrellas of woven cane to receive the mark upon their foreheads that shows to all who know what it means that they have washed away all their offences in the purifying waters of Ganga Mai.

Festivals

In the month Kartik (October-November) there is a great festival at this ghat, in honour of Kali the black goddess of darkness, whose strange image with protruding tongue is taken in procession from its shrine and accompanied by throngs of pilgrims on foot, on elephants and camels, or in carriages to the river, where at sunset it is immersed. Hundreds of smaller images of Kali are thrown in by the pilgrims. Then as night falls begins the feast of Lakshmi, the goddess of Fortune, when little lighted lamps are set afloat upon the waters to be watched until they fade into the darkness. Should a lamp go out, its owner need expect no good fortune in the coming year.

Below the temples, shrines and palaces farther along the river, their clusters of domes and spires stained deep red and tipped with gold, are other ghats; some crowded with worshippers, among whom sacred bulls garlanded with marigolds wander in and out as they please, while monkeys clamber on the cornices and brightly-plumaged birds dart here and there among the temple domes.

The Scindhia Ghat is the haunt of *sadhus*, strange wandering mystics who beg their way from shrine to shrine, smeared with ashes and marked with the coloured sect-mark upon their foreheads. Some gather funds to pay for the repair of a temple; some are learned men who have renounced the world and given themselves up to a life of self-denial.

Within the city the narrow winding streets are so crowded that only foot passengers can pass. Beneath the tall houses on both sides of the way are the open shops—mere recesses in the walls—some crammed with figures of gods and goddesses; some hung with prayer bags, embroidered with bright colours; and some full of sweetmeats and sticky cakes.

Hedda Morrison.

ON THE RIVER GANGES, BENARES

To Benares come pilgrims from all over India to bathe in the sacred river Ganges from the steps of the bathing ghats. The bathers wash all over and submerge themselves completely in the water.

TRANSPORT OLD AND NEW

Railways are the main arteries of India's transport system. The rivers, with a few exceptions, have not been used for navigation. Motor transport took its place on the roads years ago, but revolutions rarely happen in a day or a year in such problems. Here we have a picture of one of the most ancient forms of transport in the East in contrast with a more recent invention on a road in Jodhpur.

Photos: The High Commisioner for India.

In such a vast country as India many areas are entirely dependent on road transport and the old forms of travel are still in use and likely to remain so for some years. The carriage seen above is a two-wheeled vehicle known as an " ekka," drawn by a pair of bullocks. The ekka is one of several different types of bullock cart still largely used in country districts.

Blue-throated Siva, father of the gods, has his shrine covered with sculptured figures. There you can see Nandi, the sacred bull on which he rides, and Kali the terrible, wearing her necklace of skulls and her girdle of cobras, with her four hands—one bearing the head of a demon and another her keen sword.

The Golden Temple

The Golden Temple has two of its domes plated with real gold. No European may cross its holy threshold. But every man, be he Hindu or Christian, may visit the "Well of Knowledge," where a Brahmin sits with his metal ladle to pour into the palm of everyone's right hand a few drops of the precious water in return for a small offering of copper coins as his reward.

There is another part of Benares which is very different from the old city and its crooked streets thronged with folk clad in many-coloured robes. That is the modern quarter, where there are many fine buildings, among them Queen's College, which is built in the Gothic style of architecture.

Patna, Cawnpore and Lucknow

Patna, the capital of the province of Bihar and Orissa, stretches for nine miles along the banks of the Ganges. Patna is the collecting centre for the agricultural produce of the area and has given its name to a particularly high quality of rice. Not far off is Pataliputra, once the capital of an early Indian Empire of the Maurya dynasty a little after the times of Alexander the Great.

At *Cawnpore*, easily reached by train from Benares, we are in the "Manchester of India," where there are large modern cotton and woollen mills, leather industries and clothing factories. Unhappy days in India's long and eventful history are recalled by the memorial church in remembrance of those who fell during the Mutiny of 1857.

Lucknow, too, has its reminders of those perilous times. Its heroic defence has passed into our history.

The district is fertile and for the most part highly cultivated, having three harvests during the year. In the spring wheat, grain and barley; during the rainy season, rice and millet; and in the autumn various native food grains. In the town itself can be seen, as at Cawnpore, evidence of changing India in the application of modern methods of manufacture.

India and the Future

It is now time for us to leave India. As we have seen, so vast and so young a nation has still many problems to resolve. The principal industry of India is agriculture, and many of the major projects which are now in hand are aimed at increasing the fertility of the land so that the standard of living of the people may be raised.

Typical of these schemes is the Bhakra-Nangal Project, part of which (the Bhakra canal system) was opened by Mr. Nehru in July, 1954. The Bhakra canal system is said to be the largest of its kind in the world. It is based upon the new Bhakra-Nangal barrage on the river Sutlej and provides water, through more than 670 miles of canal, for nearly 4 million acres of land in the East Punjab and the adjoining parts of Rajasthan. About 650 million tiles were used to line the bed of the canal system.

India's interest in the Sutlej, which is a river of the Indus Basin, recently brought protests from her neighbour, Pakistan, who also needs these waters. This reminds us of yet another problem which has to be solved by these two countries—the future of Kashmir, the beautiful State which is claimed by both. On such matters does the future prosperity of India, and indeed of neighbouring Pakistan, depend.

PAKISTAN

THE UNIVERSITY SENATE HALL AT LAHORE

Lahore, the city we associate with Rudyard Kipling's *Kim*, rose to importance as a strong fortress in the days of the Moghul Empire. To-day it is the capital of West Punjab in the Dominion of Pakistan. Among its many fine buildings is the University Senate Hall which you see in the photograph above.

THE Moslems, who form over 85 per cent. of the people of Pakistan, are very different from the Hindus. Indeed, it was because the differences were so great that a single self-governing nation of both Hindus and Moslems could not be established in 1947. The Moslems established their own state, which they called Pakistan (meaning " land of the pure ") and which was formed from the predominantly Moslem parts of the sub-continent.

As we have already seen, some areas were not immediately brought into either India or Pakistan. An example is Kashmir, whose Hindu Maharajah wanted Kashmir to join the Indian Union, while most of his subjects were Moslem and naturally wanted Kashmir to join Pakistan. For a long while statesmen have wrestled with the prob-lem of Kashmir, and by August, 1953 India and Pakistan had agreed that a plebiscite should be held to decide the matter. Plebiscite means literally a decree of the whole people; in other words, the people themselves would decide by vote where their future lay. But no arrangements for the plebiscite had been made by October, 1954.

Exactly how do Moslems differ from Hindus ? When we visited southern India we saw that Hinduism was a religion with many gods and goddesses, and that the Hindus are divided into many castes, each of which keeps to itself. The Hindu will not kill a cow; to him it is a sacred animal. A really strict Hindu would not take a meal with a European; to him the European would be an unclean person. By con-trast, the Moslem has ways of thought much more like our own. His religion is Islam. Islam is an Arabic word which means "pious submission to the will of God" and was the name chosen for the religion by Mahomet, its founder and prophet. Hindus believe in many gods, the Moslems in one God. They have great reverence for Jesus Christ, whom they regard as a prophet of God, like Mahomet himself. They disapprove of idols and images and are forbidden to drink wine or eat pork. Anyone can be converted to Islam and become a Moslem; to be a Hindu you must be born a Hindu.

These examples are perhaps enough to show how wide the differences are and to explain why both Hindus and Moslems demanded separate and independent states when British rule in India ended in 1947.

Western and Eastern Pakistan

If you look at Pakistan on the map you will at once notice that this new country is divided into two parts: Western and Eastern Pakistan. The Western is the larger part and consists of the North-West Frontier Province, West Punjab and Sind, and Baluchistan. Many hundreds of miles distant is Eastern Pakistan, consisting of East Bengal and a small part of Assam. *Karachi*, the Dominion Capital, stands in its own "federal territory" in Western Pakistan; it is the chief seaport for the Indus basin and the North-west and an important airport on the B.O.A.C. route to India, Singapore and Australia. *Chittagong* and *Chalna* are the ports of Eastern Pakistan.

When Pakistan first came into being, many difficulties had to be overcome. An entirely new country, with new officials and new machinery of government had to be set up in a very short time. There were shortages of every kind at first: not enough office buildings, not even enough typewriters and telephones, and often not enough trained clerks to replace the Hindus and Sikhs who left banks and merchant houses in

Pakistan to find new homes and new jobs in their own Hindu India. Nor were clerks the only people on the move in those early days. Literally millions of people were uprooted. While Sikhs and Hindus left Pakistan for India, Moslems came from India into Pakistan, often without money or possessions of even the most simple kind. You can imagine what terrible times these were and how hard the leaders of Pakistan had to work to solve these and many other desperate problems.

When the problems of the moment had been met, the government of Pakistan had other serious and more permanent difficulties to face. Pakistan was virtually without industry and lacked readily available raw materials for industry. Her coal from Punjab and Baluchistan was poor in quality and small in quantity. Her oil from Balkesar and other Punjab fields was not enough for her needs. How, then, is Pakistan to build the industry she must have if she is to be fully independent?

The answer lies in water power, which is now being developed extensively within the Dominion. For example, the Swat River is harnessed at Malakand and Dargai to provide power for the North-West Frontier and West Punjab Provinces. Other projects are taking shape at Warsak and Mianwali in Western Pakistan and at Karnafuli in East Pakistan—not merely to provide electric power, but to control floods, drain flooded areas and irrigate desert lands.

New Villages and Towns

Probably the most ambitious scheme is that for the reclamation of the Thal, a great plain lying between the rivers Indus and Jhelum, where irrigation and settlement are being directed by the Thal Development Authority. Already the great Jinnah Barrage has been built across the River Indus by the small town of Kalabagh. This barrage and an extensive canal system will eventually irrigate $1\frac{1}{2}$ million acres where wheat, cotton, sugar-cane and other crops will be grown.

When the desert land has been made fertile, settlements are established. Some 250,000 settlers are to be placed on farms of about 15 acres; 900 villages with roads, houses, schools, hospitals and transport are to be built. Already 240 villages have come into existence, 7,000 houses have been built and 24,000 families settled. New market towns are being built, and of the planned 670 miles of road, 310 miles have been opened to traffic.

In the Thal region, too, an experimental livestock farm is being created with the help of Australia, New Zealand and Canada. Another important irrigation and power project is the Lower Sind Barrage, the first part of which has just been completed. The key of the scheme is the Kotri Barrage, near the city of Hyderabad on the Indus, which will irrigate desert, provide electricity and supply water to Karachi.

Paul Popper.

A COPPERSMITH OF PESHAWAR

While his craftsmen work at new pots, pans and trays, this coppersmith sits in the open front of his shop, hopefully awaiting a customer. Peshawar is the capital of the North-West Frontier Province of Pakistan and an important centre on one of the great caravan routes. More than 151,000 people live in the city.

Raw Materials for Industry

Other developments include exploration of Pakistan's mineral wealth. No one yet knows how rich the Dominion is in raw materials for industry, but an important new oil-field has been discovered at Chakwal, near Balkesar, and there are indications of other mineral wealth. Pakistan is also striving to build more factories that will turn her raw materials, such as jute and cotton, into finished products. Already she has a growing textile industry at such centres as *Jhang*, *Lyallpur* and *Multan* in the Punjab and in Eastern Pakistan. Other new undertakings include cement and fertiliser factories, paper and board mills, woollen mills, and factories producing carpets, tobacco, leather goods, dyestuffs and other products. The sugar mill at Mardan in the North-West Frontier Province is said to be the largest in Asia.

Nevertheless Pakistan is first and foremost a nation of farmers and country people. Over three-quarters of her population of about 76 millions get a living from the land. They live mostly in small villages and often have still to learn the most modern ways of growing their crops and rearing their animals. In a typical village not everyone will farm, of course; there will be tradesmen and craftsmen—a carpenter, a blacksmith, a potter and others. There may well be a village moneylender, too, although nowadays farmers can borrow money at more reasonable charges from the growing number of banks and co-operative societies.

Teaching the peasant farmers new and better ways is not an easy task. The number of people in Pakistan who cannot read or write is even greater than it is in India; before 1947 it was estimated that over 80 per cent. of the peoples of what is now India and Pakistan were illiterate. In the tribal areas of the North-West Frontier and in Baluchistan, ninety-eight out of every hundred people cannot read or write. Add to this the instinctive reluctance of the peasant farmer to make any change in how he tills his land and grows his crops and you will realise that here is a problem that will take time to solve.

Much is expected from the Village Aid Programmes, for which teachers are being trained at four agricultural-industrial institutes. These teachers will train the inhabitants of six hundred villages which will become models of what can be done to improve farming practice, encourage village industries and handicrafts, and provide better health and education services.

Travelling through Pakistan

Our visit to Pakistan begins at *Karachi*, the modern city and port of the Indus Basin and the capital of the country. It exports much wheat and cotton from

Copyright.

THE PETITION WRITER AT WORK

Lahore is both an ancient city and a new town, the old city being enclosed by walls, a reminder of the days when it was a strong fortress and one of the two capitals of the great Moghul Empire. Here is a scene taken within the precincts of the District Court at Lahore, showing a petition writer taking instructions from his clients and preparing the necessary document.

Pictorial Press.

CONTRASTS IN KARACHI

The dignified building in the background contains the port administration and customs offices of Karachi, the chief seaport and capital of Pakistan. Cars and buses may be seen in the city, but it is not unusual for camel carts to be used for bringing goods from the docks. Karachi is one of the main airports on the B.O.A.C. route to Australia.

Punjab and is the terminus of the great railway that runs north into the " Land of the Five Rivers " and has branch lines to the passes through the western mountain barriers.

Sind Province, through which the lower Indus runs to the sea, is dry country where water is the most precious thing on earth. But, thanks to great irrigation works, large crops of cotton, wheat and rice can be grown. The most famous of these irrigation works is the Sukkur Dam, which gives life to more than $3\frac{3}{4}$ million acres of thirsty land. The dam is also known as the Lloyd Barrage because it was inaugurated during Lord Lloyd's term of office as Governor of Bombay. When the scheme of which it is part is complete,

water will be provided for nearly $5\frac{1}{2}$ million acres. Meanwhile work is continuing on the Lower Sind, or Kotri Barrage, which will irrigate $2\frac{3}{4}$ million acres for the growing of rice between *Hyderabad*, the capital of Sind Province, and the sea.

From the Sukkur Dam we might travel by train and road to remarkable ruins at Mohenjo-Daro, about eight miles from Dokri. Here archæologists have laid bare the site of three ancient cities, the earliest of which dates from 3300 B.C. The plan of the cities, the houses, baths and drainage, and the pottery, statuettes and inscriptions that have been revealed, show that the people who lived here all those thousands of years ago were highly civilised.

Camera Press.

ON THE KHYBER PASS

The armed men are perhaps members of a caravan which has stopped
for provisions at this caravanserai, or inn, at the top of the Khyber
Pass. The Khyber Pass is one of the most famous gateways to
Pakistan and India. Landi Kotal, the highest point of the pass, is
about 3,500 feet above sea level.

—grim fellows in white with callouses on their cheeks made by the stocks of their rifles in frequent recoil.

The Khyber Pass

The Khyber Pass begins near Jamrud, about ten miles from Peshawar; at Ali Masjid it plunges into a deep gorge, through which the road and the railway reach Landi Kotal at the highest point of the pass, but only about 3,500 feet above sea level. This pass is low, and it has pure water supplies. It is on the direct route between Kabul and Peshawar, and is consequently the most important of all the frontier gates from the west. The others—the Malakand, the Tochi, the Gomal Valley and the Bolan—were none of them so convenient for the old commerce that flowed into India from South-western Asia.

The forces of Alexander the Great entered India by this gate in 326 B.C.; the Moghuls Babar and Humayan came this way to found Empires in India, and so in later days did the Persians.

Our next stop is Rawalpindi, where people start for Kashmir, into the North-west Frontier Province and on to its capital, *Peshawar*, the most important centre on the great caravan road, linking up Samarkand, Bokhara, Teheran and Kabul, with Lahore, Amritsar and Delhi. In the bazaar are people from all the markets of Asia, but notably those tall, lean, hook-nosed tribesmen from the frontier hills

At Landi Kotal, the summit of the Khyber, is the well-laid-out modern " fort " town, with tribal villages of the people within sight of it, each with its wall and its fortified look-out tower, where the villagers can take refuge in case of a raid. The barren hills offer little to support the tribesmen; their lean sheep and goats find coarse herbage in places that look as arid as the barren rock, but beyond these the people of this frontier region have no resources and no supplies save those they can get by trading or plunder. The frontier is less lawless and much safer for caravans than it formerly was, though it has had its troubles in quite recent times.

Afghanistan, Land of many Peoples

Beyond the North-West Frontier is the kingdom of Afghanistan, roughly triangular in shape, its frontiers bordering Persia (Iran) in the west, Soviet Russia in the north, and Pakistan in the south-east. This mountainous land, almost three times as large as Great Britain, is the home of Pathans, Turkis, Hazaras, and Tajiks as well as Sikh merchants and Hindu bankers from India. Pushtu, the tongue of the Pathans, is the official language.

There are no railways in Afghanistan and *Kabul*, the capital, stands at an ancient road centre where routes from Peshawar, Kandahar, Herat, and Soviet Russia meet. The people are mostly peasant farmers and nomad herdsmen.

The Vale of Kashmir

Our starting point for the rugged North-West Frontier was Rawalpindi. From this same centre we might travel by road up to Kashmir, the beautiful State cradled in the great mountains of the north. *Srinagar* is the summer capital, and Jammu the winter capital.

The River Jhelum flows through the Vale of Kashmir, which is so lovely that it is known all over the world as " the Happy Valley." Meadowland borders the river with lush grass and colourful wild flowers. Majestic chinar trees, cedars and walnut trees cover the lower slopes of the mountains before giving way to dark belts of pines. Higher still are the mountain pastures, then bare rock and the snow peaks.

If we wish, we can glide peacefully across the emerald-green waters in a *shikara*, a long and narrow craft paddled

E.N.A.

KABUL, THE CAPITAL OF AFGHANISTAN

The kingdom of Afghanistan is one of the most rugged and isolated countries in the world. Kabul, the capital, commands the important Khyber Pass route to Peshawar in Pakistan. Several irrigation dams and new roads are now being built in Afghanistan.

by two or three men sitting in the stern. Here and there, moored to the river bank, are the houseboats where Europeans made their homes because they were forbidden by law to buy houses in Kashmir.

Among the most beautiful places in the Vale of Kashmir is Dal Lake, on whose shores the Mogul emperors had their pleasure grounds. The Moguls are gone, but their gardens remain. The most famous is the Shalimar Bagh, laid out by the Emperor Jehangir, with its splendid pavilion of black marble.

Srinagar, a place of quaintly leaning houses, straddles the Jhelum. Here we might buy Kashmir shawls and rugs and perhaps see merchants who have come through the passes with loads of skins and carpets. For Srinagar is still a market centre for caravans from central Asia.

While in Kashmir, we should also see great Nanga Parbat, "the Naked Mountain" over 26,000 feet high, that was first climbed by a German-Austrian expedition in July, 1953.

West Punjab

We leave Kashmir and return to Rawalpindi, travelling from there by rail to Lahore, capital of the West Punjab. Those of us who have read Kipling's *Kim* will naturally want to see the gun under the tree—the Zamzamah—on which Kim is discovered sitting when the story begins. We shall find that Lahore has many links with the Mogul emperors. Here Jehangir, whose garden we saw in Kashmir, is buried, and here the emperor Aurangzeb built the Jama Masjid, or Great Mosque. In the old quarter of the city are narrow streets that seem to have changed little with the passing of the years. But Lahore does not dwell entirely in the past. It also has wide modern streets and many fine buildings.

E.N.A.

HOUSEBOATS ON THE JHELUM

The peaceful waters of the River Jhelum, flowing through the beautiful Vale of Kashmir, suggest nothing of the troubled times through which Kashmir has been passing. Most of the people of Kashmir are Moslems, but the ruling family was Hindu, and the state has been claimed by both Pakistan and India.

The Story
of the
World and
its People

In the
Dominion of
the
" Lion People "

Associated Press.

MODERN GOVERNMENT BUILDINGS AT COLOMBO

Colombo, the capital of Ceylon, is also the chief seaport of the Dominion and a city of fine streets lined with shady trees, shops, and offices. Many different nations are represented in the population of the capital, but most of the Dominion's people are Singhalese, claiming descent from the *Sinhalas* or " Lion People."

THE ISLAND OF CEYLON

LYING to the south of India from which it is separated by Palk Strait, Ceylon is a large island in the Indian Ocean which slopes upwards from the coast on all sides towards the central mountains. Its population to-day is over 8 millions, of whom over $5\frac{1}{2}$ millions are Singhalese. They are the descendants of the Hindus from the valley of the Ganges who gained authority over the aboriginal Veddahs as far back as 543 B.C.

Other races which make up the total population are the Tamils, who came from Southern India, Moors descended from the old Arab traders, Indians and

Europeans. The Portuguese landed in Ceylon in 1505 and formed settlements along the coast, but about 150 years later they were dispossessed by the Dutch. Later Britain took possession and in 1802 the island was finally ceded to the British. The King of Kandy, however, continued to rule until 1815 when he was deposed and Ceylon became a British Colony.

Ceylon was known to the Romans, who called it Taprobane, from the native name which meant " the island of dusky leaves." In later years it became famous for another and even duskier kind of leaf and to-day it produces about a sixth of the world's tea supply.

A Dominion of the Commonwealth

Various developments in its system of government took place while the island was under British rule. The culmination came in February 1948 when Ceylon attained full Dominion status and became a self-governing member of the British Commonwealth of Nations. Its first Parliament was opened by the Duke of Gloucester and at the ceremony the ancient golden throne of the kings of Kandy, the old capital of Ceylon, occupied a place of honour.

The industrial development of the island has gone ahead in recent years and many factories have been built. These produce plywood, leather and leather goods, paper, glass, and chemicals. Tea, as we know, is the main export. Originally coffee was the main crop of the plantations, but the plants were destroyed by disease, and tea was introduced so successfully that it became the chief crop of a considerable area. Rice is the chief grain. Rubber and products of the coconut palm are also important.

From the forests come satinwood and ebony. In addition to the many quarries from which precious stones such as sapphires and rubies are obtained, there are mines from which graphite is got and Ceylon probably produces about a quarter of the world's supply of this material.

Colombo is the capital of the island and, unlike many of the world's great seaports, has no disreputable or ugly water-side slums. As soon as the traveller lands here he will pass through the Fort district, where the government offices stand, and go on into a neighbourhood of fine streets lined with shady trees, shops and business offices.

Prince Street is the port's principal thoroughfare and chief shopping centre, running parallel to the sea. Here we are almost as much in Europe as in Asia, were it not for the climate. But if we go down to the Pettah or older town we are very definitely in the East, although even the Pettah is changing. Two Buddhist temples still remain, however, covered with strange and intricate carvings and multitudes of figures. Buddhism is still the chief religion on the island.

Camera Press.

A CONTRAST IN STYLES

Here we see two stewardesses of Air Ceylon, a company which operates regional services to Madras and international services to London and Sydney. The western dress of the Australian stewardess contrasts sharply with the sari worn by her Singhalese colleague.

Colombo has given its name to the Colombo Plan. This is a big plan for providing help in the form of money grants, equipment, technical advice and training for the under-developed countries of south and south-east Asia. The help is provided by the more developed countries of the West, including the United Kingdom, Australia, New Zealand, Canada and the United States, and the plan is thus a fine example of co-operation between the East and the West and of the way in which different nations can work together for the good of all.

Ceylon herself will benefit under the Plan. She urgently needs to grow more food and so, like India and Pakistan, she is using the benefits of the Plan for works like the Gal Oya irrigation scheme, which will bring more land under fruitful cultivation. She is also building more factories, extending her port of Colombo, building hydro-electric stations and improving her railways.

Camera Press.

PROPERLY TRAINED, A WILD ELEPHANT BECOMES A USEFUL WORKER

Although large areas in Ceylon have been cleared for plantations, about a fifth of the country is still forested. Wild elephants live in the forests. Some are caught and trained to become obedient and useful work animals. Here, for example, is an elephant using his trunk to carry a large rubber tree. You can probably think of some other parts of the world where man has taught the elephant how to work for him.

On the Road to Kandy

The people interest us at once, if only because of their variety: Singhalese and Moormen, Tamils and Burghers, with representatives of other Eastern races as well as Europeans, crowd the streets.

Our first trip up-country is to the ancient capital of Kandy, among the hills. We can go by train, but decide that a run by car along the fine Colombo-Kandy motor road will give us a better general idea of the country.

Almost at once the road plunges into the midst of luxuriant tropical vegetation. Coconut palms by the million grow on both sides of it; and here and there the Singhalese are busy breaking open the nuts, to get the white kernels which will be dried and exported as copra. The stout husks will be shredded up and spun into coir rope and sennit, or made into net-bags or matting, or one or other of the many things that come from coconut fibre.

H. Armstrong Roberts.

IN A SINGHALESE VILLAGE

This scene is typical of the villages and small towns of Ceylon and shows what is evidently the shopping centre of the place. Notice the dress worn by the people. Menfolk as well as women wear the *sarong*, and both sexes go about bare-footed. Shoes will be reserved for special occasions such as the rare visits to the cities.

Villages are frequent—most of them two lines of low, palm-thatched buildings on either side of the way—with their rice fields and their water buffaloes with monstrous horns and lumbering carcasses. The rice on this side of the island is sown during March, April and May, and reaped in July, August and September; but on the other side of the island, facing the north-east monsoon of the cooler months, the sowing begins in July and the harvesting in January. The rice fields here are being prepared for the coming rain; those on the other side of Ceylon are almost ready for harvest.

The village schools interest us mightily, for as we speed past their low walls we can see the dark heads of the children at their work, and the village teacher at the blackboard. Two elephants stand at the place where a small road branches off; except that they sway their huge trunks rhythmically from side to side, and occasionally flap their large ears, they might be carved in stone.

On the Tea Estates

All the time the road is winding up into the hills and at every bend a new and astonishing landscape unfolds itself now that we have left the lowlands behind. Presently, on both sides are rows upon rows of neatly-pruned bushes, which we know, without being told, are tea bushes. Here and there in the hollows are the white buildings of the tea factories. Few people are at work in the gardens, for picking ceased

A BEAUTIFUL COUNTRYSIDE

The Temple of the Tooth at Kandy contains a sacred relic, a tooth of Buddha, which is said to have been brought to Ceylon about the year A.D. 325. The relic makes the temple a place of pilgrimage.

At Peradeniya, on the road to Kandy, are the Botanical Gardens. Here you can see specimens of many tropical trees and shrubs, and this famous Palm Avenue.

Photos : Paul Popper.

These are the " lines," or houses built by an estate owner for his Tamil workpeople. They are not very pleasing to the eye, but they are probably much cleaner and more comfortable than the homes in Tamil villages in southern India. When the Tamils come from India to work on the estates, they bring their families with them. Their contract with the estate owner will probably be for a period of five years.

for the time-being a month ago; but the factories are busy enough, no doubt, packing the prepared tea for transport to the coast.

Most of the tea gardens are in Uva and the Central Province, but there are some large gardens in the south-west, in the Kelani Valley. There are about 2,400 tea estates in Ceylon; nearly half of these are situated at heights between 2,000 feet and 4,000 feet, and nearly a quarter at heights above 4,000 feet.

Height plays its part in determining the quality of the tea. The highest estates (5,000 to 7,000 feet) have cold nights and strong winds. Their tea bushes grow slowly, and flavour and quality are therefore more concentrated.

Weather conditions also affect the quality of the tea. The best teas of the Uva district, for example, are produced in August and September, when the high winds following the south-west monsoon cause the tea to take on its delightful flavour. Districts on the other side of the hills will produce their best teas in January and February, when the north-east monsoon is over and the nights are cold and the weather dry.

Each tea estate is like a little world on its own. It contains everything that the workpeople and their families will need to live useful and happy lives. In recent years the tea industry has led the way in improving the housing, health and education of the half million people it employs.

Both men and women help to tend the tea bushes, but the actual picking is usually women's work, and very skilled work it is. Both hands are used, and one picker can usually handle about 30,000 shoots in a day. Fine pickings, of two leaves and a young bud, will produce the best tea, but there may also be coarse pickings (four leaves) and medium pickings (three leaves and a bud). One bush can be picked for about ten days at a time, and it will probably go on producing tea for about fifty years. To make one pound of tea, no fewer than 3,200 shoots must be picked.

Rubber and Rice

Rubber plantations claim our attention next, each tree with its trunk carved in V-shaped patterns by the incisions made to get the white latex or milk, which is regularly collected and sent to the factory on the estate to be turned into rubber.

Camera Press.

BASKET-MAKING IS ANOTHER VILLAGE INDUSTRY

With deft fingers, these girls weave gaily-patterned baskets from the stained leaves of the wild date palm. Their dress—a simple bodice and sari—is the typical day-to-day attire of the Singhalese woman.

TEMPLE AND PALACE

Paul Popper.

This ancient rock temple reminds us that most of the people of Ceylon are Buddhists. To the left of the entrance and partly hidden by the rock is a dome capped by a curious spire. This structure is known as a *dagoba* and it was probably built as a resting place for some holy relic.

By courtesy of Christmas Humphreys, Esq.

Among Ceylon's magnificent scenery are stretches of forestland from which protrude strange rock formations like the one shown here. There was once a palace upon this rock which, defended by a Singhalese king and his soldiers, resisted the besieging armies for thirty years.

Camera Press.

A LESSON IN LACE-MAKING

This little girl is being taught the art of lace-making by her grandmother. Lace-making is one of the chief village industries in Ceylon. Only about a quarter of the people in the country live in the towns or on the estates. The remainder live in the villages where lace-making, rope-making and other crafts are carried on by the womenfolk.

At last we reach Kandy, the old capital of Ceylon, some 1,600 feet above sea-level, but in a basin among the hills, which are covered with verdure where they are not cut into marvellous terraces for paddy cultivation, and supplied with water in all sorts of ingenious ways through channels and pipes or stones, bamboo, or even mud. Kandy itself stands by a beautiful lake which, it is said, was made artificially by the last Kandyan King very early in the nineteenth century.

The Temple of the Tooth

The most interesting thing to us in Kandy is the famous " Temple of the Tooth." This old Buddhist temple has its moat, in which live the sacred tortoises. Within the shrine behind the finely-carved doors is a yellow piece of ivory mounted on a stand. This is the famous " tooth " reputed to be the tooth of Buddha, and visited as such by pious pilgrims from distant parts of Asia. As an act of devotion, these pilgrims place gold leaf upon the stone pillars surrounding the shrine, much as the pious in Burma gild the pagodas.

The highest part of Ceylon's mountain knot is Pidurutallagalla (Pedrotallagalla), which reaches an altitude of over 8,000 feet. Much better known, however, is Adam's Peak, whose cone-like summit is about 1,000 feet less— for this is sacred ground. Up there is a strange depression in the earth, about 2¾ feet wide and from 3 to 5 inches deep, which is regarded with reverence by Buddhists, Hindus and Moslems alike. Buddhists say it is the foot-print of Buddha; Hindus say that it is Siva's footmark; and the Moslems aver that it is neither of these, but in very truth the foot-print of Adam, who came to this precise spot on his expulsion from Eden.

Not far from Adam's Peak is the lovely hill-station of Nuwara Eliya (Neuralia), which is very popular in the hot season. In December and January, however, the air is distinctly chilly, for the town is some 6,000 feet above sea level, and overcoats and fires are quite in order.

The Buried Cities

The visit to Kandy makes us all the

more eager to see something of the "Buried Cities of Ceylon"—cities which were the capitals of mighty kings hundreds of years before the birth of Christ, and the centres of early and wonderful civilisations. Their glory passed and the jungle swept over them as if they had never been. In recent years, however, much time and money have been spent in clearing away the jungle growths sufficiently to reveal the main features of these ancient cities, palaces and temples.

The oldest remains are at Anuradhapura in the central part of the island, where an image of Buddha sits in lofty contemplation regardless of time and change, where temples and *dagobas*, *wiharas* (image houses) and *pansalas* (priests' houses) peep unexpectedly from the jungle, and where Buddhist priests to-day still keep watch and ward over temples that have been restored to something like their original beauty. At Anuradhapura, too, is the sacred *bo-tree*, sprung from a branch of that same tree of Gaya in the Valley of the Ganges, beneath which Gautama Buddha sat in contemplation.

An Ancient Capital

Farther south are the famous ruins at Polonnaruwa—a capital of later date, and in much better preservation than those of Anuradhapura. Its walls, 10 feet high and 10 feet thick, built of brickwork over 800 years ago, extended for twelve miles round the ancient city. Even

H. Armstrong Roberts.

A BEACH SCENE IN CEYLON

The curious sailing craft in this picture are catamarans. Notice their strangely-shaped sails and the primitive steering boards aft. They are the boats of simple fisherfolk; their masts and outriggers are held in place by cunningly fastened coir ropes. If you could see the straw hats worn by the fishermen more closely, you would probably discover that they are " pin cushions " for innumerable hooks.

to-day you can trace them in a series of irregular grassy humps, with great masses of brickwork exposed here and there.

Sigiriya, the Fortress Rock

To the west of Polonnaruwa, a short distance from the road linking Colombo with Trincomalee, is the remarkable fortress rock of Sigiriya, which was for eighteen years the stronghold of King Kasyapa I. Kasyapa killed his father, King Dhatu Sena in A.D. 477 and, abandoning Anuradhapura, which was then the capital, retired to this strange rock and built himself a palace on its summit.

The name Sigiriya means " Lion Rock," but to western eyes the rock looks more like a huge granite mushroom as it rises abruptly out of the jungle to a height of about 400 feet. The name,

in fact, did not come from the shape of the rock, but from the brick and plaster lion which Kasyapa had built on one side of the rock and which marked the way up to the summit. Only the paws of this gigantic work remain.

It is a long and arduous climb, up a staircase of nearly two thousand steps, to the summit of the rock. On the way, we would see frescoes showing a procession of Buddhist pilgrims and painted nearly 1,500 years ago. Little remains of Kasyapa's palace on the summit, but we might sit on his pink granite throne, from where, it is said, he saw the avenging armies of his brother approaching the fortress.

Glimpses of forest and jungle give us but a faint idea of Ceylon's glorious trees and marvellous flowers, and none at all of the jungle folk. To discover the real secrets of the wilds, one must penetrate deeply into the little-visited parts of the island, where herds of wild elephant and the bison (*tsaing*) live, where the fierce leopards stalk deer, and where birds of gay plumage flutter among the branches, or sip honey from the flowers. Myriads of fire-flies flit amid the velvet gloom of jungle nights, and those who seek carefully may find those strange stick insects and leaf insects, which evade their foes by successfully pretending to be what they are not. When they are motionless, it is hard to distinguish them from the branch or twig on which they are standing.

Camera Press.

THE SHRINE OF THE SEATED BUDDHA

A worshipper is seen kneeling at the Shrine of the Seated Buddha at Polonnaruwa. This ruined city in the north central part of Ceylon was the capital from the ninth to the thirteenth century. Its greatest days were during the reign of King Parakama I, who lived and ruled about the same time as King Henry II of England. The ruins of his palace can still be seen.

The Story
of the
World and
its Peoples

Lands,
near and far,
of our
Colonial Empire

Paul Popper.

KILIMANJARO'S ICE-CLAD PEAK

In Northern Tanganyika, between Lake Victoria and the coast, stands Africa's highest mountain, Kilimanjaro (19,565 feet). It includes two lesser peaks, Kibo (19,455 feet) and Mawenzi (17,300 feet), both craters of extinct volcanoes. In this photograph Kibo Peak is seen. Its lava slopes are covered to a depth of 200 feet with an ice cap.

BRITISH EAST AFRICA

IN East Africa are broad lands which form part of the colonies, protectorates and territories of the British Commonwealth and Empire. They are (1) Kenya Colony and Protectorate; (2) Uganda, which is a British Protectorate embracing several Native kingdoms; (3) Tanganyika Territory, formerly a German colony, but placed under the care of Britain by the old League of Nations and now held under United Nations' trusteeship; and (4), off the East African shore, the Islands of Zanzibar and Pemba, ruled by an Arab sultan under British protection.

Most of these lands belong to the high plateau country of East Africa, which is crossed in the west by higher mountain ranges and studded with enormous lakes, and is famous all the world over as the " Land of Big Game " —the hunter's paradise. These lands drop steeply down to the narrow, hot, wet coast-plain that fringes the Indian Ocean.

Great Lakes and Volcanic Peaks

Two mighty volcanic peaks rise from the eastern half of the plateau— Kilimanjaro (19,565 feet), in Tanganyika Territory, and Kenya (17,036 feet). The western half, too, is dotted with large volcanoes, some of which are active. Here stands the third highest mountain in Africa, Mount Stanley (16,794 feet), which rises in the Ruwenzori Range, in western Uganda. The largest lake is Victoria, whose level is 3,700 feet above the sea, and whose deeply indented shores belong partly to Kenya Colony, partly to Uganda and partly to Tanganyika Territory. Covering an area of 26,200 square miles, Victoria is the third largest stretch of inland water in the world. The other great lakes, Nyasa, Tanganyika and Albert, are long and narrow, for they are flooded parts of a deep valley formed by the sinking of part of the earth's crust to form a deep trench ; a similar trench, with lakes in it here and there, cuts across the table-land east of Lake Victoria ; both form parts of what is called the " Great African Rift Valley."

Railway Routes

The chief ports of this part of the British Commonwealth are Mombasa in Kenya and Dar es Salaam in Tanganyika. From each of them a long railway climbs up from the narrow coastal plain to the plateau and crosses it to the great lakes. The Kenya and Uganda section of the East African Railways runs from Mombasa on the Indian Ocean to Nairobi, the capital of Kenya, and on to Kisumu on Lake Victoria and thence to Butere ; and to Jinja and Kampala in Uganda, whence it is to be extended to Mityana and Lake George to serve the rich copper deposits at Kilembe in the Ruwenzori foothills ; the Tanganyika line starts at Dar es Salaam, and goes by way of Tabora to Kigoma on Lake Tanganyika and to Mwanza on Lake Victoria. A further line runs from the port of Tanga to Moshi and Arusha and joins the Mombasa line at Voi. Tanganyika also has a Southern Province Railway running from Mkwaya, near Lindi, to Nachingwea, which is joined at Ruo by a line from Mtwara, the new deep-water port.

It was the building of a railway that made possible the swift development of Kenya and Uganda. Yet when the task of building a line to link Uganda with the coast was begun in 1896, some people said that it was a harebrained project. The railway was actually described as " a lunatic line." This was small encouragement to the engineers who had the task of building the line

Paul Popper.

HOW TO MAKE A CANOE

Probably the first boat ever made by man was fashioned from a tree trunk with the aid of primitive tools. In most parts of the world this method of boat-building belongs to the very distant past. It is still used, however, in the second half of the twentieth century in some places, and here we see a native of Uganda hollowing out a tree trunk into a canoe on the shores of Lake Albert.

BRITAIN'S FIRST COLONIAL CITY

Not so many years ago Nairobi was a mere village with corrugated iron buildings and rough roadways. The building of the Kenya and Uganda Railway led to its rapid development, and in 1950 it became the first city in the Colonial Empire by Royal Charter. To-day Nairobi has wide, well-laid streets and imposing buildings. In this picture is seen Government Road, one of the chief shopping centres.

Photos : Paul Popper.

Lake Victoria, or Victoria Nyanza, was discovered by the explorer, Speke, in 1858. As a fresh-water lake it is second only in size to Lake Superior. The East African Railways and Harbours Administration run a regular service of sailing round the Lake and this photograph shows the steamship *Usoga* moored alongside at a port of call on the Lake.

across very difficult country, where water was sometimes scarce and where disease and wild animals killed numbers of their workpeople and transport animals. But they carried the job through, despite all setbacks and dangers, the cattle watering place on the Athi Plain, which was once their advanced workshop base, becoming the city of Nairobi.

Nairobi

Nairobi stands over 5,400 feet above sea-level and is about 330 miles from Mombasa. A hundred miles away to the north is the snowy cone of Mount Kenya. Everybody who comes to Kenya, whether for big-game hunting, or for coffee-planting, or to see the country, comes to Nairobi, for it is the capital and the heart of things in the colony. It received its City Charter on March 30th, 1950, from H.R.H. the Duke of Gloucester, who became Nairobi's first Freeman. Although Nairobi is clearly still in its growing stage, there are many fine buildings along its wide straight streets among others that are in process of erection.

You will also see in Nairobi a fine bronze statue of Lord Delamere, who worked hard for the European settlers in Kenya and became their leader. Among the many research and farming ventures which he started was co-operative dairy farming, and to-day practically all Kenya's butter and much of her cheese is produced by the Kenya Co-operative Creameries which he founded. He was also a great believer in training for the Africans and helped to establish the Trade School and Teacher Training School at Kabete.

Coffee thrives on the highlands of East Africa and in the neighbourhood of Nairobi are many coffee plantations, ranging in size from about fifty acres to several hundred and owned by European planters. Typical coffee-growing districts are Kiambu, Thika and Ruiru. Coffee is an important crop in Kenya, but is more important still in Uganda, which is the leading coffee producer in the British Commonwealth. During 1951 about £10 million worth of coffee was exported from Uganda. Tanganyika also grows coffee, and East Africa as a whole produces about 70,000 tons each year. Other important East African crops are sisal, tea and tobacco.

While cattle and sheep are reared in large numbers in Kenya, most successful farmers there operate mixed farms. Wheat, maize, and barley are widely grown, and dairy herds can also be seen. Kenya is the world's chief producer of pyrethrum. The higher ground is used widely for the growing of this daisy-like plant, whose flowers yield a dust that is fatal to insects, although its importance is less now that such artificial insecticides as D.D.T. have been invented. The great danger to farming is erosion. Soil is washed away down the rivers by tropical rain, and strenuous efforts are being made to impress on farmers, both European and African, the need for keeping the fertile soil under control. As might be expected, Kenya has many industries linked with her agriculture. But there are also secondary industries such as boot and shoe, clothing and furniture, which are being developed. Gold and other minerals are mined.

Past Nairobi, the railway climbs up through hilly country dotted with the farms of Europeans and the *manyalta* (camps) of the Masai people, who are a nomadic people who live by their cattle on the Masai Reserve—territory specially set apart for their use by the Government—and whose famous lion-hunts have often appeared on the screens of British cinemas. At last we arrive at the port of Kisumu on Lake Victoria, where we find regular services of lake steamers linking up the native ports and towns around the lake shores.

From Kisumu we can travel by steamer to Jinja, at the northernmost tip of Lake Victoria. Here, in 1862, the British explorer Speke came across the source of the great River Nile : " It was a sight that attracted one to it for hours —the roar of the waters, the thousands

A UGANDA FISHING PARTY

There are flourishing African-owned fisheries along the north-eastern shores of Lake Edward and in the long Kazinga Channel which joins that lake and Lake George. Here we see a typical fishing party paying out their nets. Do you see the line of net-floats on the far side of the canoe?

Crown Copyright.

The fishing industry illustrated on this page supports about 2,000 Africans—most of them Baganda from the northern and north-eastern shores of Lake Victoria. Before selling their catch, the fishermen put it in brine pits, and after several days lay it out to dry for about a week.

of passenger-fish, leaping at the falls with all their might ; the Wassago and Waganda fishermen coming out in boats and taking post on all the rocks with rod and hook, hippopotami and crocodiles lying sleepily on the water, the ferry at work above the falls, and cattle driven down to drink at the margin of the lake. . . ."

To-day the Nile is being harnessed. Near Jinja, the Owen Falls Dam has been built across the Victoria Nile. This new dam and its power station will provide electricity for Jinja, Kampala and Entebbe, the capital of Uganda, and for the Kilembe copper mine and other industrial undertakings.

Cotton and the Buganda Kingdom

Around the north-western shores of Lake Victoria lies one of the African states of the Uganda Protectorate. This is the Kingdom of Buganda, where dwell 1,300,000 Baganda Africans ruled by their *Kabaka* or king. Their homes are rectangular huts with white-washed walls and roofs of thatch or corrugated iron, built on the hillsides amid dark green banana plantations. Their clothes are mostly long white robes of cotton; for next to coffee, cotton is Uganda's most important crop.

The main growing areas are Buganda and the Eastern Provinces. It is not large-scale cultivation; the entire crop is produced on small plots of land cared for by the African peoples of the Protectorate.

So far only two of the African peoples of East Africa have been mentioned— the Masai and the Baganda, but it would be very wrong to imagine that these are the only peoples native to this part of the continent. There are something like 18 million Africans living in East Africa and they belong to more than 200 different tribes. Any one tribe will differ greatly from the others—in appearance, in language, in religion and in their way of life. Some tribes are quick to learn and very progressive; examples are the Kikuyu of Kenya and

the Chagga of Tanganyika, and the Baganda and Teso of Uganda ; other tribes, like the Masai, have taken slowly to the new ways brought by Europeans. All these differences mean that governing and teaching the Africans in East Africa is not the simple and straightforward job it might at first appear.

To see what is being done to teach the African, let us go to *Kampala*, the largest town in the Uganda Protectorate, and its chief commercial and missionary centre. North-west of the town is Makerere College, a centre for higher education which ranks as a university college. Here teachers and leaders are trained, some of whom may well find their work in the new towns which progress will bring into being in East Africa. Makerere is but one training centre ; at Nairobi, in Kenya, there is the Royal Technical College, serving students of all races, and at Mombasa the Institute of Muslim Education. Schools have been established in most communities and much is done by travelling teams of teachers, by mobile cinemas and by wireless programmes to bring education to the masses ; an important part in this work is taken by the East African Literature Bureau.

Tanganyika Territory

Once a German colony, Tanganyika is the second largest country in the British Colonial Empire ; four times as large as Great Britain, it is second in size only to Nigeria. Its chief port, main railway terminus and capital is *Dar es Salaam* (" Haven of Peace "), a town built during the last seventy years or so, which to-day has a population of about 70,000. Besides handling modern shipping, the harbour at Dar es Salaam, like that of Mombasa, is often a port of call for picturesque coastal and sea-going Arab dhows. Arabs have been trading along this coast and inland for centuries and numbers of them still live in East Africa.

The new deep-water port of *Mtwara* was opened in 1954. With its railway,

PROBLEMS IN EAST AFRICA

The problem of water supply is one that explorers have always had to face when travelling through country some distance from rivers or lakes. In East Africa the task of opening up the country and discovering its natural resources frequently entails the employment of large numbers of bearers, and in this picture, taken in Uganda, part of a file of water carriers is seen.

Photos : Paul Popper.

In this photograph another problem of equatorial lands is vividly illustrated. African carriers are walking through a flying swarm of locusts near the borders of Kenya and Uganda. On the last occasion when locusts invaded East Africa they did £7,000,000 worth of damage to crops and thousands of cattle died after the grass had been eaten up. Determined efforts are being made to exterminate the pest.

PEOPLE OF EAST AFRICA

One of the most advanced tribes in Uganda are the Baganda people, who are keenly interested in European customs. Here is a close-up of the bride and her attendants at a wedding.

The fine features, characteristic expression and elaborate decoration of this Masai woman mark her out as a person of high caste. The leather thongs and ear-rings weigh over a pound.

Photos : Paul Popper.

At one time the Masai tribe occupied a considerable part of the plains of Kenya, Tanganyika and British East Africa. Sinewy and tall, they are, or were, of warlike character. A warrior who has killed a male lion in single-handed combat has his own particular shield and spear and is entitled to wear a head-dress made from the lion's mane. The shield decorations have their special meaning.

ON THE ISLAND OF CLOVES

Most of the world's cloves come from Zanzibar and Pemba, and scientific study of the clove tree began on the former island in 1932 with the opening of the Kizimbani Experimental Station. The station now studies all the main food crops of the Protectorate. Here, for example, are young papaw trees.

Rice, maize, millet, cassava, sweet potatoes and yams are among the main food crops of Zanzibar which are studied at the Kizimbani Experimental Station. In this picture we see selected vegetable seed at the station being dried before it is issued to farmers and small growers on the island. In the background is a fine grove of raphia palms.

it will help in the development of the Southern Province.

Tanganyika's most important crop is sisal, a plant with sword-shaped leaves that provide fibre for making rope and string. Most of the crop is grown in Tanga and the Northern Provinces and shipped through the port of *Tanga*, but a considerable quantity is grown in the coastal belt around Dar es Salaam and shipped from that port. The average yearly yield of sisal in Tanganyika is about 140,000 tons—that is, about a third of the total world production. East Africa as a whole produces about half the world's supply.

Like Kenya, Tanganyika produces some gold and her diamonds from the rich field at Shinyanga are important. One of the most valuable diamonds from the Williamson Mine at Mwadui was presented by Dr. Williamson, the Canadian geologist who discovered the mine, to Queen Elizabeth II on the occasion of her marriage. There are large deposits of coal, but they have not yet been fully developed because of transport difficulties. The main fields are : *Tukuyu*, north-west of Lake Nyasa ; *Ruhuhu*, east of the same lake, and *Ufipa* near Lake Tanganyika. *Mpanda*, 200 miles south-west of Tabora, is a lead-mining centre which is connected by a new 127-mile railway to the main line at Kaliua.

Zanzibar

Now let us take a peep at Zanzibar and Pemba, the " islands of cloves "— for most of the world's cloves are grown there. We find Zanzibar a town of tall white, flat-topped houses, of mosques and towers, set amid the deep green of waving palms, and " the myrtle-like green of giant clove trees." We go ashore and lose ourselves in the maze of dark crooked streets, which are crowded with people of all sorts, reminding us in many ways of the thronged bazaars in Indian cities. At the clove market every Monday, all the East congregates. Men with snowy turbans folded round

A TOWNSHIP IN UGANDA   *Paul Popper.*

Changes are taking place in East Africa; roads have been and still are being made through parts of the country which until comparatively recently were to a large extent unknown. Many hundreds of miles of all-weather roads have been made in the past twenty years. Here is a typical township, just over the border from Kenya and in Uganda near Lake Victoria.

fine embroidered caps ; bearded men hung with gold chains, and eager, fine-faced men in white robes—Arabs and Persians, Greeks, Jews and Gentiles—bid for the stacks of cloves which glut the stores, bursting from the high-piled sacks.

Both Zanzibar and Pemba have a long history dating from the first century ; and from the sixteenth century onwards it is largely one concerning the East Coast Arabs whose island of Zanzibar became one of the last strongholds of slavery.

But Zanzibar's golden age was during the early nineteenth century when it was the great centre of East African commerce, a place of such power and importance that Arabs coined the proverb : " If you play on the flute at Zanzibar, everyone as far as the Lakes dances."

Cloves from Zanzibar

It was about this time that the clove was brought to Zanzibar from either Mauritius or Réunion ; and although Zanzibar and Pemba are among the leading producers of copra along the East African coast, their major crop is cloves of which they produce some eighty per cent. of the world supply. It has been estimated that there are some four million clove-bearing trees on the islands ; each tree yields about six pounds of dried buds, and it is these that we find in the clove market in Zanzibar.

Scientists have been hard at work discovering the cause of a disease called " sudden death " which has been devastating the clove plantations. It was said recently that " sudden death," which is probably caused by a fungus parasite,

Paul Popper.

A CLOSE CROP

Even in Britain a visit to the barber's for a hair-cut is rarely regarded by young boys as a pleasant amusement. This youngster, who lives in the Uluguru Mountains of Tanganyika, is undergoing the same ordeal, but instead of scissors a large kitchen knife is slowly removing his locks and giving him a close crop.

has killed more than half the clove trees on Zanzibar Island.

The language we need here is Swahili, which we found useful in speaking to the natives in Kenya, and which naturally has here been affected by Arabic ; but in Zanzibar it seems possible to find people of every seafaring race, and along the water-front you can hear the tongues of many of the nations that " go down to the sea in ships."

Among other advantages Zanzibar has the best water supply on the east coast of Africa, and it is much in demand for shipping services.

BRITISH WEST AFRICA

A GOLD COAST CASTLE

F. Deaville Walker.

The Portuguese, and other colonising nations, built strong forts along the Gold Coast which in those distant times was a region favoured by the Slave Traders. Many of these old strongholds can be seen to-day. Here, for example, is Christianborg Castle, near Accra, which is now the residence of the British Governor.

VERY different from South Africa are those lands of the British Commonwealth in West Africa between Cape Verde and the Bight of Biafra—Nigeria and the Gold Coast facing the great Gulf of Guinea, and Sierra Leone and Gambia facing the Atlantic where it is narrowest between Africa and South America.

In many parts of South Africa, Europeans have made their homes ; but in West Africa, Europeans administer and guide, direct business, run plantations and carry on trade, to leave the country as soon as their work is done. They do not make homes and bring up their families there, for it is not at all a white man's country. You can see that clearly if you look at any book that tells you the population of Nigeria, for instance ; over 25 millions of people live there, but of these, only a few thousands are Europeans. The British West African lands, in fact, are all within fifteen degrees of the Equator, and the climate is too hot for Europeans to live there in comfort all their lives.

Rivers and Ports

The great river of West Africa is the Niger, some of whose tributaries are many times longer than the English Thames. The story of how it was explored by Mungo Park, a young Scottish surgeon, in 1796, is told elsewhere in these volumes. Like other large African rivers, its lower courses are spoilt by falls and swift rapids, but it has several hundreds of miles of open navigation, and is still one of the chief ways of taking goods from place to place. Many other rivers come down to the Gulf of Guinea, and along them the palm oil, the groundnuts, rubber and other West African products are brought to the ports. Few of these ports, however, are really good, for the Atlantic beats all along this coast in heavy surf, so that in many cases steamers must anchor a mile or two out, and send goods ashore or take them aboard by the surf boats manned by the sturdy black Kru men, who are the best sailors in Africa. A great artificial deep water harbour was, however, opened at the port of *Takoradi* on the Gold Coast in 1928, a little to the west of the old port of Sekondi. Another really fine deep-water harbour is the French port of *Dakar*, under the shelter of Cape Verde. The finest natural harbour on the West African coast is *Freetown*, the port of Sierra Leone.

The Walled City of Kano

Lagos, the capital of Nigeria, is the port for the walled city of Kano to which it is joined by a 700-mile-long railway. This railway goes via *Ibadan*, which has a population of 459,000 and is the largest Negro city in the whole of Africa, and on from Kano to Nguru. *Kano* is the biggest trading centre in West Africa, famous for its cloth, dyeing, and leatherwork for over a thousand years. To Kano come the long camel caravans of the Tuareg and other desert tribes as they have done for many centuries. For before West Africa was opened up to seaborne trade, Kano's leather goods, made from sheep and goatskins, found their outlet by camel caravan to the ports of the Barbary shore where they became famous as " Morocco leather." Twelve miles of adobe walls encircle this ancient city, within which Europeans are not allowed to live. But Kano does not linger in the past. The walled city has electric light and a modern water supply, and the hospital there is one of the best in this region.

The 13½ million people who live in Kano and the Northern Region of Nigeria are very different from those of other parts of West Africa. They are mostly Mohammedans ruled by their own Emirs or Sultans. In West Africa generally there are the same differences

F. Deaville Walker.

IN THE WALLED CITY OF KANO

Kano, in Northern Nigeria, is the biggest trading centre in West Africa, famous for its cloth, dyeing, and leatherwork for more than a thousand years. The city is encircled by twelve miles of adobe (clay) walls, and some typical Kano architecture is seen in this picture. But Kano also has electric light, a modern water supply, and a fine hospital.

between the various people that we noticed in East Africa. West Africa has a population of some 32 millions, about forty major tribes and a great number of minor tribes. There are differences of race, speech, religion, dress and way of life. There are, too, differences arising from the spread of education ; you may meet a simple peasant farmer who cannot read and is quite content to live as his forefathers lived, and find that his son has been educated at a university.

But the influence of the tribe remains and its most typical representative is probably the peasant farmer of the West African countryside. He grows his own food—grain, yams, cassava and similar crops—and lives in a thatched mud house, which his friends have helped him to build. If he lives in northern Nigeria or in the Northern Territories of the Gold Coast he may be a herdsman tending cattle, or may earn money by growing groundnuts. If he does not wish to lead this sort of life, he may leave his own locality and its peasant farming and work in the mines or some other industry. Perhaps he is ambitious and not content with the ways of the past ; if so, he may well study and in time become a lawyer, doctor, teacher or business man.

Among the schools and colleges where West Africans of the future are being taught and trained is the University College of the Gold Coast, near Achimota, for the building of which the Gold Coast Government granted more than £2 million. A further £400,000 came from Colonial Development sources, while the Gold Coast cocoa farmers themselves contributed £1,900,000. Nigeria has a similar college at Ibadan. Both these colleges are linked with the University of London, and as a result a West African can take his examinations in the Gold Coast or Nigeria and, if he is successful, receive his degree from distant London University.

Cocoa and the Gold Coast

Fifty years before Columbus dis-covered America, the Gold Coast was beginning its long history as a centre of the cruel trade in " black ivory," in slaves. Slavery was not considered inhuman in those distant times, and under the Portuguese pioneers the Slave Trade so flourished that they built strong forts along the coast to strengthen their hold on this land of " black cargoes." Later, English and Dutch adventurers, men like Sir John Hawkins, fought to win a share of this profitable business in human lives, adding their own forts and castles to those built by the Portuguese. Many of these old strongholds can be seen to-day along the Gold Coast. One of the most interesting is Elmina Castle, which is probably one of the first prefabricated buildings the world has known. It came, in numbered sections, from Portugal over five hundred years ago.

The Gold Coast got its name from the gold found in its streams, but it is much more important to-day as the land which supplies much of the cacao used in the world's cocoa and chocolate factories.

The Cocoa Farmer

To start his farm, the cocoa farmer hacks and burns out a part of the bush, leaving enough trees to provide shade and retain moisture for his crop. When the beans he has planted have become seedlings, he replants them 10 to 15 feet apart in cleared ground and for five years keeps the land well hoed so that the weeds cannot spoil his young cacao trees. At the end of this time the trees will have so grown that their branches meet and the area beneath the trees is humid and shady. When the small flowers have dropped, the pods appear; they are green at first, but soon change to a vivid yellow.

The main harvest takes place from October to December, and there is a second harvest between March and May. The beans are put in heaps covered with leaves and left a short time to mature, after which they are dried and packed in

Shell Photographic Unit.

YOUNG MECHANICS AT A NIGERIAN TRADE SCHOOL
Much has been done recently to provide academic and technical education for the peoples of British West Africa. Both Nigeria and the Gold Coast now have their university colleges and there are also several trade schools. This picture, taken at the Enugu Trade Centre, Nigeria, shows young apprentice mechanics under instruction.

bags for sale to the Gold Coast Marketing Board. In the old days before boards were set up in the Gold Coast and Nigeria, the cocoa farmer was at the mercy of the sudden price changes that then occurred and could never be sure of a proper reward for his toil.

Most of the cocoa harvest is taken to the ports by lorry or train, but in the more remote districts you can still see Africans carrying the bags of cocoa to market on their heads. The harbour of Takoradi is much more convenient for shipping the cacao than the old port of Accra, where surf boats and lighters must be used. At Accra, even passengers who wish to land must be swung from the deck of the liner in " mammy chairs," lowered into the surf boat that rises and falls on the big rolling swells, and taken ashore through the boiling surf by boatmen.

The Gold Coast and Nigeria together produce about half the world's supply of cocoa. One of the worst blows which can fall on a cocoa farmer in these countries is to have his trees stricken by " swollen shoot," a virus disease that has recently become most serious. There is at present no known cure, and the only way to check the spread of the disease is to cut down the infected trees and all other trees within a certain area.

Kumasi, about 170 miles from the coast, is the chief town of Ashanti, which is a British protectorate.

Towards Self-Government

The policy followed by successive British governments has been to educate peoples, once referred to as backward races, to the stage where they can carry on their own government as members of the British Commonwealth.

In the Gold Coast Colony a step nearer this goal was taken in 1951 when the first General Election for the Legislative Assembly took place. Throughout the towns and villages of the Colony trained teams were sent

E.N.A.

A VILLAGE IN NORTHERN NIGERIA

This picture shows us an up-country village whose dwellings, made from mud and thatch, provide a striking contrast with the Nigeria of the future that is now emerging. Here is something that will one day be of Nigeria's past. The future lies in such wealth as the Enugu coalfield, the tin mines of the Bauchi tableland, and the Sokoto cottonfields, and in the new way of life which the West is bringing to native Africa.

before the elections to explain and instruct those who were entitled to vote how an election by secret ballot is carried out.

Elections were also held in Nigeria in 1951, but because Nigeria is such a large country (the largest in the British Colonial Empire) and contains so many different peoples, the system had to be different. The country has therefore been divided into three regions, each with its own assemblies containing elected members. The regions then appoint all members, save twelve, of the House of Representatives for the whole country.

Palm-Oil from West Africa

It was in West Africa that Europeans discovered palm-oil—the valuable vegetable fat obtainable from the pulp and kernels of the fruit of the oil palm. This oil, used in the manufacture of margarine, soap, and many other things, is still an important export from Nigeria where the palms which provide it grow in the hot, wet forestlands of the south. Here the Yoruba people climb the palms

and hew off the clusters of fruit which will later be pressed and crushed to yield the oil.

Another valuable contribution made by West Africa to our food supplies is its groundnut crop. Great efforts have been made to grow groundnuts in East Africa, but the result has been only partially successful. In British West Africa a large groundnut crop is grown annually.

West Africa grows about half of the world's cacao ; its forests are rich in mahogany and ebony, and the tin mines of the Bauchi tableland of Nigeria are among the richest in the British Commonwealth.

Nigeria has also important cottonfields in Sokoto Province and coal from the Enugu coalfield comes down to Port Harcourt, in the Niger delta, for shipment. Uranium ore is also known to exist in Nigeria, and manganese and gold are important Gold Coast products.

The Volta River

The most ambitious development to

be carried out concerns the Volta, the biggest river of the Gold Coast. Near *Ajena* a dam and hydro-electric power station are to be built, and an artificial lake, 200 miles long, created. Power from Ajena will be used for the large-scale manufacture of aluminium from the bauxite deposits at *Mpraeso* and *Yenahin*. Water from the Volta will also be used to irrigate the Accra Plains to the south. This scheme, which involves the building of new railways and of a new port at *Tema*, is expected to cost £150 million.

Sierra Leone

When the world turned from slavery, many of the freed Negroes were settled in West Africa where they later formed the free and independent Republic of Liberia. English settlers had also taken a part in giving freed slaves a home in their native continent and, in 1788, had bought a piece of land for this purpose from a native King. In time, this small territory became the British colony and protectorate of Sierra Leone which has, to this day, people descended from the freed slaves among its inhabitants.

Most of the population of the colony work at palm-oil production and industrial diamonds are mined, but its importance lies more in the great natural harbour and naval base of Freetown.

Freetown has more than seven miles of good anchorage for ships, where the water has an average depth of not less than 30 feet, and a new 1,200-foot long deep-water quay has been built at Fourah Bay. With the hot sun overhead, the seas look inviting as your ship steams past low, sandy Cape Sierra Leone into the great harbour, and you might feel tempted to bathe. But there are sharks here to make you pause before trusting yourself to the green depths, although the Africans who meet the boat in frail canoes and gladly dive for the coins you toss overboard do not seem to consider the risk.

Freetown is the home of the Fourah

E.N.A.

A VILLAGE MAIN STREET, SIERRA LEONE

A short train journey from the port of Freetown will take you to such a village as the one shown in this picture. Here, amid vivid greenery, corrugated iron and old petrol tins now find more favour than mud and thatch when it comes to home building, though native habits remain—as witness the two women (left) who carry their loads on their heads.

Bay College which at one time (before Achimota College was opened) was the only place where Africans could receive higher education. Sponsored by a religious missionary body, it trains Africans to hold responsible positions in the service of their people. Fourah Bay College has long been linked with the University of Durham. The European part of the town is on the higher ground where it is healthier for those not born to this climate.

The production of palm-oil as well as the development of other industries is being encouraged in Sierra Leone under a planning scheme which has been carefully mapped out by the Legislative Council. The scheme gives priority to the construction of new roads which are badly needed.

From Freetown, a railway runs into the interior to the oil palm forests. The main line runs some 230 miles to Pendembu, near the frontier of Liberia;

and there is a branch line from Bauyu Junction to Makeni.

North of Sierra Leone is Gambia where English traders first did business with the peoples of the West African coastlands. *Bathurst*, its port, is a link in the air route to Latin America. The Cameroons and Togoland are trusteeship Territories held jointly by Britain and France. The British sections are attached to Nigeria and the Gold Coast respectively.

Sandwiched between Sierra Leone and the Ivory Coast (which is part of French West Africa and adjoins the Gold Coast) is the Independent Republic of Liberia which grew out of a settlement of freed American slaves and is an exclusively Negro State. *Monrovia* is the capital.

Spain has the Rio de Oro, a wide coastal stretch opposite the Canary Islands, south of which are lands of the French Union, including Senegal, and Portuguese Guinea.

Keystone.

PREPARING FOR THE FIRST GENERAL ELECTION

For the first time in its history the Gold Coast Colony held a General Election in 1951. To instruct the people in the meaning of democratic government and the method of voting, the British authorities sent trained teams round the country. In this photograph an African official, a member of one of the teams, is explaining to villagers just what they have to do on Election Day.

THE BRITISH WEST INDIES

Paul Popper.

MAHEAN BAY, TRINIDAD

Trinidad has beautiful coastal scenery, as you can see from this picture of palm-fringed Mahean Bay where the brilliant green foliage seems to descend to the very brink of the deep blue seas. The island has very rich soil which yields fine crops of cane-sugar, cacao, coconuts and all kinds of tropical fruits.

IT is strange how names "stick" even though they are quite wrong. When Christopher Columbus, one fine day in October, 1492, sighted the island of San Salvador (now called Watlings Island, one of the Bahamas), he believed he had reached the Indies off south-eastern Asia, and the name West Indies soon came to be applied not only to the islands, but to the mainland of America. The islands were not the "Indies," nor were the natives whom Columbus found there "Indians," but both names persist.

The West Indies fall into three great groups: (1) the Greater Antilles, consisting of the large islands of Cuba, Hispaniola, Jamaica and Puerto Rico; (2) the Lesser Antilles, which include the long festoon of volcanic or coral islands stretching away from Puerto Rico to the mainland of South America;

and (3) the low coral islands of the Bahamas to the north of Cuba. Practically all of these were first discovered by Columbus on one or other of the four great voyages between 1492 and 1502.

Peoples of the Indies

The Spaniards almost crushed out of existence most of the native peoples of these lovely islands, setting them to work in the mines of Hispaniola. Then they followed the example of the Portuguese and brought in large numbers of Negro slaves from West Africa—a foul trade in which English seamen took a leading part, although in after years England redeemed herself by leading the movement to abolish slavery.

Most of the people of the West Indies to-day are the Negro descendants

419

27—2

of freed slaves. They are wonderful gardeners and excellent plantation workers. At one time large numbers of East Indians and many Chinese people went to work in the islands, and there are still a great many of their descendants there to this day. You will find innumerable East Indians in Trinidad, Jamaica and St. Lucia, for example.

Volcanic Outbursts

The British West Indies consist of the Bahamas, Jamaica, Barbados, Trinidad and Tobago, the Leeward Islands and the Windward Islands. The Bahamas and Barbados are low coral islands with no great depth of soil; nearly all the rest are volcanic, and are really the upstanding portions of great sunken mountain chains. The terrible forces that cause sudden and appalling changes in the earth's crust are still alive there from time to time; Kingston, the capital of Jamaica, was overwhelmed by an earthquake in 1907, when 1,500 lives were lost and property destroyed to the value of nearly two million pounds. In 1902 the great volcano of the Soufrière on the island of St. Vincent burst into sudden violence, destroying farms and homes and killing 1,300 of the inhabitants; and, at the same time, an even more frightful volcanic eruption of Mont Pelée took place on the neighbouring French island of Martinique, where the loss of life was still more appalling.

The large island of Trinidad, very near the South American mainland, has a remarkable " pitch lake," which makes one feel as one looks at it as if he were witnessing part of the earth's crust in process of manufacture.

Sugar and Rum

The West Indies were once the headquarters of ruthless buccaneers, but to-day their chief business is sugar-planting and the production of sugar and rum. Banana-growing is very important, too, and so is the cultivation of oranges,

spices, coffee, cotton, tobacco, and other tropical products. Most of the really important things grown in the West Indies are got from plants which are not native to the islands, but which have been imported from time to time. The Spaniards introduced the sugar-cane in the sixteenth century, and the cacao tree, too. Coffee, cinnamon, nutmegs, bananas, oranges and ginger were all brought into the islands from other lands.

No one who has ever been to the West Indies forgets to tell his friends about the magnificent palms which flourish in many of the islands. The great Royal Palm grows to a height of 100 feet, and an avenue of royal palms is a sight to be ever afterwards remembered.

Jamaica

Jamaica is the largest and the richest of all the British West Indies, and gets its name from the native *Xaymaca* meaning " the island of springs." It is about twice the size of Lancashire, and lies south of Cuba, almost on the direct route from Europe and the United States to the Panama Canal. Its divisions bear names that are familiar to Britons—Middlesex, Surrey and Cornwall. The beautiful Blue Mountains rise inland to twice the height of Snowdon, and it is on their slopes, between three and four thousand feet above the tropical sea, that splendid coffee is grown, known all the world over for its exquisite flavour.

Jamaica grows pimento (" allspice "), sugar and tobacco, bananas and oranges, grape fruit and limes, coconuts, and even tea. From its tropical forests are got ebony and dyewoods. Many factories are established on the island —tobacco and cigar factories and others where banana " figs " and banana flour are made. The new Monymusk sugar factory at Vere is said to be the largest of its kind in the British Commonwealth.

Kingston, the capital, has fine wide streets laid out on the chess-board plan,

King Street is its main thoroughfare. Kingston Harbour is one of the finest natural harbours in the world.

Jamaican Bauxite

Jamaica's deposits of bauxite have been estimated at between 200 and 315 million tons, and in January, 1953, an important new mining plant was opened by the Governor. The company owning the plant not only mines bauxite, but has some 50,000 acres of good farming land where high-quality cattle are bred and experiments carried out in farming methods that will restore the land to its fertility after the bauxite has been taken. It is expected that within ten years Jamaica will be producing three million tons of bauxite annually.

Trinidad has rich volcanic soil in which enormous quantities of sugar-cane are grown. Cacao is at its best here. Coconuts and all kinds of tropical fruits flourish. The capital is Port of Spain on the flat plain at the foot of the Santa Anna Mountains. It is very up to date with its electric light, electric cars and good telephone services. As a result of the American use of Port of Spain as a base during the war, the harbour and dock equipment have been vastly improved, and can now accommodate the largest ships.

Trinidad is probably the most pros-

E.N.A.

FISHING CRAFT AT BRIDGETOWN, BARBADOS

Barbados is noted for its sugar and its rum, but cotton is also grown on nearly all the large estates. The harbour of Bridgetown, the capital, is known as the Careenage, and here you will find fishing craft of the kind shown in the picture. Larger vessels lie off the port and load and discharge passengers and cargo by launch and lighter.

perous of the West Indies. The island is one of the main producers of mineral oil in the colonial parts of the British Commonwealth, and her sugar factory, the Usine Sainte Madeleine, is one of the largest in the world. At Trinidad, too, are the Imperial College of Tropical Agriculture and the Central Research Station of the Cotton Growing Corporation to which come students from all parts of the Commonwealth.

Columbus discovered Trinidad in 1498 at a time when his ships were desperately short of water. Columbus thereupon vowed that he would dedicate the first land he came across to the Holy Trinity. Shortly after, a look-out sighted the peaks of the island, which was accordingly named by Columbus " La Trinidado."

When Sir Walter Raleigh came to Trinidad in 1595, he not only discovered the famous Pitch Lake, but noticed a " salt river that had store of oysters upon the branches of the trees and were very salt and well tasted. All their oysters grow upon these boughs and sprays, and not on the ground." If you visit Trinidad, you will still find oysters " growing upon trees "—the trees are mangrove and the oysters grow upon their roots.

Trinidad and the West Indies generally are world-famous for their *calypso* singers who are surely the spiritual descendants of the minstrels and troubadours of history. They compose songs, both words and music, dealing with current events in the islands and in the world. *Calypso* singers often give themselves curious and highsounding names such as " Attila the Hun " and " the Lord Redeemer," and the usual rule seems to be that the more fantastic and spectacular names are chosen by those with the loudest and most penetrating voices.

Twenty-seven miles to the north-east of Trinidad is the island of *Tobago* which is administered from Trinidad. Tobago is a fertile farming island,

Fox Photos.

THE SPONGE FLEET IN HARBOUR

The Bahamas are a base for sponge-fishing and here, at a Nassau quayside, we see some of the trim vessels of the sponge fleet. The boats usually stay out some weeks, and the crews sometimes take a dog or a pig with them—as company, and to eat up the scraps. Very large sponges are rare, but sponges 6 feet in circumference and capable of absorbing 16 gallons of water have occasionally been found.

TRINIDAD AND JAMAICA

The pitch in some parts of Trinidad's famous Pitch Lake is rather like treacle. But most of the surface is hard enough to bear the lorries which come to collect the pitch.

Carrying four large stems of bananas, this Jamaican runner is on his way to the collecting station. His load may weigh 200 lbs. and be carried for half a mile.

Photos : Paul Popper.

This market-place in Dominica is thronged with buyers and sellers. The latter have spread their wares upon the cobblestones. Notice that nearly everyone wears a shady hat. The chief town of Dominica is Roseau. Citrus fruits, cocoa, copra and rum are some of the products of this small island colony.

although much of its area is covered by thick forests.

Tobago is sometimes said to be the original of the island described by Defoe in " Robinson Crusoe," although Alexander Selkirk, the original of the hero, was not marooned in Tobago, but thousands of miles away in the Pacific ocean on an island of the Juan Fernandez group, off the coast of Chile.

Barbados

Barbados is the outermost of the West Indies, and the nearest to Europe. It is about as big as the Isle of Wight. Its name probably came from the Spanish word *barbudo*, which means " a vine transplanted with roots " and was perhaps used to describe the banyan tree which grows well on the island. Bridgetown is its capital; its inner harbour is usually crowded with island schooners which have brought vegetables and other things from the neighbouring islands. Along the water front is the busy market where coloured folk bargain and chatter joyously in the sunshine.

Sugar laid the foundation of Barbados' fortunes. Sugar plantations cover large parts of the island and among the dark green of the growing canes you can still see the old windmills that provided power for the former type of crushing-mills, although large and up-to-date crushing-plants are now the rule. Some cotton is grown, and on the cotton plantations at picking-time you witness much the same scenes as those which are common on the cotton-fields of the southern States of North America.

Fox Photos.

BLEACHING AND CURING SPONGES IN THE BAHAMAS

The sponges have to be prepared for market after they have been brought home by the sponge fishers, and here we see sponges being put out in the sun for bleaching and curing. Once the chief industry of the Bahamas, sponge-fishing has greatly declined in recent years.

The Bahamas

The archipelago of coral islands which is called the *Bahamas* is the northernmost of the British West Indies. Nassau, on the island of New Providence, is the capital and is a favourite winter resort for American and Canadian sunseekers. The chief exports are lumber and tomatoes, which go mainly to the United States and Canada. The Bahamas once had the largest sponge-market in the world. Nowadays sponge-fishing and the growing of sisal are of less importance. Tomato-growing for export is now a leading industry. Many crawfish are also exported.

Among the other islands of the British West Indies are the *Leeward Islands*, mountainous and many years ago volcanic : and the *Windward Islands* (Grenada, St. Vincent, St. Lucia and Dominica) where traces of former French colonisation are found in the French patois spoken by the peasants, and where there is some of the most beautiful scenery in the West Indies.

In recent years the British West Indies have received large money grants from the Motherland to help restore their trade and prosperity. These were given mainly as a result of the Moyne Report of 1938 and the Stockdale Report of 1943. For beautiful though the West Indies are, they are faced with serious problems of poverty and employment, of food, health and education.

West Indian Federation

For some years now statesmen have been considering bringing the British territories of the West Indies into a single unit or federation within the Commonwealth. Our lands in the Caribbean

Paul Popper.

MAKING A CANOE

These Caribs in Dominica are making a canoe from the hollowed trunk of a Gommier tree. Stones and water are put into the trunk to widen it before the canoe is finished and taken down to the shore. The island of Dominica is one of Britain's Caribbean colonies and should not be confused with the Dominican Republic, which is an independent state.

area have many common problems; and while full self-government could not easily be given to a large number of small isolated communities, a single federal community could shape its own life and take an independent part, as a self-governing unit, in international affairs.

Since 1945 there has been steady progress towards federation, a principle which has been accepted by all the territories concerned except two: British Guiana and British Honduras. In April, 1953, a Conference took place in London to consider " the Federation of British Caribbean Territories," and it was decided that a Federation should be formed, with its own Governor-General, elected House of Assembly, Senate and Council of State.

BRITAIN IN THE AMERICAS

H. J. Shepstone.

SWAMP INDIANS OF BRITISH GUIANA

The people native to British Guiana are Indians, many of whom live in Reservations—lands specially set apart for them by the Government. The Swamp Indians live in riverside huts and are expert at making dug-out canoes, each canoe being laboriously turned and carved from a single tree-trunk.

THE only British Commonwealth territory on the mainland of South America is British Guiana, which is about the same size as Great Britain and is the *Eldorado* which beckoned adventurers to the New World in the sixteenth century.

" God of Waters "

The Guianas—British, Dutch and French—are hot, wet lands within a few degrees of the Equator, and a great deal of their surface is covered with dense tropical forest. It is only in the lowlands near the coast that white planters, employing Asiatic as well as native labour, have made their plantations of sugar-cane, rice, cacao, coffee, spices and coconuts. The greater part of the country still belongs to the forest, which is very difficult to penetrate, except by way of the rivers, which with their tributaries form a great network of waterways ; but these are full of falls and cataracts that hinder free use of them as highways. The numerous rivers explain the name of the territory, for Guiana is an Amerindian word meaning " Land of the Waters."

The most magnificent falls in British Guiana are the Kaieteur Falls on the upper Potaro River, which is one of the tributaries of British Guiana's great river, the Essequibo. They are nearly five times as high as Niagara, and the deep voice of the roaring waters can be heard miles away. The Indians call the Falls " God of Waters."

Sugar-Cane and Rice

British Guiana has areas of grasslands —for instance, the Rupununi district in the far south-west—but four-fifths of her area is covered by forest. Most of the population of about 437,000 live in a narrow coastal strip which is low-lying and protected from flooding by sea walls and breakwaters. The two main crops—sugar-cane and rice—are grown in the coastal areas and much is to be done to increase production by proper irrigation and drainage. Dams and weirs are being built, for example, to bring into cultivation 23,000 acres of coastland between the Essequibo and Demerara rivers so that more rice can be grown. Another area between the Corentyne and Berbice rivers is to be similarly controlled for rice-growing and stock-breeding.

British Guiana has rich mineral resources, including gold, manganese ore, diamonds and mica. Particularly important are her huge deposits of bauxite (the ore of aluminium). Bauxite is second only to sugar in the colony's exports ; of the total of just over 2 million tons of bauxite exported in 1950, nearly $1\frac{1}{2}$ million tons went to Canada.

Georgetown, the Capital

Although the Essequibo is by far the greatest river, it is the Demerara that is most important, for at its mouth stands *Georgetown*, the capital of the colony. In Georgetown you may see not only British and other European people, but also Chinese, East Indians and Negroes, as well as some of the native people of Guiana, who work for the white men. Chinese, East Indians and Negroes have come to Guiana to work on the plantations, just as they went to Natal and to Kenya Colony for the same reason. Europeans, indeed, form only about 5 per cent. of the people, but the East Indians include nearly half of the total population of British Guiana.

Peoples of the Guianas

The natives of Guiana are the Amerindians, coppery-brown people with lank black hair, broad, flat faces with dark, narrow eyes, and very muscular. They are the descendants of the earliest known inhabitants of South America. They live in their villages up-country, according to their tribes, unless they have come to work in the lowlands for

Paul Popper.

THE MAJESTIC KAIETEUR FALLS IN BRITISH GUIANA

In the heart of British Guiana, on the Potaro River, are these majestic falls, which are almost five times the height of Niagara. They are nearly 300 feet wide and have a sheer drop of 741 feet. The most comfortable way of reaching the falls is by flying-boat from Georgetown, the capital of this British colony.

the white men, or pilot boats on the rivers, or to act as carriers in the forests.

The Swamp Indians live a timid, squalid life in their riverside huts on the lowlands, but they are clever makers of dug-out canoes. The Arawaks are a much finer people ; many speak English and dress in European clothes. They are good boatmen and expert foresters. Other tribes live in the forest depths, and are clever in the use of the blowpipe and in the making of poisoned arrows.

Because the Amerindians are so different from the other peoples living in British Guiana, and because so many of them live in the remoter parts of the colony, it has not been easy to teach them civilised ways of life. At present there are many Amerindian Reservations, areas set aside by the Government in which the Amerindians may live in their own way. In time these will be reduced in number to three large districts, each with its district and area councils.

British Guiana is among the British

Paul Popper.

Forest industries are important in British Honduras. Here we see a train of mahogany logs on its way to the sawmills. Other important timbers are pine, cedar and sapodilla.

colonial territories that are moving towards self-government. The new Constitution introduced in 1953 gave the adults of all races in British Guiana (except Amerindians) the right to vote and established a State Council and a House of Assembly. All the members of the latter, except three, were to be popularly elected.

The first general election was held in April, 1953, but Communist intrigues led to a suspension of the Constitution in October of the same year.

Many of the Guianese are simple peasant farmers with more interest in local farming problems than understanding of politics. Unfortunately many do not even know of the efforts being made to raise their standard of living or of the money contributed by Britain to the present £10 million development scheme.

What is this scheme providing ? The answer is found in more and better houses, in the large new sawmill opened by the Colonial Development Corporation at Georgetown, in land settlement and similar projects. Another hopeful sign is the development of *Mackenzie*, on the Demerara River, where the Canadian bauxite company has its mine.

The most interesting time to visit British Guiana is in spring, for it is then that the East Indians have their festivals—the Pagwa, during which they anoint themselves with a purplish coloured dye, and the Tadja, which is an occasion for general rejoicing. At Georgetown, the capital, you would see the Botanic Gardens with their wonderful palms, orchids, and lotus lilies, and be offered all sorts of interesting souvenirs of your visit—parrots, stuffed alligators, blowpipes, and colourful plumed head-dresses.

British Honduras

The only part of the British Empire in Central America is British Honduras. It is bounded on the north by Mexico and on the west and south by the republic of Guatemala. Its coastlands are

Photos : Paul Popper.

The bark of the sapodilla tree contains chicle-gum, from which chewing gum is made. The bark is scored with deep cuts to a height of 30 feet.

When the trees have been tapped in this way, the *chicelero* collects and boils the chicle to reduce the water content. Here we see the chicle being stretched as it sets.

low, marshy and fever-smitten ; but inland the ground rises rapidly into mountains clad in dense tropical forest where mahogany, log-wood and cedar are cut for export. When they have been cut, the heavy logs are hauled to the nearest stream by bullock teams and floated down to the sea when the heavy rains set in. Other exports are chicle-gum (used in making chewing gum) and bananas.

Recently British Honduras has been striving to develop her agriculture, particularly in the Stann Creek Valley, where thousands of acres are devoted to oranges and bananas. More land is also being used to grow maize and rice.

The people of the colony are of several races : Creoles, who are descended from the early settlers, Europeans, American Indians and Caribs. In all they number about 69,000, and some 27,000 of them live in *Belize*, the capital, which stands on a river of the same name.

In the Steps of the Buccaneers

The mangrove cays or coastal reefs which guard the seaward approach to Belize were once the haunt of a Scottish pirate named Wallace or Willis, and some say that it was a corruption of his name which produced the name Belize. This was the Spaniards' name for the colony and it remains with us as the name of the capital city. But it is more easy to believe the evidence of an old map which shows " Bullys River "; the " bullys " were bullet or bullywood trees. This seems to be much nearer " belize " than the name of the obscure Scottish buccaneer.

But the story of British Honduras extends far into the remote past, along with that of many other parts of Central America. In the south of the colony are the foliage-hidden ruins of a Mayan city, and in the central district are ruins dating from the period 3000 B.C. to A.D. 1700.

Natural beauty is to be found in the Roaring Creek Falls and the remarkable caves along the course of the Manatee River.

BRITAIN'S ISLAND COLONIES

E.N.A.

HAMILTON, CAPITAL OF BERMUDA

The group of islands called Bermuda has more tourists than population. Each year about 80,000 Americans travel by air to this favourite holiday place, while others make the pleasant sea voyage to Hamilton, whose waterfront is shown in this picture. Bermuda consists of two or three hundred small islands rising far out to sea on top of an old undersea volcano.

SIX hundred miles from North Carolina's Cape Hatteras is a group of two or three hundred small islands which are known as Bermuda, or the Bermudas. It seems strange to find them so far from mainland, for the sea-bed here is twelve to fifteen thousand feet below the surface. But geologists have explained that the limestone and coral Bermudas sit on the top of an old undersea volcano.

The Bermudas have more tourists than they have population. Each year about 80,000 Americans fly to one or other of the fifteen or sixteen islands in the group that are inhabited to have their holidays.

The largest island of the group is Great Bermuda, also known as Long or Main Island, on which stands Hamilton, the chief town and capital. The first settlement, about 1612, was made on the island of St. George where many of the streets bear the very names that they had in the seventeenth century— Shinbone Alley, One Gun Lane, Featherbed Alley, and many others. At Bermuda's Aquarium is one of the world's finest collections of tropical fish, and here you can hire a diving helmet and explore the underwater mysteries of Harrington Sound, seeing the beautiful sea anemones, sponges, and sea fans, and such exotic fish as sergeant-majors, grunts, and squirrel-fish in the marvellous setting of their natural home.

The British Commonwealth has many colonial outposts scattered over the Seven Seas, many of them guarding important trade routes. One of the most famous is Gibraltar, which surveys the western entrance to the Mediterranean. Another such outpost in the same sea is Malta, which has a long history as an island fortress and which still guards our sea routes of Commonwealth.

The George Cross Island

There are three islands really— Comino, Gozo, and Malta, but we think at once of *Malta*, the fortress island commanding the sea passage of the central Mediterranean, rather than of the group. In its long history, Malta has been held by Phoenicians, Greeks, Carthaginians, Romans, Arabs, Normans, French, and the British. For many years it was a stronghold of the Knights of St. John whose fortifications can be seen to-day in *Valletta*, the capital of the island. Malta is not the barren and unfriendly island that it seems at first sight from the sea ; it is actually one of the most intensively farmed areas in Europe. Beyond the limit of its towns you will see patches

Topical Press.

FORTRESS GIBRALTAR GUARDS THE MEDITERRANEAN'S WESTERN GATEWAY

Towering majestically into the clear sky, Britain's fortress "Rock" guards the western entrance to the Mediterranean. Its name comes from Tarik, an Arab Corsair, who built a fortress on the Rock which he called *Jebel Tarik*—the Hill of Tarik. In 1704, it was captured from the Spanish and has been a British possession since, defying Franco-Spanish forces in the famous siege of 1779–83. The Rock is about two miles long and 1,400 feet high; it is separated from Spain by a small strip of neutral territory.

431

of farmland, each enclosed by a stone wall, which yield fine crops of grain, potatoes, onions, fruit and vegetables.

Malta's key position has made it an important air and naval base. Its heroic resistance to long and persistent attack during the war was acknowledged by a George Cross which was awarded to the island for its gallantry in one of the greatest of modern sieges.

Cyprus, Perim and the Seychelles

Eastwards now to the Levant, " region of the sunrise," where *Cyprus* lies off the main shipping routes about forty miles from the Turkish coast to the north and sixty miles from the shore of Syria. Like Malta, Cyprus has a history of varied ownership, but the Greeks who were among the earliest inhabitants predominate among Cypriot people. To Cyprus came peoples from all parts of the Levant to whom the island was a natural meeting and market-place. Famagusta, the island's chief port, was once renowned for its riches and belied the meaning of its name—" hidden in the sands." *Nicosia* is the capital and is connected by railway to Famagusta. Larnaca and Limassol, both in the south, are other ports. Cyprus is a peasant island of craftsmen, fishermen and farmers who fight a hard struggle to gain a living from the sea and soil.

If we continue southwards, through the Suez Canal, we reach the British island of *Perim* which guards the southern entrance to the Red Sea, the *Bab-el-Mandeb* or Gate of Tears as it was called by sailors of ancient times who were wrecked there.

North-east of Perim is the colony and protectorate of *Aden* occupying a small coastal strip of south-western Arabia. Aden is an important naval and re-fuelling base and a warehouse for goods from Arabia, from British Somaliland,

Keystone.

A VILLAGE IN CYPRUS

This is a typical mountain village in Cyprus, rising in tiers up a steep hillside. In many of the houses a bedroom and kitchen will often be the home of a family of ten or more, and in some houses the family dwelling-room will be shared by the animals. Bigger and better houses are now gradually replacing the older ones, but it will be some time before such living conditions are a thing of the past.

MALTA—THE GEORGE CROSS ISLAND

Beneath the frowning walls of ancient fortifications, dating perhaps from the times of the Knights of St. John, sailing craft unload food and wine they have brought to Valletta, Malta, from Sicily. From the sea Malta appears a barren island, but it is actually one of the most intensively farmed areas in Europe, producing grain, potatoes, fruit and vegetables.

Photos : Keystone.

A Grand Master of the Knights of St. John provided the money for St. John's Co-Cathedral at Valletta, Malta. Its plain design was meant to express the self-denying poverty of the Knights.

Builders of Valletta solved the problem of steep hillsides with streets of steps. St. John's Street (above) is typical. Its buildings are close enough to provide shade when the sun is at its height.

and from the island of Socotra, which produces "dragon's blood," a gum obtained from the dragon tree. Socotra is part of the Aden protectorate, which also includes the Hadhramaut.

Aden's importance will be increased when her large new oil refinery is completed. This refinery, which will take about two years to build, will handle every year 5 million tons of crude oil brought from the Persian Gulf in large tankers. The new oil port will cover 50 acres, and the refinery 270 acres. About 2,300 engineers and workpeople will be needed to work the installation, and a complete small town will be built for them by the oil company. During the early stages of construction, all those responsible for its building have been using the liner *Dorsetshire*, in which they sailed to Aden, as their floating camp.

Far to the south are the ninety-two islands of the Seychelles, whose chief port is on the island of Mahé. Assistance from the Colonial Development Fund has given the Seychelles a dis-

tillery which treats eucalyptus and other oil crops. Government farms are leading the way in increasing food production, and fishery and re-afforestation schemes have been started.

From Mauritius to Hong Kong

Still farther south, five hundred miles east of Madagascar, is *Mauritius* which has been called "a land of waterfalls and rainbows." Mauritius might also be called the sugar-bowl of the Indian Ocean, for sugar is the most important product of the island and during the period 1951–52 formed 97 per cent. of the total value of all exports.

Our journey round the island colonies now takes us across the Indian Ocean, through the Malacca Straits to *Singapore*, which has been a separate colony since the dissolution of the Straits Settlements colony in 1946. The Cocos or Keeling Islands and Christmas Island, in the Indian Ocean, were a part of the colony of Singapore until 1951, when it was agreed that they should be transferred to Australia.

ADEN FROM THE AIR   *E.N.A.*

Aden lies in a hot, dry part of the world where there is harsh sunshine all the year round. The high mountains hemming the city in are part of an extinct volcano. Aden is a British colony and an important refuelling station for ships on the route to the East. A large oil refinery is now being built.

Hedda M. Morrison.

HONG KONG'S MOST PROMINENT BUILDING

This striking building houses the Hong Kong and Shanghai Bank offices and is the most conspicuous building in Hong Kong. The smaller building (right foreground) contains the Courts of Justice.

Singapore was founded in the early nineteenth century by Sir Stamford Raffles, who rented the island at the southern tip of the Malay Peninsula that was a pirates' lair and transformed it into a flourishing free port. The name Singapore was ready-made for him; once before a rich city had stood there— Singapura, " City of the Lion."

The island is separated from the State of Johore, on the mainland, by a narrow strait which is to-day crossed by a granite causeway bearing road and railway. Three-quarters of the colony's population of just over a million live in the city of Singapore itself (the status of city was conferred by King George VI in 1951). The port covers 36¼ square miles; the great wharves and dry docks, more than 690 acres.

From Singapore are shipped the tin and rubber of Malaya, teak from Siam, cloth from India and China, oil from Sumatra and Borneo, and goods and supplies to south-east Asia from all parts of the world. No other Malayan port can vie with Singapore as the clearing house for the seaborne trade of south-east Asia. Moreover, the colony now has its place in world air routes, for Singapore is an important stopping place on the air route to Australia.

Britain has another important trading colony in the East. This is *Hong Kong* (" Fragrant Harbour "), a small island at the mouth of the Canton River, which has one of the world's finest harbours. On the mainland opposite is a much greater territory, Kowloon, which was leased from China in 1898

IN THE HADHRAMAUT

The Hadhramaut, in southern Arabia, is part of the British Protectorate of Aden. It includes the Kathiri state of Seiyun, whose chief town, which is called Seiyun, is seen in this picture. Notice the three white buildings in the background; the central one is the Sultan's palace.

Photos : E.N.A

Although it is more than a hundred years old, this palace at Shibam is not unlike some of the lofty buildings of to-day. It is built of sun-baked bricks, and has flat roofs, which are sleeping quarters in hot weather. Notice (left) the minaret of a mosque.

SINGAPORE & SARAWAK

H. Armstrong Roberts.

The curious craft moored along this stretch of the Singapore waterfront are sampans. Singapore city, on the island of Singapore at the southern tip of the Malay Peninsula, is the export and import centre for the peninsula and south-east Asia. Singapore has been a separate colony since 1946.

E.N.A.

Once the kingdom of the White Rajahs, Sarawak has been a British colony since 1946. This picture shows us the waterfront at Kuching, with the Matang Hills in the background. Near Kuching there are gold and mercury mines, but oil from such places as Miri and Seria is more important.

and now forms part of the colony. Small though the colony is, it had a population of over a million before the war, and this has now been swollen by the arrival of refugees from China to an estimated figure of over 2¼ millions.

Hong Kong is a vast depot of Far-Eastern trade, a clearing house for goods to China and other Far-Eastern lands and an export centre (in normal times) for Chinese products. Naturally enough for so great a seaport, the most important activities are shipbuilding and ship repairing. Did you know that there is no actual city of Hong Kong? The capital of the colony is the city of Victoria.

North Borneo, Brunei and Sarawak

Several hundred miles east of Singapore lies the large island of Borneo, whose northern part is a British colony which includes Brunei (where there is still a native sultan) and Sarawak. Sarawak was the kingdom of the White Rajahs whose ancestor, James Brooke, received this territory as a gift from the Sultan of Brunei over a century ago. It was ceded to the British Crown in 1946.

Much of British Borneo is dense jungle with rivers like the Batang Rajang as its only real highways. The jungle is the home of strange animals: the red-haired orang-utans and many kinds of monkey; the *pelandok*, or mouse-deer, which is about the same size as a hare ; wild pigs and oxen, rhinoceroses and porcupines, birds of many kinds, and even flying lizards. Where there is cultivation the crops are rice, sago and coconuts. Cutch is obtained from the bark of the mangrove. Rubber is the chief export product.

Oil is produced at Seria in Brunei and Miri in Sarawak, and the combined production from these sources is now more than that of Trinidad. There are coal deposits and gold is mined.

Camera Press.

A DYAK LONG-HOUSE

Many of the village people in Borneo live in long-houses. Each long-house is really a complete village under one roof. Each family has its own private room (on the left in this picture), and all the families share the verandah. Long-houses are usually built on the river banks, are sometimes 600 feet long, and may contain as many as sixty families.

Camera Press.

A TEACHERS' TRAINING COLLEGE IN FIJI

This is a craftwork lesson in the Teachers' Training College at Nasinu, near Suva. The training course lasts for two years and is taken by about three hundred Fijian and Indian student teachers at a time. Indians are now the largest racial group in Fiji.

Many tribes and races make up the people of British Borneo. In the towns, like *Jesselton* (capital of North Borneo) and *Kuching* (capital of Sarawak), are many Chinese. You will also see Malays, who are the fishermen and rice-farmers of this part of the world. But much more numerous are the native peoples : the Dusuns, who are farmers; the Muruts, who not so long ago were head-hunters; the seafaring Bajaus and Suluks, and the Dyaks, and people of many lesser tribes or races.

Life in a Long-house

How would you like to live in the same house as sixty other families ? It would probably seem very crowded to any European, to say the least, but it is the way in which many of the villagers of Borneo live. Their homes are often long-houses of wood, palm leaves and thatch, built on piles on the banks of a river and accommodating from ten to sixty families. Each family has its own bedroom, but the other rooms are shared.

The only entrance to the long-house is by way of a ladder. In charge of the long-house is the house-chief, who is judge, priest and ruler to the inhabitants.

To find out why the villagers have become accustomed to the long-house way of life, you must look back to the old days of the past when tribe fought tribe. Tribal warfare meant constant danger of attack; to live together in a single house raised from the ground and with only one entrance was the best safe-guard against a surprise raid from enemies.

Among the Pacific Islands

Britain's islands of the Pacific are small groups sprinkled across the blue waters as though from a pepper pot—the Gilbert and Ellice Island Colony, the Solomon Islands Protectorate, the New Hebrides (Anglo-French Condominium), the Tonga group or Friendly Islands which form the last surviving independent kingdom of the Pacific, and the Fiji Islands. Some, like the Solomons, are of volcanic origin, mountainous and thickly forested; others, like the Gilbert and Ellice, are flat coral belts girdling lagoons; some, like Fiji, are fertile; others are barren. And everywhere we see the coconut palm which could almost be described as the trademark of the south Pacific.

These islands are the home of three distinct peoples—the dark-skinned fuzzy-haired Melanesians such as we find in Fiji, the Solomons, and the New Hebrides; the light-skinned Polynesians who live in Tonga and the central and east Pacific and who are among the most artistic of native peoples; and the Micronesians such as are found in the Gilbert and Ellice Islands. Besides copra, their island homes yield sugar, vegetables, and fruit, and from the shore waters, pearls and pearl shell. In some islands— Ocean Island in the Gilbert and Ellice, and Nauru (administered by Australia) —there are large deposits of phosphate rock.

The two hundred and fifty islands of the Fiji group are the most important. Their capital is Suva on the island of Viti Levu. Here we can see not only the modern buildings of a growing colonial capital, but along the waterfront, the dugout canoes of native

fishermen filled perhaps with an unusual harvest of the sea—small octopuses and great green sea crabs. We shall also see something of the wonderful coral reefs which abound in this island group.

The Fiji Islands are a thriving centre of the sugar industry which relies on Indian workers brought from their native land towards the end of the last century: but copra, bananas and pineapples are exported, and also gold from the Vatukoula mines in Viti Levu.

Fiji is the headquarters of the Western Pacific High Commission, which administers Britain's scattered territories in the Pacific and conducts her relations with the independent kingdom of Tonga.

Tonga is the only independent island kingdom in the Pacific and it has flourished under British protection since 1900. The sovereign is the wise and popular Queen Salote Tupou, G.B.E., who came to the throne in 1918, at the age of eighteen. Tonga has a Constitution very like that of the United Kingdom, but life there is certainly much less complicated than it is in Britain. For Tonga has no towns and great industries. The people are peasant farmers, with copra and bananas as their main crops. Most of the people are members of the

Fox Photos.

A ROYAL OCCASION IN THE FRIENDLY ISLANDS

The Tonga group, or Friendly Islands, form the last surviving independent kingdom of the Pacific Islands. The kingdom is ruled, under British protection, by Queen Salote Tupou who is here seen reviewing her warriors. Queen Salote visited Britain for the Coronation in 1953.

FIJI AND THE SOLOMONS

Aerofilms.

The people of Fiji are very fond of dancing, feasting and ceremonial. There are many occasions when the ritual laid down by ancient custom must be followed. But while Fijians, such as the warriors in this picture, keep their traditional customs, they are also rapidly learning to progress.

E.N.A.

The coconut palm might almost be described as the trademark of the Pacific. From copra, the dried kernel of the nut, the valuable coconut oil is obtained. Here we see Solomon-Islanders removing the tough and fibrous outer husk by using a sharp-pointed stake.

Wesleyan Free Church of Tonga, whose head is Queen Salote herself.

"Bounty" Island

Many miles to the east lies little Pitcairn Island which owes its fame, and its existence as a British colony, to the mutiny on His Majesty's Ship *Bounty* in April, 1789. Commanded by Lieutenant Bligh, the *Bounty* was bound from Tahiti to the West Indies with a cargo of young bread-fruit trees. Led by Fletcher Christian, the crew mutinied and eight of the mutineers, including their leader, sailed with a number of Polynesian natives to little Pitcairn where they burned the *Bounty* and made their home. From this curious beginning sprang the present colony which has a population of just over a hundred and thirty persons.

Islands of the Atlantic

Continuing eastwards and rounding Cape Horn, we come to the Falkland Islands lying in the belt of the " Wester-lies." West Falkland and East Falkland are the two main islands and the capital is Port Stanley. Sheep-farming is the main industry, but whaling is also carried on, with South Georgia as the base.

Half-way between South America and the Cape of Good Hope is Tristan da Cunha, whose original inhabitants were soldiers and sailors from the garrison of the island of St. Helena. St. Helena itself is, like Tristan da Cunha, volcanic in origin, and is famous as the island of Napoleon's exile.

Longwood House, where he lived, was presented to the French by Queen Victoria, and to-day the tricolor flies above its roofs.

Ascension Island is seven hundred miles north-west of St. Helena. During the war it was a refuelling base on the air route from Natal, Brazil, to West Africa.

Photo : E.N.A.

THE HOME OF AN EXILED EMPEROR

After the Battle of Waterloo, the French Emperor was exiled to lonely St. Helena. Longwood House, where he died in 1821, with its grounds, was given to the French by Queen Victoria and to-day the tricolor flies over the scene of Napoleon's last years. Jamestown is the only town on St. Helena whose chief industry is the growing of New Zealand flax.

MALAYA: LAND OF RUBBER AND TIN

Paul Popper.

MINING TIN IN MALAYA

This picture shows part of the gravel pump method of tin mining. A pit has been dug to the level of the tin-ore gravels. Powerful water jets are then used to break up the surface. The mixture of sand and clay, ore and water, which then forms at the bottom of the pit, is pumped to the head of a " flume," where the heavy tin ore is deposited. The lighter sand and clay are carried away by the water.

THE Malay Peninsula stretches its long body southwards from Siam. Its neck is Thailand, but the rest of the peninsula is Malaya where British interests prevail and which, before the war, consisted of (1) the Straits Settlements, governed by a British governor; (2) the Federated Malay States, which were under British protection; and (3) the Unfederated Malay States, which were ruled by native sultans or princes who had British advisers at their courts. These all now form part of the Federation of Malaya which came into being on February 1st, 1948. The Federation has a British High Commissioner and a Constitution protecting the rulers of the Malay States and the people.

The whole peninsula is practically one vast tropical forest, which rolls in great waves across the country covering the mountain ranges in an ocean of green. It is true that here and there men have built villages, towns and even cities, and in some places they have stripped away patches of forest to get at the rich tin deposits, or grow their plantations of rubber and spices ; but these clearings are only the tiniest of spots in that great ocean of forest which stretches from sea to sea on either side.

In the Green Jungle

The railways and the roads are bordered by dense forest; mines, towns, plantations and villages are hemmed in by it as by a wall. The villages, usually by the side of a river, consist of a row of neat houses of wood and thatch, often on stilts, overshadowed by fruit trees. Behind them are the wet paddy (rice) fields; in front is the river. But beyond the cultivated land and the village, " the dark heavy line of the forest uprears itself around and above it like the walls of a prison."

Trees, ferns, creepers and other plant-life grow rapidly in the warm, wet climate of Malaya, creating the vast tangle of forest and jungle that covers four-fifths of the country. This is the realm of monkeys, tigers and elephants; snakes, lizards, butterflies and insects of many kinds live in the dark stillness of the jungle; the swamps and pools are potential breeding grounds for mosquitoes which, if given the chance, would once more spread malaria across the country.

Only half a century ago Malaya was one of the worst areas in the world for this terrible disease. But at this same time, a doctor in the Malay Medical Service was studying the species of mosquito that transmitted malaria and applying the methods laid down by Sir Ronald Ross to wipe them out. His name was Watson, and he is now Sir Malcolm Watson and a leading authority

on malaria control. He showed that malaria could be conquered by finding the breeding places of the mosquito and spraying them with insecticides. His methods have made Malaya one of the more healthy areas of the tropics.

Even now, searching and spraying continue. And so they must, if malaria is not to return.

The People of Malaya

Who are the people of this forest land of Malaya ? The chief are the Malays, who number about 2½ millions. They are lithe and well-built brown people with shining black hair, who live in the villages by the water-side, and grow rice and fruit. Those who live near the sea are expert sailors and fishermen; those inland are clever hunters as well as farmers. The Malays are mostly Mohammedans; they are very polite and very particular, very cheerful but very quick tempered, brave fighters and firm friends. You will find Malays all over the south-eastern shorelands of Asia from Ceylon to the East Indies. They are not, as a rule, too fond of hard work; the work in the rich tin-fields in Malaya is mainly done by Chinese, of whom there are nearly two millions ; and the labour on the rubber and coconut plantations is provided chiefly by Tamil people from India, who number over half a million. The Malay hates to work for a master; he leaves that to those he regards as inferior folk.

The Malay likes gaily coloured clothing. At the end of the day he will put on his *songkok*, or velvet hat, and bright *baju*, a loose-sleeved garment made of cotton, which will also be worn for holidays and festivals. His amusements will include kite-flying, spinning tops and cock-fighting.

The houses in a typical Malay village are made of wood and thatched with palm fronds. If the village is by a river or on the sea-shore, the houses will probably be built on piles over the water. Every Malay is loyal to his

Paul Popper.
HUNTING WITH A BLOWPIPE
These Sakai people of the mountains of Pahang are setting out on a hunting expedition, armed with a bamboo blowpipe.

Sultan, and every village respects and obeys its penghulu, or headman.

Growing Rice

The Malay farmer plants his rice seed in a small " nursery plot," where the soil has been made rich with manure and fertiliser and where the rain-water is kept in by low mud walls. The heavy rains make the seed grow well and the farmer is now very busy preparing the ground into which the young crop will presently be transplanted. This land will also be surrounded by low mud walls, for the rice, or paddy, must have plenty of water. Although there are now cultivating machines which the farmer can use for preparing his land, many farmers still use water-buffaloes to drag their ploughs and other implements across the flooded land to get it ready for transplanting.

By the time this work is done, the rice in the nursery plot will probably be about 9 inches high. The farmer and his family now have a very busy time pulling up the young rice and tying it in bundles, and then planting it out in the fields with the help of a wooden dibber or small fork. Once this has been done, the farmer's chief task is to make sure that his rice has enough water. If the rains are not enough, he will irrigate his fields from a *parit* or waterway. If too much water comes, he will drain some off by opening one of the mud walls.

In about three or four months his rice will be ready for harvest, and once again everyone in the family helps. When the crop has been cut, gathered, threshed

Malayan Information Agency.

DRYING AND PACKING RUBBER

The rubber tree was brought to Malaya from Central America, flourished and gave rise to a great industry on which the fortunes of such towns as Kuala Lumpur were founded. When the trees have been tapped, the juice is taken to the factory, strained, and then mixed with a little water and some formic acid. The set rubber is squeezed by rollers, dried on racks, then sent to the smoke house to be finished and packed.

and stored, there will be harvest celebrations—feasts, music, dancing and shadow-plays.

The best of the crop will probably be kept for planting next year, and the remainder will be eaten by the farmer and his family. Some farmers in the north-east grow more than they need for themselves and have a surplus to sell in the nearest town. But only about half the rice that Malaya needs is grown by her own farmers; the rest has to be brought in from abroad.

Chinese and Indians

In some parts of Penang, and other places, a traveller would find it easy to believe that he had suddenly been transported from Malaya to China. The signs hanging outside the small shops would be in Chinese characters, and the shopkeepers themselves would be Chinese.

The Chinese are among the workers and traders of Malaya. Their money and toil helped to develop the tin

Paul Popper.

A COUNTRY WEDDING

Wearing ornate robes and head-dresses, bride
and groom have to sit still for many hours to
ensure happiness and good luck.

industry, of which they still hold about
a third; their shops and business houses
can be seen in many towns. Some of
them have come to Malaya from China;
others have been born in Malaya and
are known as "Straits-born Chinese."
Chinese are found in many walks of
life; they are doctors, lawyers, miners
and farmers.

There are also many Indians. The
term "Indian" is used in Malaya to
describe Tamils, Pathans, Sikhs and
Sinhalese. So the Indian community
really comes not only from India itself,
but from Pakistan and Ceylon as well.
Among the other peoples living in
Malaya are Arabs. They have a special
place in the history of the peninsula
because they brought the Moslem religion to Malaya.

Forest People

In the forest country, where civilisation has not yet reached, live the
Sakai, who are great hunters and
clever trackers of wild animals, using
their blow-pipes and poisoned darts
with deadly accuracy. A Sakai blowpipe is made of bamboo and may be
6 feet in length, perhaps seven. The
pipe is carefully hollowed out and
polished inside. The darts are long
thorns, to which some palm-fluff is
attached, and the poison in which they
are sometimes dipped is prepared from
the upas tree.

Some of the Sakai grow a little millet
and rice and fruits on land cleared by
burning; when this is exhausted they
clear a new patch. Like the Veddahs
of Ceylon and the Todas of Southern
India, the Sakai are animists who
believe their world to be filled with
spirits—mostly evil, and therefore to
be pleased by strange offerings in
lonely places. When the white man
wants to build a new railway or cut a
new road through the living forest he
generally employs bands of these Sakai
to clear away the dense tangle of
vegetation as only these little brown
people can.

Wilder and shyer even than the
Sakai are the small, black, short and
woolly-haired Negrito people of the
remotest forests, who grow nothing, but
live entirely by hunting, or by grubbing
up roots, finding wild honey and fruits,
and rooting out tortoises and burrowing
animals from their secret haunts.

Kuala Lumpur is the "rubber city"
of Malaya; its fortunes are founded on
the rubber plantations, just as those of
Johannesburg are on gold, and those of
Kimberley on diamonds.

Its port is Port Swettenham on the
Straits, and rubber and tin exporting is
the chief business there.

Kuala Lumpur is the chief city of
Selangor and the capital of Malaya;
it has fine broad streets and many
beautiful roads. Roads and railways
connect it with the many rubber plantations and with the tin-fields. Its
population is at least 136,000.

Tin Mining in Malaya

Malaya supplies much of the world

output of tin. Her richest mines are in the Kinta valley, east of the Kledang Mountains, and there are other important mines in the nearby Perak valley. In both valleys, they mine for alluvial tin: that is to say, tin ore which is mixed with alluvium, a silt brought down by the rivers. Heavy machinery is needed for this kind of mining, and power for this machinery is provided by harnessing the swift floods of such rivers as the Perak, whose Chenderoh Dam supplies power to the mines of the Larut and Kinta valleys.

Ipoh

One great modern centre of the mining industry is the town of *Ipoh* which, as you can tell from its rectangular blocks of buildings and straight streets, is one of the newest of Malayan towns. Ipoh is the home of the miners of the Kinta valley and of many Chinese and Indians.

Tin is also obtained in Malaya by lode mining, and the lode mine at Pahang is one of the most productive tin ore mines in the world.

Broadly speaking, there are two types of tin mine: the dredge mine and the gravel pump mine. The first method requires a very expensive machine called a tin dredger and is used mostly when there is much tin ore to be extracted from the silt. The tin dredger works on a large pool or lake and is really nothing more or less than an unusual kind of boat. It may have a tall funnel, but its engine, instead of being used to move the "boat" from place to place, is used to turn large wheels which move a chain carrying big buckets. These buckets go down into the water and bring up a load of gravel and water, which is emptied on to mechanical washing trays as the buckets pass over a wheel high up in the middle of the dredger. These washing trays separate the black-grained tin ore from the gravel, and meanwhile the buckets have passed down again.

E.N.A.

A TIN DREDGER AT WORK

The tin dredger is really nothing more than an unusual sort of boat. A bucket chain brings up gravel and water from the bed of the pool or lake, and washing trays on the dredger separate the tin ore from the gravel. Many of the workpeople in the mines are Chinese.

The gravel-pump mine begins with a large pit dug down to where the gravels containing the tin ore have been found. These gravels are then washed by water into a pool, whence they are pumped (as a mixture of water and gravel) to water troughs at the top of the pit. Here, in sluices, the tin ore is collected.

Malayan Pineapple

The story of rubber is told elsewhere in these volumes. Another famous product of Malaya is canned pineapple. Pineapple farming is found mostly in Johore, in southern Malaya, and two crops are raised each year and processed in the canneries of Johore Bahru and Singapore Island.

The pineapple plantations suffered greatly during the war, for they were largely allowed to revert to jungle during the Japanese occupation. But there has recently been much replanting and the value of pineapple exports from Malaya is now greater than ever before.

The chief port of Malaya is not in the Federation at all! Can you guess its name? It is the great trading port of Singapore, a separate Crown Colony which has already been described, and it is linked with the mainland by the causeway to Johore Bahru. Nearly three-quarters of the imports and 63 per cent. of the exports of Malaya are handled by Singapore.

Tin and rubber are also shipped from George Town, a deep water port at the northern end of Penang Island. This port also serves Thailand.

The fight against terrorism in Malaya has been going on since 1948, when the Malayan Communists, using jungle hide-outs, began their campaign to bring chaos and revolution to the country. Law and order are slowly winning the battle, but it has been a hard struggle because the jungle favours the hit-and-run tactics of the terrorists.

Pictorial Press.

PINEAPPLES FOR A MALAYAN CANNERY

The Chinese built up the pineapple industry in Malaya. Most of the plantations are in Johore. This picture shows pineapples being delivered to a cannery, where the rough skins and hard cores will be removed by machine. The fruit is cut into slices or chunks, then cooked and sweetened, and finally canned.